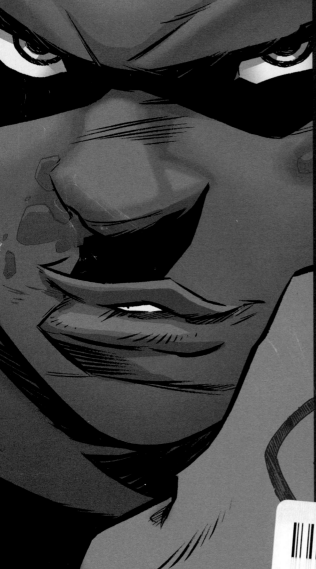

VOLUME 1
THE
VIGILANTE
BUSINESS

WE ARE ROBIN

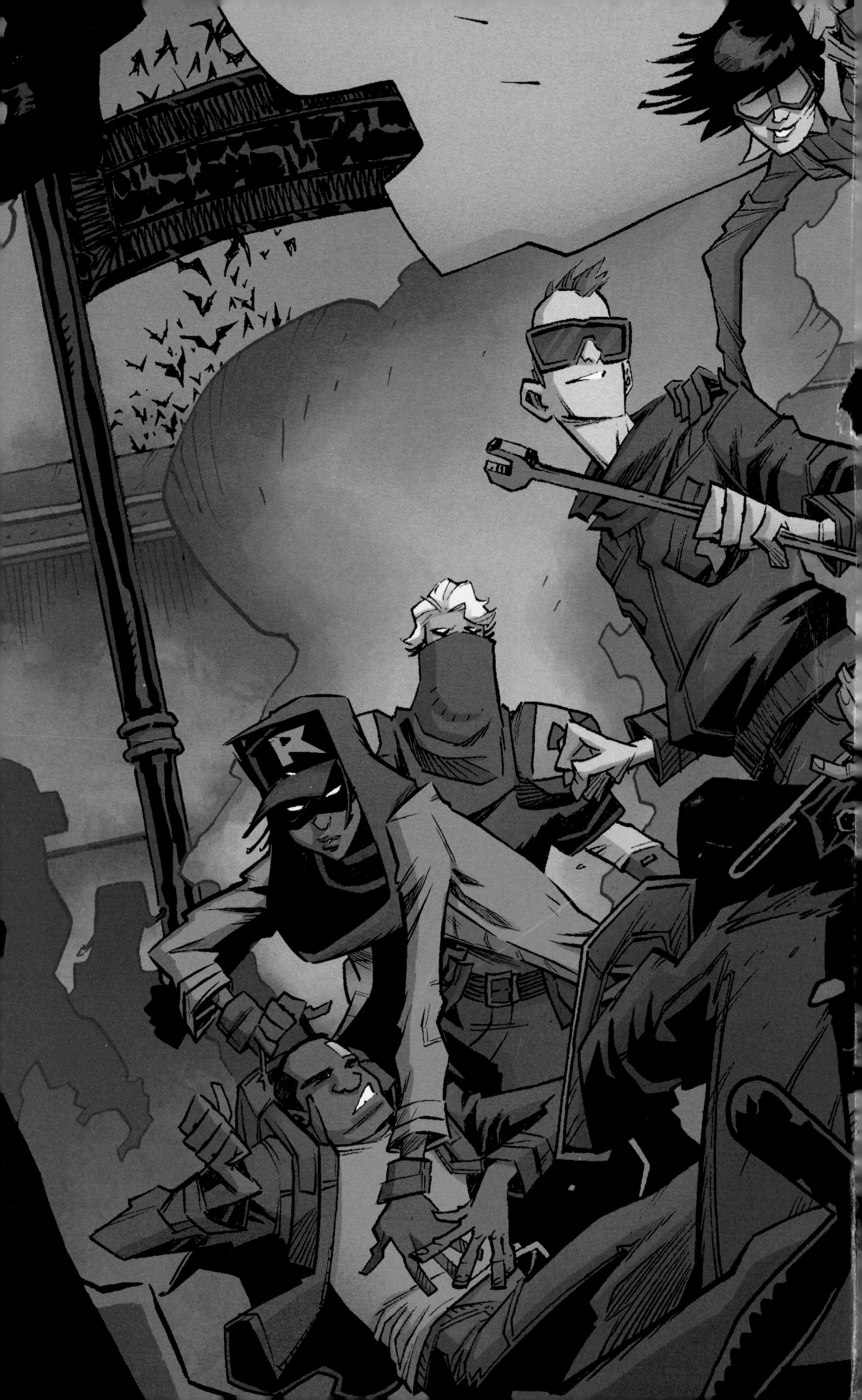

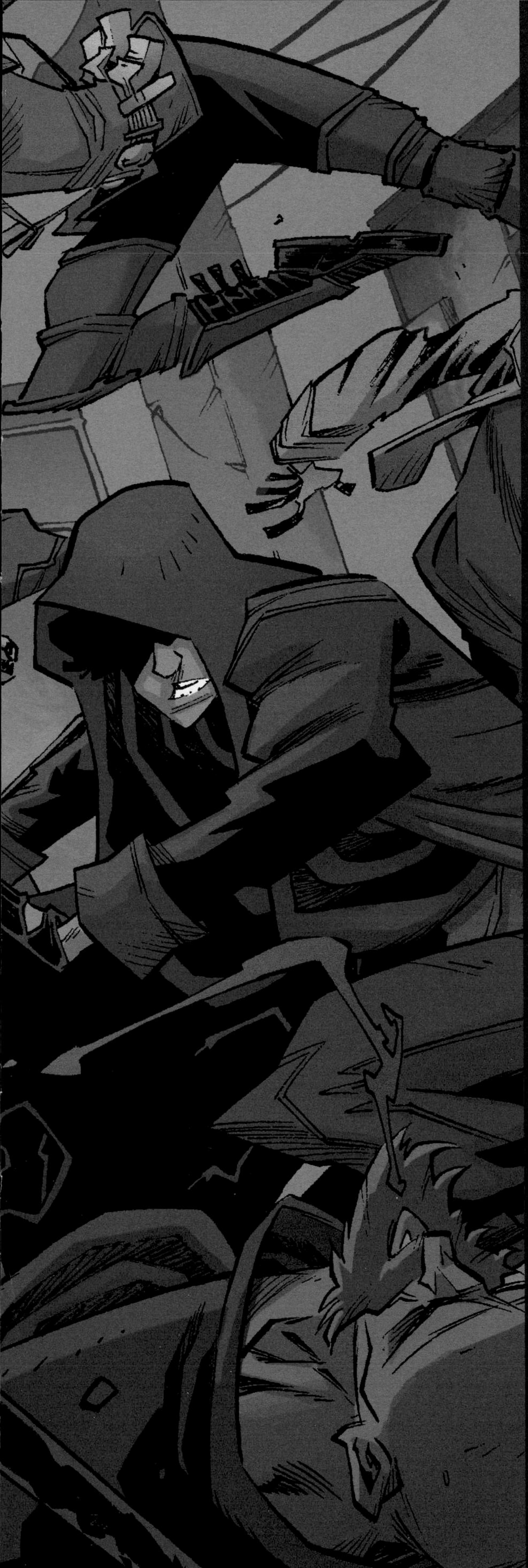

WE ARE ROBIN

VOLUME 1
THE VIGILANTE BUSINESS

WRITTEN BY
LEE BERMEJO

ART BY
JORGE CORONA
ROB HAYNES
KHARY RANDOLPH
JAMES HARVEY
CARMINE DI GIANDOMENICO

COLORS BY
TRISH MULVIHILL
EMILIO LOPEZ
JAMES HARVEY
CHRISTINE DUART PETER
ALLEN PASSALAQUA
MAT LOPES

LETTERS BY
JARED K. FLETCHER

COVERS BY
LEE BERMEJO

BATMAN CREATED BY
BOB KANE with BILL FINGER

WE ARE ROBIN VOLUME 1: THE VIGILANTE BUSINESS

Published by DC Comics. Compilation and all new material Copyright © 2016 DC Comics. All Rights Reserved.

Originally published in single magazine form in WE ARE ROBIN 1-6 and online in DC COMICS SNEAK PEEK: WE ARE ROBIN 1 Copyright © 2015 DC Comics. All Rights Reserved. All characters, their distinctive likenesses and related elements featured in this publication are trademarks of DC Comics. The stories, characters and incidents featured in this publication are entirely fictional. DC Comics does not read or accept unsolicited submissions of ideas, stories or artwork.

DC Comics, 2900 West Alameda Avenue, Burbank, CA 91505
Printed by RR Donnelley, Salem, VA, USA. 2/26/16. First Printing.
ISBN: 978-1-4012-5982-2

Library of Congress Cataloging-in-Publication Data is Available.

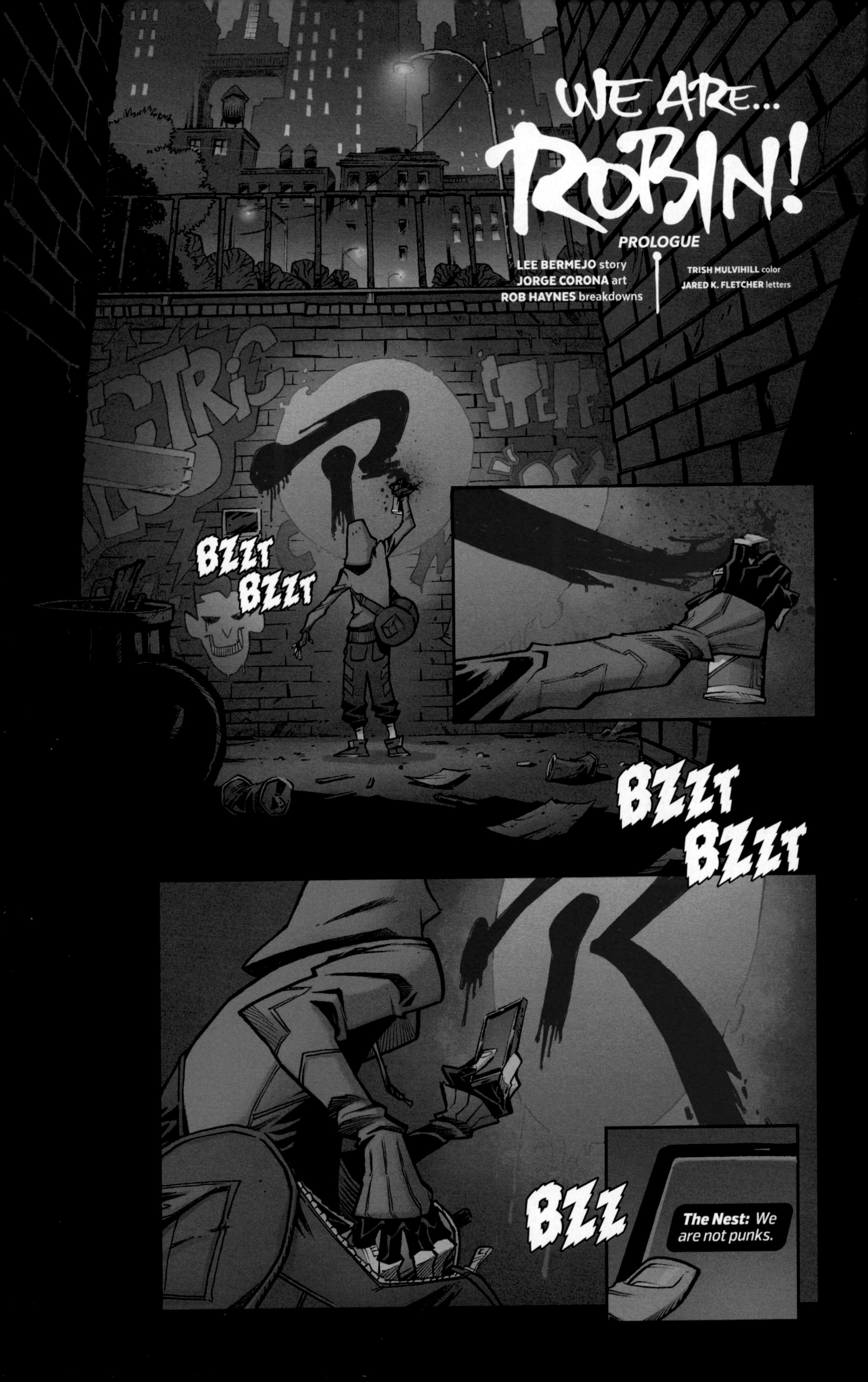
WE ARE...
ROBIN!
PROLOGUE
LEE BERMEJO story
JORGE CORONA art
ROB HAYNES breakdowns
TRISH MULVIHILL color
JARED K. FLETCHER letters
BZZT BZZT
BZZT BZZT
BZZ
The Nest: We are not punks.

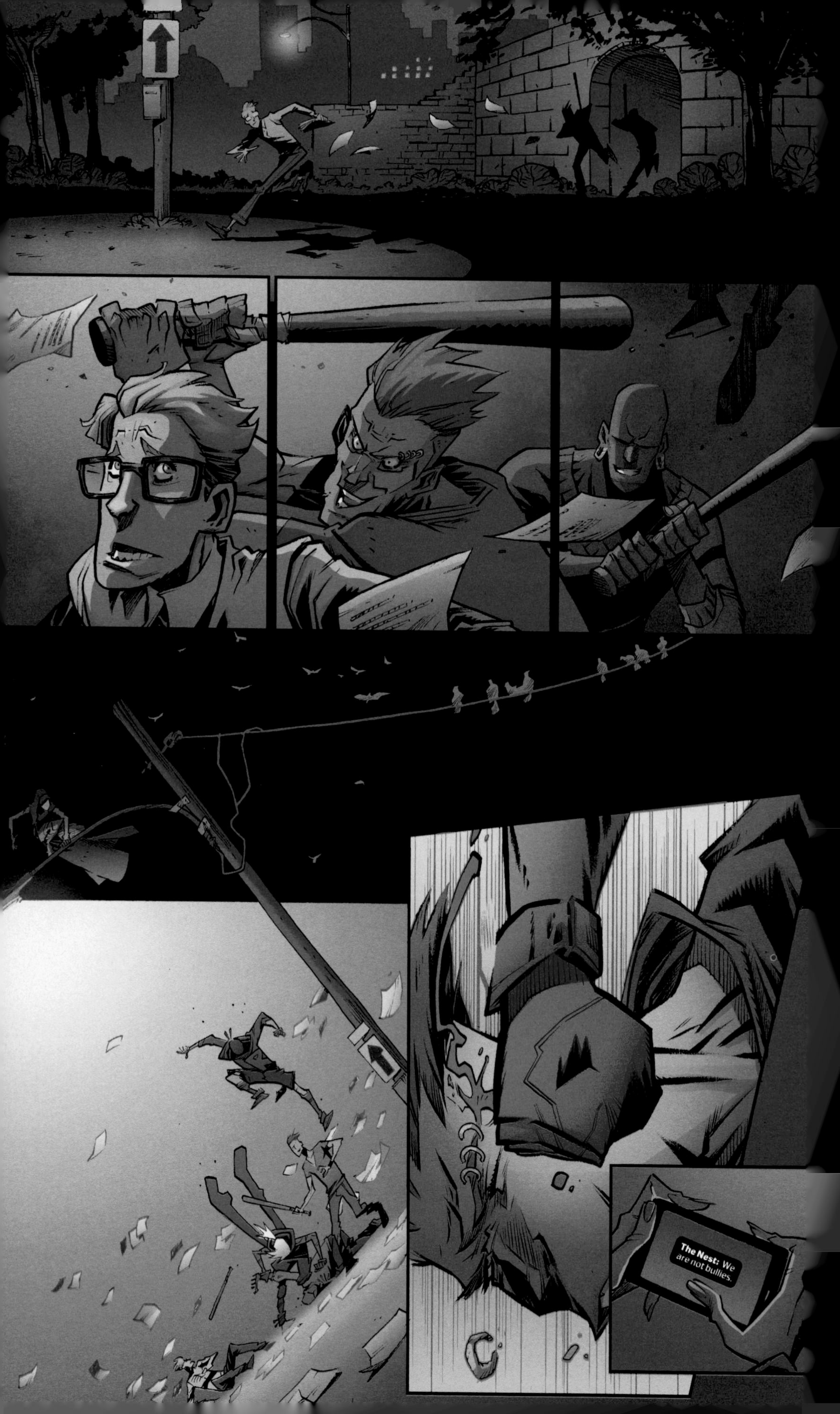
The Nest: We are not bullies.

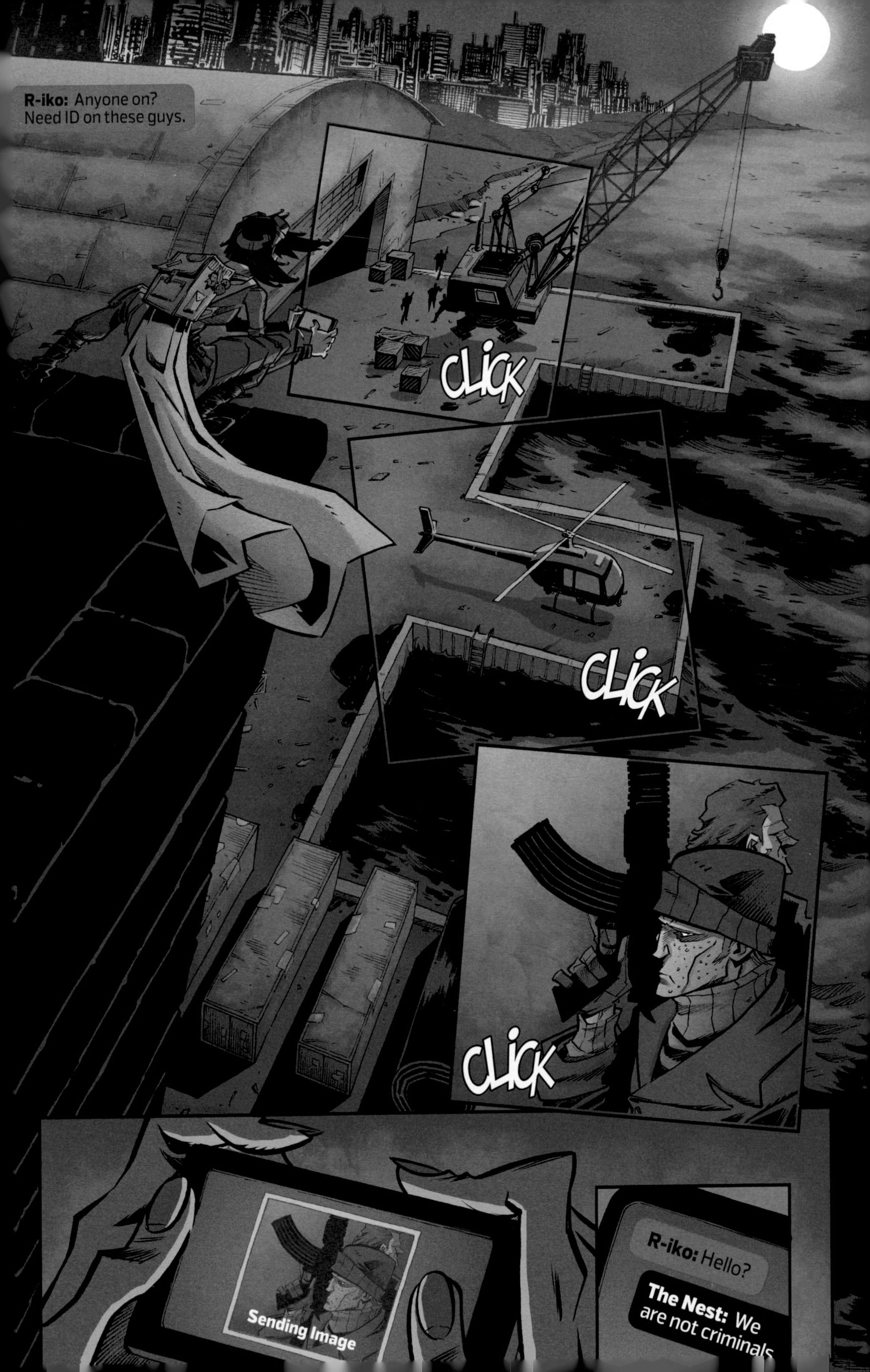
R-iko: Anyone on? Need ID on these guys.
CLICK
CLICK
CLICK
Sending Image
R-iko: Hello?
The Nest: We are not criminals

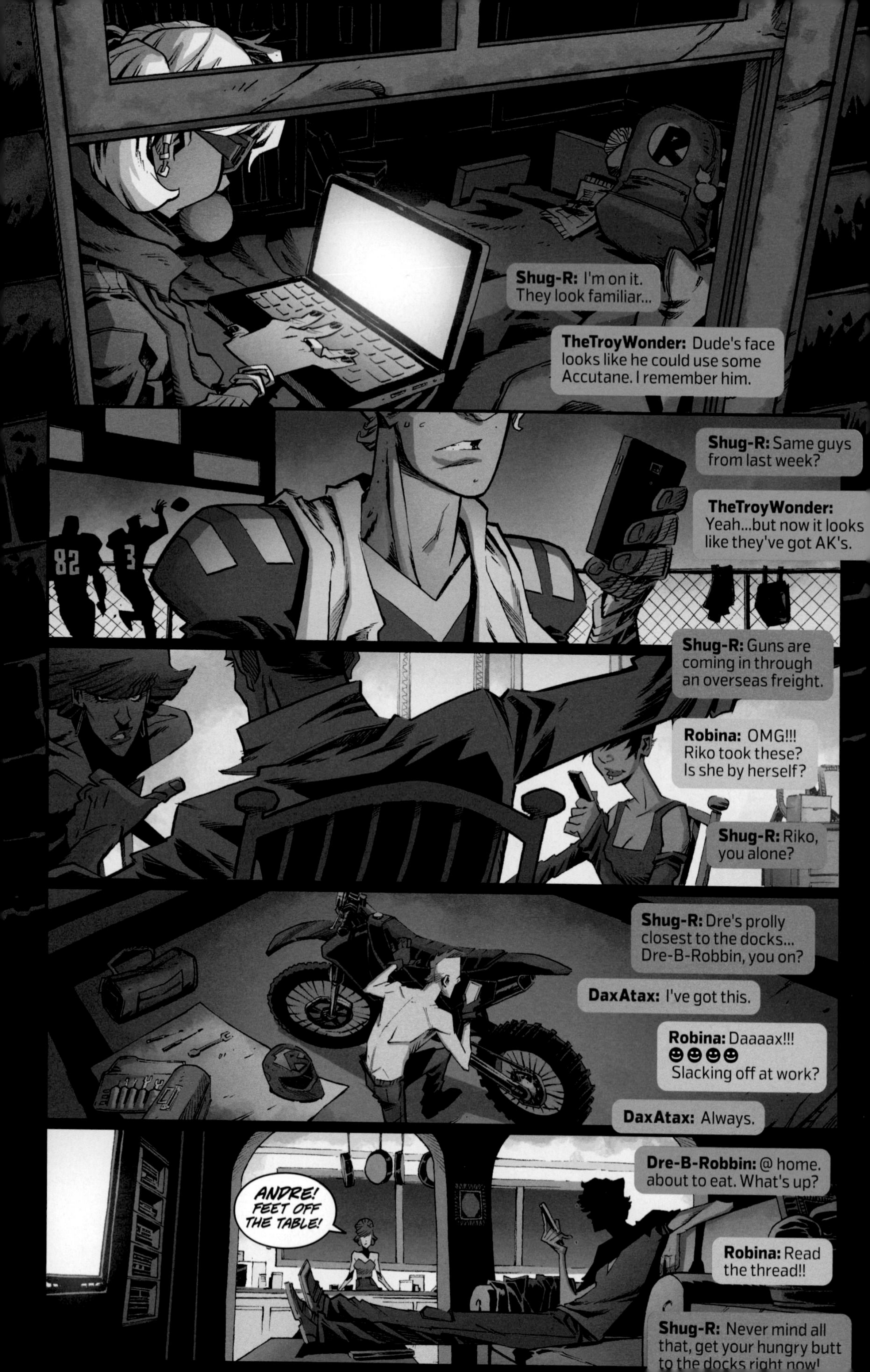

Shug-R: I'm on it. They look familiar...
TheTroyWonder: Dude's face looks like he could use some Accutane. I remember him.
Shug-R: Same guys from last week?
TheTroyWonder: Yeah...but now it looks like they've got AK's.
82
3
Shug-R: Guns are coming in through an overseas freight.
Robina: OMG!!! Riko took these? Is she by herself?
Shug-R: Riko, you alone?
Shug-R: Dre's prolly closest to the docks... Dre-B-Robbin, you on?
DaxAtax: I've got this.
Robina: Daaaax!!! ☻☻☻☻ Slacking off at work?
DaxAtax: Always.
Dre-B-Robbin: @ home. about to eat. What's up?
ANDRE! FEET OFF THE TABLE!
Robina: Read the thread!!
Shug-R: Never mind all that, get your hungry butt to the docks right now!

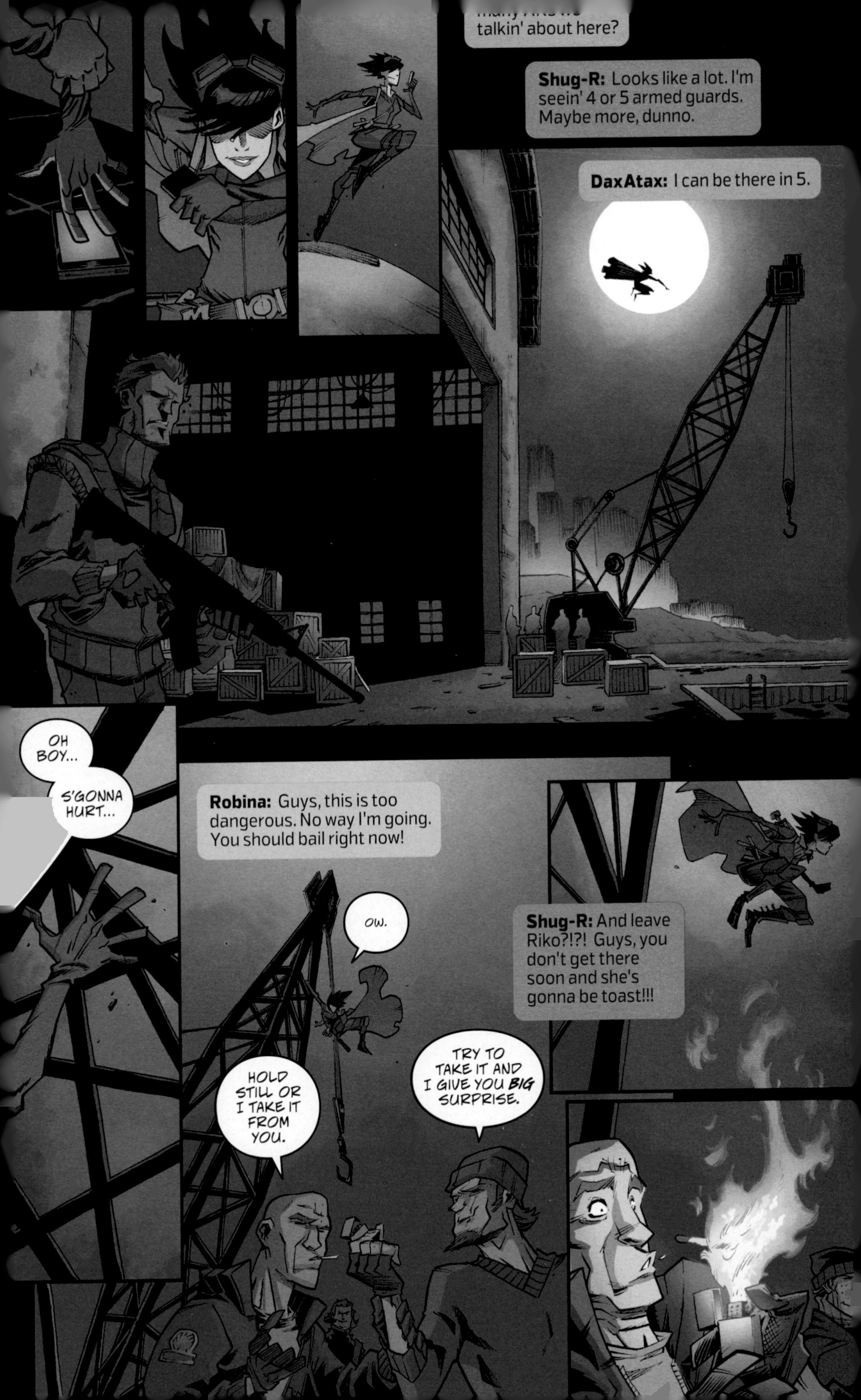

talkin' about here?
Shug-R: Looks like a lot. I'm seein' 4 or 5 armed guards. Maybe more, dunno.
DaxAtax: I can be there in 5.
OH BOY...
S'GONNA HURT...
Robina: Guys, this is too dangerous. No way I'm going. You should bail right now!
Shug-R: And leave Riko?!?! Guys, you don't get there soon and she's gonna be toast!!!
OW.
HOLD STILL OR I TAKE IT FROM YOU.
TRY TO TAKE IT AND I GIVE YOU BIG SURPRISE.

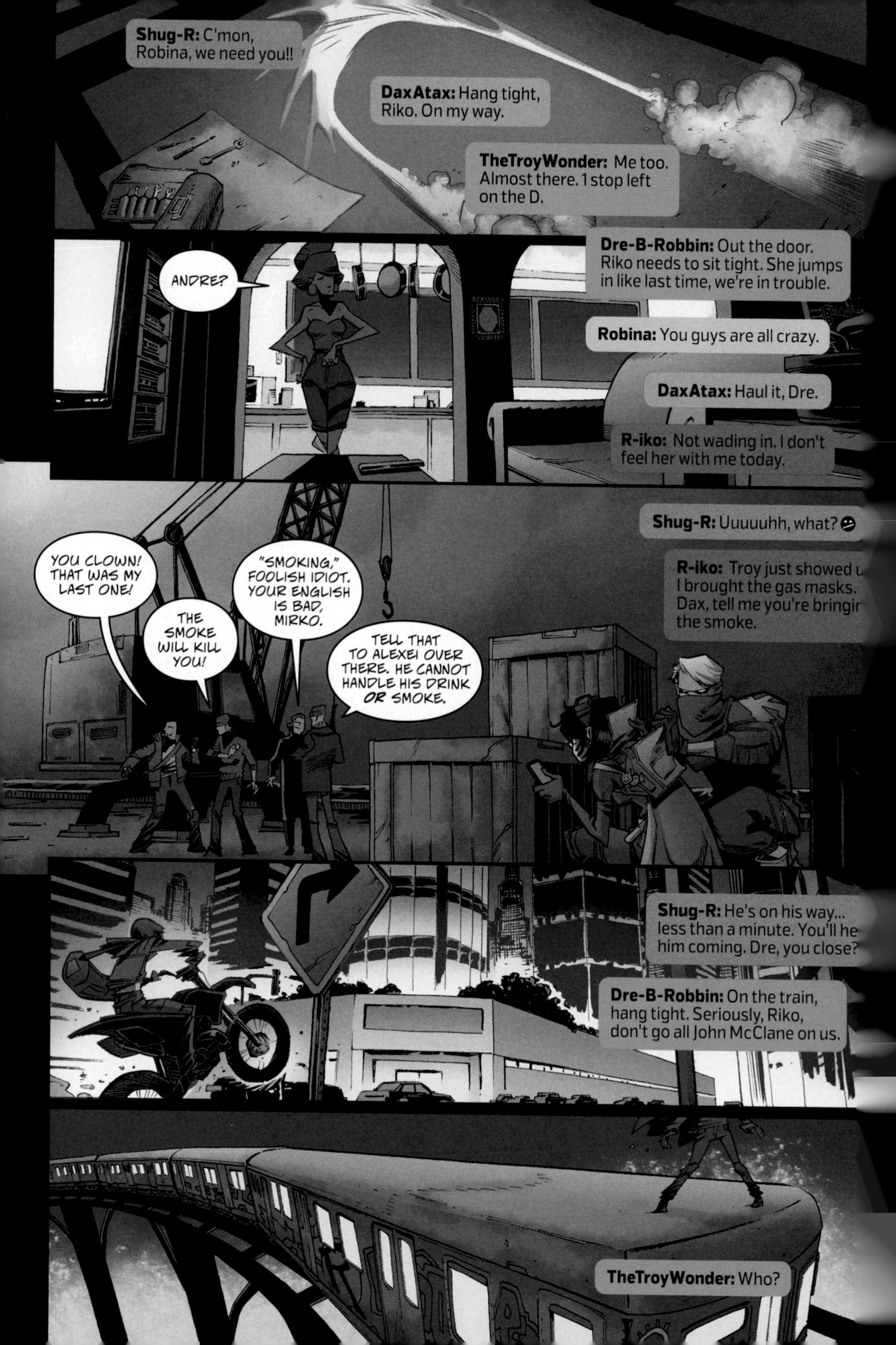
Shug-R: C'mon, Robina, we need you!!
DaxAtax: Hang tight, Riko. On my way.
TheTroyWonder: Me too. Almost there. 1 stop left on the D.
ANDRE?
Dre-B-Robbin: Out the door. Riko needs to sit tight. She jumps in like last time, we're in trouble.
Robina: You guys are all crazy.
DaxAtax: Haul it, Dre.
R-iko: Not wading in. I don't feel her with me today.
Shug-R: Uuuuuhh, what?
R-iko: Troy just showed u
I brought the gas masks.
Dax, tell me you're bringir
the smoke.
YOU CLOWN! THAT WAS MY LAST ONE!
THE SMOKE WILL KILL YOU!
"SMOKING," FOOLISH IDIOT. YOUR ENGLISH IS BAD, MIRKO.
TELL THAT TO ALEXEI OVER THERE. HE CANNOT HANDLE HIS DRINK OR SMOKE.
Shug-R: He's on his way... less than a minute. You'll he
him coming. Dre, you close?
Dre-B-Robbin: On the train, hang tight. Seriously, Riko, don't go all John McClane on us.
TheTroyWonder: Who?

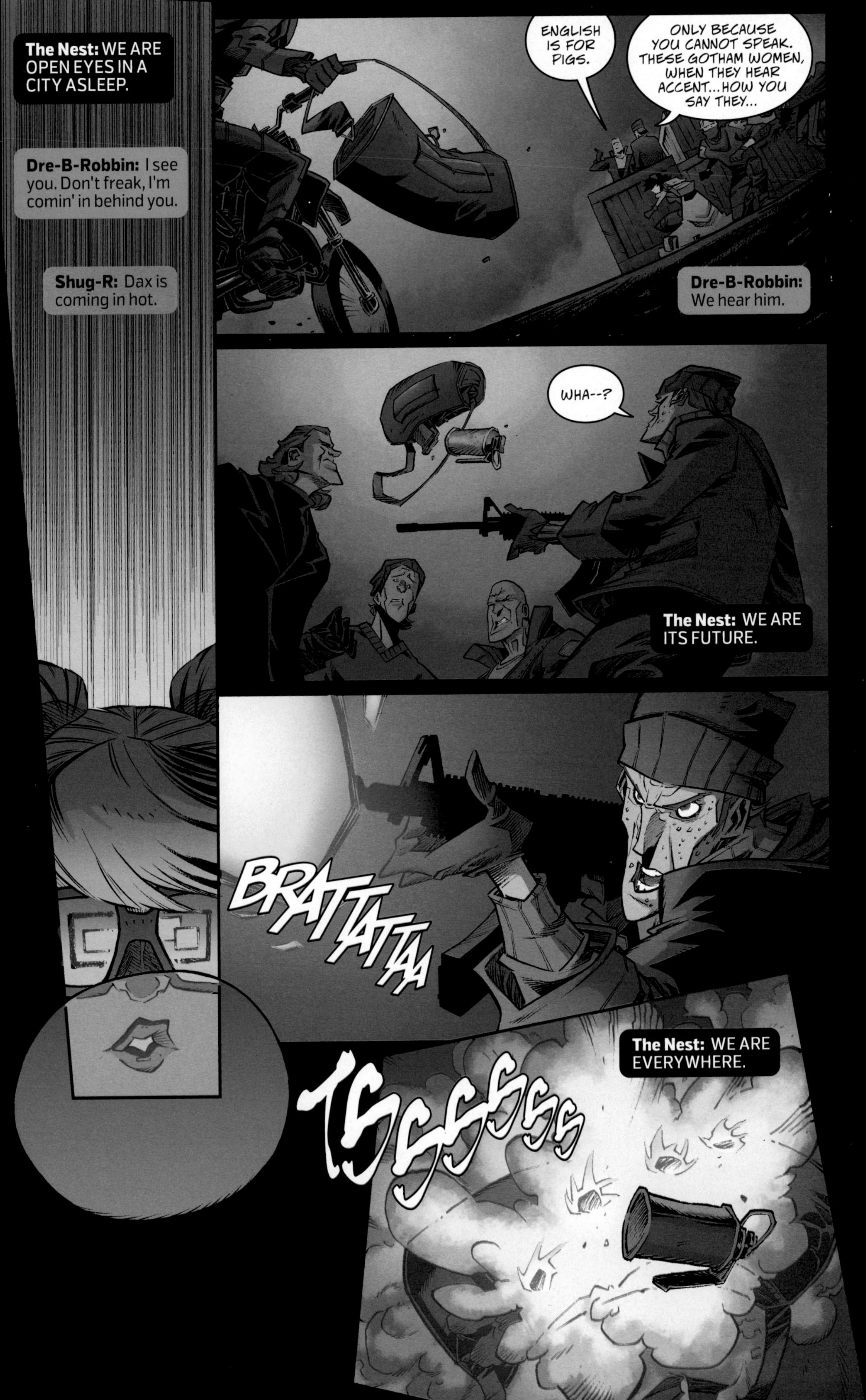
The Nest: WE ARE OPEN EYES IN A CITY ASLEEP.
Dre-B-Robbin: I see you. Don't freak, I'm comin' in behind you.
Shug-R: Dax is coming in hot.
ENGLISH IS FOR PIGS.
ONLY BECAUSE YOU CANNOT SPEAK. THESE GOTHAM WOMEN, WHEN THEY HEAR ACCENT...HOW YOU SAY THEY...
Dre-B-Robbin: We hear him.
WHA--?
The Nest: WE ARE ITS FUTURE.
BRATTATTAA
The Nest: WE ARE EVERYWHERE.
TSSSSSS

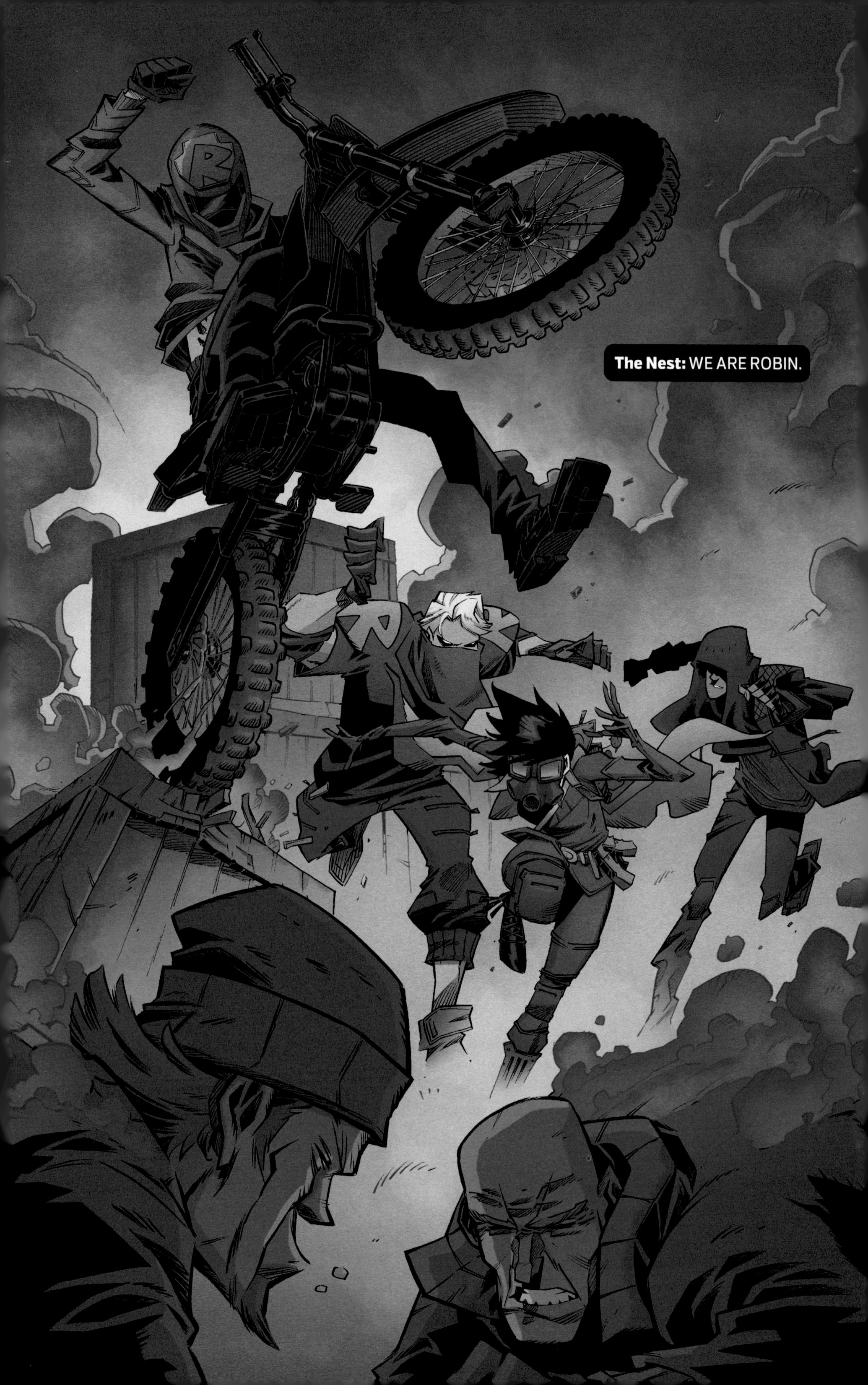
The Nest: WE ARE ROBIN.

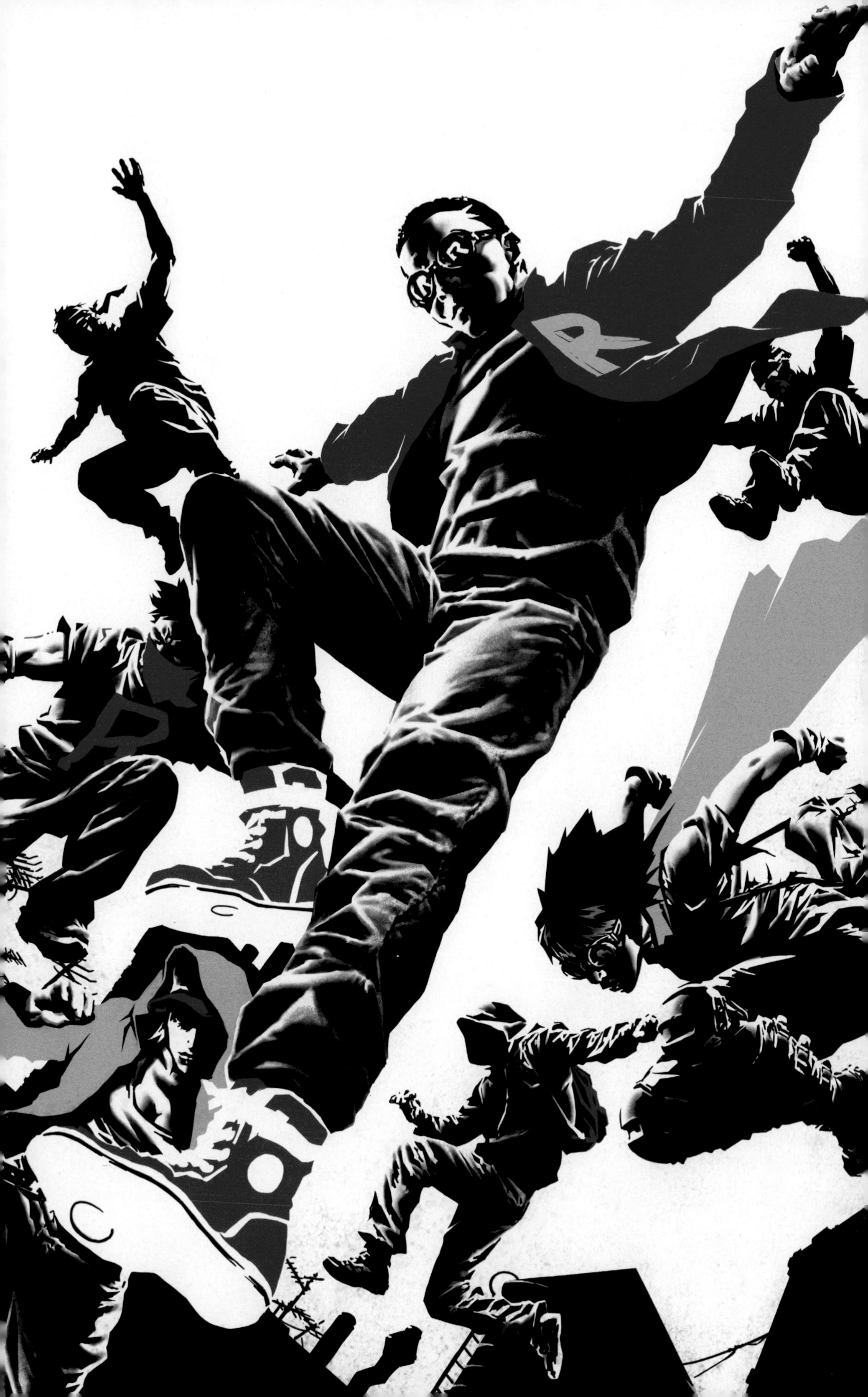

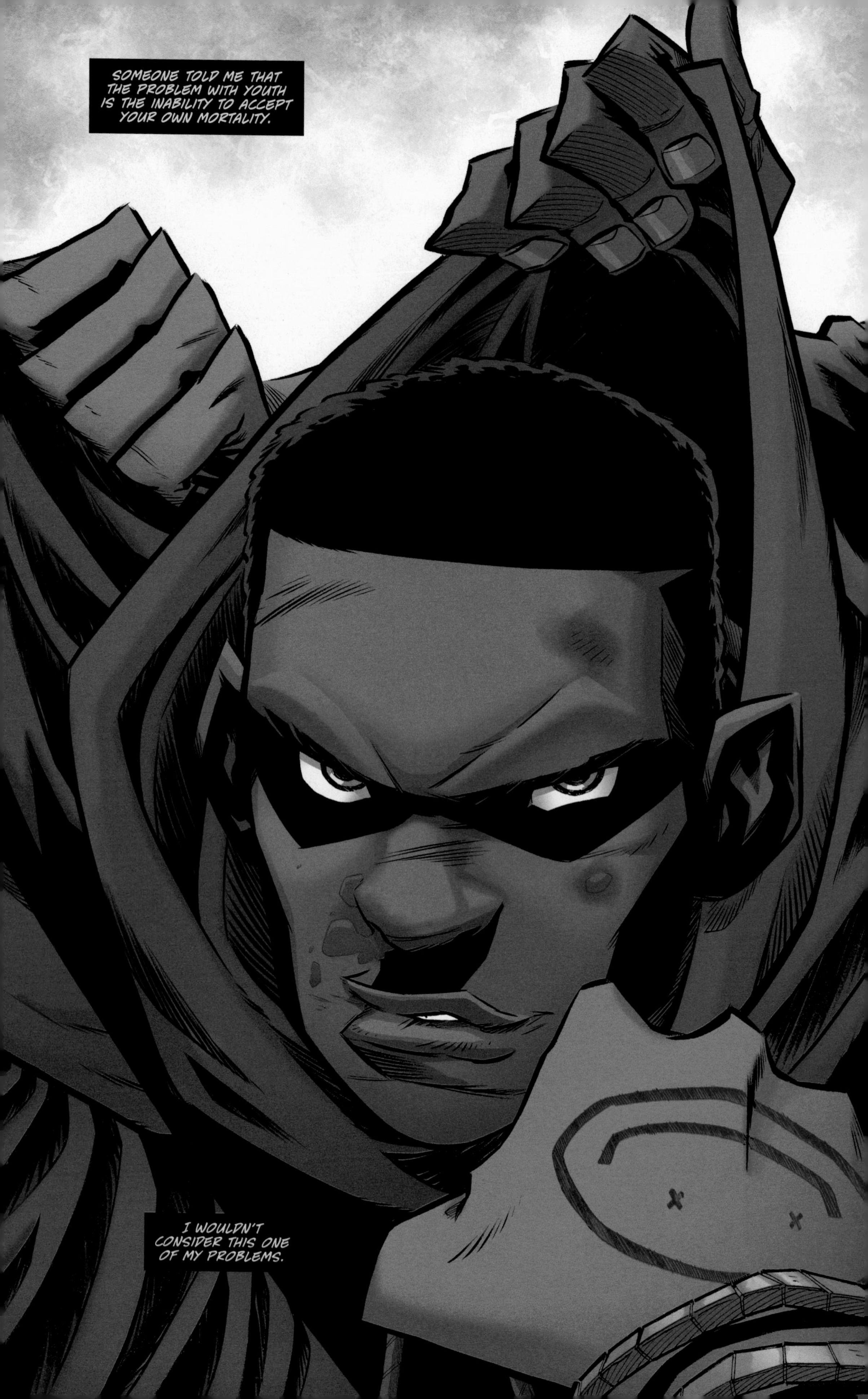
SOMEONE TOLD ME THAT THE PROBLEM WITH YOUTH IS THE INABILITY TO ACCEPT YOUR OWN MORTALITY.
I WOULDN'T CONSIDER THIS ONE OF MY PROBLEMS.

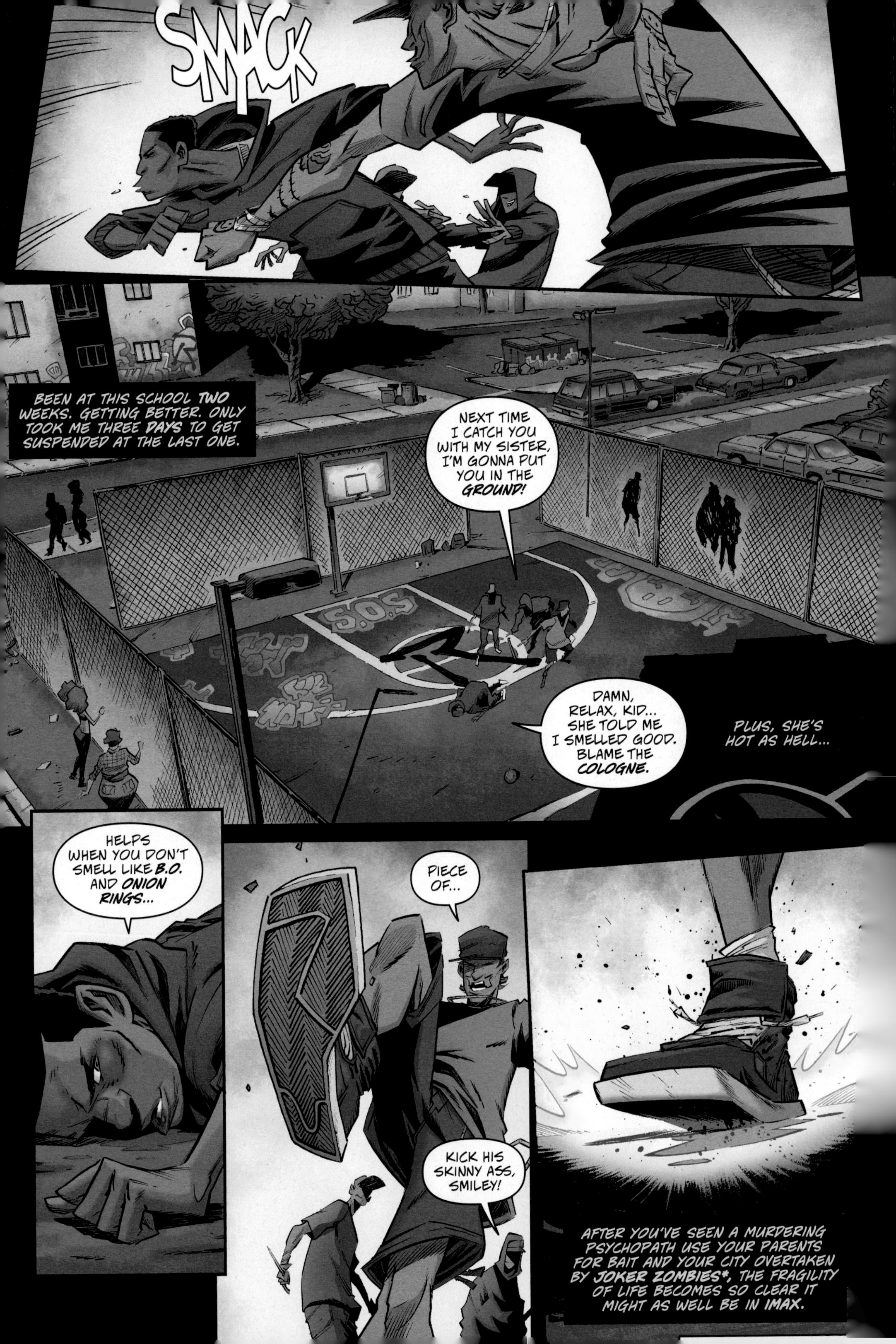
SMACK
BEEN AT THIS SCHOOL TWO WEEKS. GETTING BETTER. ONLY TOOK ME THREE DAYS TO GET SUSPENDED AT THE LAST ONE.
NEXT TIME I CATCH YOU WITH MY SISTER, I'M GONNA PUT YOU IN THE GROUND!
DAMN, RELAX, KID... SHE TOLD ME I SMELLED GOOD. BLAME THE COLOGNE.
PLUS, SHE'S HOT AS HELL...
HELPS WHEN YOU DON'T SMELL LIKE B.O. AND ONION RINGS...
PIECE OF...
KICK HIS SKINNY ASS, SMILEY!
AFTER YOU'VE SEEN A MURDERING PSYCHOPATH USE YOUR PARENTS FOR BAIT AND YOUR CITY OVERTAKEN BY JOKER ZOMBIES*, THE FRAGILITY OF LIFE BECOMES SO CLEAR IT MIGHT AS WELL BE IN IMAX.

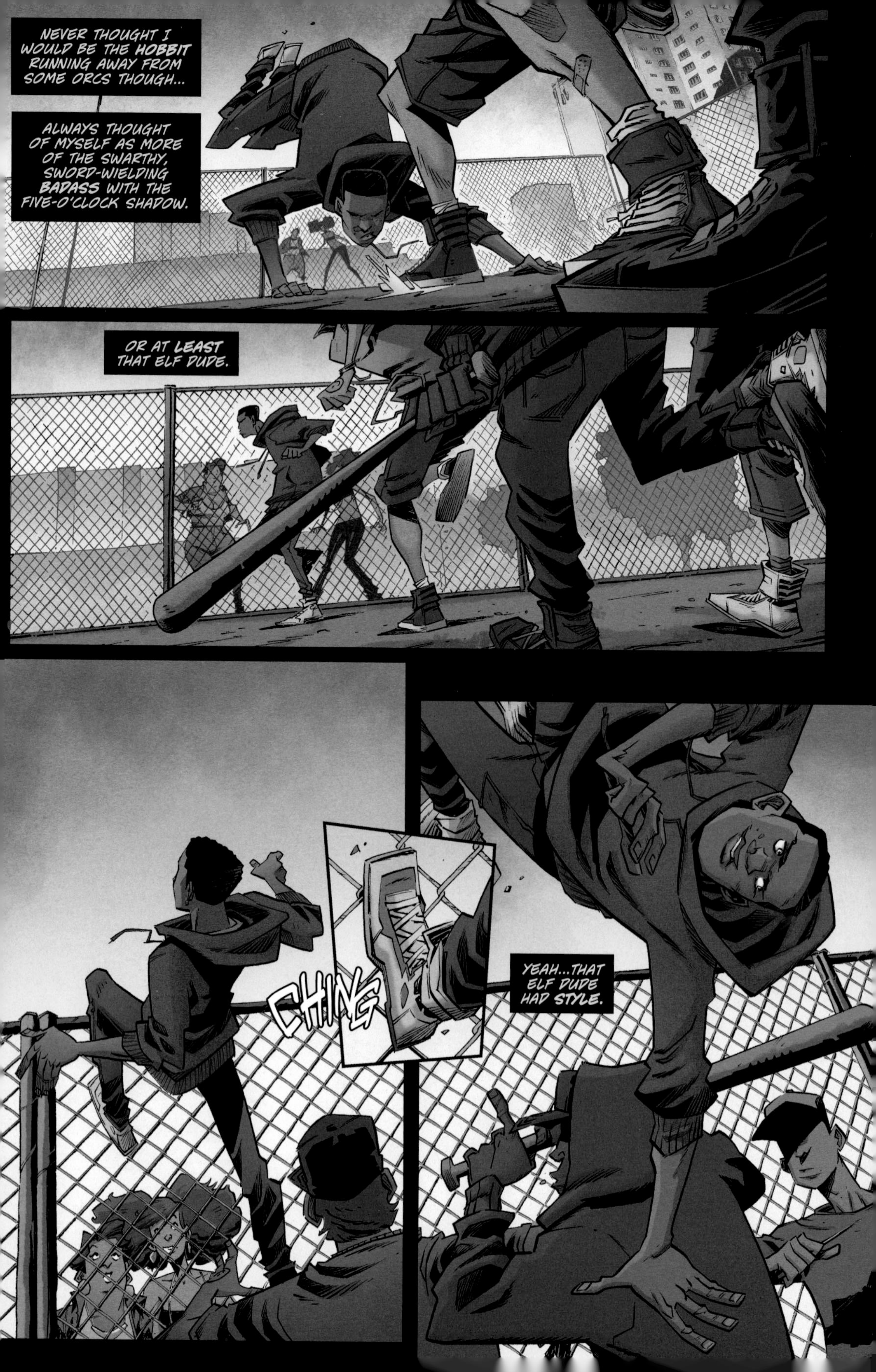
NEVER THOUGHT I WOULD BE THE HOBBIT RUNNING AWAY FROM SOME ORCS THOUGH...
ALWAYS THOUGHT OF MYSELF AS MORE OF THE SWARTHY, SWORD-WIELDING BADASS WITH THE FIVE-O'CLOCK SHADOW.
OR AT LEAST THAT ELF DUDE.
CHING
YEAH...THAT ELF DUDE HAD STYLE.

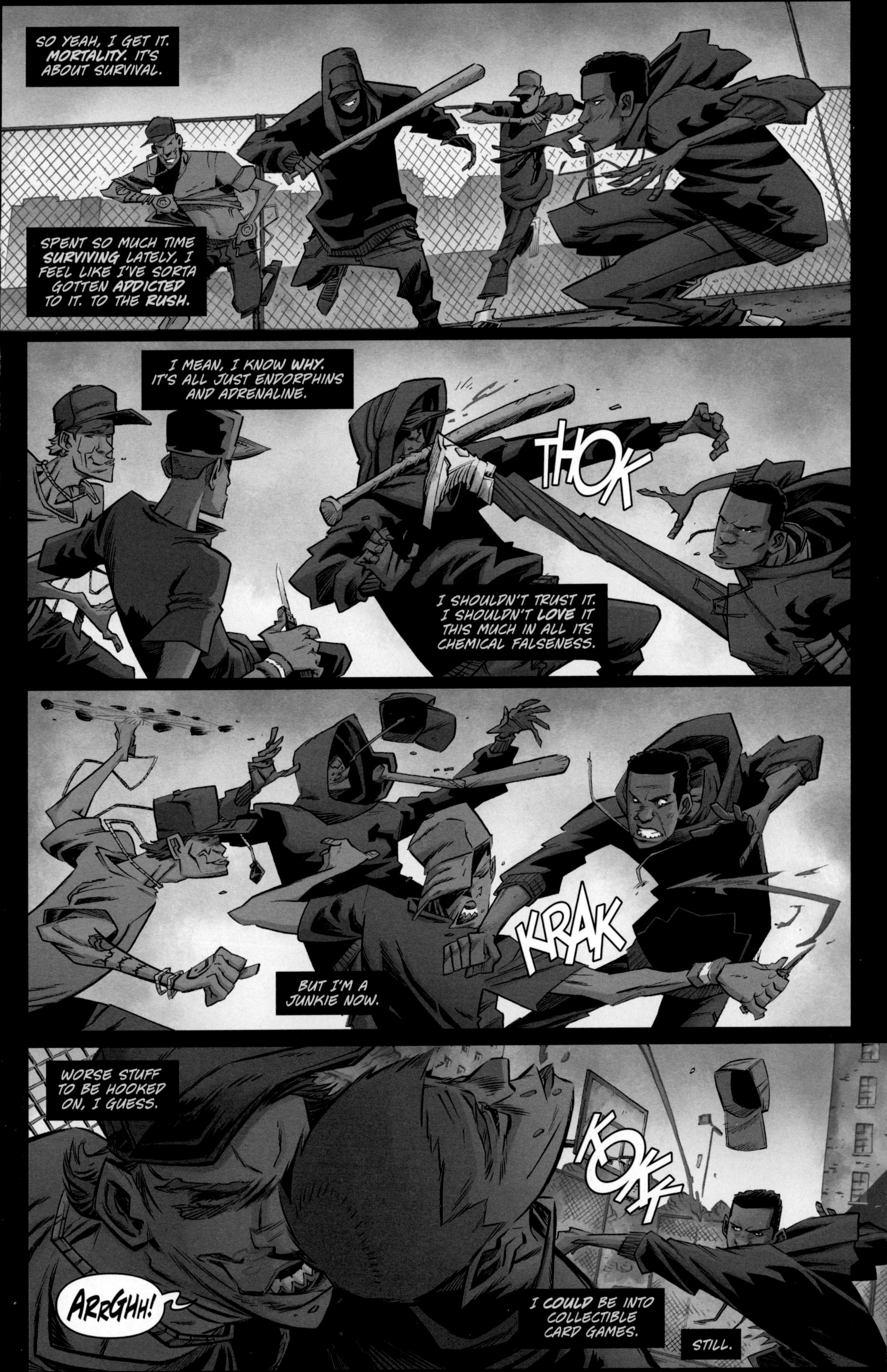

SO YEAH, I GET IT. MORTALITY. IT'S ABOUT SURVIVAL.
SPENT SO MUCH TIME SURVIVING LATELY, I FEEL LIKE I'VE SORTA GOTTEN ADDICTED TO IT. TO THE RUSH.
I MEAN, I KNOW WHY. IT'S ALL JUST ENDORPHINS AND ADRENALINE.
THOK
I SHOULDN'T TRUST IT. I SHOULDN'T LOVE IT THIS MUCH IN ALL ITS CHEMICAL FALSENESS.
KRAK
BUT I'M A JUNKIE NOW.
WORSE STUFF TO BE HOOKED ON, I GUESS.
KOKK
ARRGHH!
I COULD BE INTO COLLECTIBLE CARD GAMES.
STILL.

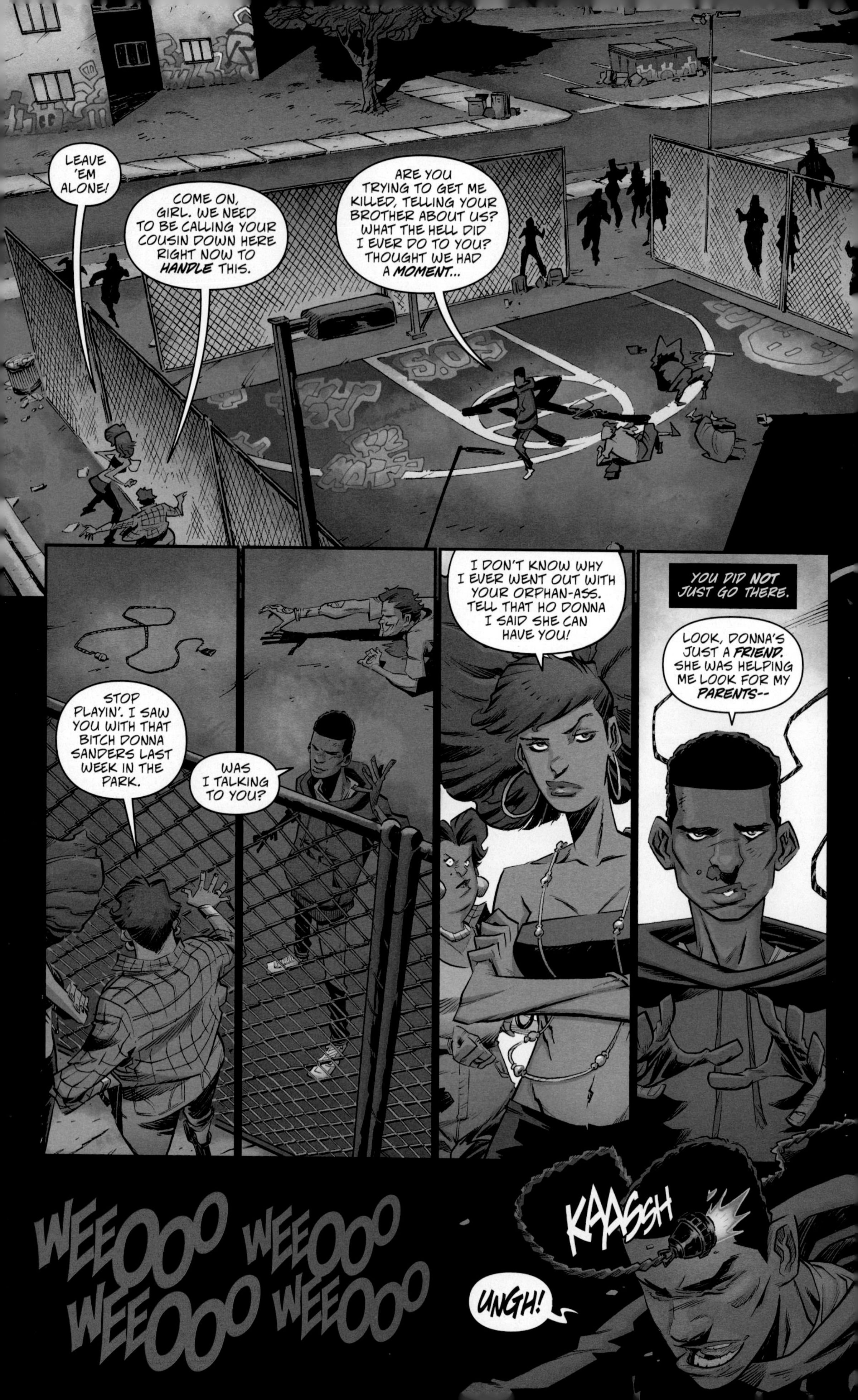
LEAVE 'EM ALONE!
COME ON, GIRL. WE NEED TO BE CALLING YOUR COUSIN DOWN HERE RIGHT NOW TO HANDLE THIS.
ARE YOU TRYING TO GET ME KILLED, TELLING YOUR BROTHER ABOUT US? WHAT THE HELL DID I EVER DO TO YOU? THOUGHT WE HAD A MOMENT...
STOP PLAYIN'. I SAW YOU WITH THAT BITCH DONNA SANDERS LAST WEEK IN THE PARK.
WAS I TALKING TO YOU?
I DON'T KNOW WHY I EVER WENT OUT WITH YOUR ORPHAN-ASS. TELL THAT HO DONNA I SAID SHE CAN HAVE YOU!
YOU DID NOT JUST GO THERE.
LOOK, DONNA'S JUST A FRIEND. SHE WAS HELPING ME LOOK FOR MY PARENTS--
WEEOOO WEEOOO WEEOOO WEEOOO
KAASSH
UNGH!

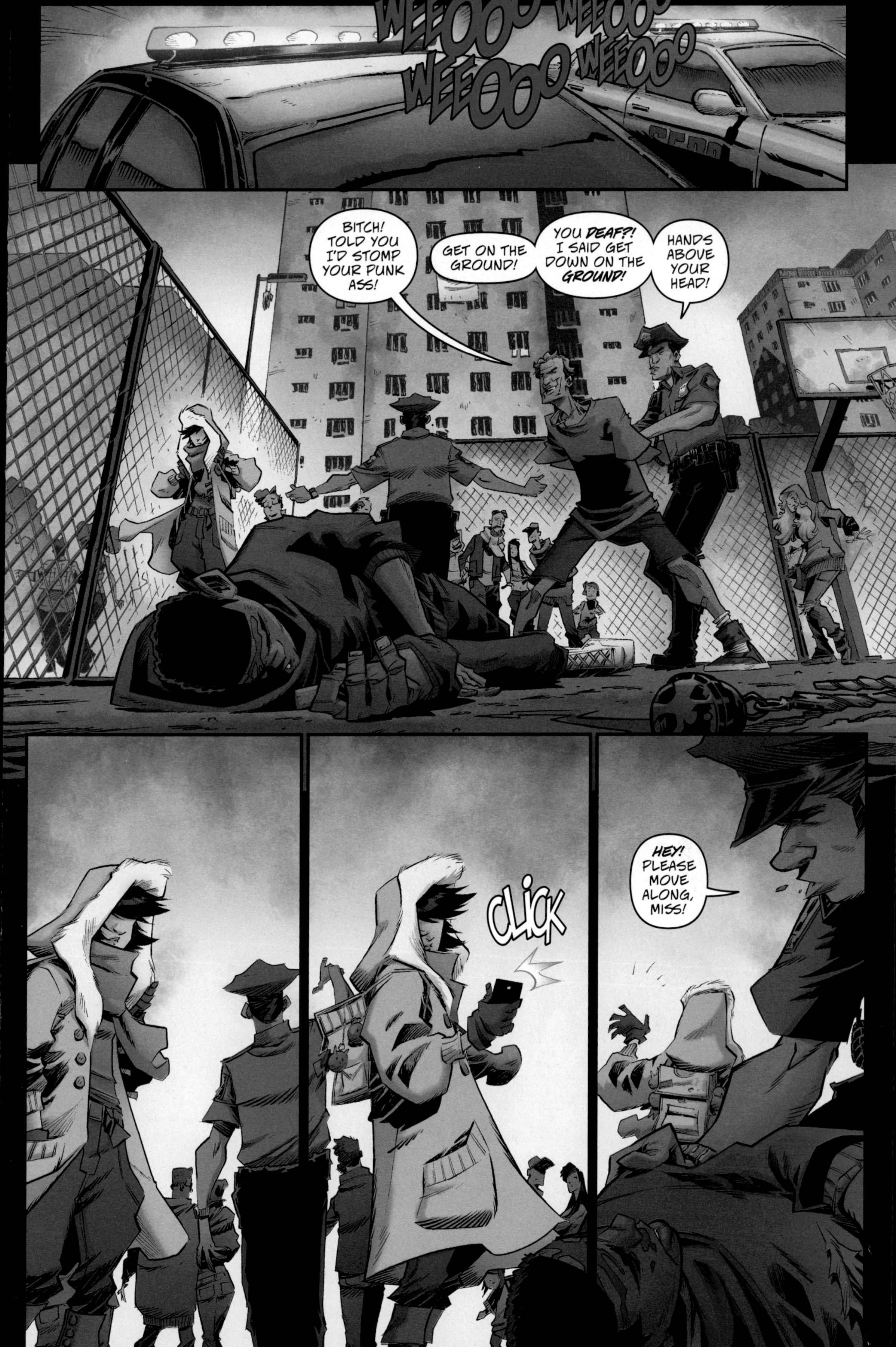
WEEOOO WEEOOO
WEEOOO WEEOOO
BITCH! TOLD YOU I'D STOMP YOUR PUNK ASS!
GET ON THE GROUND!
YOU **DEAF?!** I SAID GET DOWN ON THE **GROUND!**
HANDS ABOVE YOUR HEAD!
CLICK
HEY! PLEASE MOVE ALONG, MISS!

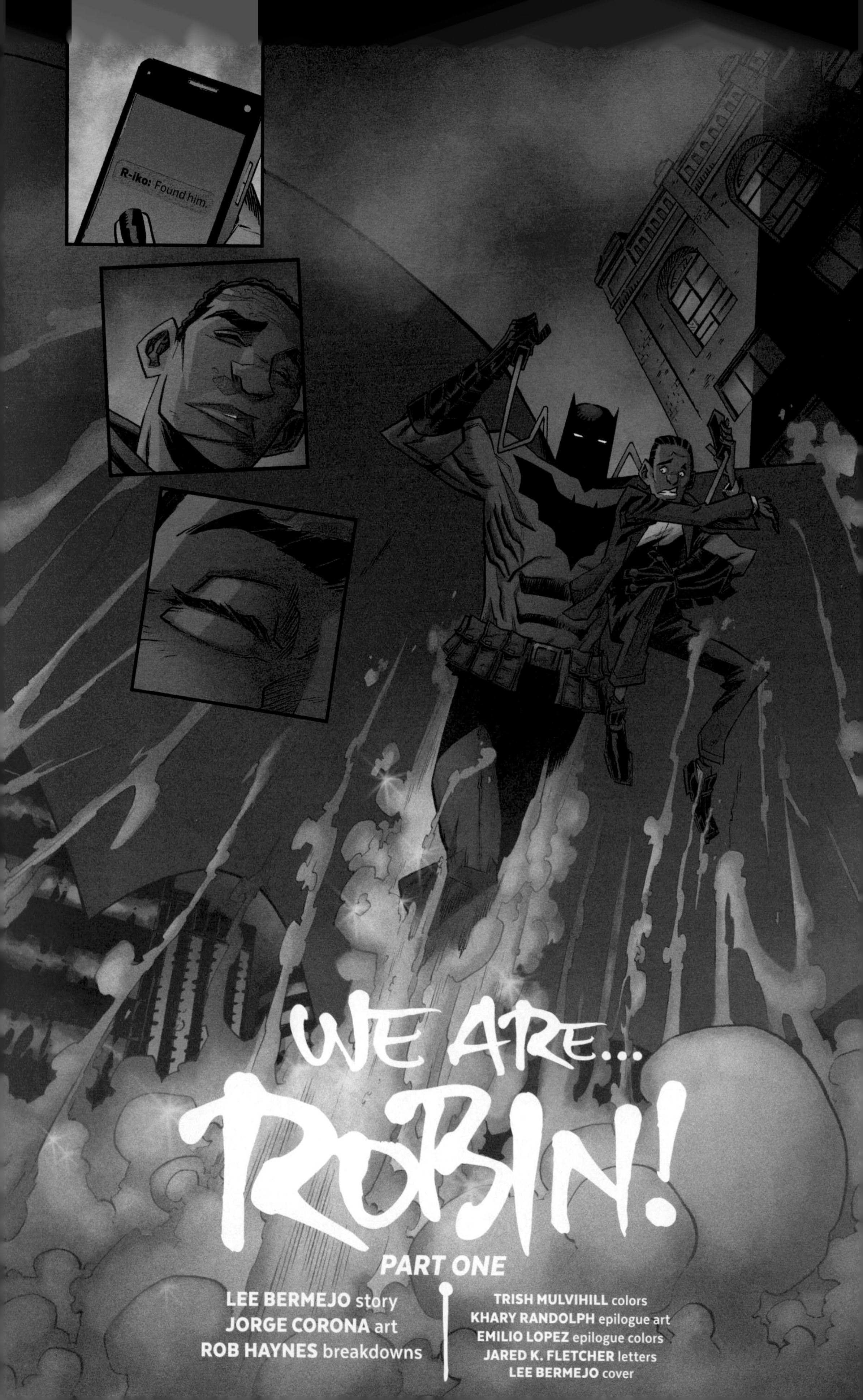
R-iko: Found him.
WE ARE...
ROBIN!
PART ONE
LEE BERMEJO story
JORGE CORONA art
ROB HAYNES breakdowns
TRISH MULVIHILL colors
KHARY RANDOLPH epilogue art
EMILIO LOPEZ epilogue colors
JARED K. FLETCHER letters
LEE BERMEJO cover

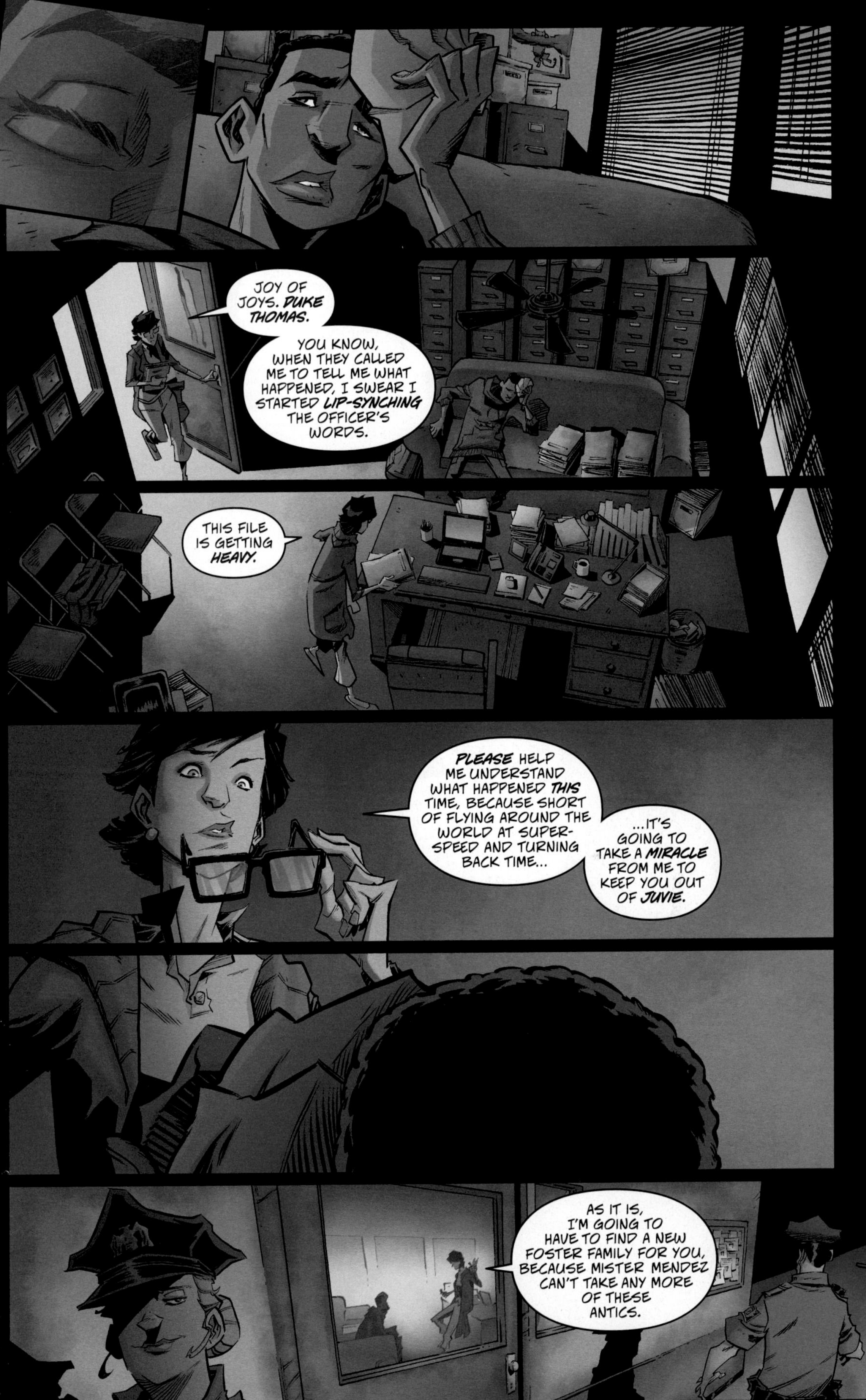

JOY OF JOYS. DUKE THOMAS.
YOU KNOW, WHEN THEY CALLED ME TO TELL ME WHAT HAPPENED, I SWEAR I STARTED LIP-SYNCHING THE OFFICER'S WORDS.
THIS FILE IS GETTING HEAVY.
PLEASE HELP ME UNDERSTAND WHAT HAPPENED THIS TIME, BECAUSE SHORT OF FLYING AROUND THE WORLD AT SUPER-SPEED AND TURNING BACK TIME...
...IT'S GOING TO TAKE A MIRACLE FROM ME TO KEEP YOU OUT OF JUVIE.
AS IT IS, I'M GOING TO HAVE TO FIND A NEW FOSTER FAMILY FOR YOU, BECAUSE MISTER MENDEZ CAN'T TAKE ANY MORE OF THESE ANTICS.

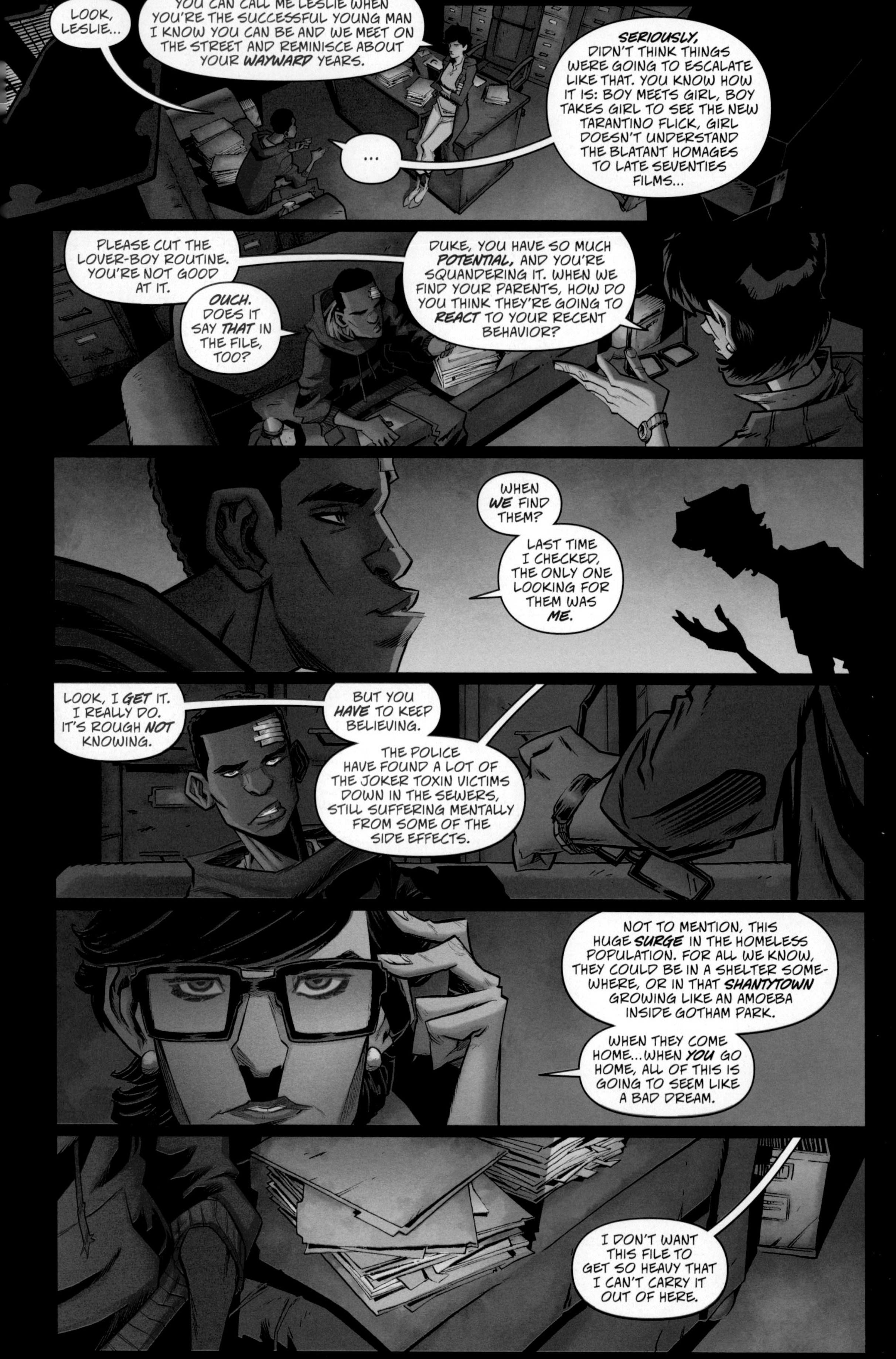
LOOK, LESLIE...
IT'S DOCTOR THOMPKINS. YOU CAN CALL ME LESLIE WHEN YOU'RE THE SUCCESSFUL YOUNG MAN I KNOW YOU CAN BE AND WE MEET ON THE STREET AND REMINISCE ABOUT YOUR WAYWARD YEARS.
...
SERIOUSLY, DIDN'T THINK THINGS WERE GOING TO ESCALATE LIKE THAT. YOU KNOW HOW IT IS: BOY MEETS GIRL, BOY TAKES GIRL TO SEE THE NEW TARANTINO FLICK, GIRL DOESN'T UNDERSTAND THE BLATANT HOMAGES TO LATE SEVENTIES FILMS...
PLEASE CUT THE LOVER-BOY ROUTINE. YOU'RE NOT GOOD AT IT.
OUCH. DOES IT SAY THAT IN THE FILE, TOO?
DUKE, YOU HAVE SO MUCH POTENTIAL, AND YOU'RE SQUANDERING IT. WHEN WE FIND YOUR PARENTS, HOW DO YOU THINK THEY'RE GOING TO REACT TO YOUR RECENT BEHAVIOR?
WHEN WE FIND THEM?
LAST TIME I CHECKED, THE ONLY ONE LOOKING FOR THEM WAS ME.
LOOK, I GET IT. I REALLY DO. IT'S ROUGH NOT KNOWING.
BUT YOU HAVE TO KEEP BELIEVING.
THE POLICE HAVE FOUND A LOT OF THE JOKER TOXIN VICTIMS DOWN IN THE SEWERS, STILL SUFFERING MENTALLY FROM SOME OF THE SIDE EFFECTS.
NOT TO MENTION, THIS HUGE SURGE IN THE HOMELESS POPULATION. FOR ALL WE KNOW, THEY COULD BE IN A SHELTER SOMEWHERE, OR IN THAT SHANTYTOWN GROWING LIKE AN AMOEBA INSIDE GOTHAM PARK.
WHEN THEY COME HOME...WHEN YOU GO HOME, ALL OF THIS IS GOING TO SEEM LIKE A BAD DREAM.
I DON'T WANT THIS FILE TO GET SO HEAVY THAT I CAN'T CARRY IT OUT OF HERE.

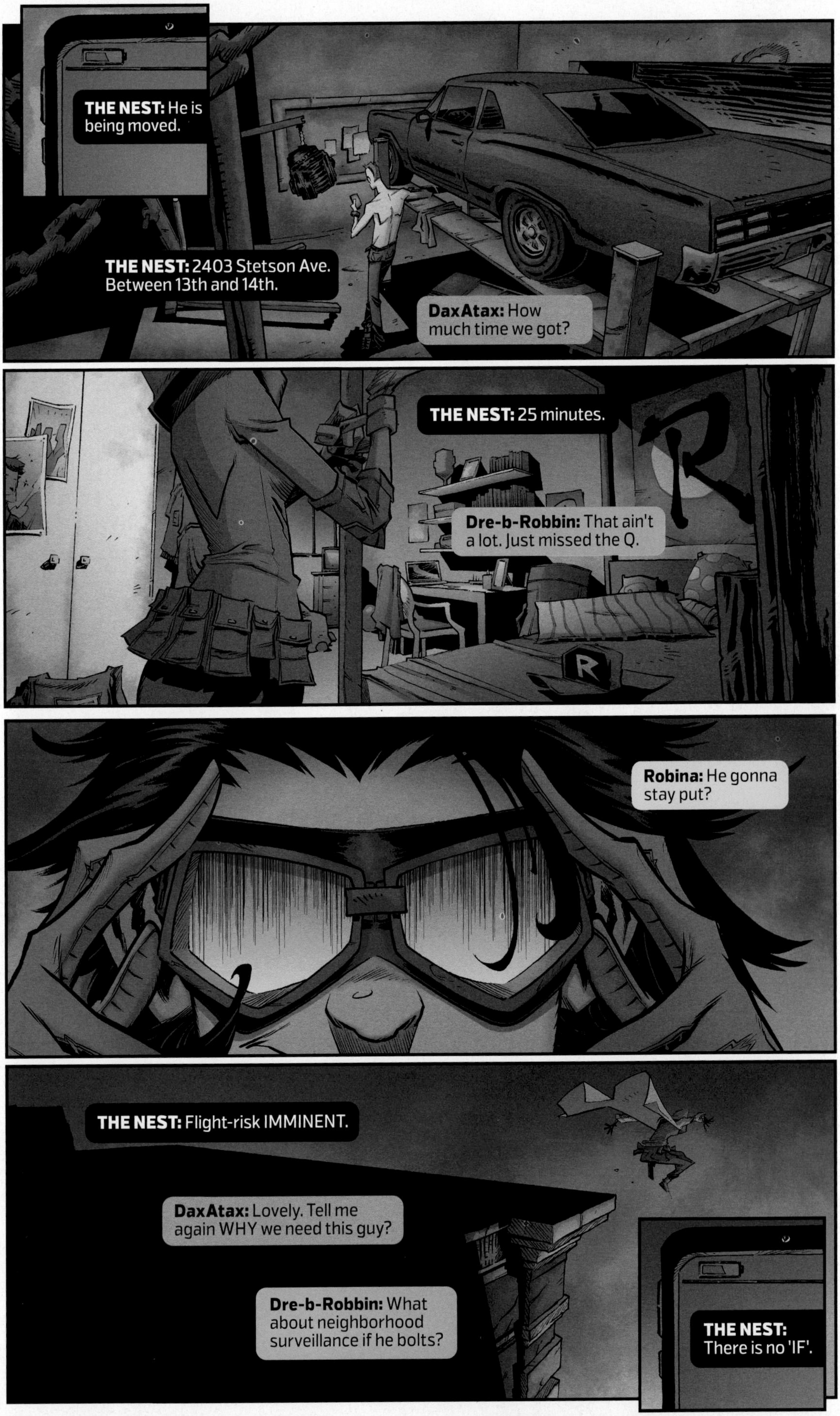
THE NEST: He is being moved.
THE NEST: 2403 Stetson Ave. Between 13th and 14th.
DaxAtax: How much time we got?
THE NEST: 25 minutes.
Dre-b-Robbin: That ain't a lot. Just missed the Q.
Robina: He gonna stay put?
THE NEST: Flight-risk IMMINENT.
DaxAtax: Lovely. Tell me again WHY we need this guy?
Dre-b-Robbin: What about neighborhood surveillance if he bolts?
THE NEST: There is no 'IF'.

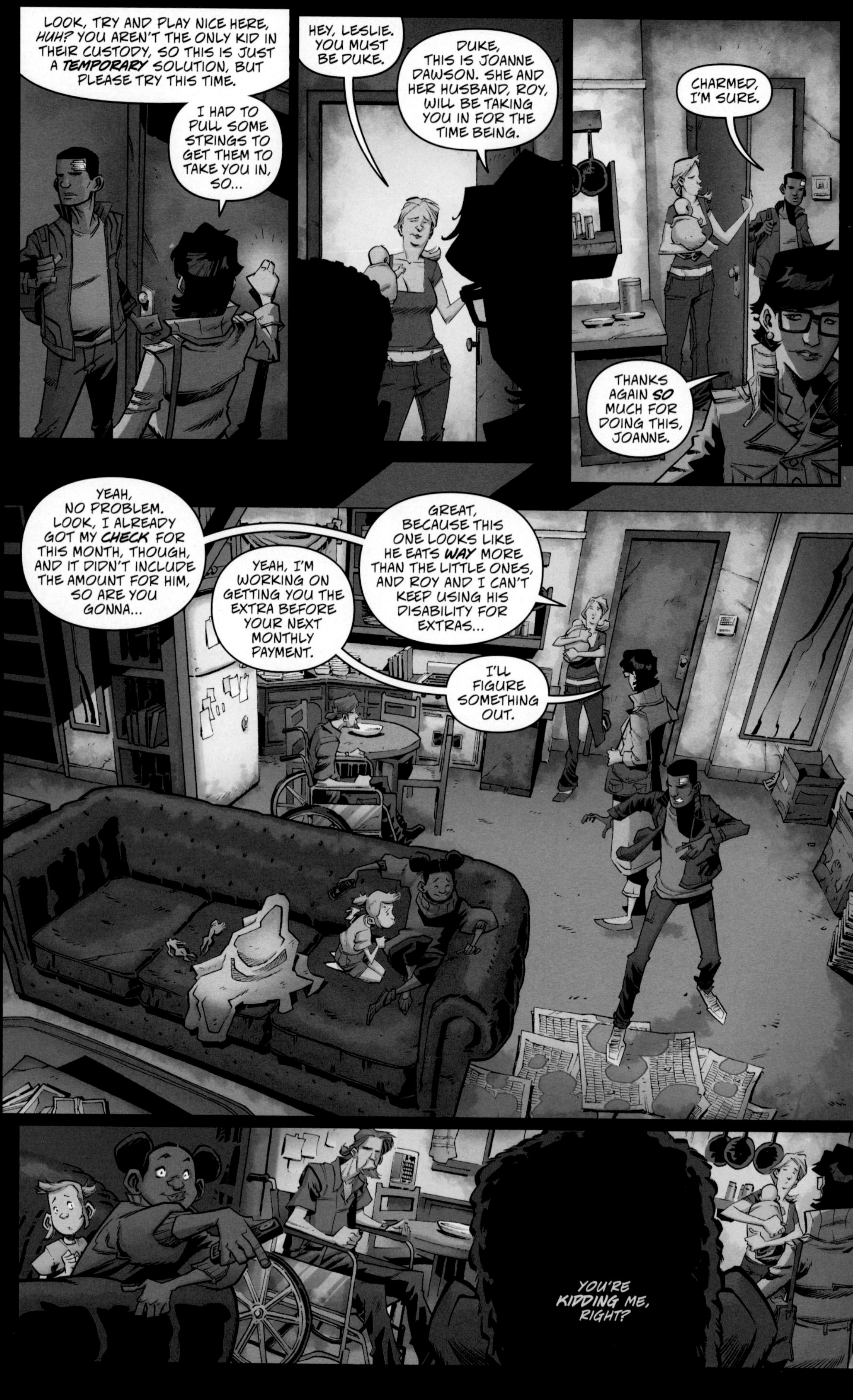
LOOK, TRY AND PLAY NICE HERE, HUH? YOU AREN'T THE ONLY KID IN THEIR CUSTODY, SO THIS IS JUST A TEMPORARY SOLUTION, BUT PLEASE TRY THIS TIME.
I HAD TO PULL SOME STRINGS TO GET THEM TO TAKE YOU IN, SO...
HEY, LESLIE. YOU MUST BE DUKE.
DUKE, THIS IS JOANNE DAWSON. SHE AND HER HUSBAND, ROY, WILL BE TAKING YOU IN FOR THE TIME BEING.
CHARMED, I'M SURE.
THANKS AGAIN SO MUCH FOR DOING THIS, JOANNE.
YEAH, NO PROBLEM. LOOK, I ALREADY GOT MY CHECK FOR THIS MONTH, THOUGH, AND IT DIDN'T INCLUDE THE AMOUNT FOR HIM, SO ARE YOU GONNA...
YEAH, I'M WORKING ON GETTING YOU THE EXTRA BEFORE YOUR NEXT MONTHLY PAYMENT.
GREAT, BECAUSE THIS ONE LOOKS LIKE HE EATS WAY MORE THAN THE LITTLE ONES, AND ROY AND I CAN'T KEEP USING HIS DISABILITY FOR EXTRAS...
I'LL FIGURE SOMETHING OUT.
YOU'RE KIDDING ME, RIGHT?

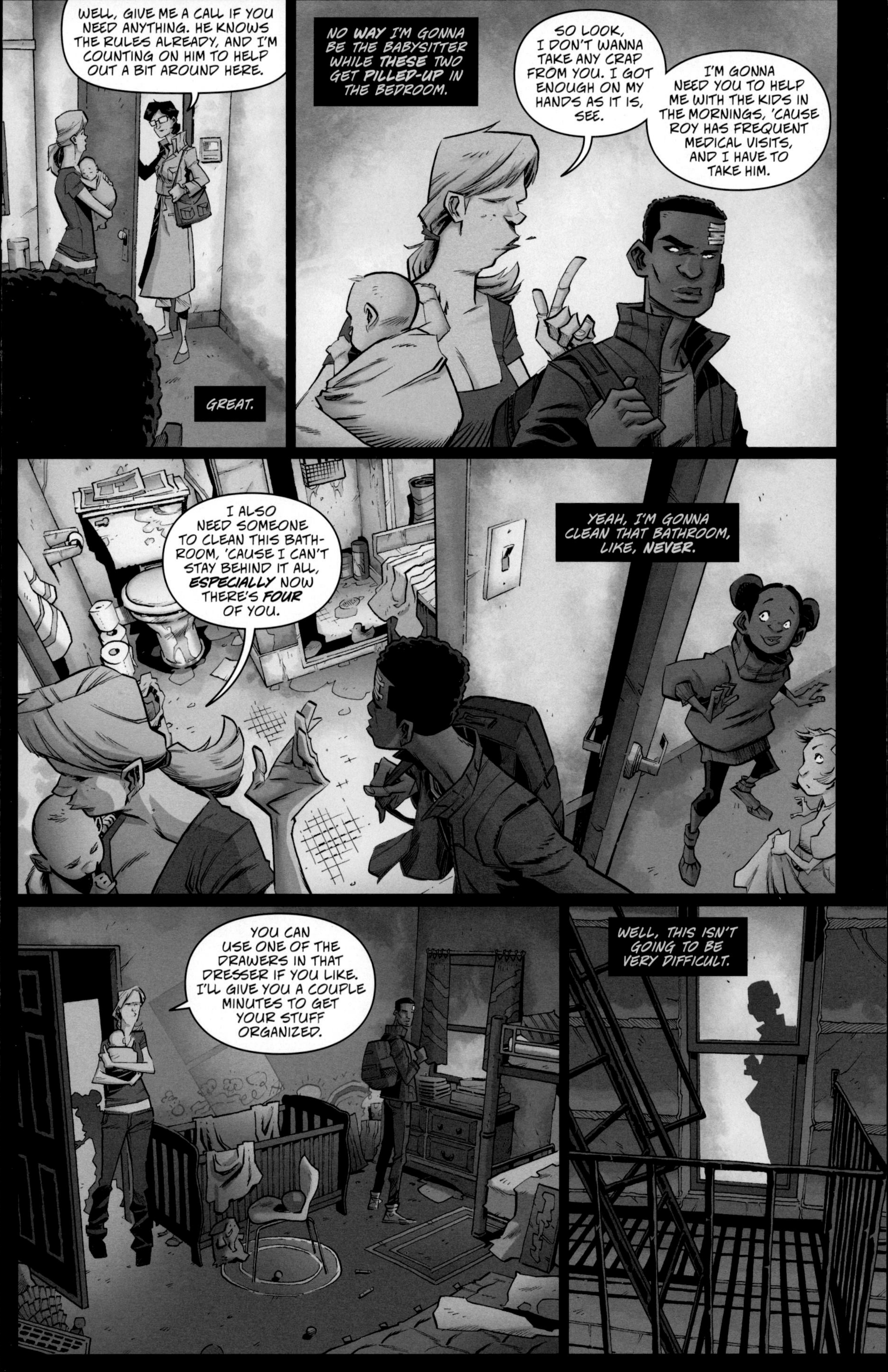

WELL, GIVE ME A CALL IF YOU NEED ANYTHING. HE KNOWS THE RULES ALREADY, AND I'M COUNTING ON HIM TO HELP OUT A BIT AROUND HERE.
GREAT.
NO WAY I'M GONNA BE THE BABYSITTER WHILE THESE TWO GET PILLED-UP IN THE BEDROOM.
SO LOOK, I DON'T WANNA TAKE ANY CRAP FROM YOU. I GOT ENOUGH ON MY HANDS AS IT IS, SEE.
I'M GONNA NEED YOU TO HELP ME WITH THE KIDS IN THE MORNINGS, 'CAUSE ROY HAS FREQUENT MEDICAL VISITS, AND I HAVE TO TAKE HIM.
I ALSO NEED SOMEONE TO CLEAN THIS BATH-ROOM, 'CAUSE I CAN'T STAY BEHIND IT ALL, ESPECIALLY NOW THERE'S FOUR OF YOU.
YEAH, I'M GONNA CLEAN THAT BATHROOM, LIKE, NEVER.
YOU CAN USE ONE OF THE DRAWERS IN THAT DRESSER IF YOU LIKE. I'LL GIVE YOU A COUPLE MINUTES TO GET YOUR STUFF ORGANIZED.
WELL, THIS ISN'T GOING TO BE VERY DIFFICULT.

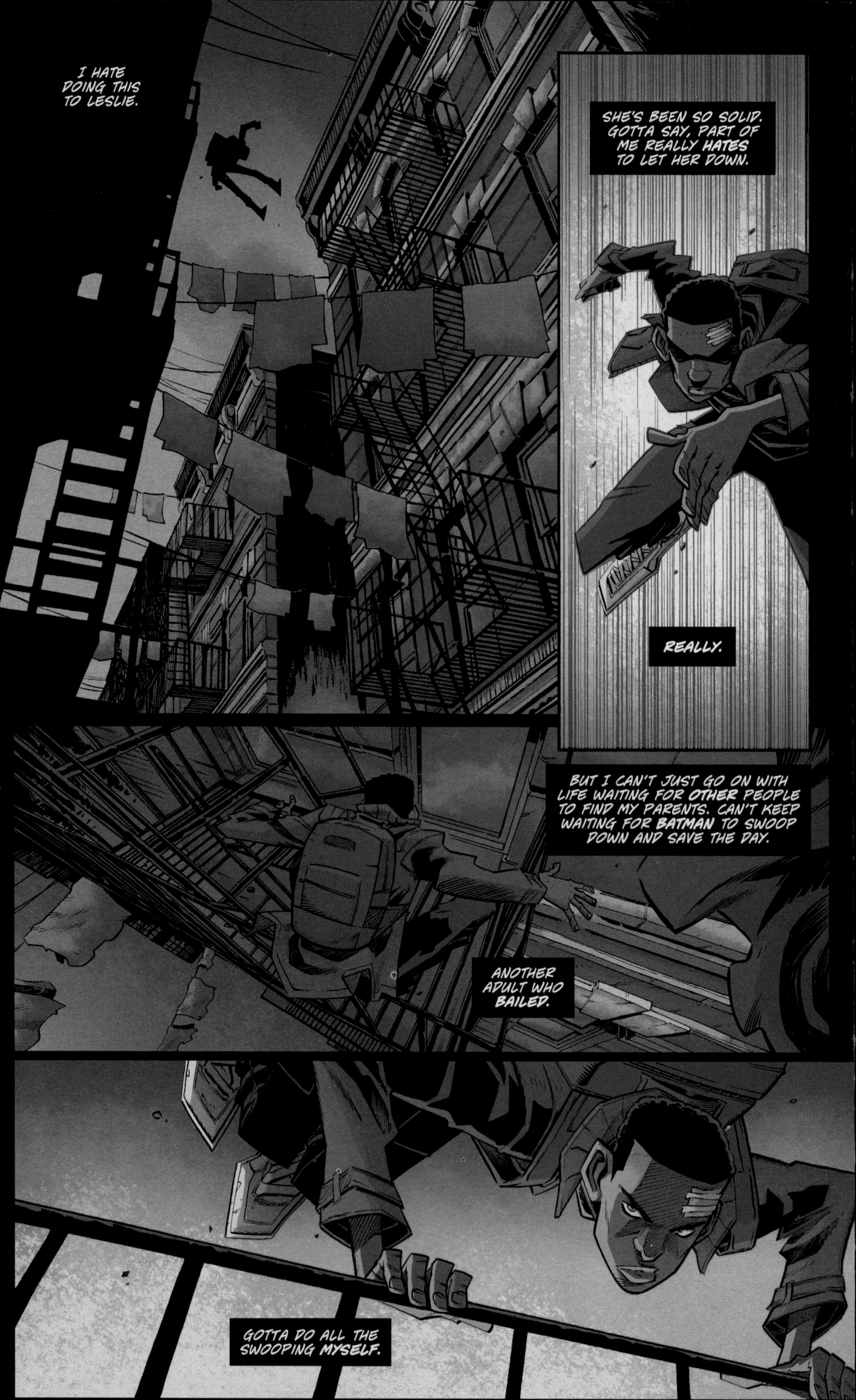
I HATE DOING THIS TO LESLIE.
SHE'S BEEN SO SOLID. GOTTA SAY, PART OF ME REALLY HATES TO LET HER DOWN.
REALLY.
BUT I CAN'T JUST GO ON WITH LIFE WAITING FOR OTHER PEOPLE TO FIND MY PARENTS. CAN'T KEEP WAITING FOR BATMAN TO SWOOP DOWN AND SAVE THE DAY.
ANOTHER ADULT WHO BAILED.
GOTTA DO ALL THE SWOOPING MYSELF.

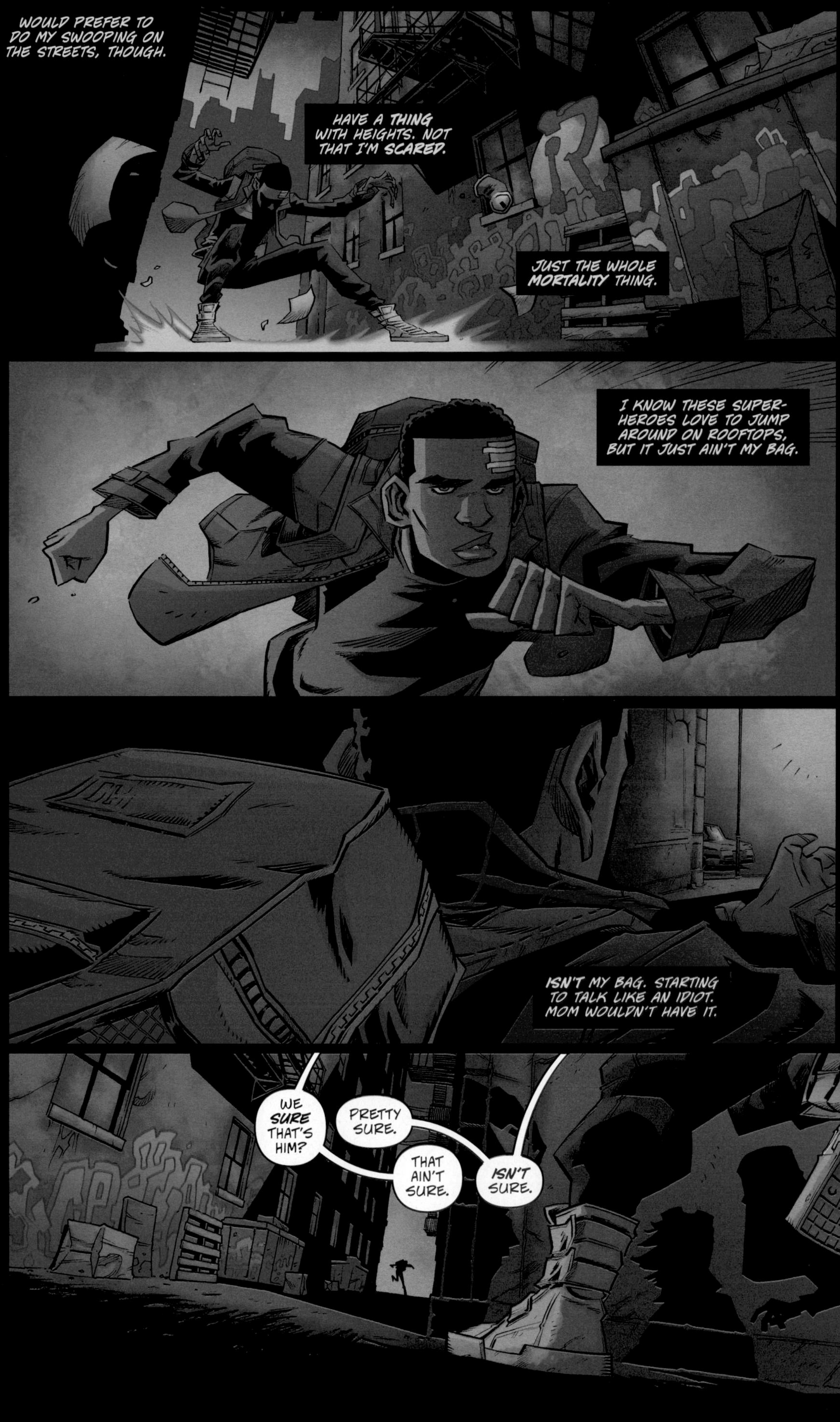
WOULD PREFER TO DO MY SWOOPING ON THE STREETS, THOUGH.
HAVE A THING WITH HEIGHTS. NOT THAT I'M SCARED.
JUST THE WHOLE MORTALITY THING.
I KNOW THESE SUPER-HEROES LOVE TO JUMP AROUND ON ROOFTOPS, BUT IT JUST AIN'T MY BAG.
ISN'T MY BAG. STARTING TO TALK LIKE AN IDIOT. MOM WOULDN'T HAVE IT.
WE SURE THAT'S HIM?
PRETTY SURE.
THAT AIN'T SURE.
ISN'T SURE.

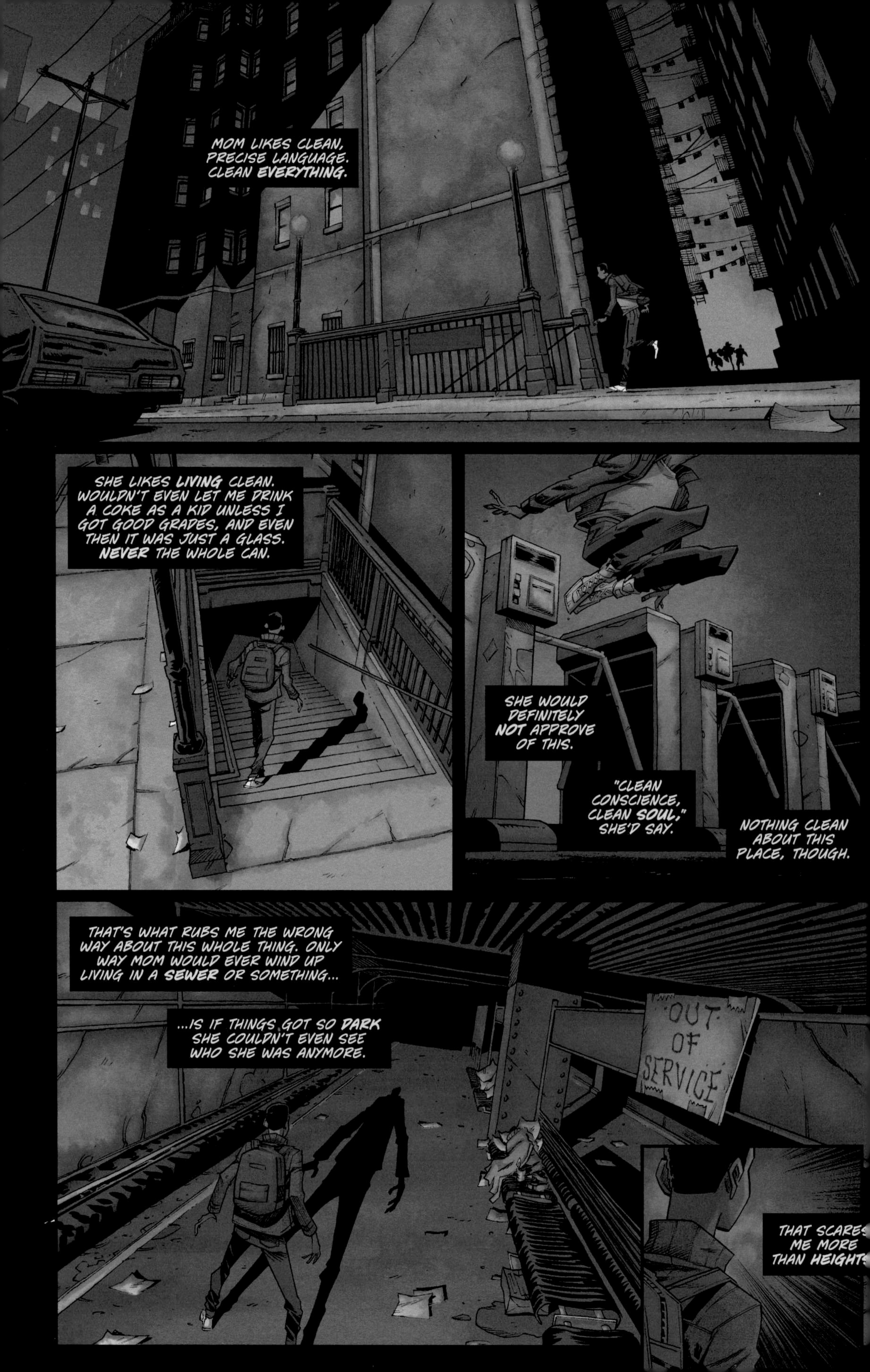
MOM LIKES CLEAN, PRECISE LANGUAGE. CLEAN EVERYTHING.
SHE LIKES LIVING CLEAN. WOULDN'T EVEN LET ME DRINK A COKE AS A KID UNLESS I GOT GOOD GRADES, AND EVEN THEN IT WAS JUST A GLASS. NEVER THE WHOLE CAN.
SHE WOULD DEFINITELY NOT APPROVE OF THIS.
"CLEAN CONSCIENCE, CLEAN SOUL," SHE'D SAY.
NOTHING CLEAN ABOUT THIS PLACE, THOUGH.
THAT'S WHAT RUBS ME THE WRONG WAY ABOUT THIS WHOLE THING. ONLY WAY MOM WOULD EVER WIND UP LIVING IN A SEWER OR SOMETHING...
...IS IF THINGS GOT SO DARK SHE COULDN'T EVEN SEE WHO SHE WAS ANYMORE.
OUT OF SERVICE
THAT SCARES ME MORE THAN HEIGHTS

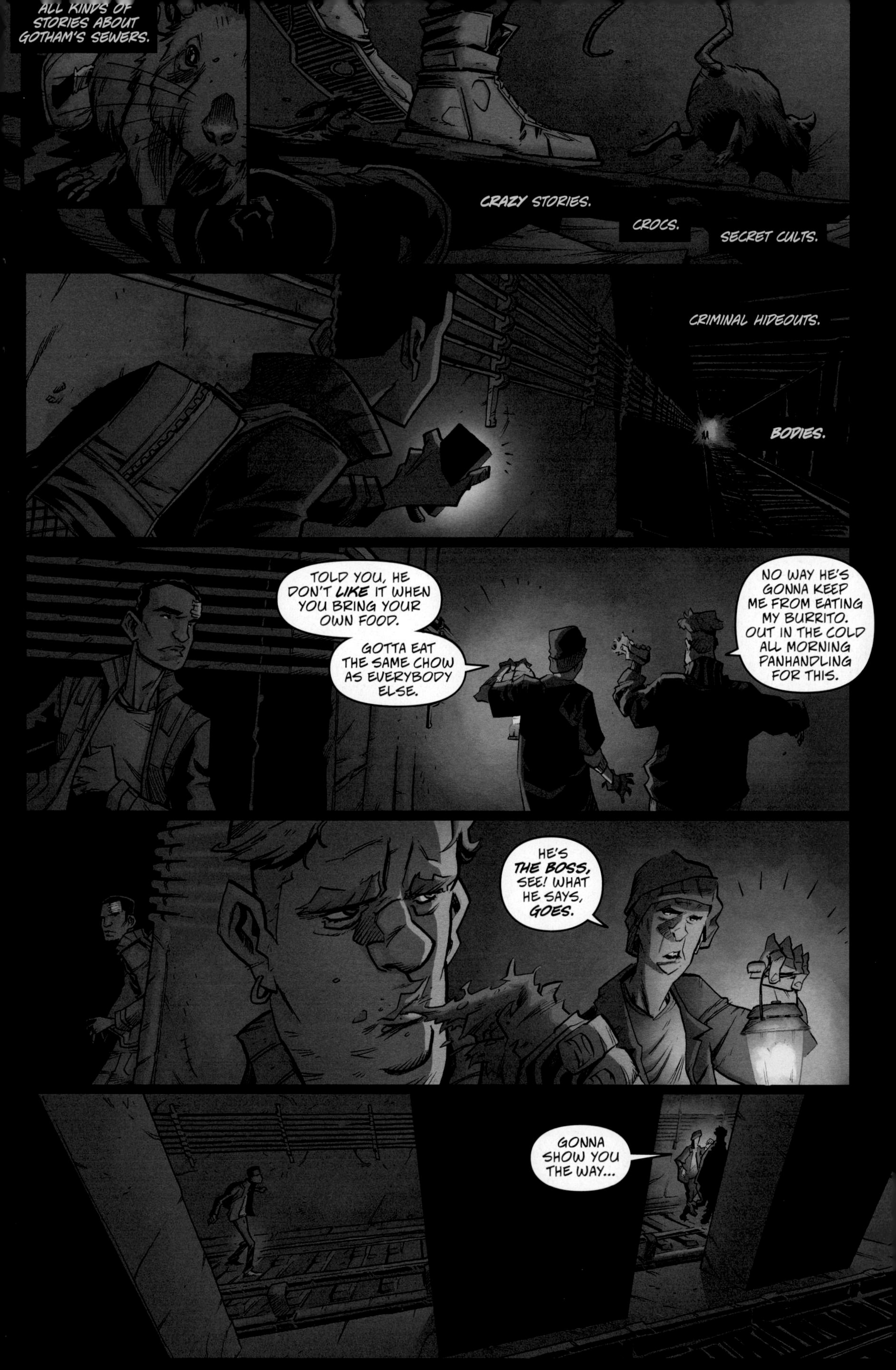
ALL KINDS OF STORIES ABOUT GOTHAM'S SEWERS.
CRAZY STORIES.
CROCS.
SECRET CULTS.
CRIMINAL HIDEOUTS.
BODIES.
TOLD YOU, HE DON'T LIKE IT WHEN YOU BRING YOUR OWN FOOD.
GOTTA EAT THE SAME CHOW AS EVERYBODY ELSE.
NO WAY HE'S GONNA KEEP ME FROM EATING MY BURRITO. OUT IN THE COLD ALL MORNING PANHANDLING FOR THIS.
HE'S THE BOSS, SEE! WHAT HE SAYS, GOES.
GONNA SHOW YOU THE WAY...

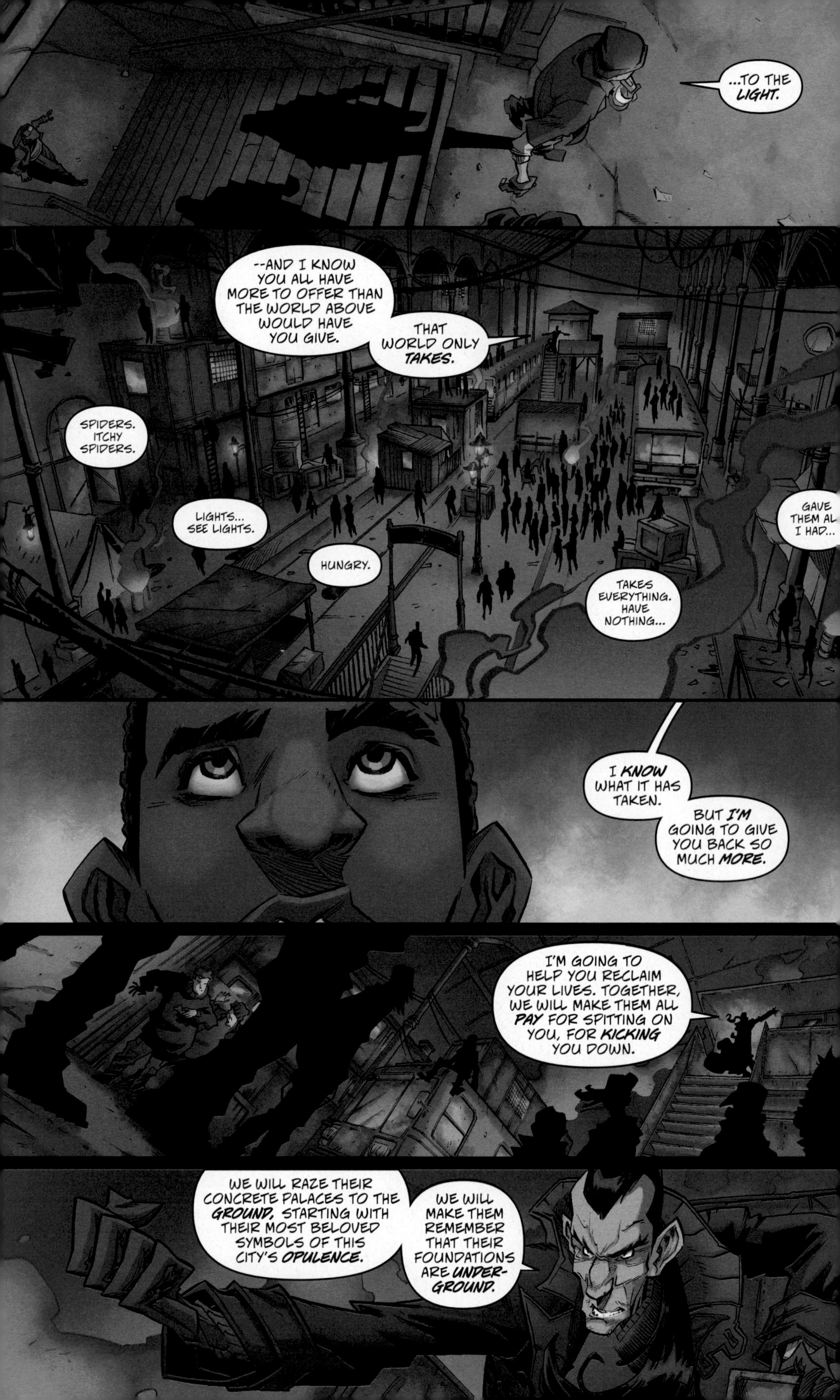
...TO THE LIGHT.
--AND I KNOW YOU ALL HAVE MORE TO OFFER THAN THE WORLD ABOVE WOULD HAVE YOU GIVE.
THAT WORLD ONLY TAKES.
SPIDERS. ITCHY SPIDERS.
LIGHTS... SEE LIGHTS.
HUNGRY.
TAKES EVERYTHING. HAVE NOTHING...
GAVE THEM AL I HAD...
I KNOW WHAT IT HAS TAKEN.
BUT I'M GOING TO GIVE YOU BACK SO MUCH MORE.
I'M GOING TO HELP YOU RECLAIM YOUR LIVES. TOGETHER, WE WILL MAKE THEM ALL PAY FOR SPITTING ON YOU, FOR KICKING YOU DOWN.
WE WILL RAZE THEIR CONCRETE PALACES TO THE GROUND, STARTING WITH THEIR MOST BELOVED SYMBOLS OF THIS CITY'S OPULENCE.
WE WILL MAKE THEM REMEMBER THAT THEIR FOUNDATIONS ARE UNDER-GROUND.

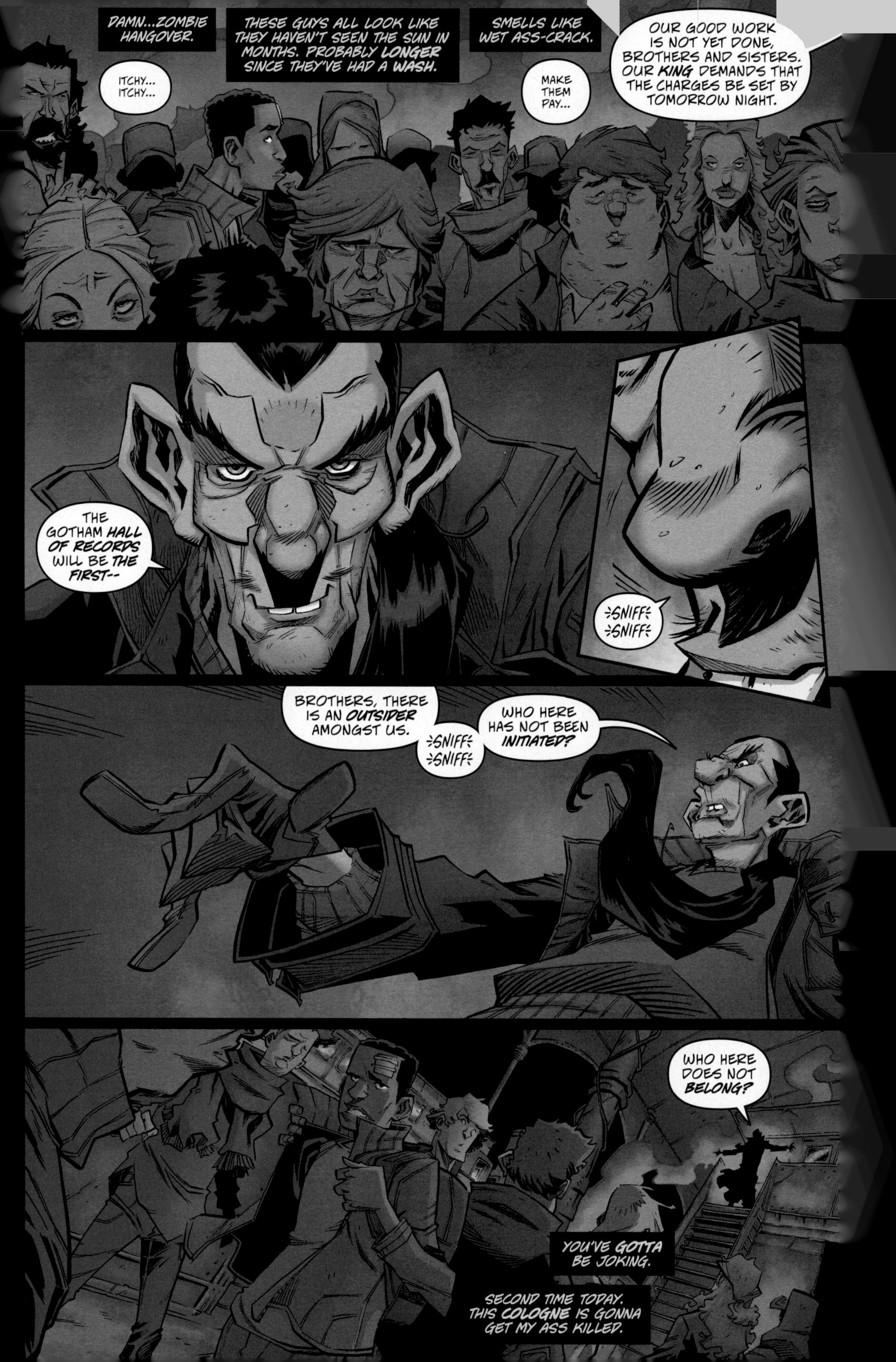
DAMN...ZOMBIE HANGOVER.
ITCHY... ITCHY...
THESE GUYS ALL LOOK LIKE THEY HAVEN'T SEEN THE SUN IN MONTHS. PROBABLY LONGER SINCE THEY'VE HAD A WASH.
SMELLS LIKE WET ASS-CRACK.
MAKE THEM PAY...
OUR GOOD WORK IS NOT YET DONE, BROTHERS AND SISTERS. OUR KING DEMANDS THAT THE CHARGES BE SET BY TOMORROW NIGHT.
THE GOTHAM HALL OF RECORDS WILL BE THE FIRST--
SNIFF SNIFF
BROTHERS, THERE IS AN OUTSIDER AMONGST US.
SNIFF SNIFF
WHO HERE HAS NOT BEEN INITIATED?
WHO HERE DOES NOT BELONG?
YOU'VE GOTTA BE JOKING.
SECOND TIME TODAY. THIS COLOGNE IS GONNA GET MY ASS KILLED.

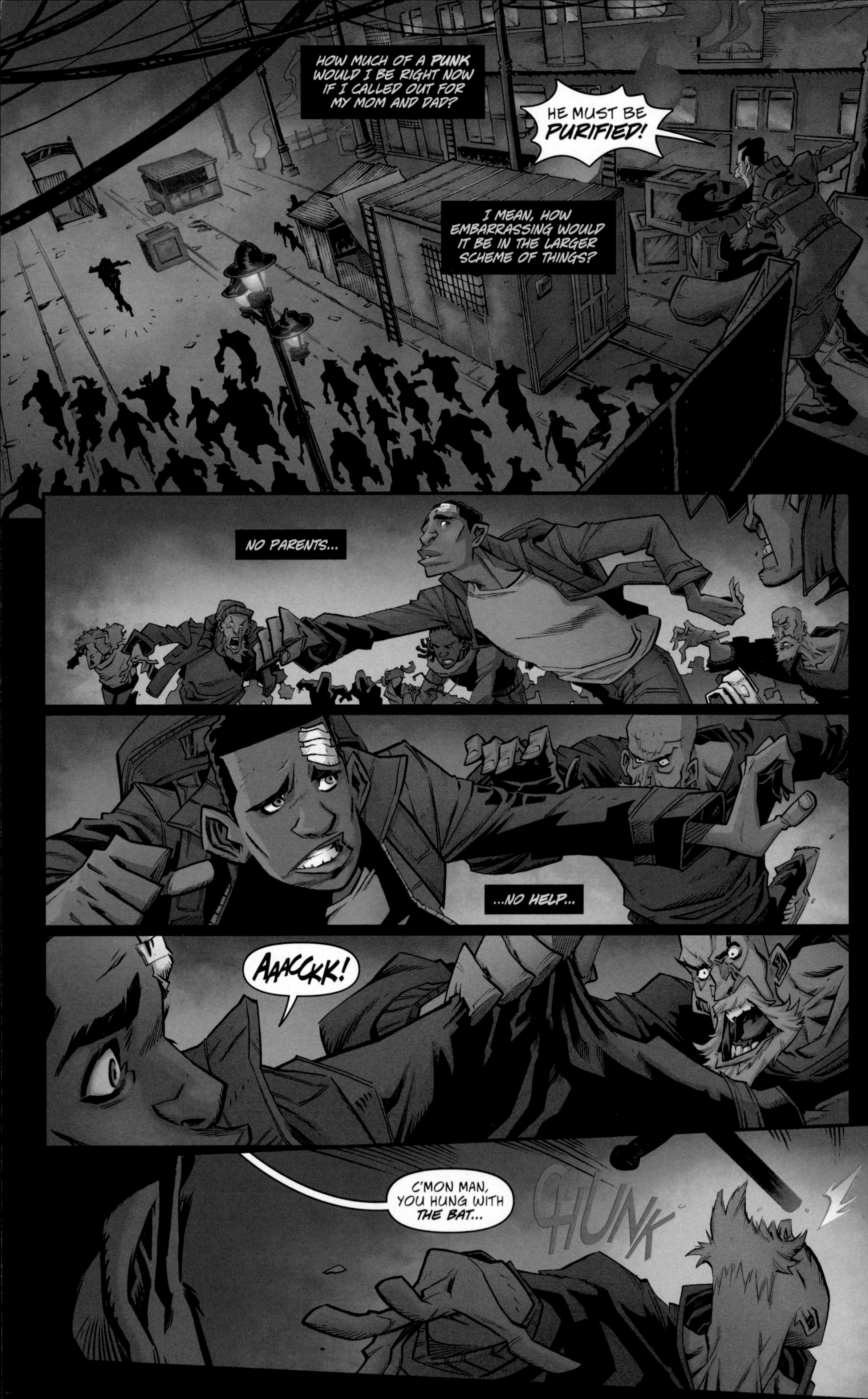
HOW MUCH OF A PUNK WOULD I BE RIGHT NOW IF I CALLED OUT FOR MY MOM AND DAD?
HE MUST BE PURIFIED!
I MEAN, HOW EMBARRASSING WOULD IT BE IN THE LARGER SCHEME OF THINGS?
NO PARENTS...
...NO HELP...
AAACKK!
C'MON MAN, YOU HUNG WITH THE BAT...
CHUNK

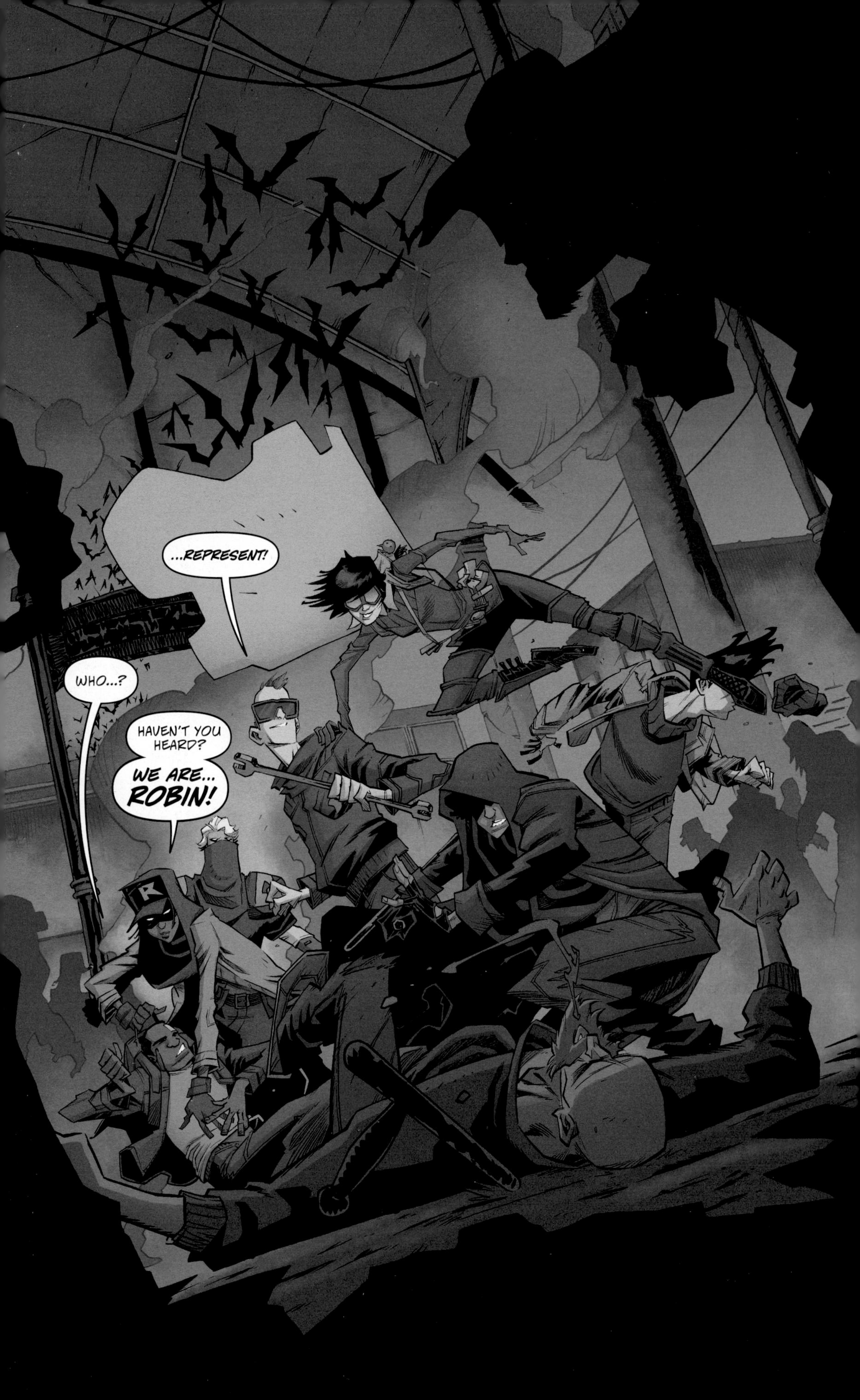
...REPRESENT!
WHO...?
HAVEN'T YOU HEARD?
WE ARE... ROBIN!

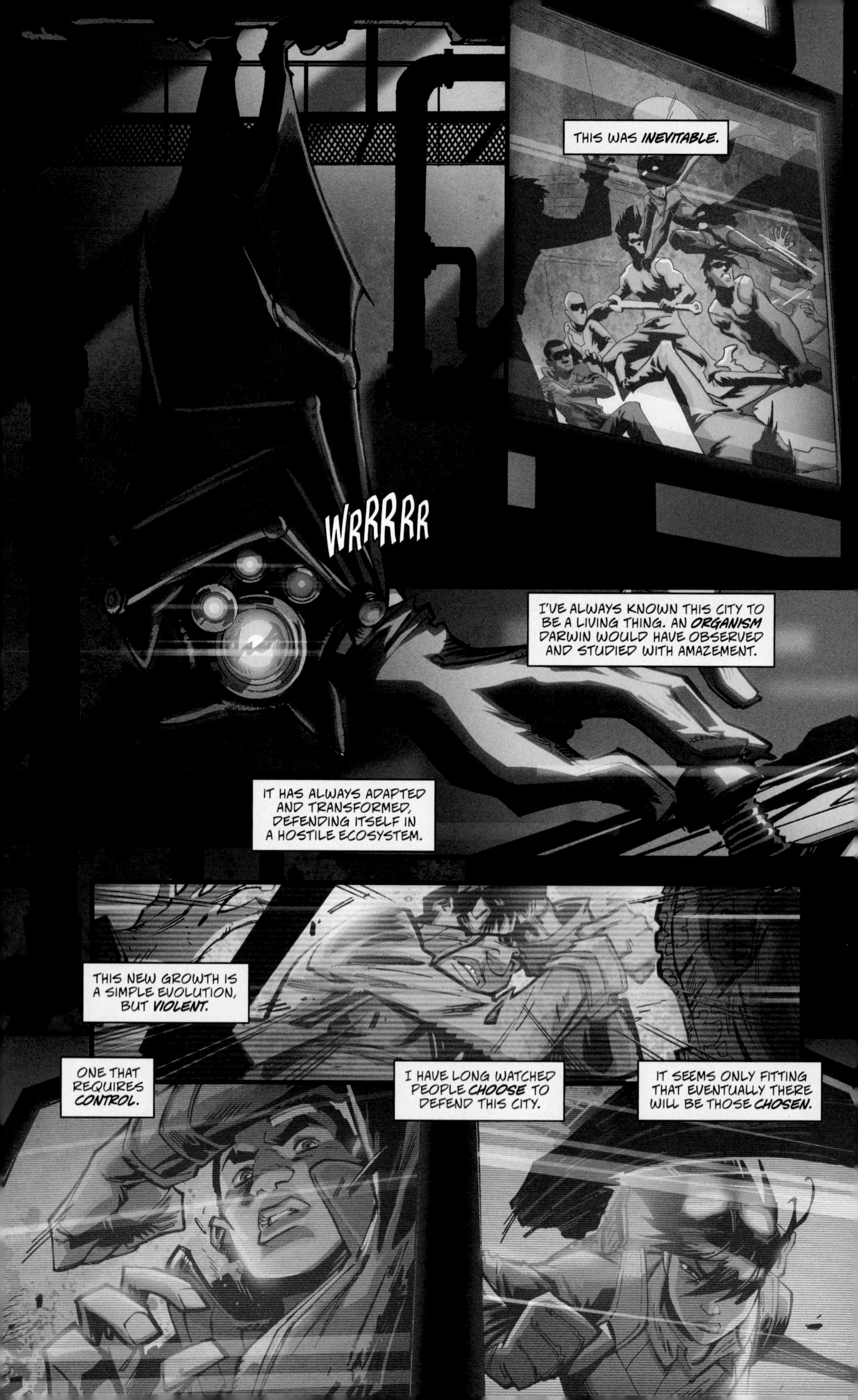
THIS WAS INEVITABLE.
WRRRRR
I'VE ALWAYS KNOWN THIS CITY TO BE A LIVING THING. AN ORGANISM DARWIN WOULD HAVE OBSERVED AND STUDIED WITH AMAZEMENT.
IT HAS ALWAYS ADAPTED AND TRANSFORMED, DEFENDING ITSELF IN A HOSTILE ECOSYSTEM.
THIS NEW GROWTH IS A SIMPLE EVOLUTION, BUT VIOLENT.
ONE THAT REQUIRES CONTROL.
I HAVE LONG WATCHED PEOPLE CHOOSE TO DEFEND THIS CITY.
IT SEEMS ONLY FITTING THAT EVENTUALLY THERE WILL BE THOSE CHOSEN.

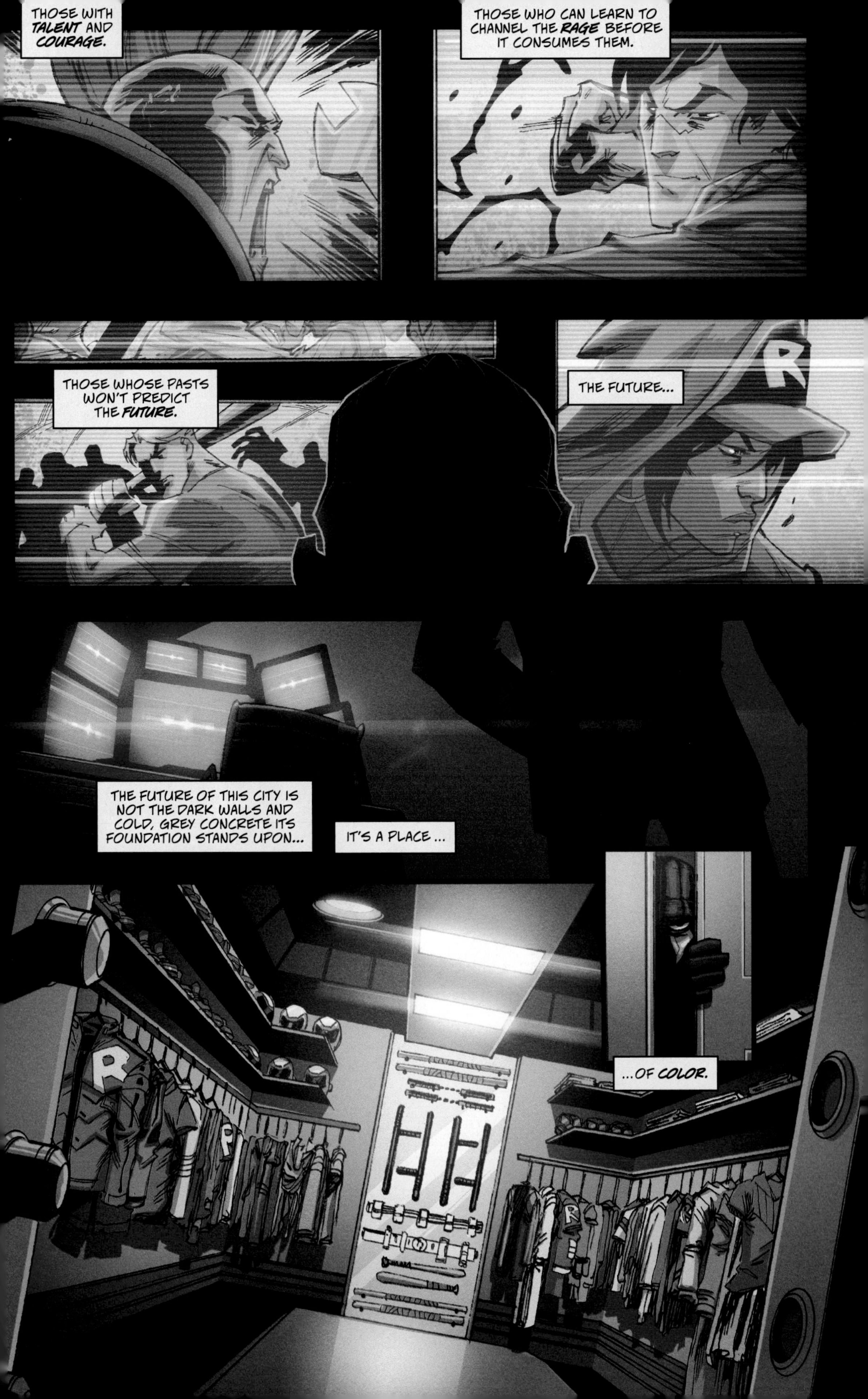
THOSE WITH *TALENT* AND *COURAGE*.
THOSE WHO CAN LEARN TO CHANNEL THE *RAGE* BEFORE IT CONSUMES THEM.
THOSE WHOSE PASTS WON'T PREDICT THE *FUTURE*.
THE FUTURE...
THE FUTURE OF THIS CITY IS NOT THE DARK WALLS AND COLD, GREY CONCRETE ITS FOUNDATION STANDS UPON...
IT'S A PLACE ...
...OF *COLOR*.

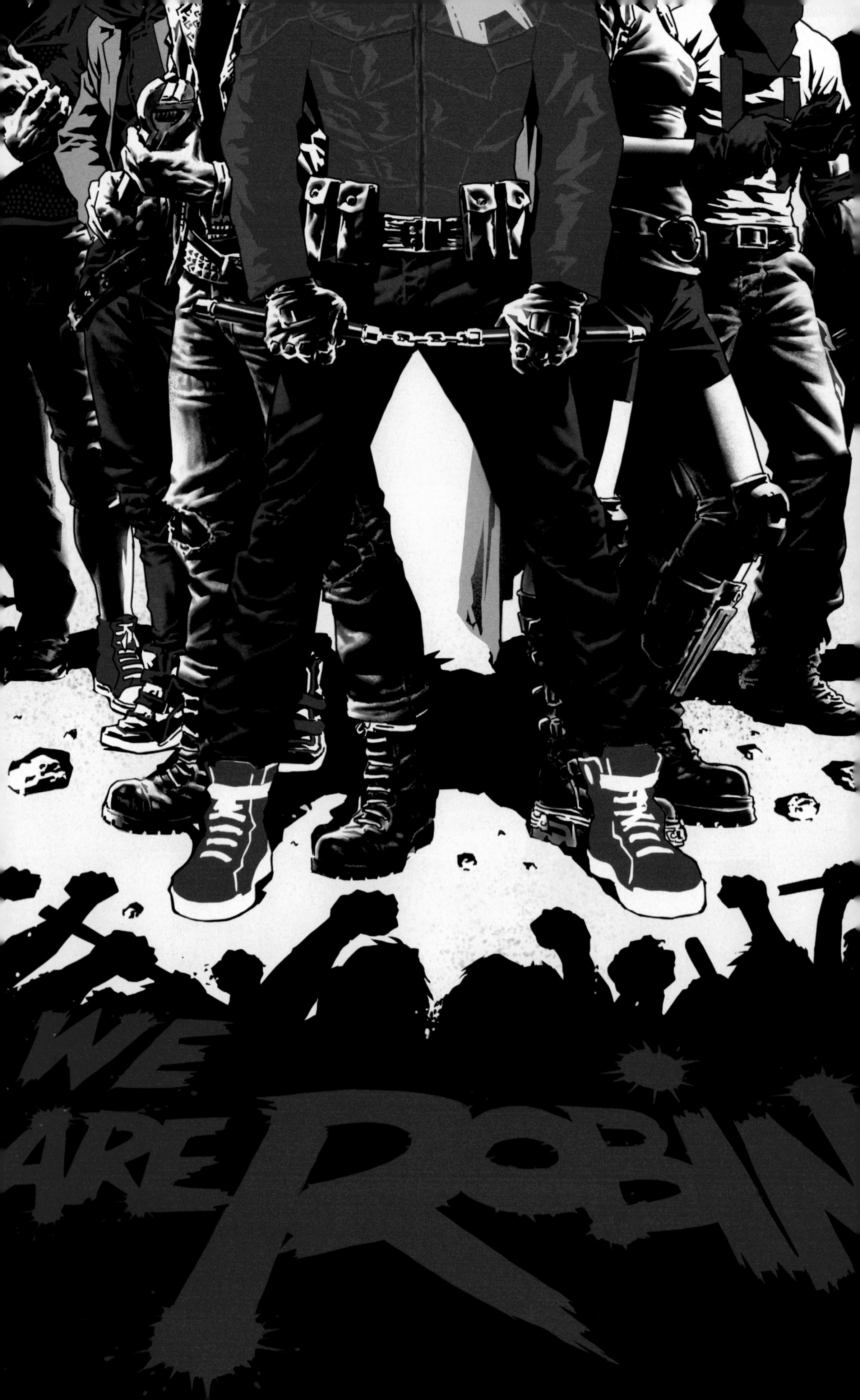
WE ARE ROBIN

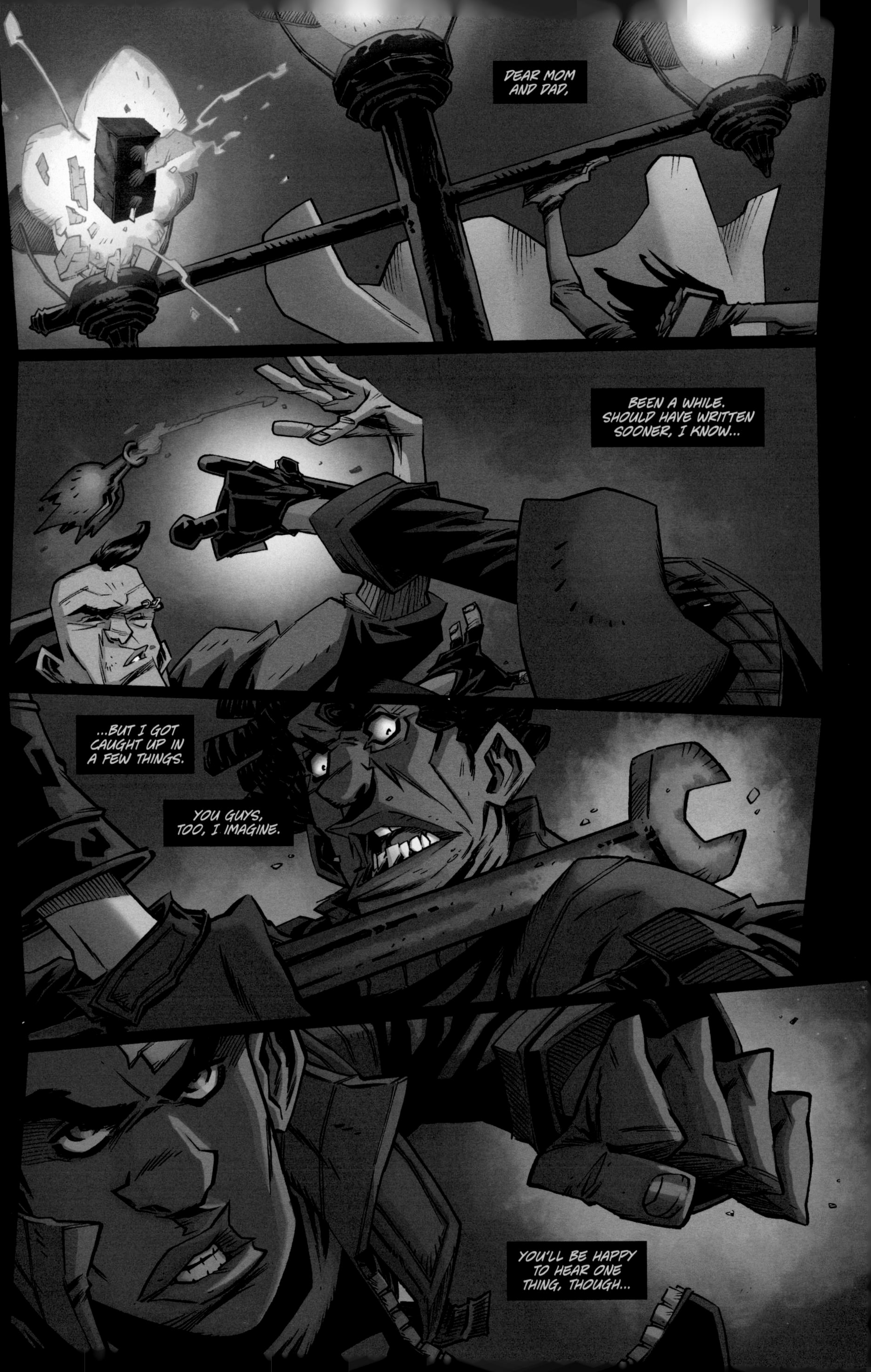
DEAR MOM AND DAD,
BEEN A WHILE. SHOULD HAVE WRITTEN SOONER, I KNOW...
...BUT I GOT CAUGHT UP IN A FEW THINGS.
YOU GUYS, TOO, I IMAGINE.
YOU'LL BE HAPPY TO HEAR ONE THING, THOUGH...

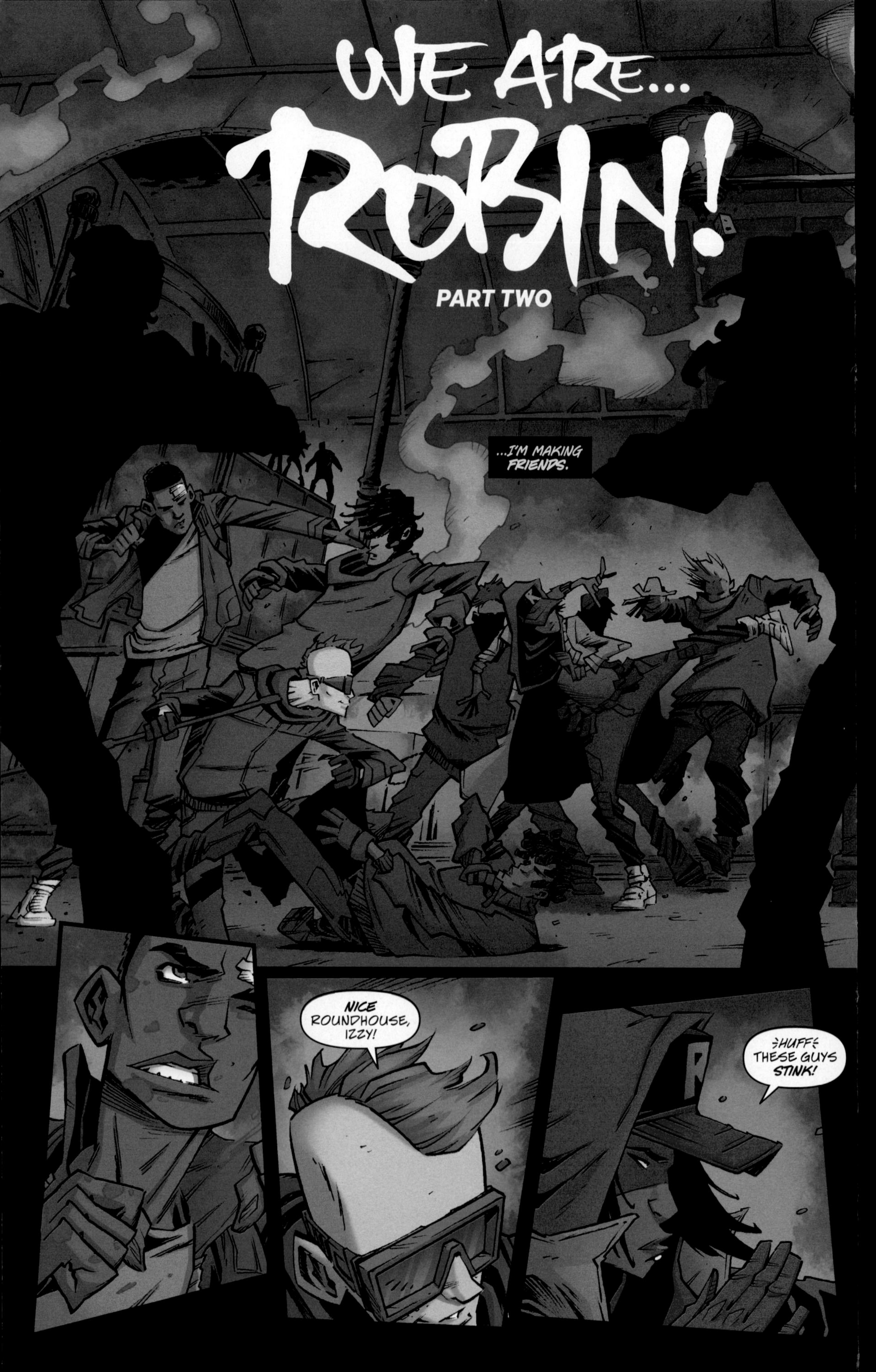
WE ARE...
ROBIN!
PART TWO
...I'M MAKING FRIENDS.
NICE ROUNDHOUSE, IZZY!
HUFF THESE GUYS STINK!

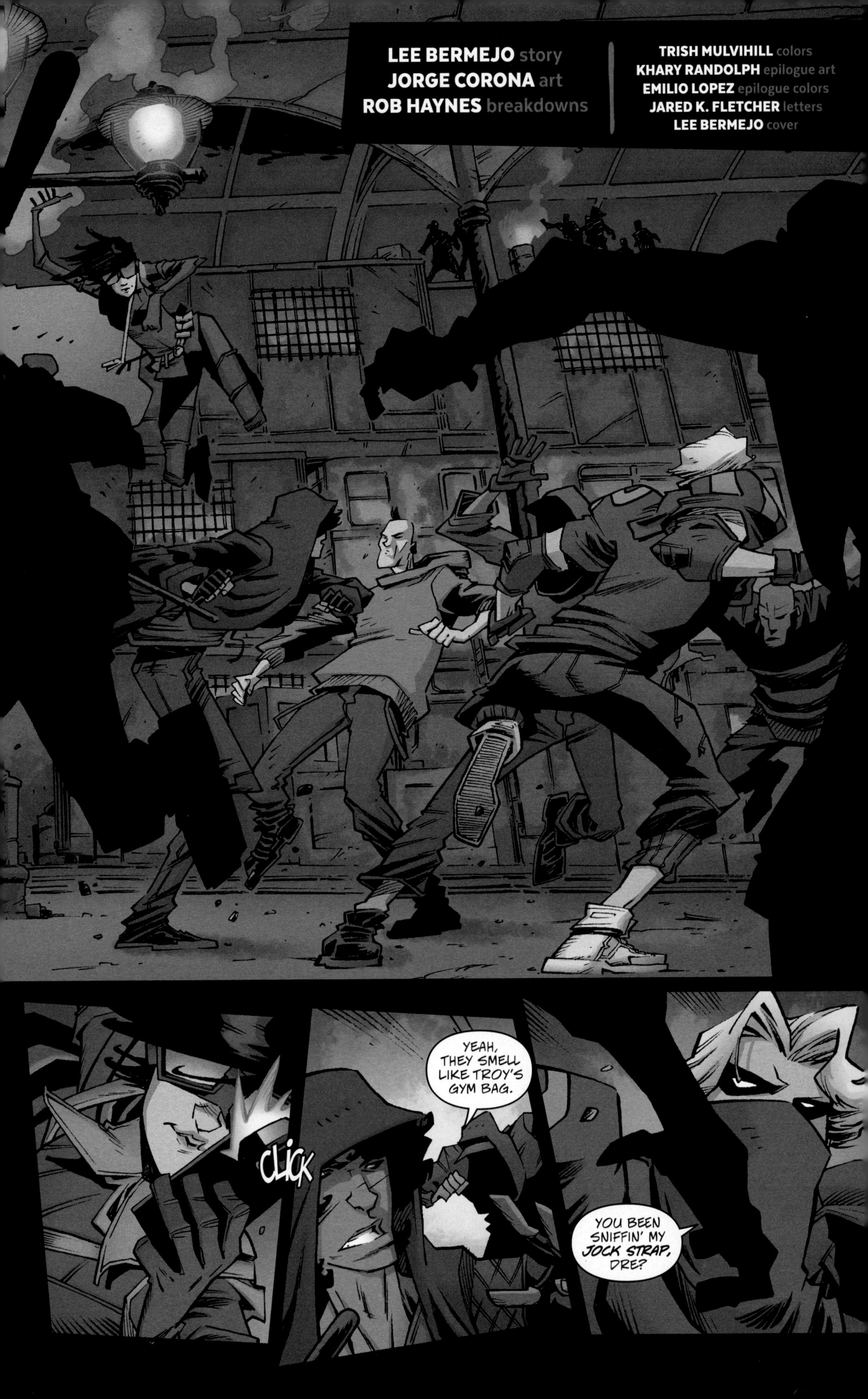
LEE BERMEJO story
JORGE CORONA art
ROB HAYNES breakdowns
TRISH MULVIHILL colors
KHARY RANDOLPH epilogue art
EMILIO LOPEZ epilogue colors
JARED K. FLETCHER letters
LEE BERMEJO cover
CLICK
YEAH, THEY SMELL LIKE TROY'S GYM BAG.
YOU BEEN SNIFFIN' MY JOCK STRAP, DRE?

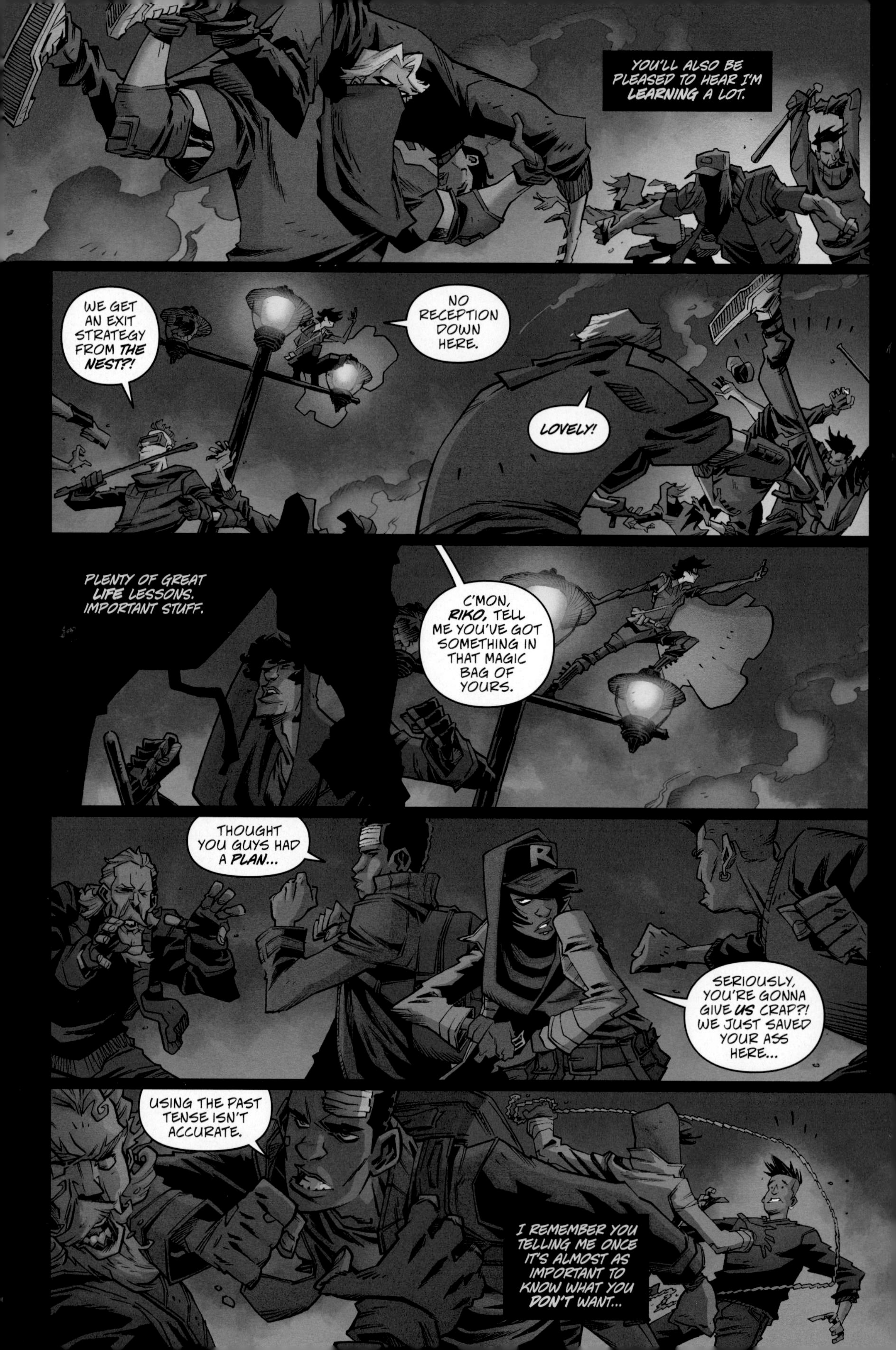
YOU'LL ALSO BE PLEASED TO HEAR I'M LEARNING A LOT.
WE GET AN EXIT STRATEGY FROM THE NEST?!
NO RECEPTION DOWN HERE.
LOVELY!
PLENTY OF GREAT LIFE LESSONS. IMPORTANT STUFF.
C'MON, RIKO, TELL ME YOU'VE GOT SOMETHING IN THAT MAGIC BAG OF YOURS.
THOUGHT YOU GUYS HAD A PLAN...
SERIOUSLY, YOU'RE GONNA GIVE US CRAP?! WE JUST SAVED YOUR ASS HERE...
USING THE PAST TENSE ISN'T ACCURATE.
I REMEMBER YOU TELLING ME ONCE IT'S ALMOST AS IMPORTANT TO KNOW WHAT YOU DON'T WANT...

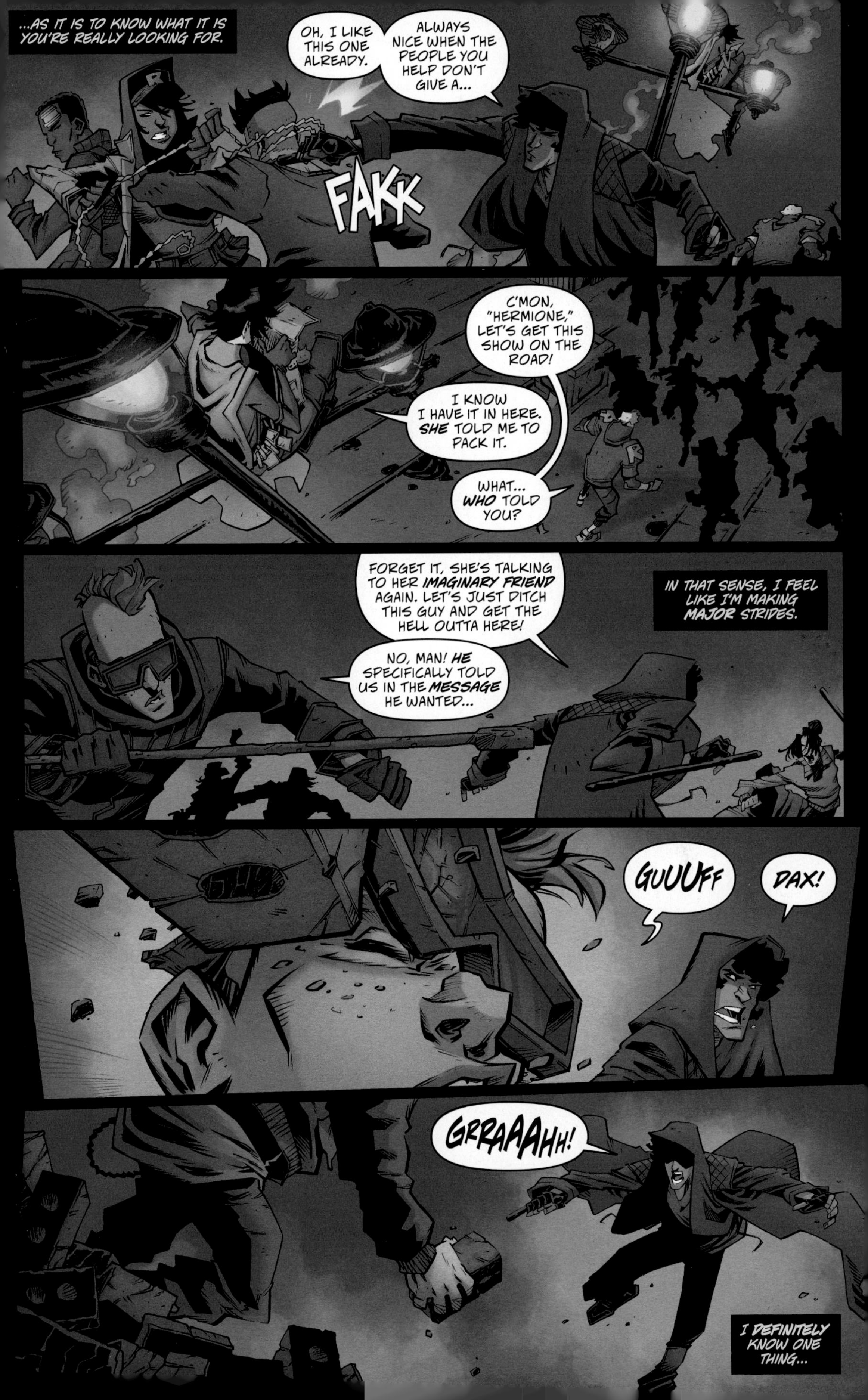
...AS IT IS TO KNOW WHAT IT IS YOU'RE REALLY LOOKING FOR.
OH, I LIKE THIS ONE ALREADY.
ALWAYS NICE WHEN THE PEOPLE YOU HELP DON'T GIVE A...
FAKK
C'MON, "HERMIONE," LET'S GET THIS SHOW ON THE ROAD!
I KNOW I HAVE IT IN HERE. SHE TOLD ME TO PACK IT.
WHAT... WHO TOLD YOU?
FORGET IT, SHE'S TALKING TO HER IMAGINARY FRIEND AGAIN. LET'S JUST DITCH THIS GUY AND GET THE HELL OUTTA HERE!
NO, MAN! HE SPECIFICALLY TOLD US IN THE MESSAGE HE WANTED...
IN THAT SENSE, I FEEL LIKE I'M MAKING MAJOR STRIDES.
GUUUFF
DAX!
GRRAAAHH!
I DEFINITELY KNOW ONE THING...

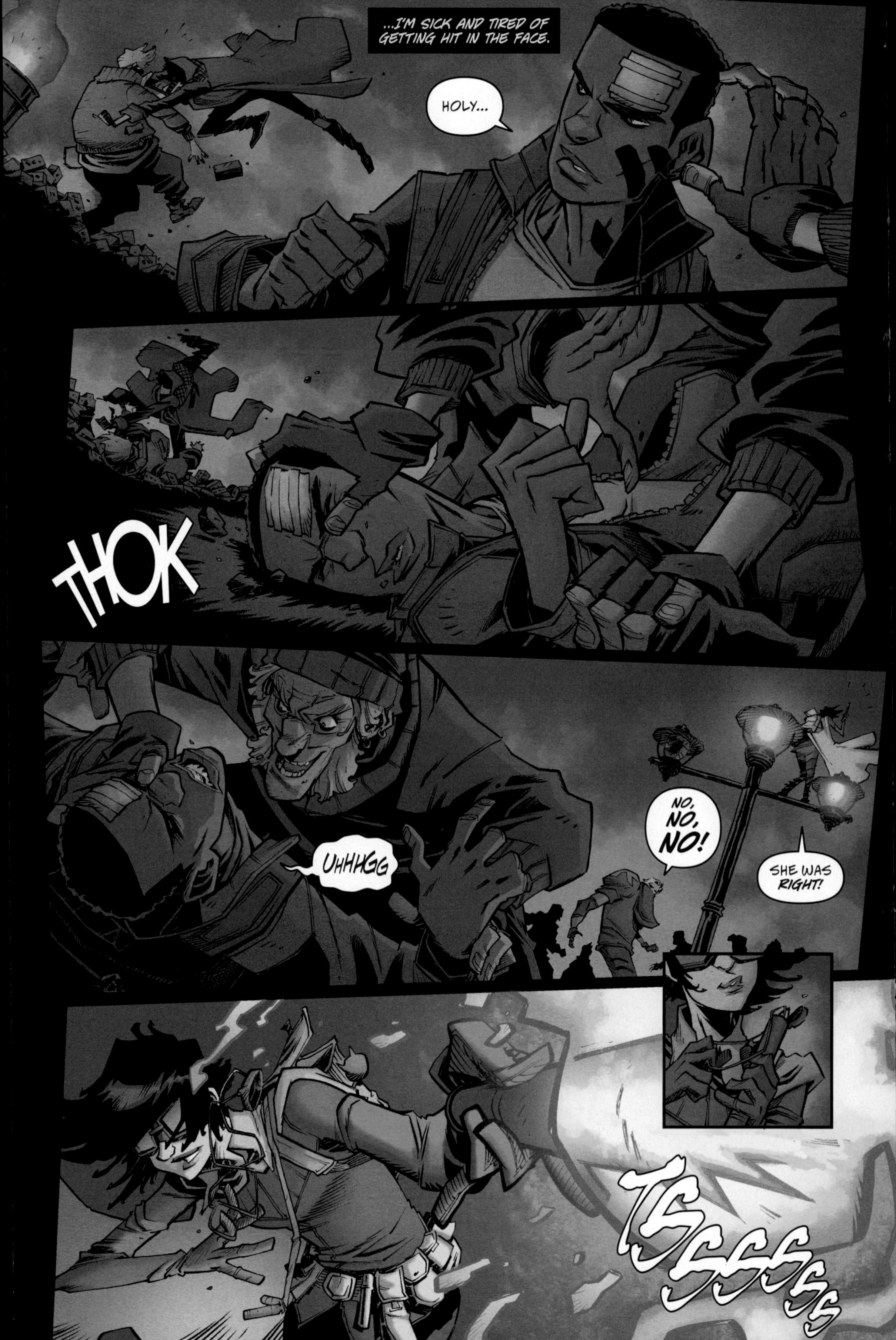
...I'M SICK AND TIRED OF GETTING HIT IN THE FACE.
HOLY...
THOK
UHHHGG
NO, NO, NO!
SHE WAS RIGHT!
TSSSSSS

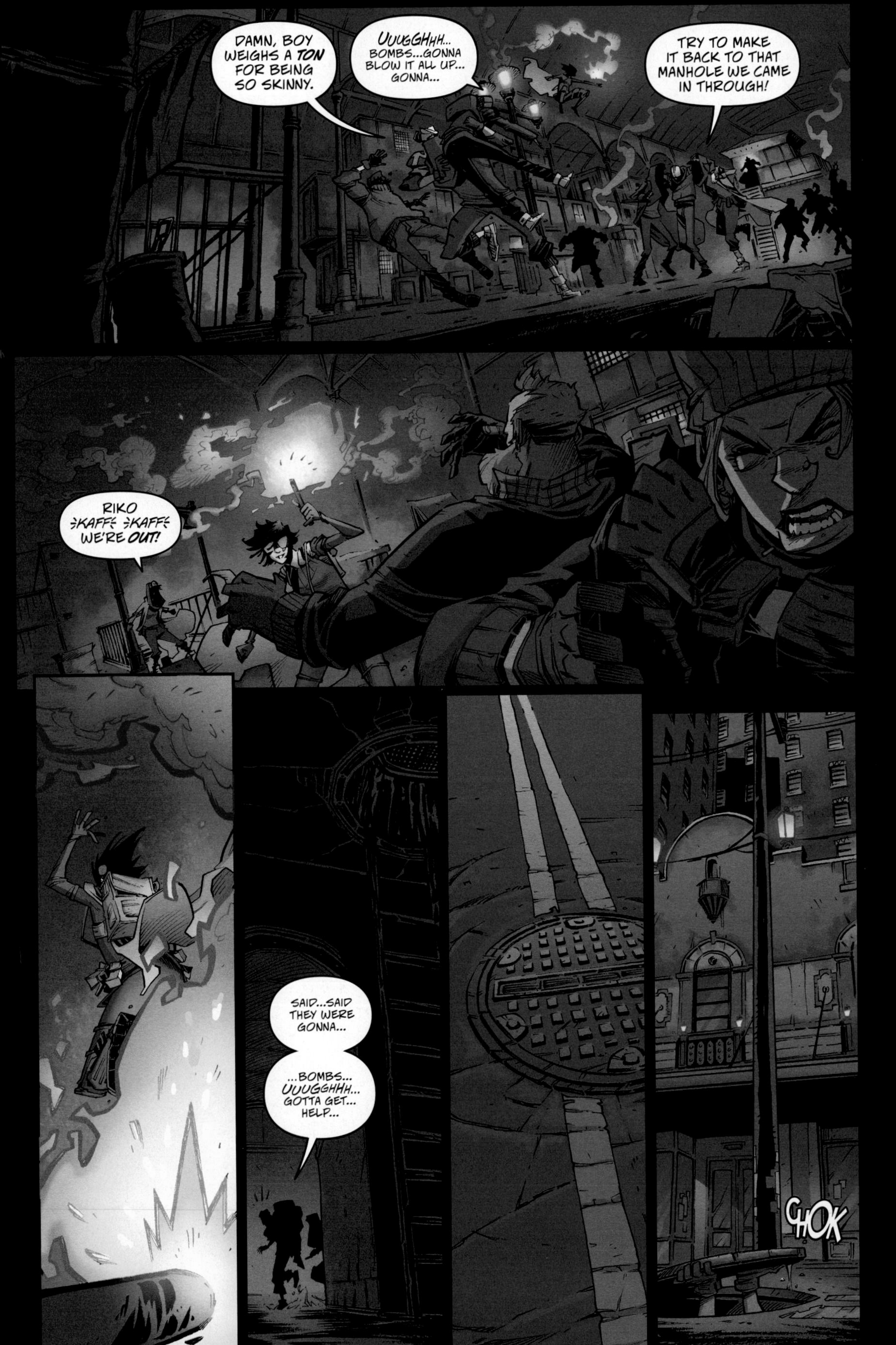
DAMN, BOY WEIGHS A TON FOR BEING SO SKINNY.
UUUGGHHH... BOMBS...GONNA BLOW IT ALL UP... GONNA...
TRY TO MAKE IT BACK TO THAT MANHOLE WE CAME IN THROUGH!
RIKO *KAFF* *KAFF* WE'RE OUT!
SAID...SAID THEY WERE GONNA...
...BOMBS... UUUGGHHH... GOTTA GET... HELP...
CHOK

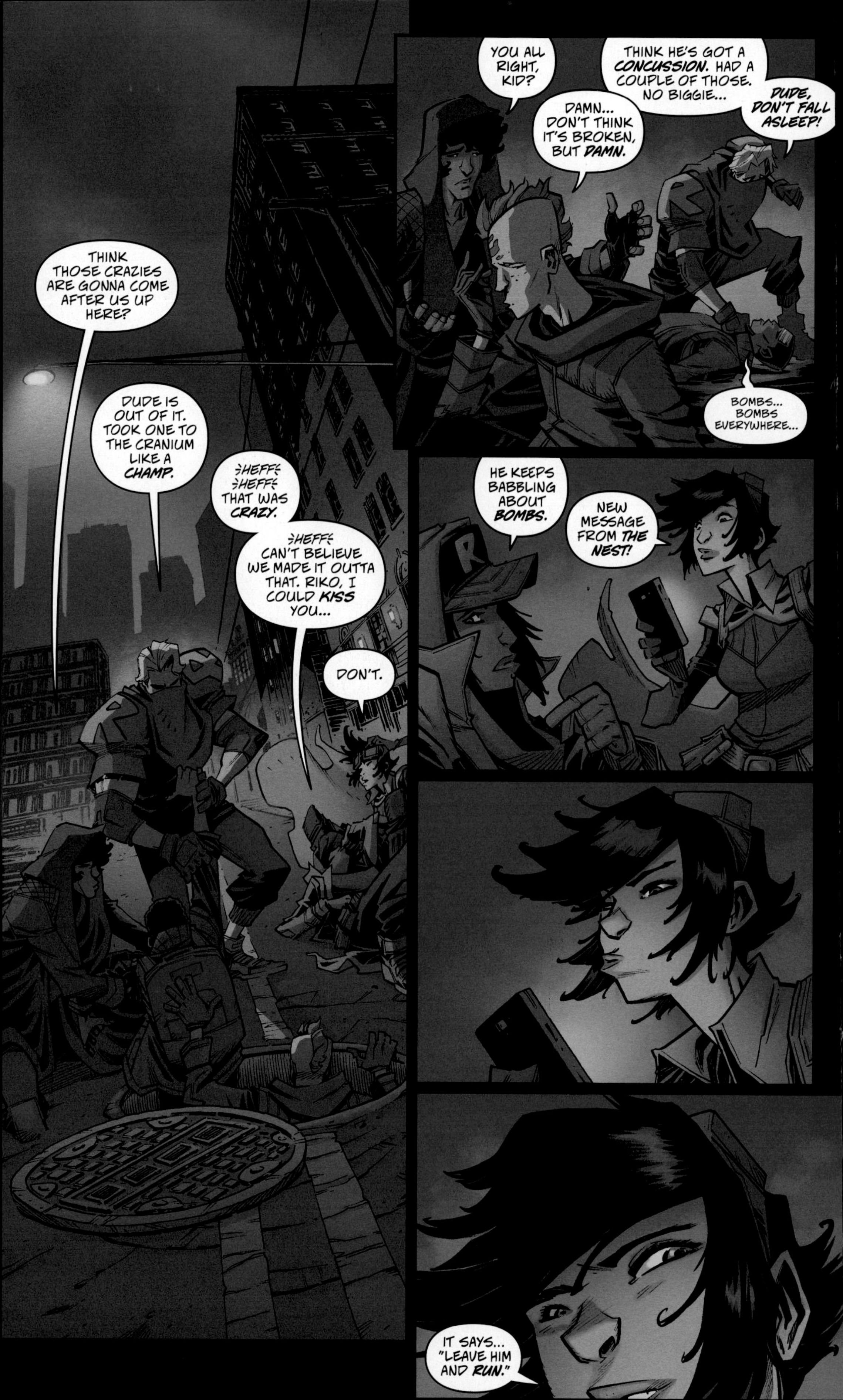
THINK THOSE CRAZIES ARE GONNA COME AFTER US UP HERE?
DUDE IS OUT OF IT. TOOK ONE TO THE CRANIUM LIKE A CHAMP.
HEFF HEFF THAT WAS CRAZY.
HEFF CAN'T BELIEVE WE MADE IT OUTTA THAT. RIKO, I COULD KISS YOU...
DON'T.
YOU ALL RIGHT, KID?
DAMN... DON'T THINK IT'S BROKEN, BUT DAMN.
THINK HE'S GOT A CONCUSSION. HAD A COUPLE OF THOSE. NO BIGGIE...
DUDE, DON'T FALL ASLEEP!
BOMBS... BOMBS EVERYWHERE...
HE KEEPS BABBLING ABOUT BOMBS.
NEW MESSAGE FROM THE NEST!
IT SAYS... "LEAVE HIM AND RUN."

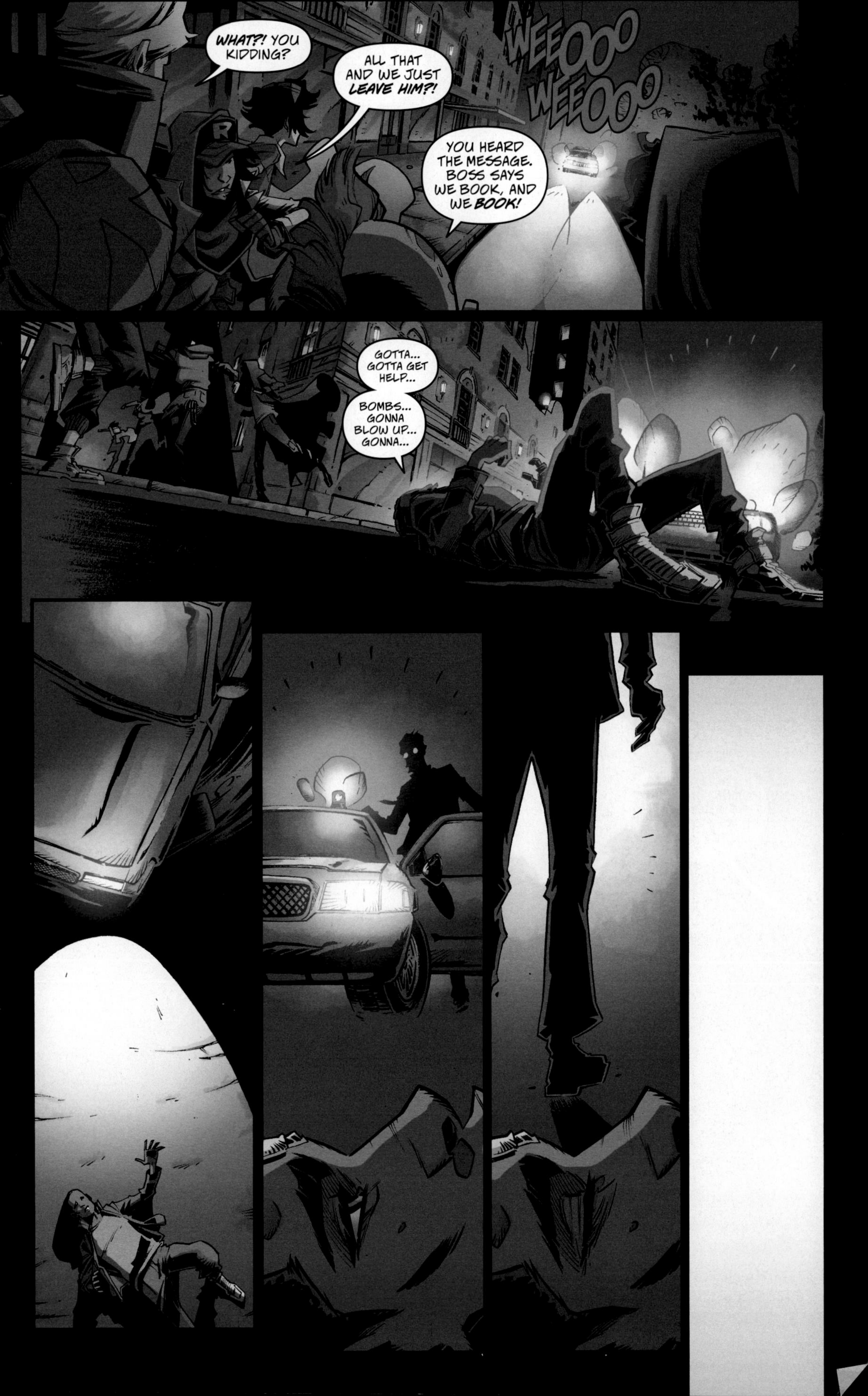
WHAT?! YOU KIDDING?
ALL THAT AND WE JUST LEAVE HIM?!
WEEOOO WEEOOO
YOU HEARD THE MESSAGE. BOSS SAYS WE BOOK, AND WE BOOK!
GOTTA... GOTTA GET HELP...
BOMBS... GONNA BLOW UP... GONNA...

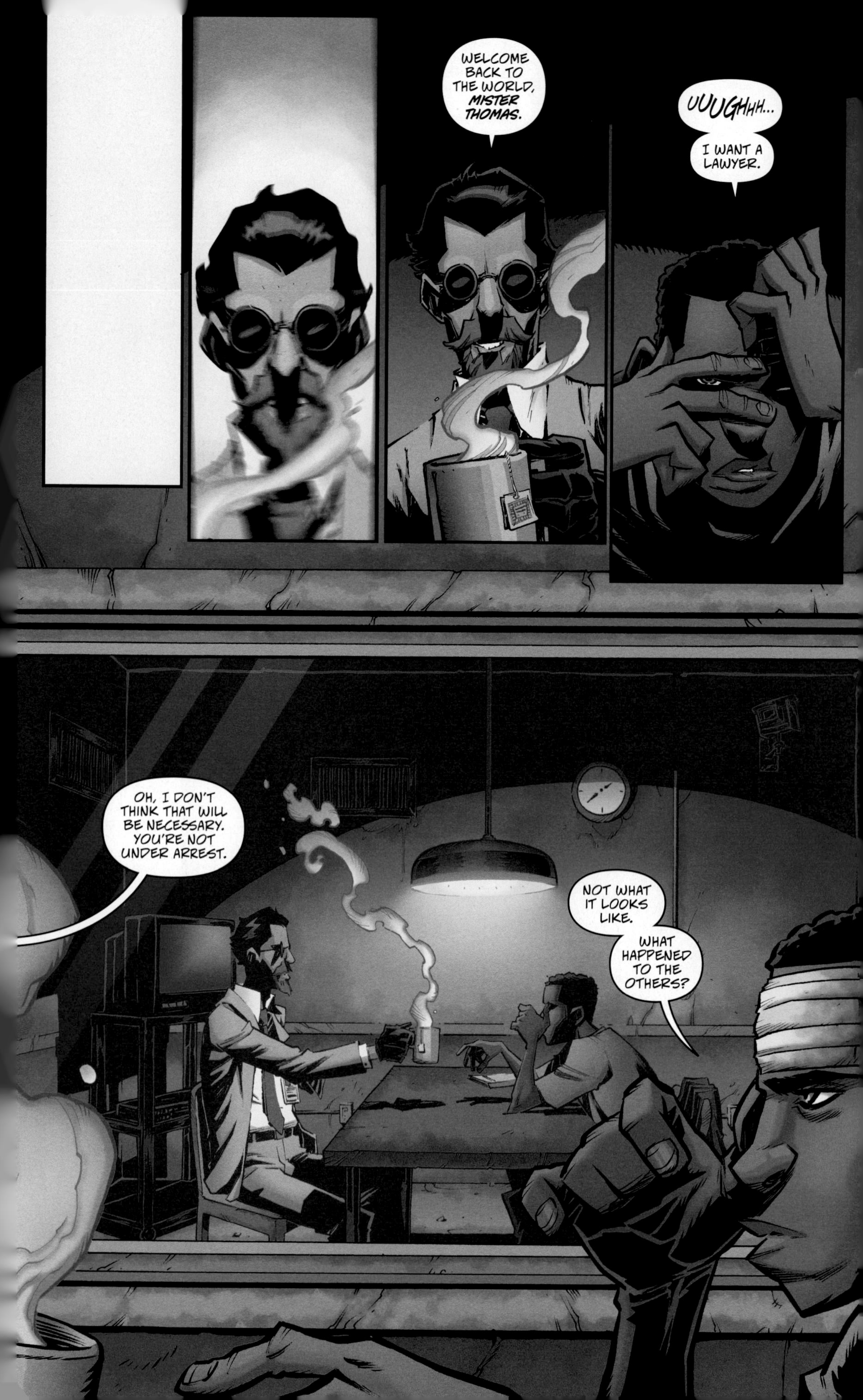
WELCOME BACK TO THE WORLD, MISTER THOMAS.
UUUGHHH...
I WANT A LAWYER.
OH, I DON'T THINK THAT WILL BE NECESSARY. YOU'RE NOT UNDER ARREST.
NOT WHAT IT LOOKS LIKE.
WHAT HAPPENED TO THE OTHERS?

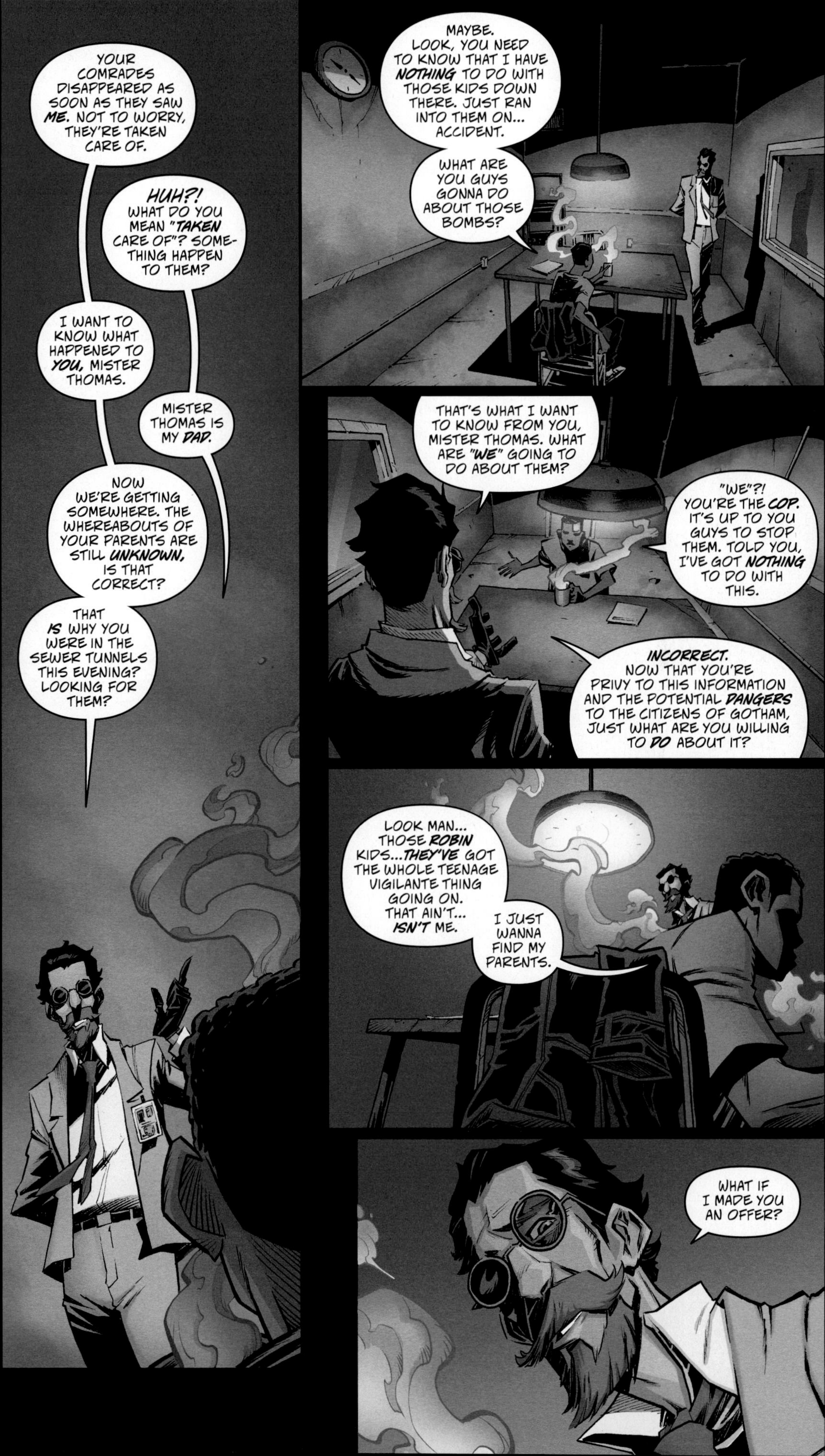
YOUR COMRADES DISAPPEARED AS SOON AS THEY SAW ME. NOT TO WORRY, THEY'RE TAKEN CARE OF.
HUH?! WHAT DO YOU MEAN "TAKEN CARE OF"? SOME-THING HAPPEN TO THEM?
I WANT TO KNOW WHAT HAPPENED TO YOU, MISTER THOMAS.
MISTER THOMAS IS MY DAD.
NOW WE'RE GETTING SOMEWHERE. THE WHEREABOUTS OF YOUR PARENTS ARE STILL UNKNOWN, IS THAT CORRECT?
THAT IS WHY YOU WERE IN THE SEWER TUNNELS THIS EVENING? LOOKING FOR THEM?
MAYBE. LOOK, YOU NEED TO KNOW THAT I HAVE NOTHING TO DO WITH THOSE KIDS DOWN THERE. JUST RAN INTO THEM ON... ACCIDENT.
WHAT ARE YOU GUYS GONNA DO ABOUT THOSE BOMBS?
THAT'S WHAT I WANT TO KNOW FROM YOU, MISTER THOMAS. WHAT ARE "WE" GOING TO DO ABOUT THEM?
"WE"?! YOU'RE THE COP. IT'S UP TO YOU GUYS TO STOP THEM. TOLD YOU, I'VE GOT NOTHING TO DO WITH THIS.
INCORRECT. NOW THAT YOU'RE PRIVY TO THIS INFORMATION AND THE POTENTIAL DANGERS TO THE CITIZENS OF GOTHAM, JUST WHAT ARE YOU WILLING TO DO ABOUT IT?
LOOK MAN... THOSE ROBIN KIDS...THEY'VE GOT THE WHOLE TEENAGE VIGILANTE THING GOING ON. THAT AIN'T... ISN'T ME.
I JUST WANNA FIND MY PARENTS.
WHAT IF I MADE YOU AN OFFER?

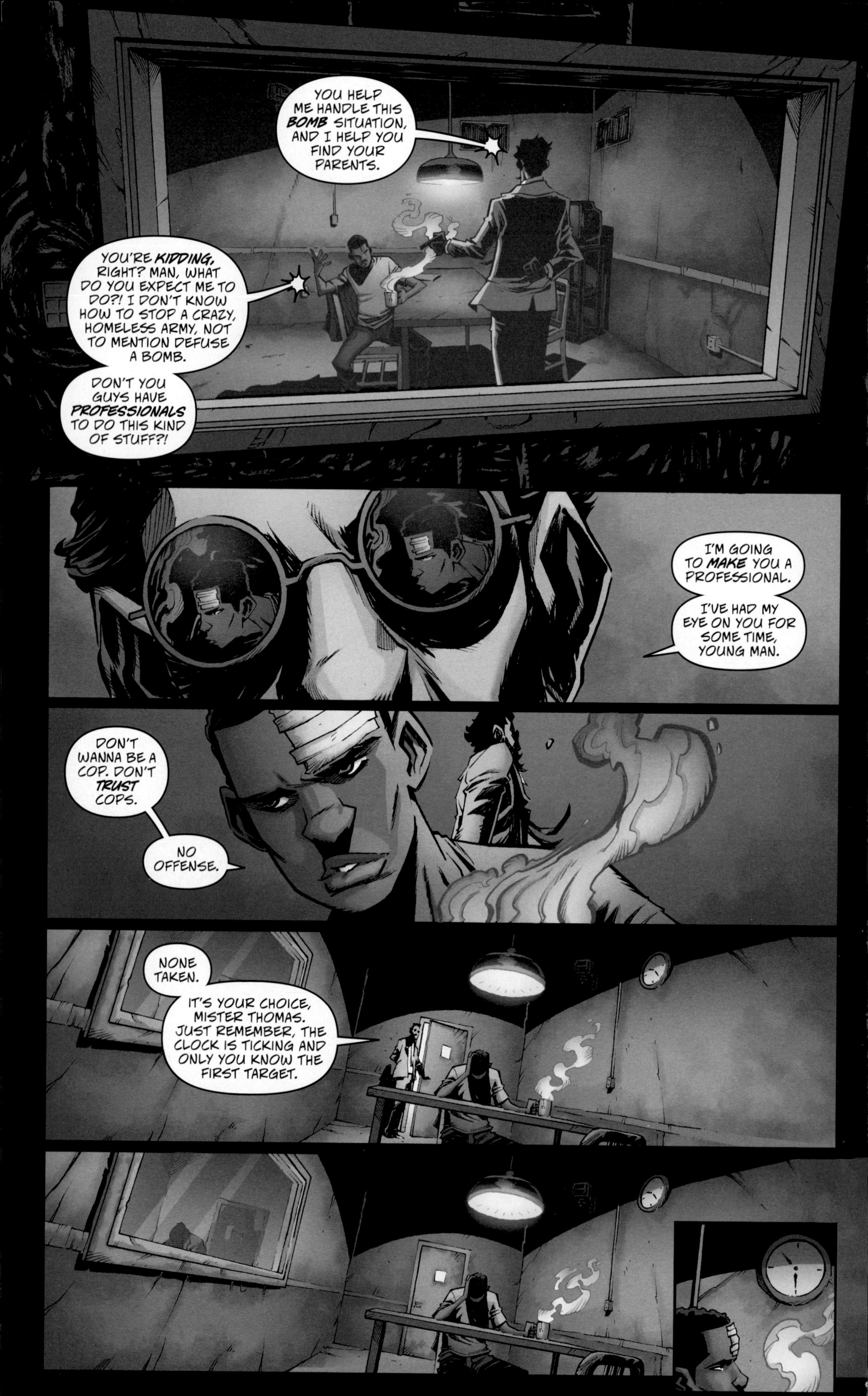

YOU HELP ME HANDLE THIS BOMB SITUATION, AND I HELP YOU FIND YOUR PARENTS.
YOU'RE KIDDING, RIGHT? MAN, WHAT DO YOU EXPECT ME TO DO?! I DON'T KNOW HOW TO STOP A CRAZY, HOMELESS ARMY, NOT TO MENTION DEFUSE A BOMB.
DON'T YOU GUYS HAVE PROFESSIONALS TO DO THIS KIND OF STUFF?!
I'M GOING TO MAKE YOU A PROFESSIONAL.
I'VE HAD MY EYE ON YOU FOR SOME TIME, YOUNG MAN.
DON'T WANNA BE A COP. DON'T TRUST COPS.
NO OFFENSE.
NONE TAKEN.
IT'S YOUR CHOICE, MISTER THOMAS. JUST REMEMBER, THE CLOCK IS TICKING AND ONLY YOU KNOW THE FIRST TARGET.

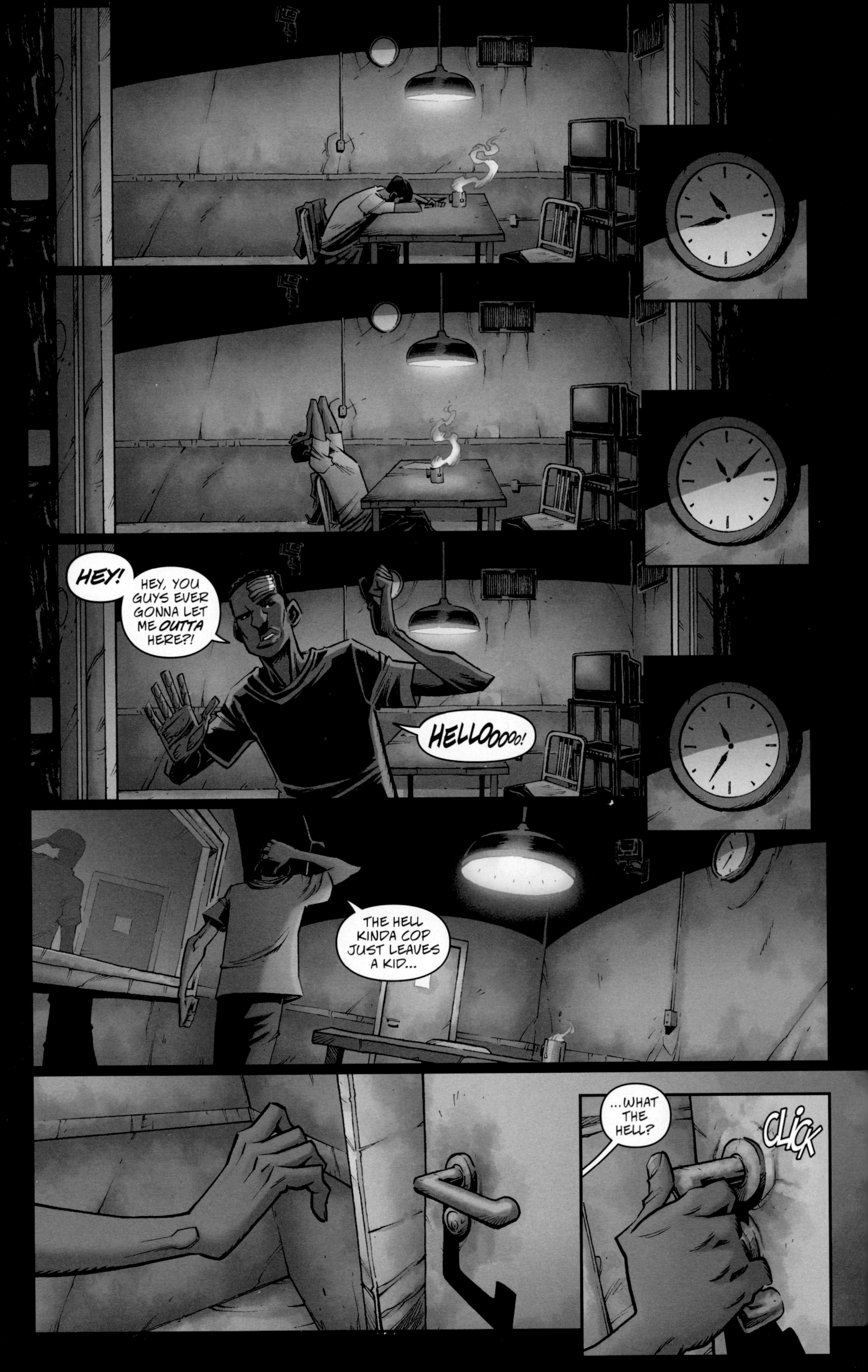
HEY!
HEY, YOU GUYS EVER GONNA LET ME OUTTA HERE?!
HELLOoooo!
THE HELL KINDA COP JUST LEAVES A KID...
...WHAT THE HELL?
CLICK

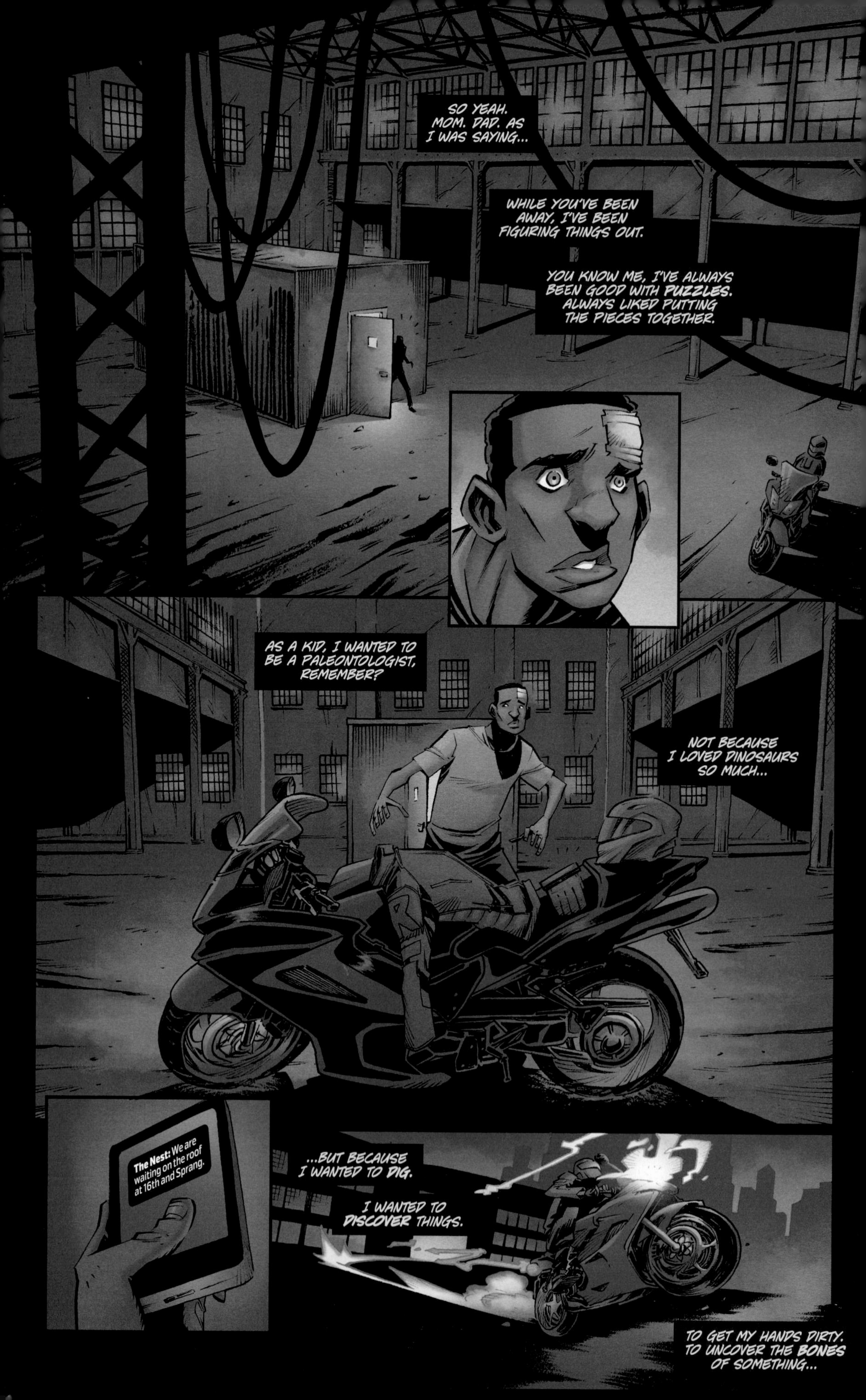
SO YEAH. MOM. DAD. AS I WAS SAYING...
WHILE YOU'VE BEEN AWAY, I'VE BEEN FIGURING THINGS OUT.
YOU KNOW ME, I'VE ALWAYS BEEN GOOD WITH PUZZLES. ALWAYS LIKED PUTTING THE PIECES TOGETHER.
AS A KID, I WANTED TO BE A PALEONTOLOGIST, REMEMBER?
NOT BECAUSE I LOVED DINOSAURS SO MUCH...
The Nest: We are waiting on the roof at 16th and Sprang.
...BUT BECAUSE I WANTED TO DIG.
I WANTED TO DISCOVER THINGS.
TO GET MY HANDS DIRTY. TO UNCOVER THE BONES OF SOMETHING...

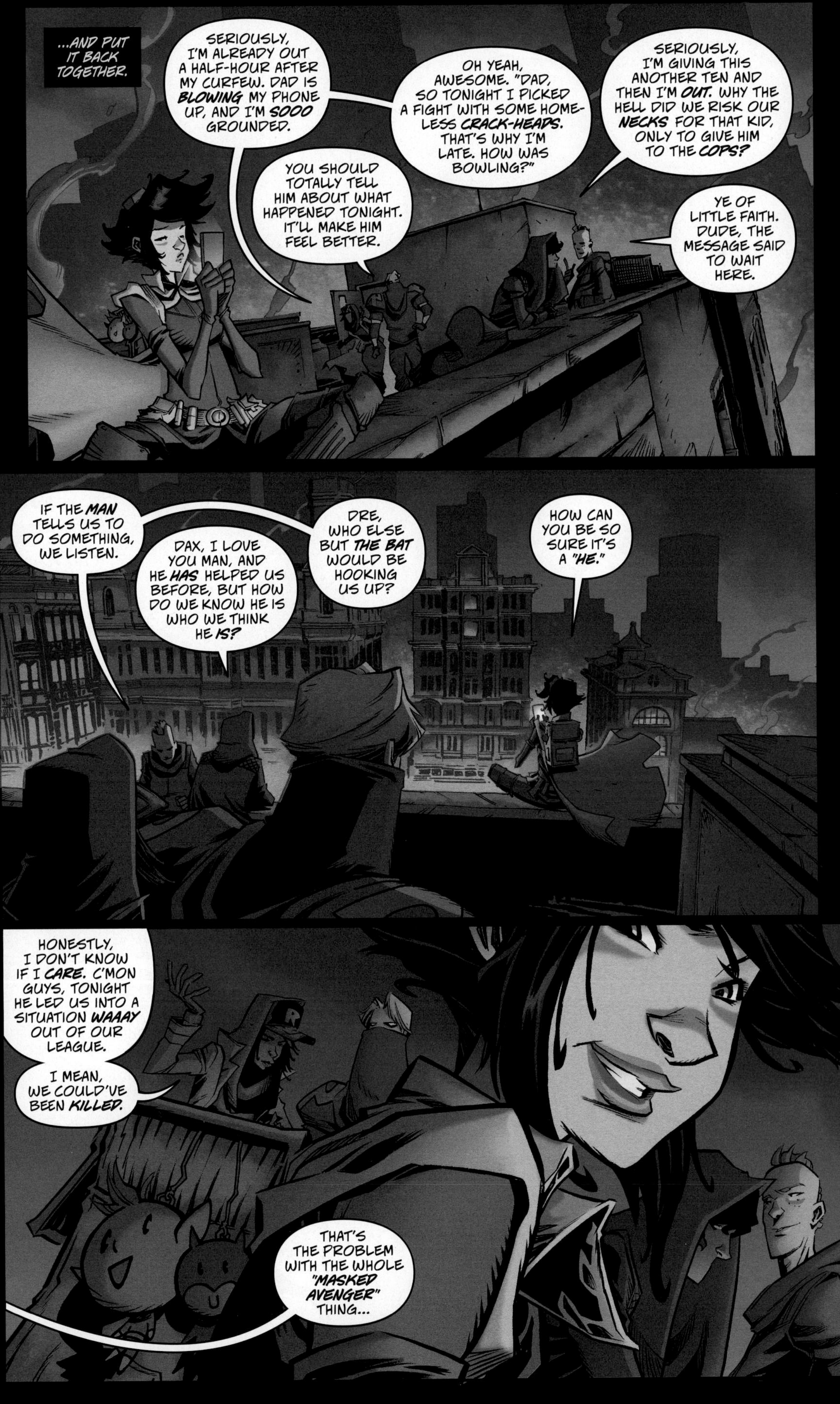

...AND PUT IT BACK TOGETHER.
SERIOUSLY, I'M ALREADY OUT A HALF-HOUR AFTER MY CURFEW. DAD IS BLOWING MY PHONE UP, AND I'M SOOO GROUNDED.
YOU SHOULD TOTALLY TELL HIM ABOUT WHAT HAPPENED TONIGHT. IT'LL MAKE HIM FEEL BETTER.
OH YEAH, AWESOME. "DAD, SO TONIGHT I PICKED A FIGHT WITH SOME HOME-LESS CRACK-HEADS. THAT'S WHY I'M LATE. HOW WAS BOWLING?"
SERIOUSLY, I'M GIVING THIS ANOTHER TEN AND THEN I'M OUT. WHY THE HELL DID WE RISK OUR NECKS FOR THAT KID, ONLY TO GIVE HIM TO THE COPS?
YE OF LITTLE FAITH. DUDE, THE MESSAGE SAID TO WAIT HERE.
IF THE MAN TELLS US TO DO SOMETHING, WE LISTEN.
DAX, I LOVE YOU MAN, AND HE HAS HELPED US BEFORE, BUT HOW DO WE KNOW HE IS WHO WE THINK HE IS?
DRE, WHO ELSE BUT THE BAT WOULD BE HOOKING US UP?
HOW CAN YOU BE SO SURE IT'S A "HE."
HONESTLY, I DON'T KNOW IF I CARE. C'MON GUYS, TONIGHT HE LED US INTO A SITUATION WAAAY OUT OF OUR LEAGUE.
I MEAN, WE COULD'VE BEEN KILLED.
THAT'S THE PROBLEM WITH THE WHOLE "MASKED AVENGER" THING...

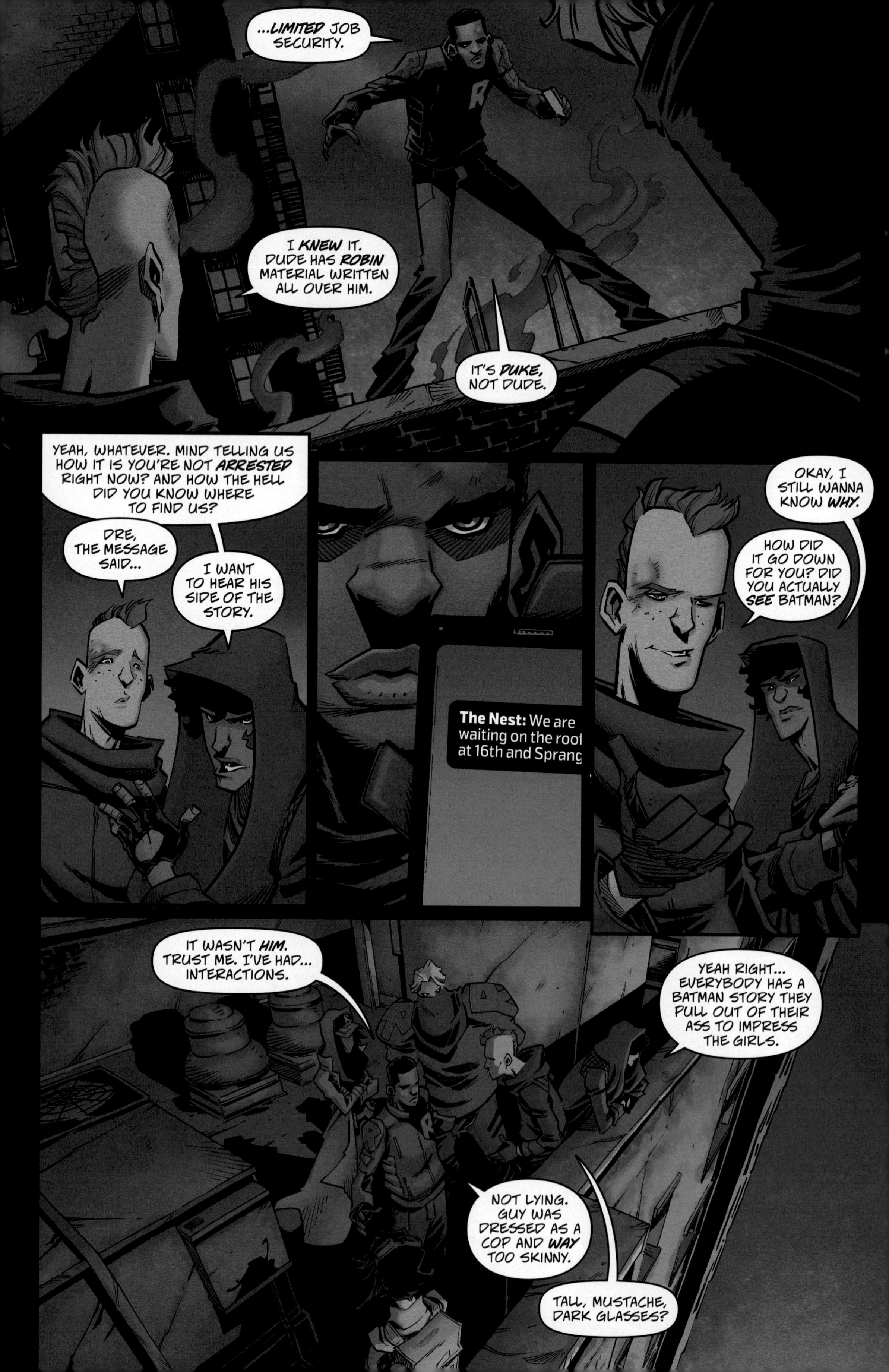

...LIMITED JOB SECURITY.
I KNEW IT. DUDE HAS ROBIN MATERIAL WRITTEN ALL OVER HIM.
IT'S DUKE, NOT DUDE.
YEAH, WHATEVER. MIND TELLING US HOW IT IS YOU'RE NOT ARRESTED RIGHT NOW? AND HOW THE HELL DID YOU KNOW WHERE TO FIND US?
DRE, THE MESSAGE SAID...
I WANT TO HEAR HIS SIDE OF THE STORY.
The Nest: We are waiting on the roof at 16th and Sprang
OKAY, I STILL WANNA KNOW WHY.
HOW DID IT GO DOWN FOR YOU? DID YOU ACTUALLY SEE BATMAN?
IT WASN'T HIM. TRUST ME. I'VE HAD... INTERACTIONS.
YEAH RIGHT... EVERYBODY HAS A BATMAN STORY THEY PULL OUT OF THEIR ASS TO IMPRESS THE GIRLS.
NOT LYING. GUY WAS DRESSED AS A COP AND WAY TOO SKINNY.
TALL, MUSTACHE, DARK GLASSES?

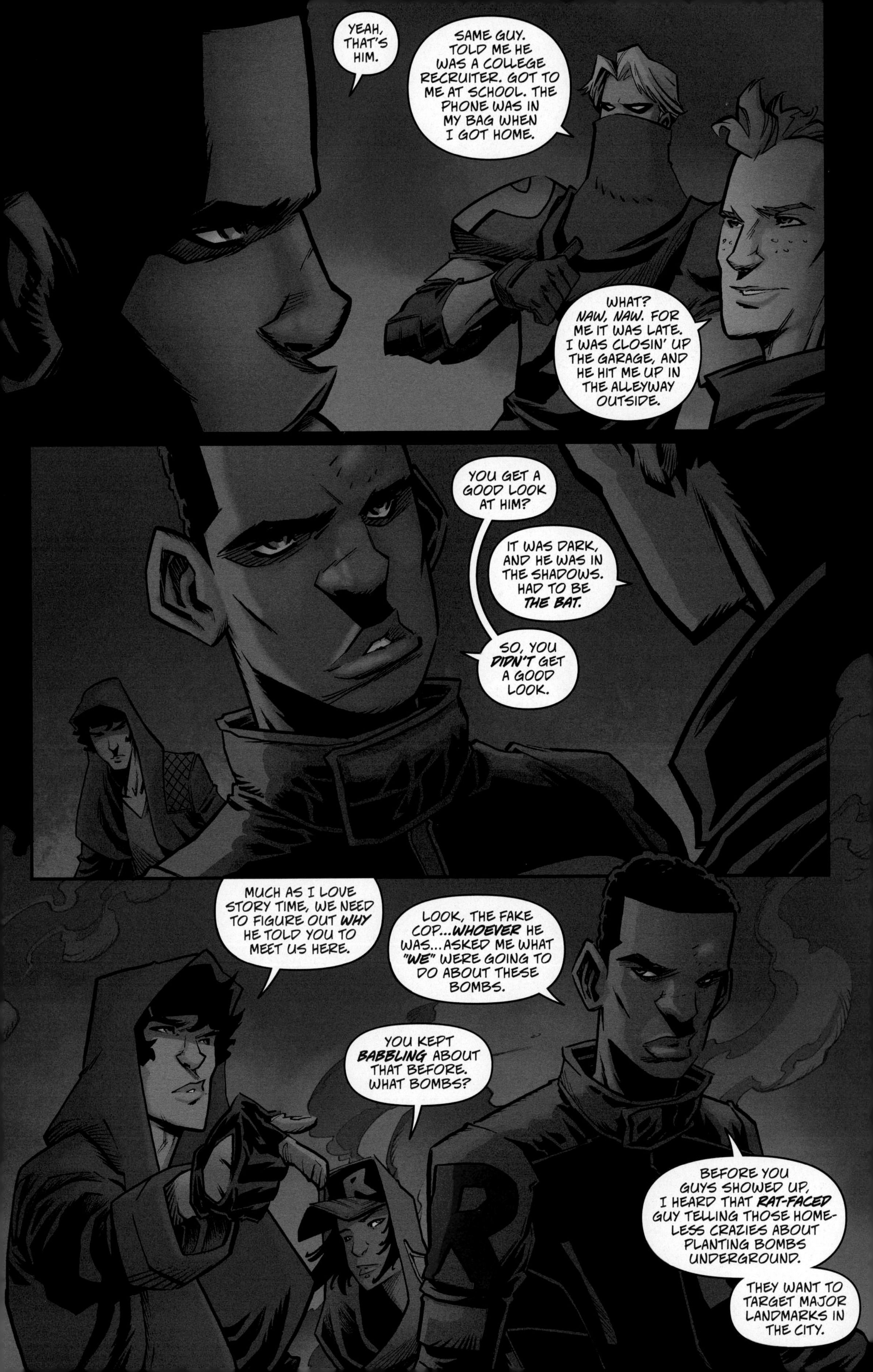
YEAH, THAT'S HIM.
SAME GUY. TOLD ME HE WAS A COLLEGE RECRUITER. GOT TO ME AT SCHOOL. THE PHONE WAS IN MY BAG WHEN I GOT HOME.
WHAT? NAW, NAW. FOR ME IT WAS LATE. I WAS CLOSIN' UP THE GARAGE, AND HE HIT ME UP IN THE ALLEYWAY OUTSIDE.
YOU GET A GOOD LOOK AT HIM?
IT WAS DARK, AND HE WAS IN THE SHADOWS. HAD TO BE THE BAT.
SO, YOU DIDN'T GET A GOOD LOOK.
MUCH AS I LOVE STORY TIME, WE NEED TO FIGURE OUT WHY HE TOLD YOU TO MEET US HERE.
LOOK, THE FAKE COP...WHOEVER HE WAS...ASKED ME WHAT "WE" WERE GOING TO DO ABOUT THESE BOMBS.
YOU KEPT BABBLING ABOUT THAT BEFORE. WHAT BOMBS?
BEFORE YOU GUYS SHOWED UP, I HEARD THAT RAT-FACED GUY TELLING THOSE HOME-LESS CRAZIES ABOUT PLANTING BOMBS UNDERGROUND.
THEY WANT TO TARGET MAJOR LANDMARKS IN THE CITY.

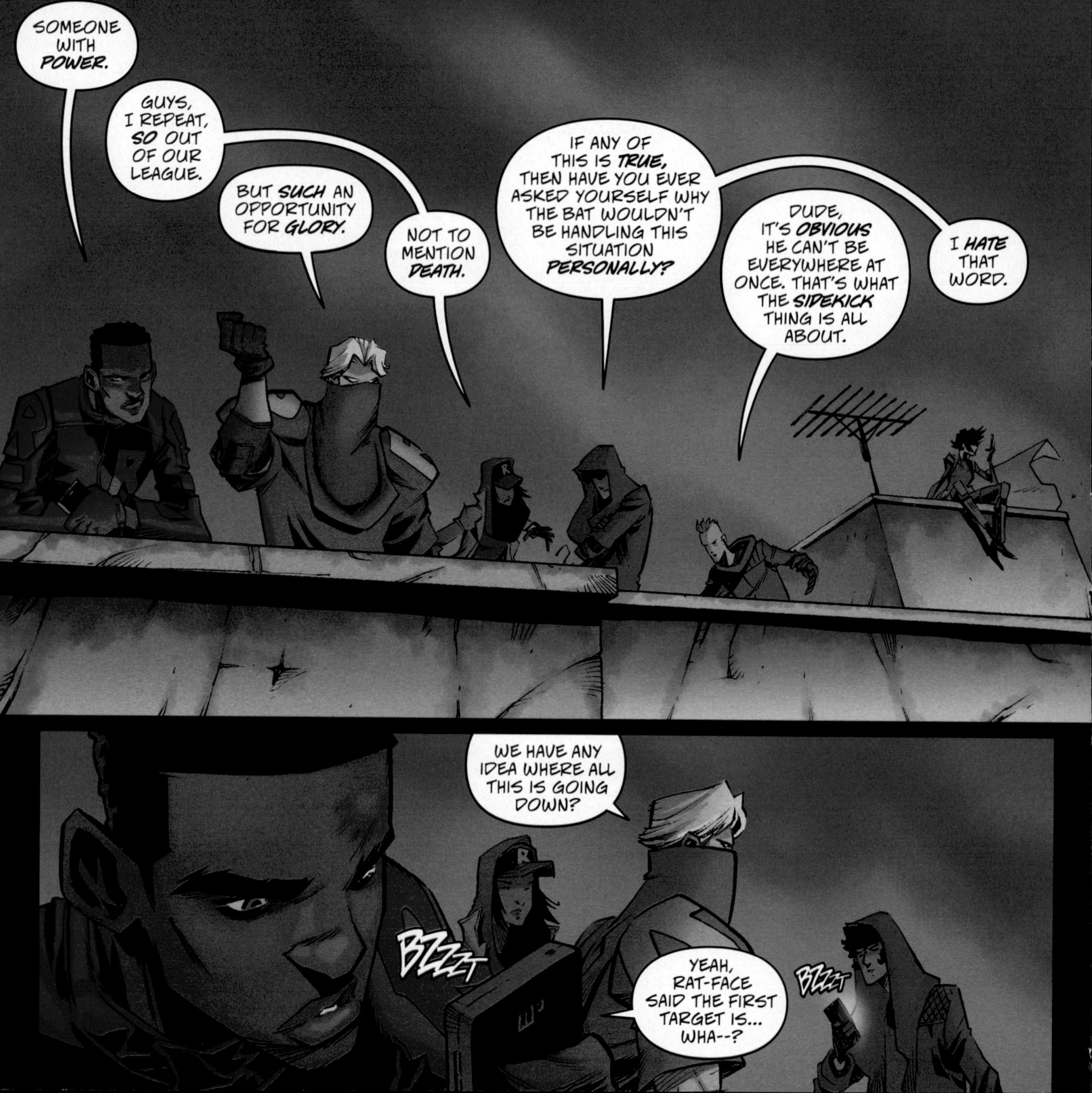
SOMEONE WITH POWER.
GUYS, I REPEAT, SO OUT OF OUR LEAGUE.
BUT SUCH AN OPPORTUNITY FOR GLORY.
NOT TO MENTION DEATH.
IF ANY OF THIS IS TRUE, THEN HAVE YOU EVER ASKED YOURSELF WHY THE BAT WOULDN'T BE HANDLING THIS SITUATION PERSONALLY?
DUDE, IT'S OBVIOUS HE CAN'T BE EVERYWHERE AT ONCE. THAT'S WHAT THE SIDEKICK THING IS ALL ABOUT.
I HATE THAT WORD.
WE HAVE ANY IDEA WHERE ALL THIS IS GOING DOWN?
BZZZT
YEAH, RAT-FACE SAID THE FIRST TARGET IS... WHA--?
BZZZT

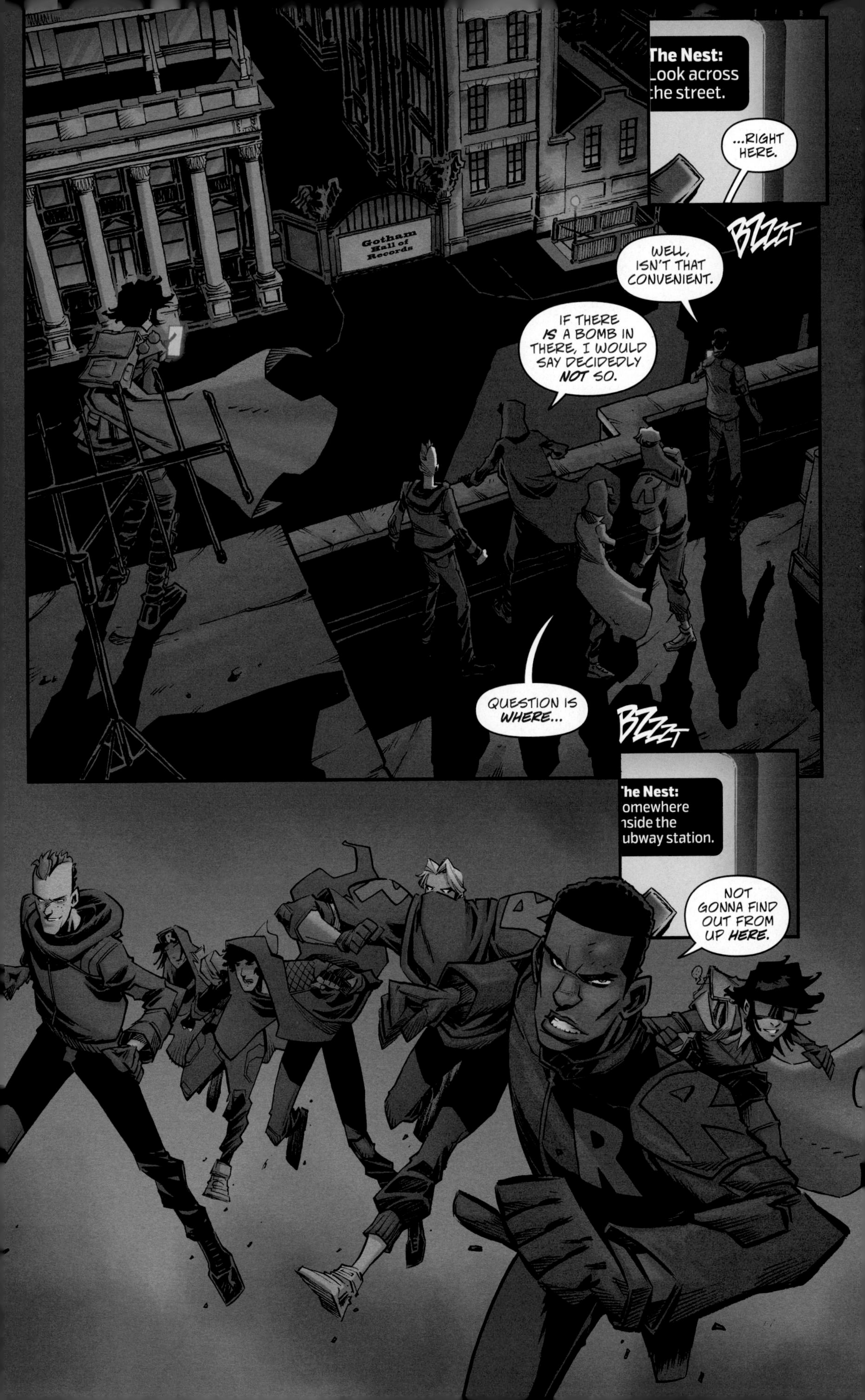
The Nest:
Look across
the street.
...RIGHT HERE.
BZZZT
WELL, ISN'T THAT CONVENIENT.
IF THERE *IS* A BOMB IN THERE, I WOULD SAY DECIDEDLY *NOT* SO.
Gotham Hall of Records
QUESTION IS *WHERE*...
BZZZT
The Nest:
omewhere
nside the
ubway station.
NOT GONNA FIND OUT FROM UP *HERE*.

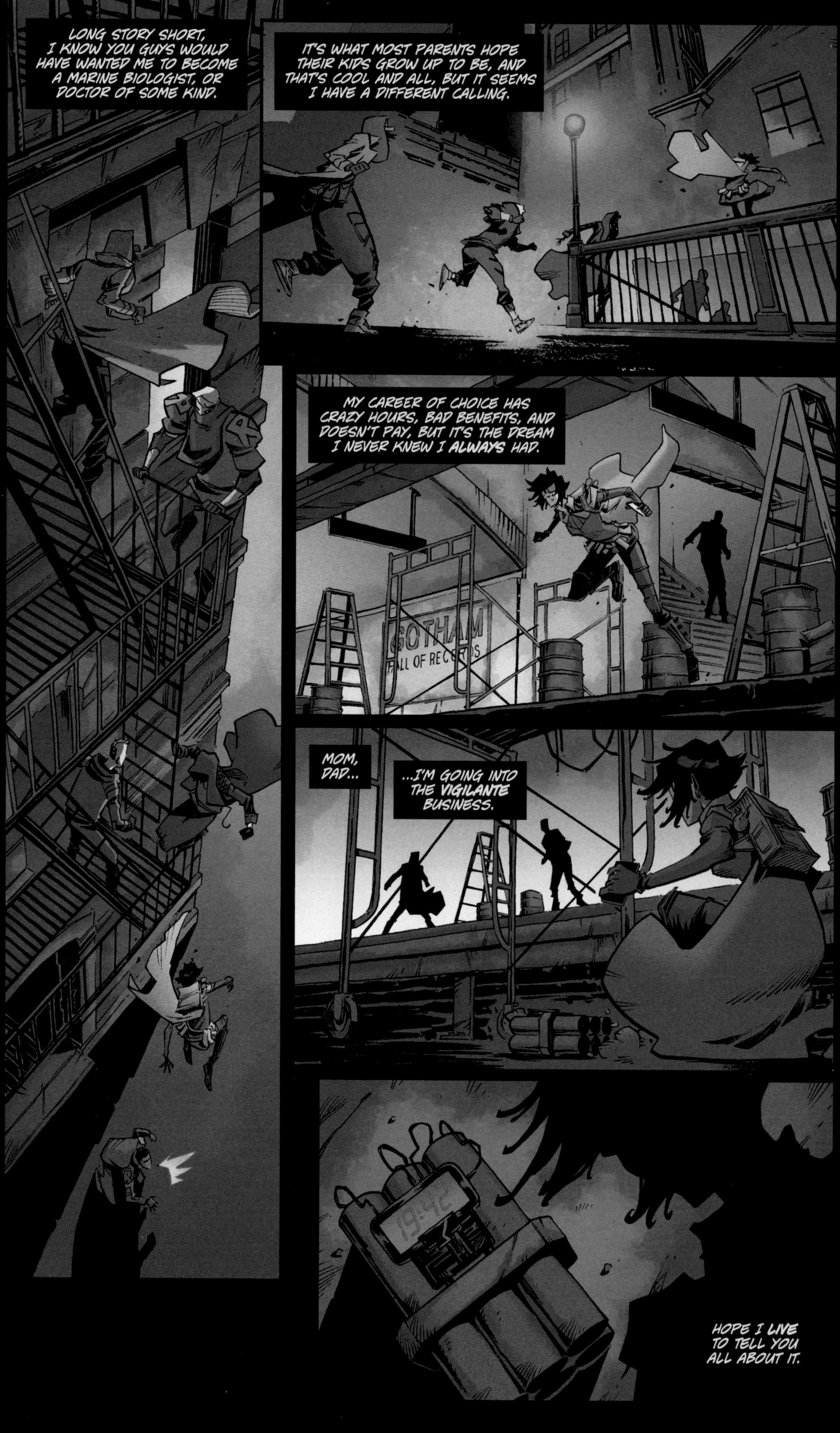
LONG STORY SHORT, I KNOW YOU GUYS WOULD HAVE WANTED ME TO BECOME A MARINE BIOLOGIST, OR DOCTOR OF SOME KIND.
IT'S WHAT MOST PARENTS HOPE THEIR KIDS GROW UP TO BE, AND THAT'S COOL AND ALL, BUT IT SEEMS I HAVE A DIFFERENT CALLING.
MY CAREER OF CHOICE HAS CRAZY HOURS, BAD BENEFITS, AND DOESN'T PAY, BUT IT'S THE DREAM I NEVER KNEW I ALWAYS HAD.
GOTHAM HALL OF RECORDS
MOM, DAD...
...I'M GOING INTO THE VIGILANTE BUSINESS.
19:42
HOPE I LIVE TO TELL YOU ALL ABOUT IT.

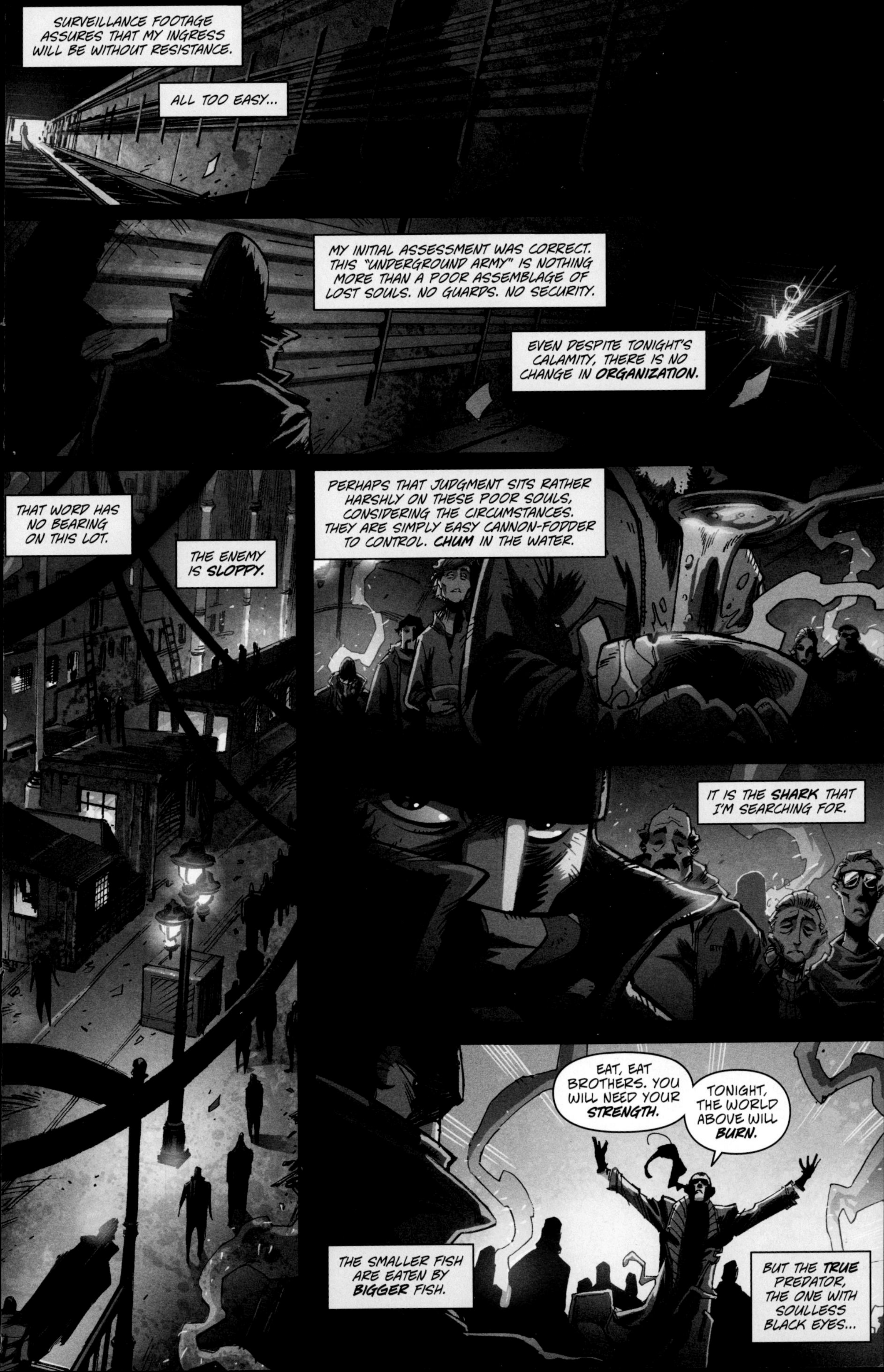
SURVEILLANCE FOOTAGE ASSURES THAT MY INGRESS WILL BE WITHOUT RESISTANCE.
ALL TOO EASY...
MY INITIAL ASSESSMENT WAS CORRECT. THIS "UNDERGROUND ARMY" IS NOTHING MORE THAN A POOR ASSEMBLAGE OF LOST SOULS. NO GUARDS. NO SECURITY.
EVEN DESPITE TONIGHT'S CALAMITY, THERE IS NO CHANGE IN ORGANIZATION.
THAT WORD HAS NO BEARING ON THIS LOT.
THE ENEMY IS SLOPPY.
PERHAPS THAT JUDGMENT SITS RATHER HARSHLY ON THESE POOR SOULS, CONSIDERING THE CIRCUMSTANCES. THEY ARE SIMPLY EASY CANNON-FODDER TO CONTROL. CHUM IN THE WATER.
IT IS THE SHARK THAT I'M SEARCHING FOR.
EAT, EAT BROTHERS. YOU WILL NEED YOUR STRENGTH.
TONIGHT, THE WORLD ABOVE WILL BURN.
THE SMALLER FISH ARE EATEN BY BIGGER FISH.
BUT THE TRUE PREDATOR, THE ONE WITH SOULLESS BLACK EYES...

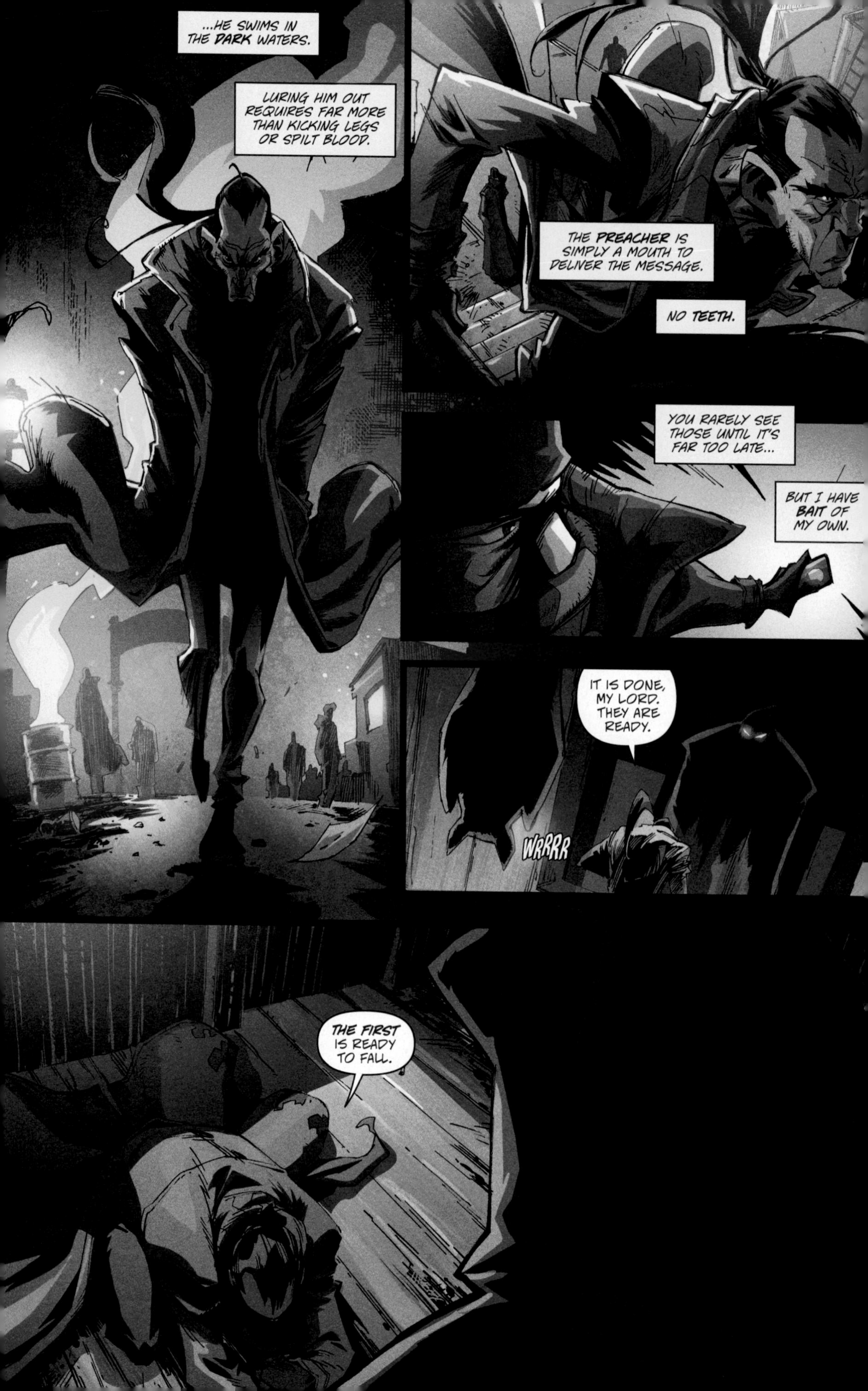
...HE SWIMS IN THE DARK WATERS.
LURING HIM OUT REQUIRES FAR MORE THAN KICKING LEGS OR SPILT BLOOD.
THE PREACHER IS SIMPLY A MOUTH TO DELIVER THE MESSAGE.
NO TEETH.
YOU RARELY SEE THOSE UNTIL IT'S FAR TOO LATE...
BUT I HAVE BAIT OF MY OWN.
IT IS DONE, MY LORD. THEY ARE READY.
WRRRR
THE FIRST IS READY TO FALL.

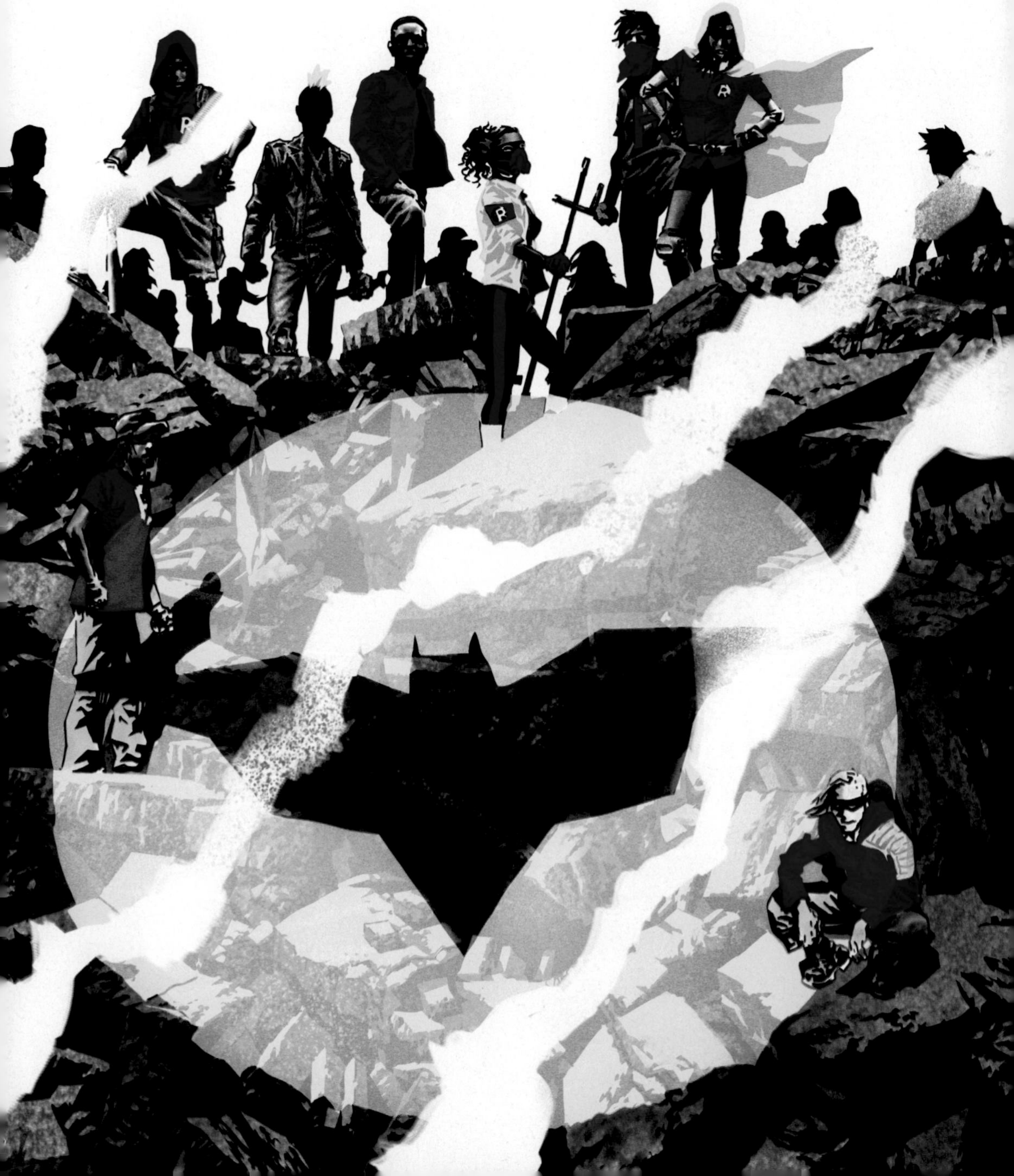

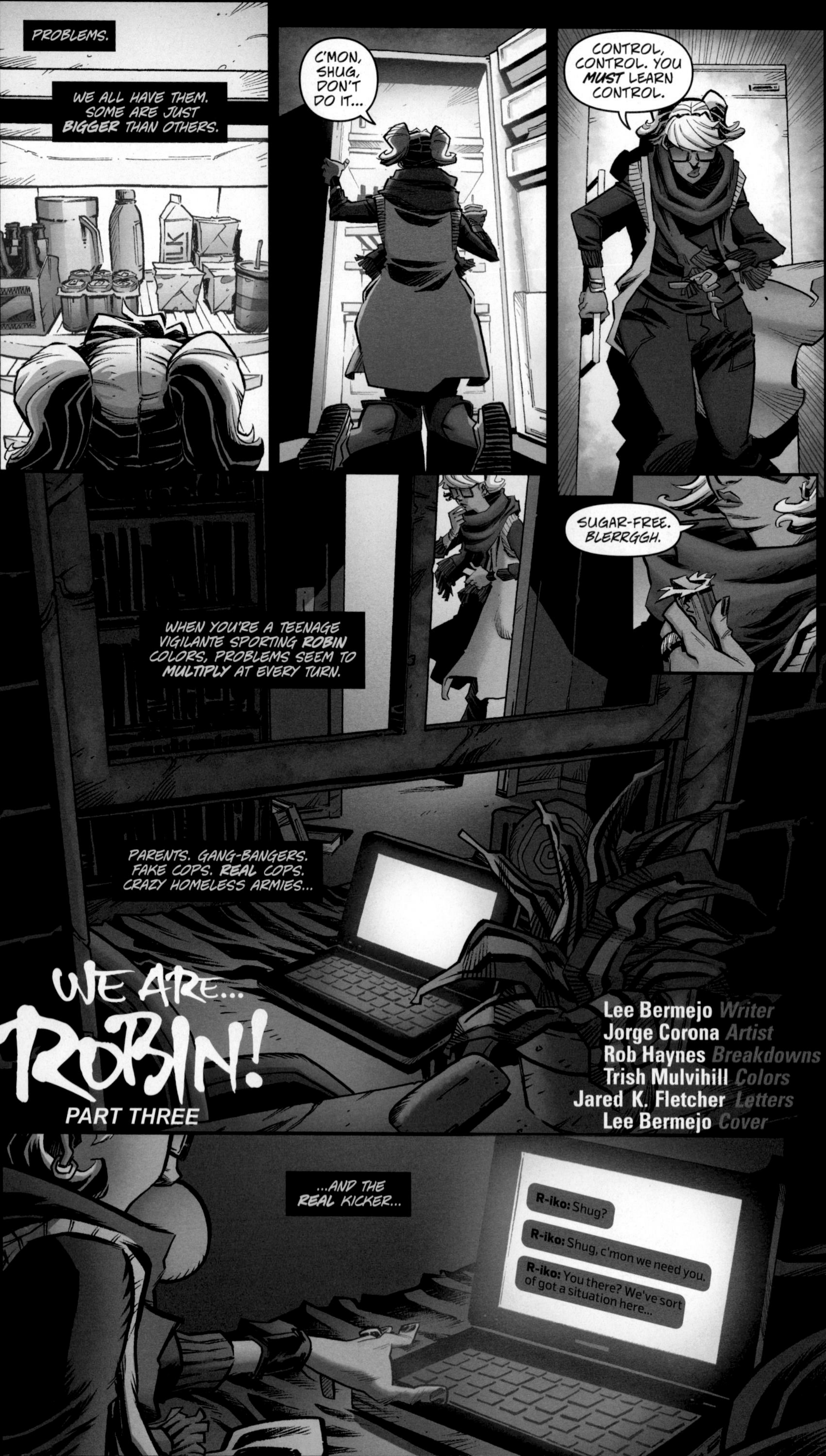
PROBLEMS.
WE ALL HAVE THEM. SOME ARE JUST BIGGER THAN OTHERS.
C'MON, SHUG, DON'T DO IT...
CONTROL, CONTROL. YOU MUST LEARN CONTROL.
SUGAR-FREE. BLERRGGH.
WHEN YOU'RE A TEENAGE VIGILANTE SPORTING ROBIN COLORS, PROBLEMS SEEM TO MULTIPLY AT EVERY TURN.
PARENTS. GANG-BANGERS. FAKE COPS. REAL COPS. CRAZY HOMELESS ARMIES...
WE ARE... ROBIN!
PART THREE
Lee Bermejo Writer
Jorge Corona Artist
Rob Haynes Breakdowns
Trish Mulvihill Colors
Jared K. Fletcher Letters
Lee Bermejo Cover
...AND THE REAL KICKER...
R-iko: Shug?
R-iko: Shug, c'mon we need you.
R-iko: You there? We've sort of got a situation here...

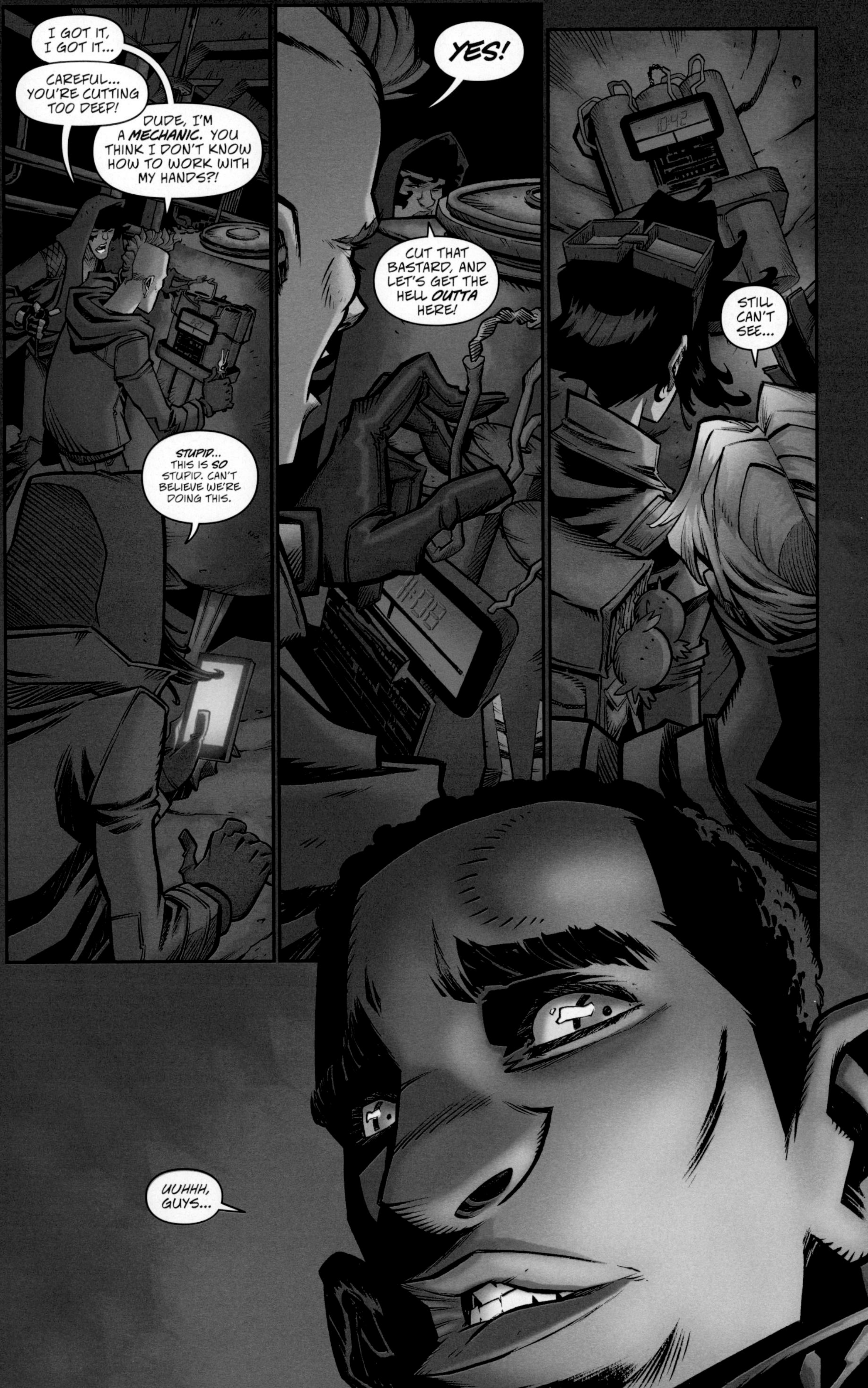
I GOT IT, I GOT IT...
CAREFUL... YOU'RE CUTTING TOO DEEP!
DUDE, I'M A **MECHANIC.** YOU THINK I DON'T KNOW HOW TO WORK WITH MY HANDS?!
STUPID... THIS IS **SO** STUPID. CAN'T BELIEVE WE'RE DOING THIS.
YES!
CUT THAT BASTARD, AND LET'S GET THE HELL **OUTTA** HERE!
STILL CAN'T SEE...
UUHHH, GUYS...

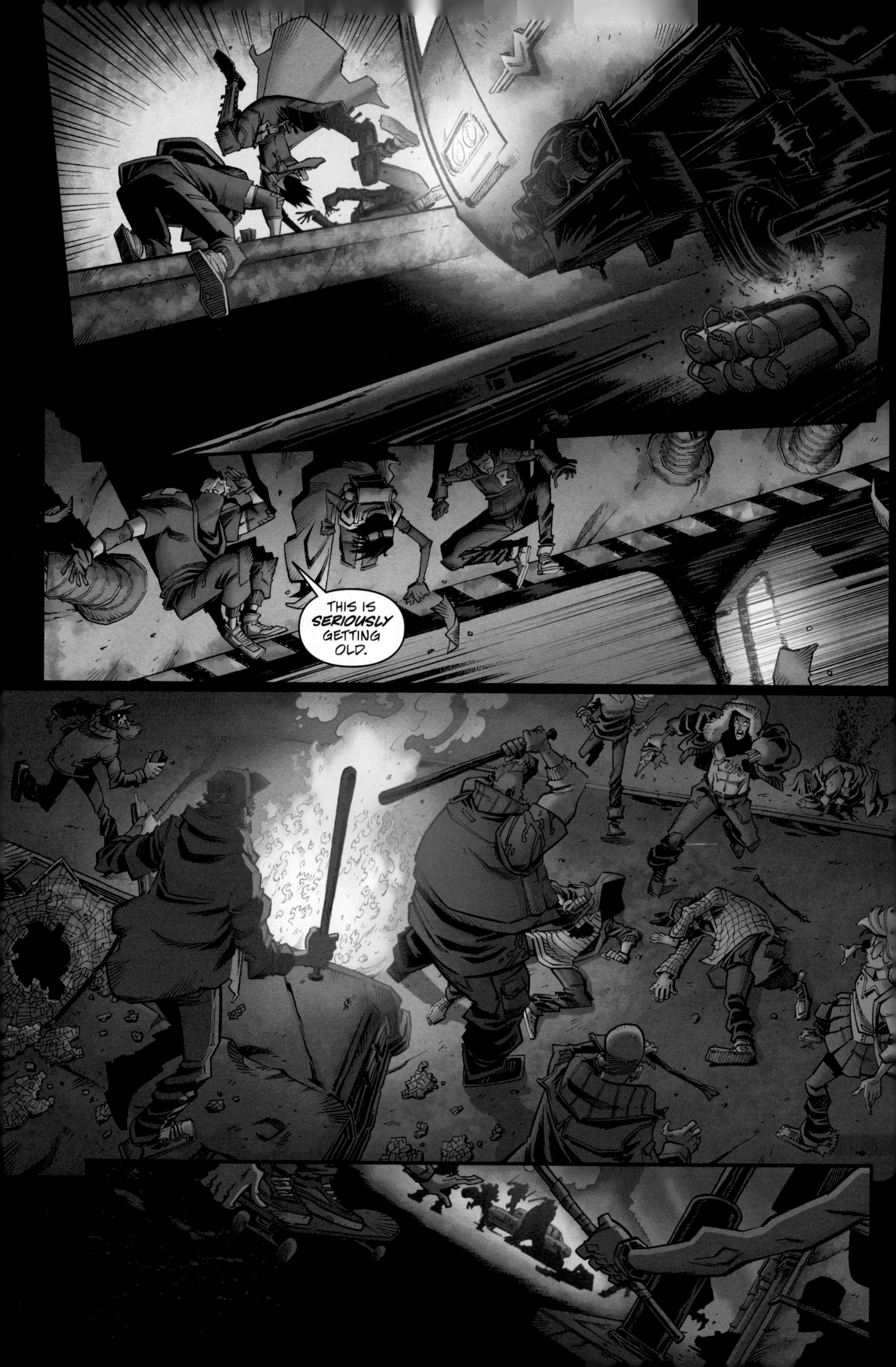
THIS IS SERIOUSLY GETTING OLD.

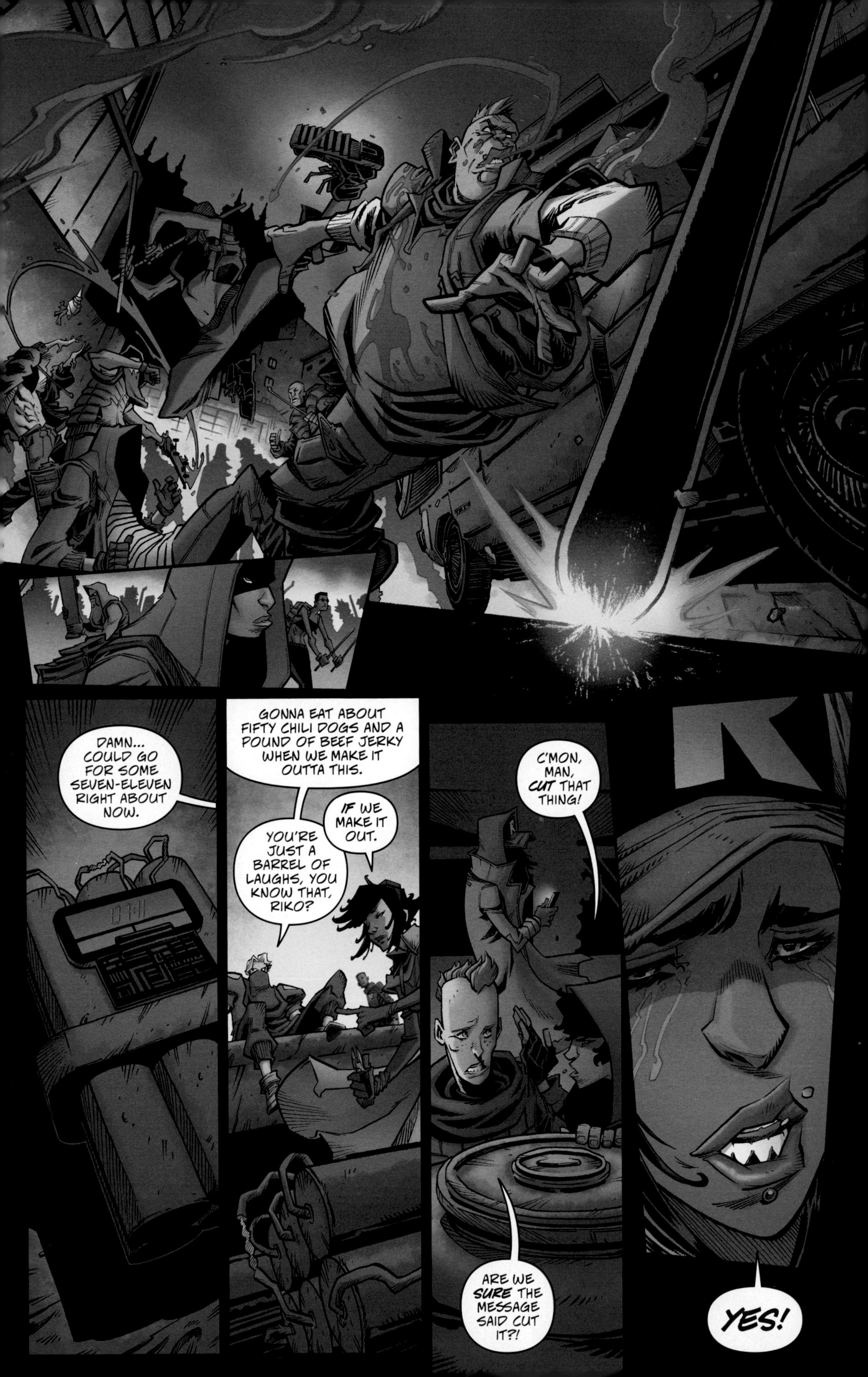
DAMN... COULD GO FOR SOME SEVEN-ELEVEN RIGHT ABOUT NOW.
GONNA EAT ABOUT FIFTY CHILI DOGS AND A POUND OF BEEF JERKY WHEN WE MAKE IT OUTTA THIS.
IF WE MAKE IT OUT.
YOU'RE JUST A BARREL OF LAUGHS, YOU KNOW THAT, RIKO?
C'MON, MAN, CUT THAT THING!
ARE WE SURE THE MESSAGE SAID CUT IT?!
YES!

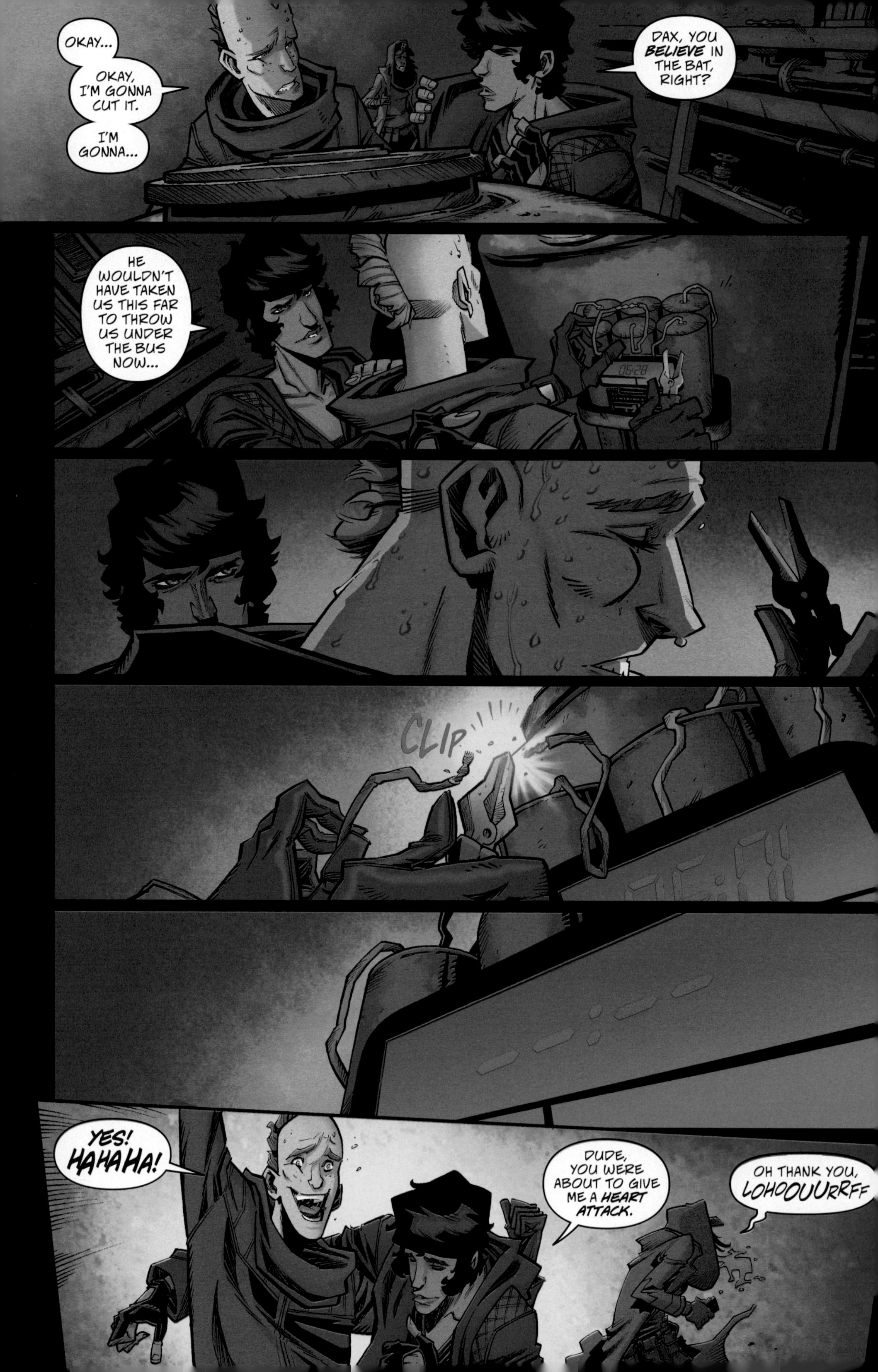

OKAY...
OKAY, I'M GONNA CUT IT.
I'M GONNA...
DAX, YOU *BELIEVE* IN THE BAT, RIGHT?
HE WOULDN'T HAVE TAKEN US THIS FAR TO THROW US UNDER THE BUS NOW...
06:28
CLIP
YES! HAHAHA!
DUDE, YOU WERE ABOUT TO GIVE ME A *HEART ATTACK*.
OH THANK YOU, LOHOOUURRFF

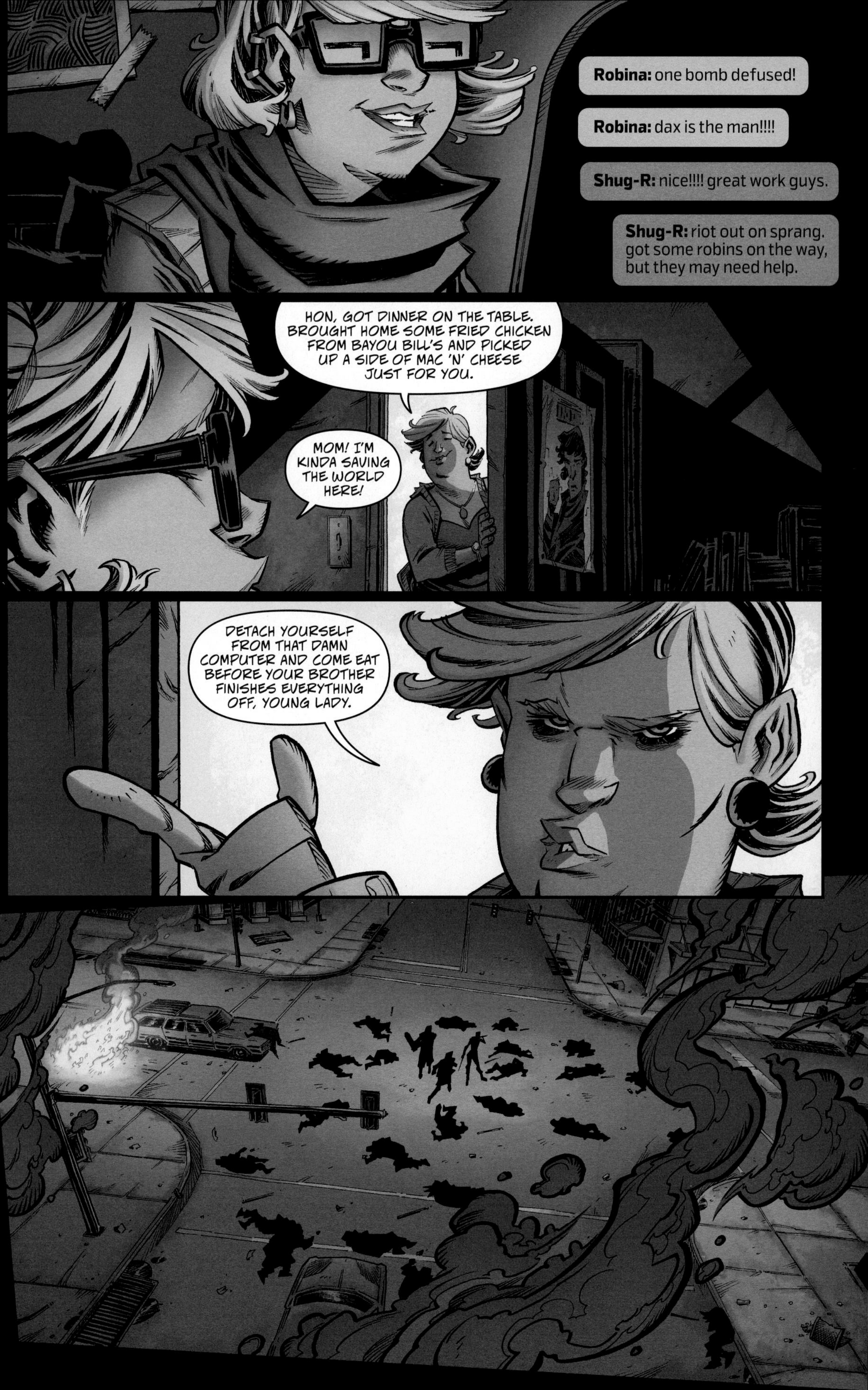
Robina: one bomb defused!
Robina: dax is the man!!!!
Shug-R: nice!!!! great work guys.
Shug-R: riot out on sprang. got some robins on the way, but they may need help.
HON, GOT DINNER ON THE TABLE. BROUGHT HOME SOME FRIED CHICKEN FROM BAYOU BILL'S AND PICKED UP A SIDE OF MAC 'N' CHEESE JUST FOR YOU.
MOM! I'M KINDA SAVING THE WORLD HERE!
DETACH YOURSELF FROM THAT DAMN COMPUTER AND COME EAT BEFORE YOUR BROTHER FINISHES EVERYTHING OFF, YOUNG LADY.

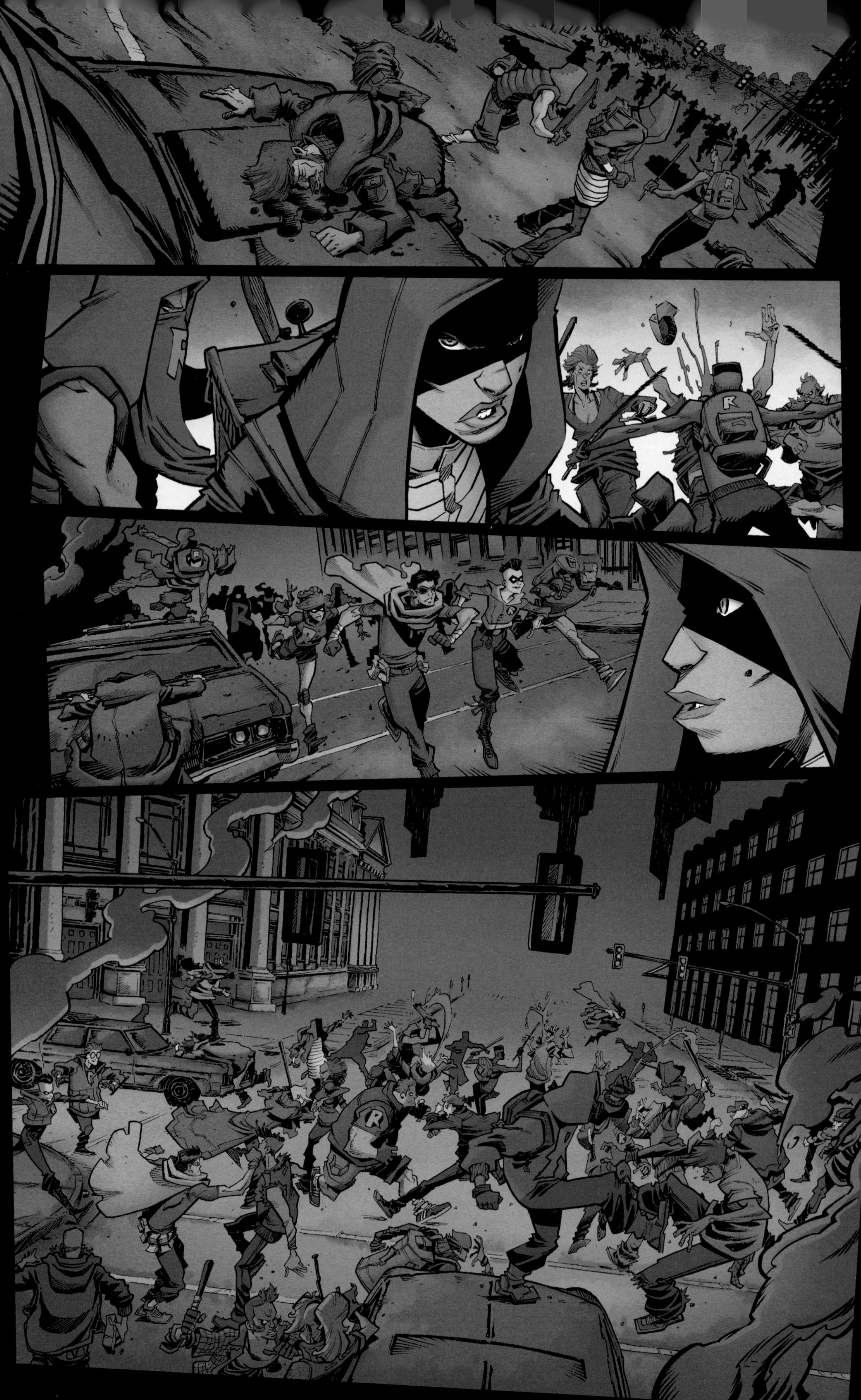

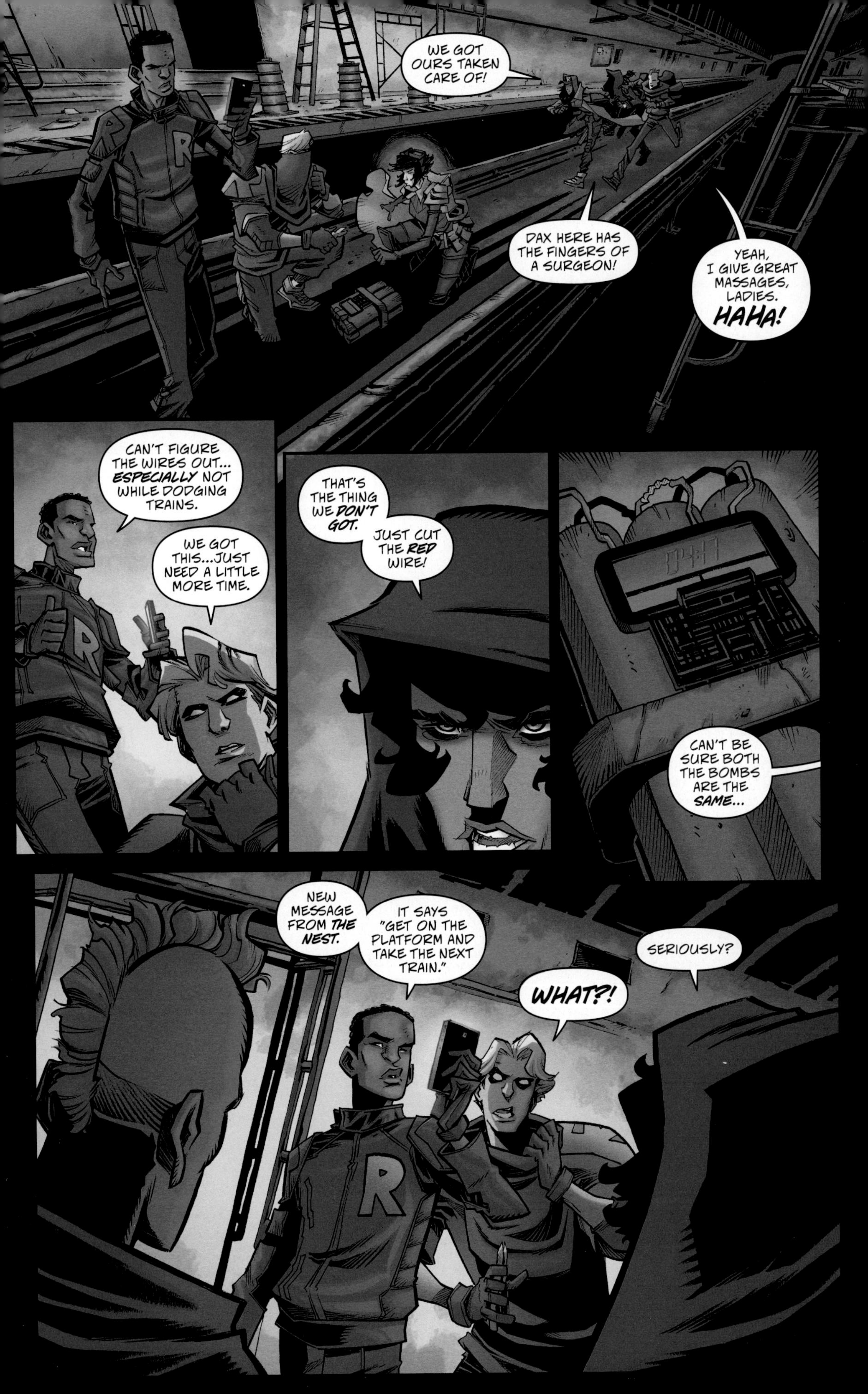

WE GOT OURS TAKEN CARE OF!
DAX HERE HAS THE FINGERS OF A SURGEON!
YEAH, I GIVE GREAT MASSAGES, LADIES. HAHA!
CAN'T FIGURE THE WIRES OUT... ESPECIALLY NOT WHILE DODGING TRAINS.
WE GOT THIS...JUST NEED A LITTLE MORE TIME.
THAT'S THE THING WE DON'T GOT.
JUST CUT THE RED WIRE!
CAN'T BE SURE BOTH THE BOMBS ARE THE SAME...
NEW MESSAGE FROM THE NEST.
IT SAYS "GET ON THE PLATFORM AND TAKE THE NEXT TRAIN."
WHAT?!
SERIOUSLY?

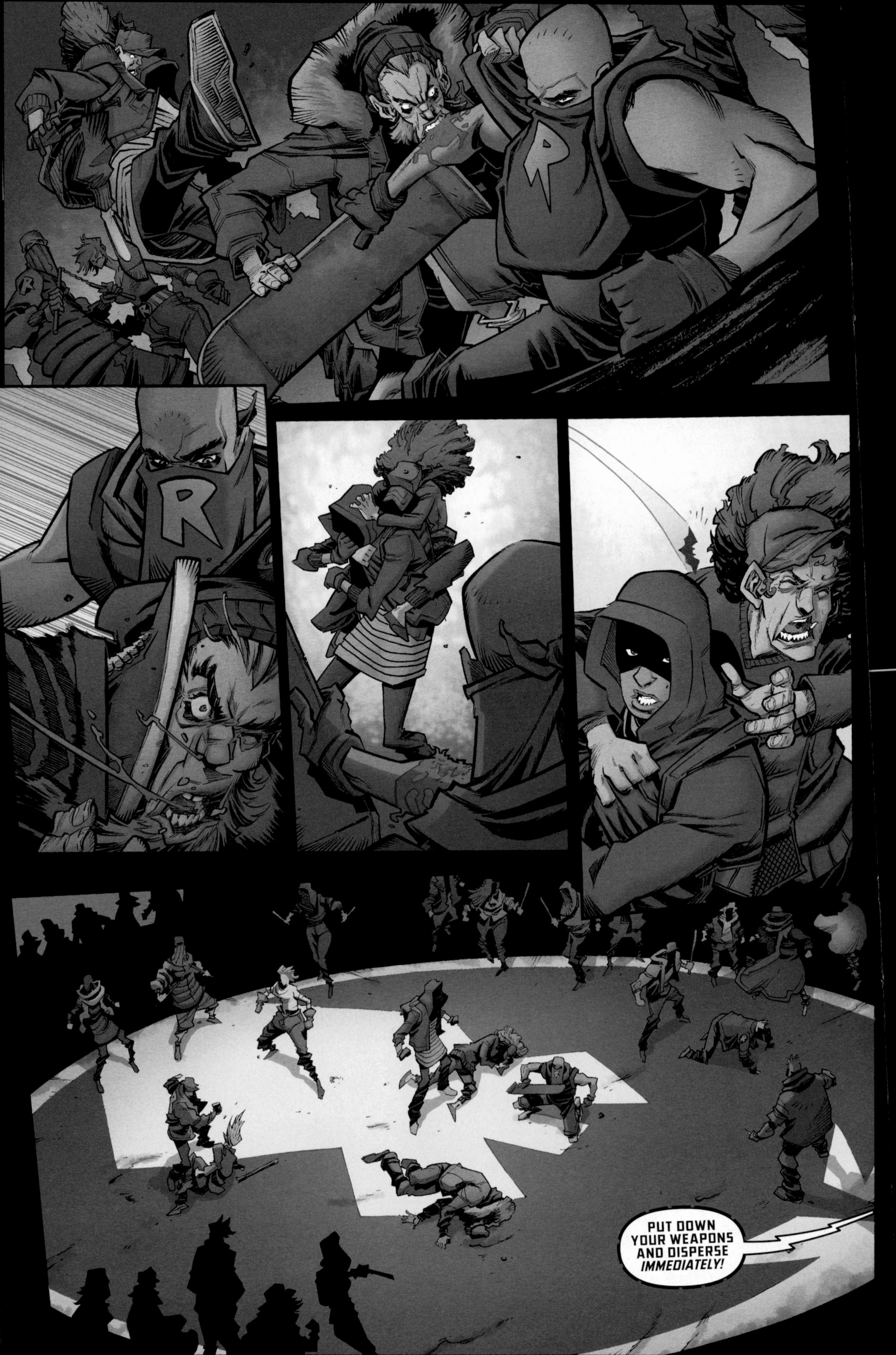
PUT DOWN YOUR WEAPONS AND DISPERSE IMMEDIATELY!

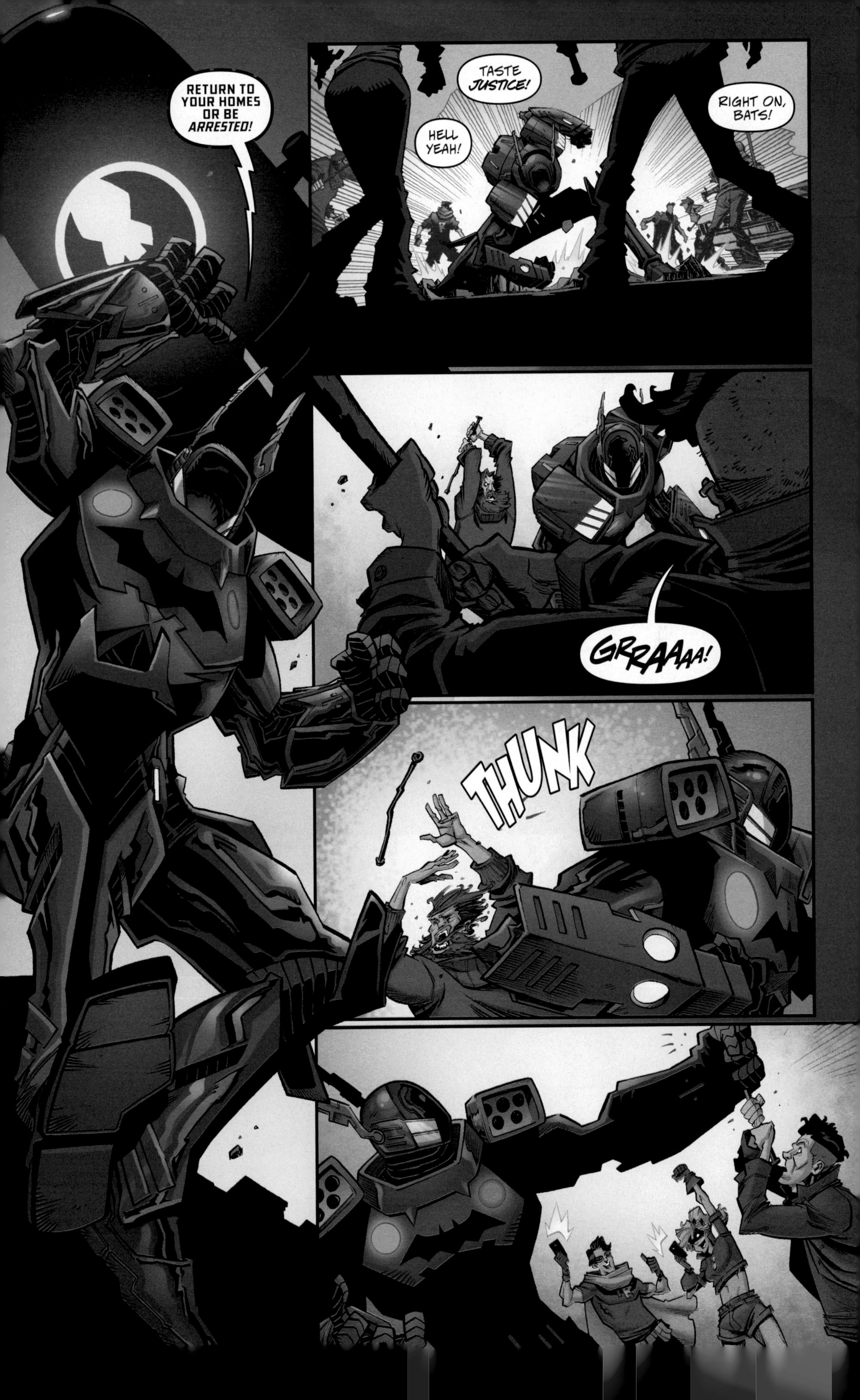
RETURN TO YOUR HOMES OR BE ARRESTED!
TASTE JUSTICE!
HELL YEAH!
RIGHT ON, BATS!
GRRAAAA!
THUNK

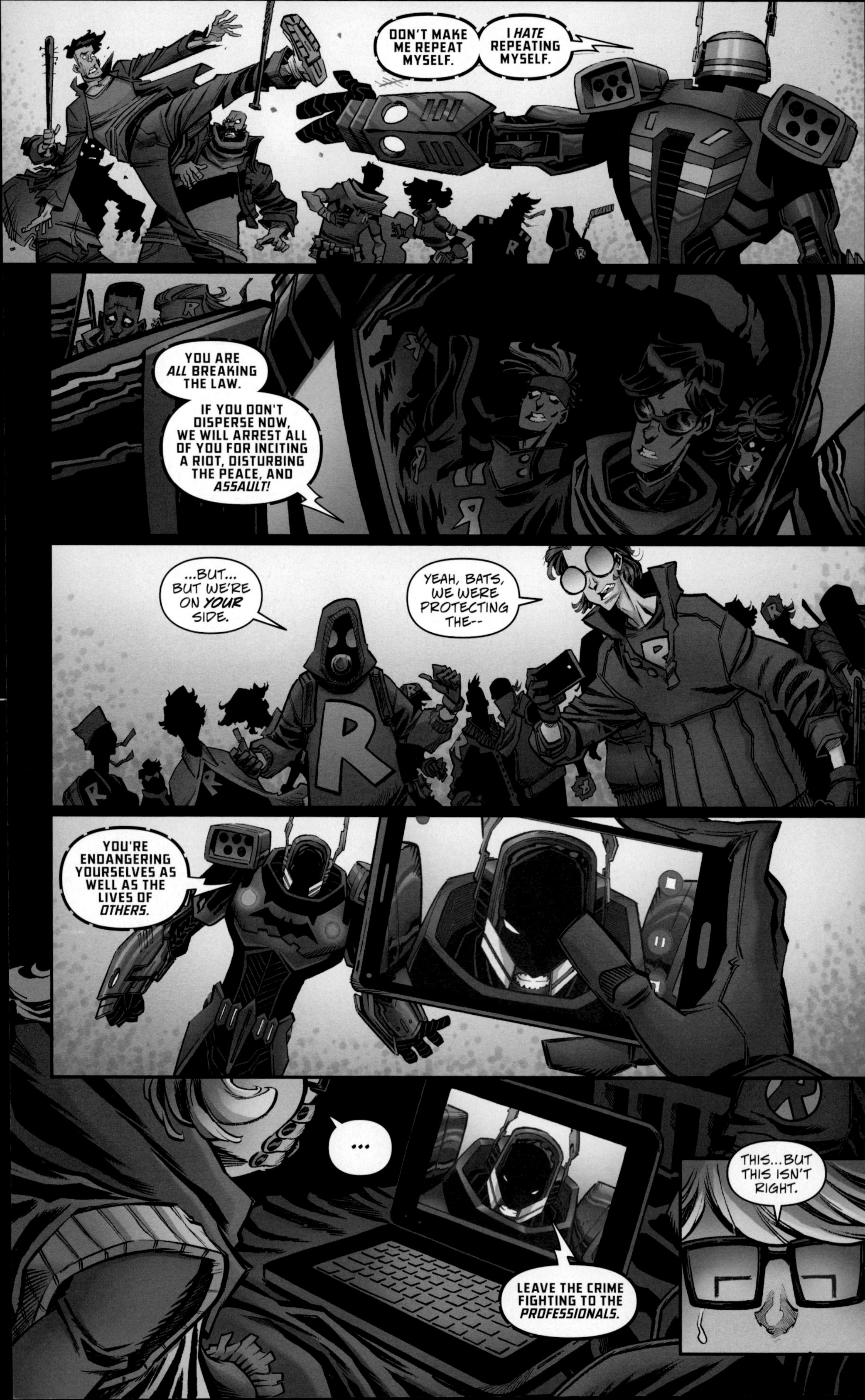

DON'T MAKE ME REPEAT MYSELF.
I *HATE* REPEATING MYSELF.
YOU ARE *ALL* BREAKING THE LAW.
IF YOU DON'T DISPERSE NOW, WE WILL ARREST ALL OF YOU FOR INCITING A RIOT, DISTURBING THE PEACE, AND *ASSAULT!*
...BUT... BUT WE'RE ON *YOUR* SIDE.
YEAH, BATS, WE WERE PROTECTING THE--
YOU'RE ENDANGERING YOURSELVES AS WELL AS THE LIVES OF *OTHERS.*
...
LEAVE THE CRIME FIGHTING TO THE *PROFESSIONALS.*
THIS...BUT THIS ISN'T RIGHT.

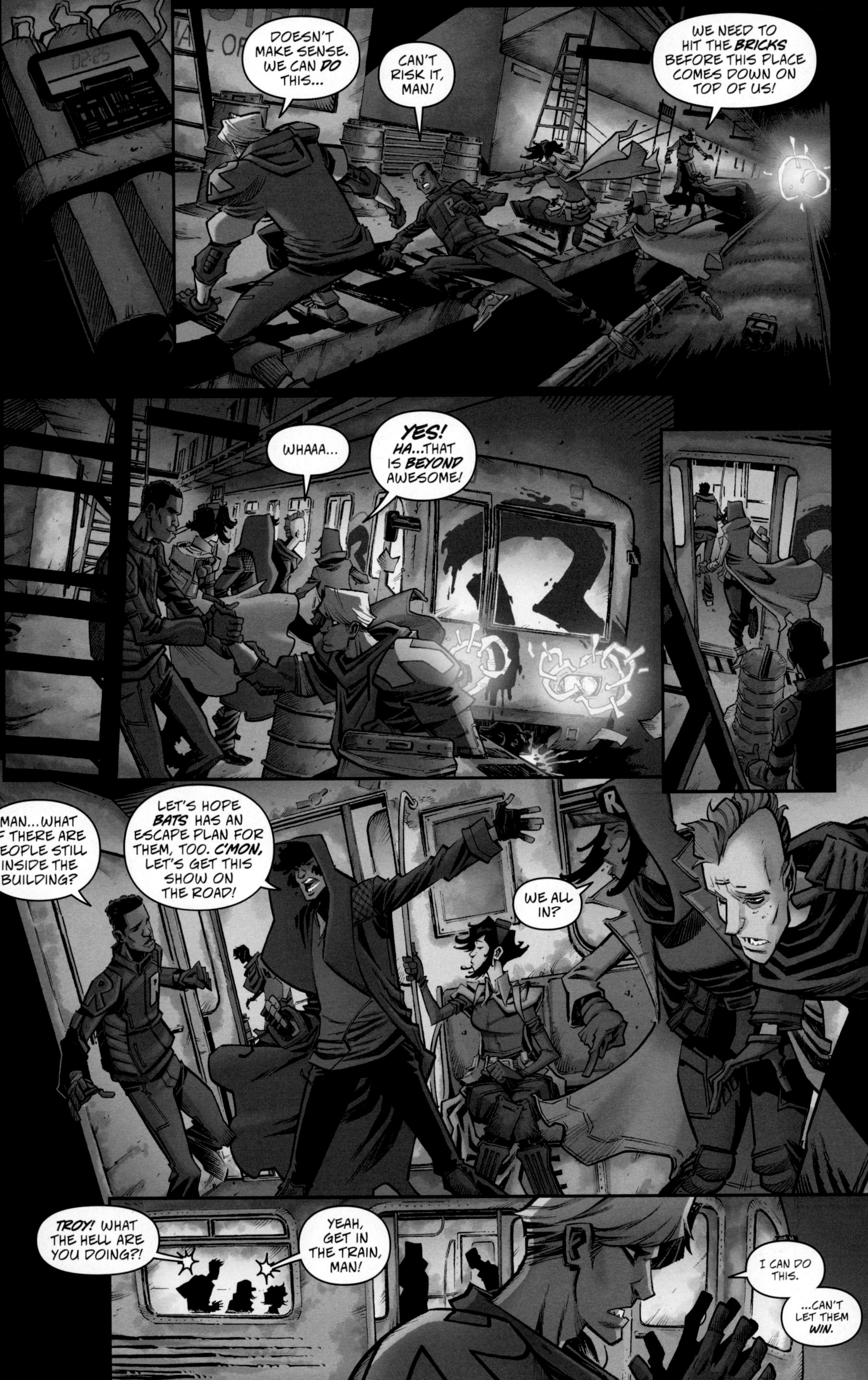
DOESN'T MAKE SENSE. WE CAN DO THIS...
CAN'T RISK IT, MAN!
WE NEED TO HIT THE BRICKS BEFORE THIS PLACE COMES DOWN ON TOP OF US!
WHAAA...
YES! HA...THAT IS BEYOND AWESOME!
MAN...WHAT IF THERE ARE PEOPLE STILL INSIDE THE BUILDING?
LET'S HOPE BATS HAS AN ESCAPE PLAN FOR THEM, TOO. C'MON, LET'S GET THIS SHOW ON THE ROAD!
WE ALL IN?
TROY! WHAT THE HELL ARE YOU DOING?!
YEAH, GET IN THE TRAIN, MAN!
I CAN DO THIS.
...CAN'T LET THEM WIN.

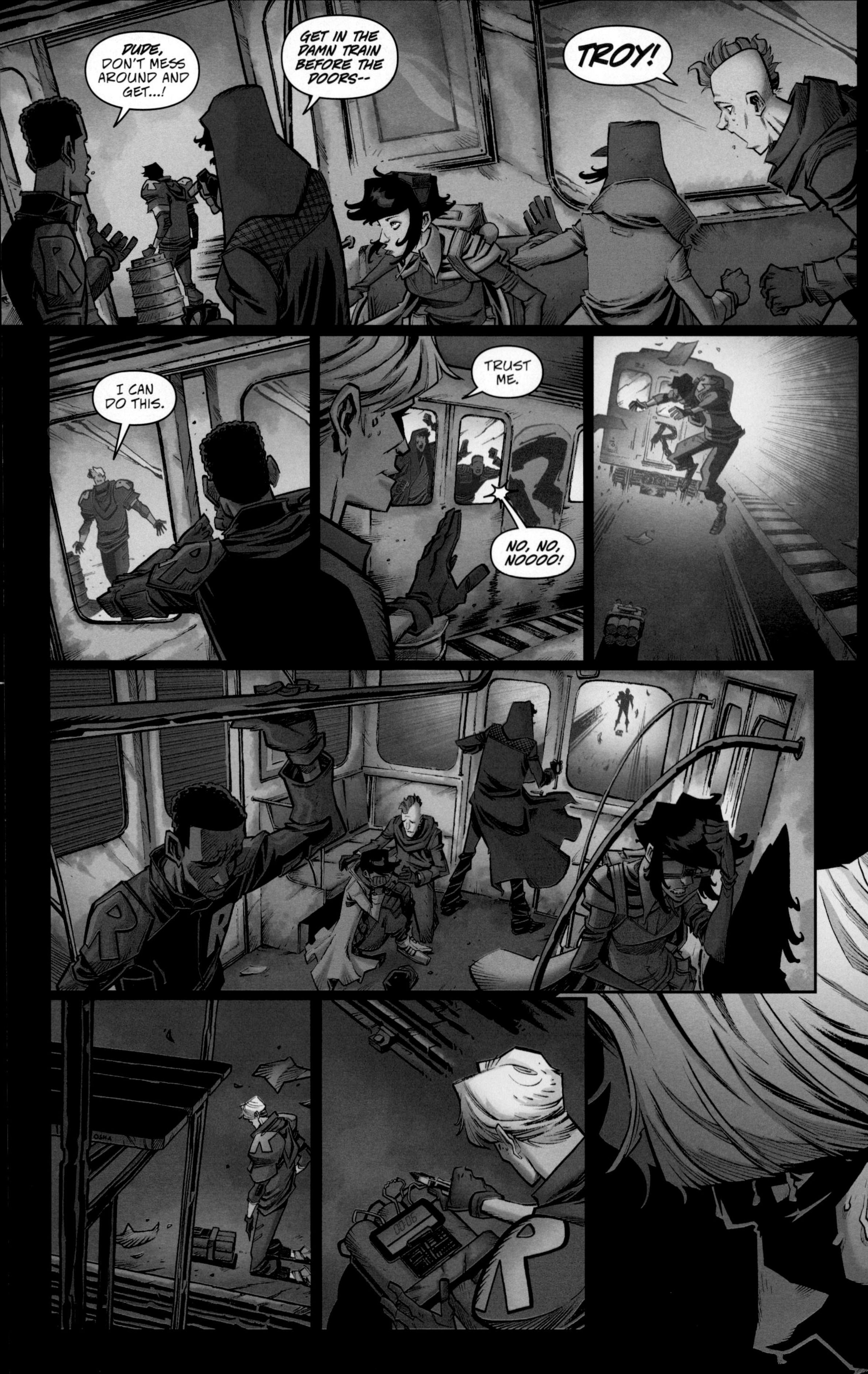
DUDE, DON'T MESS AROUND AND GET...!
GET IN THE DAMN TRAIN BEFORE THE DOORS--
TROY!
I CAN DO THIS.
TRUST ME.
NO, NO, NOOOO!

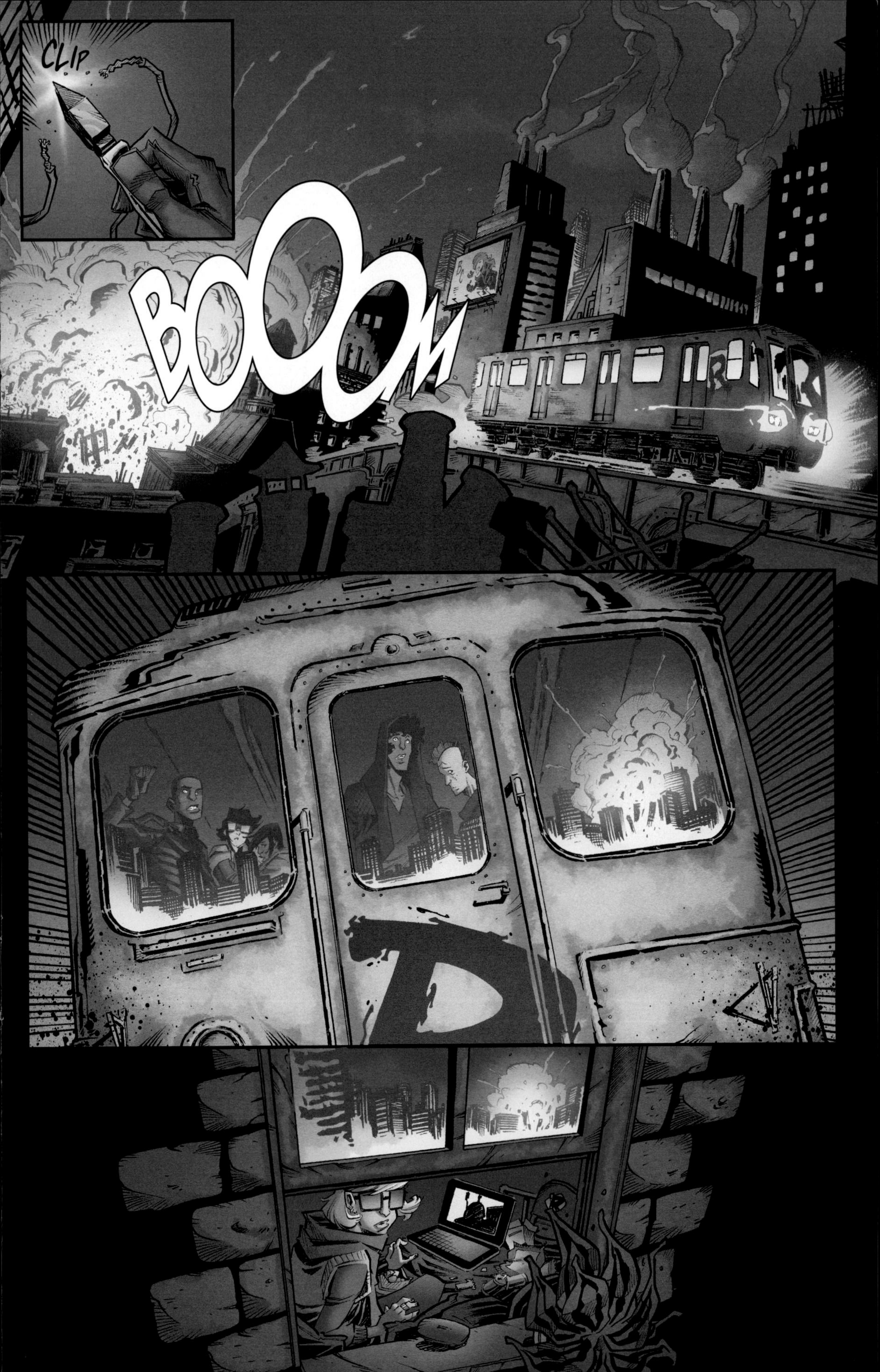
CLIP
BOOOM

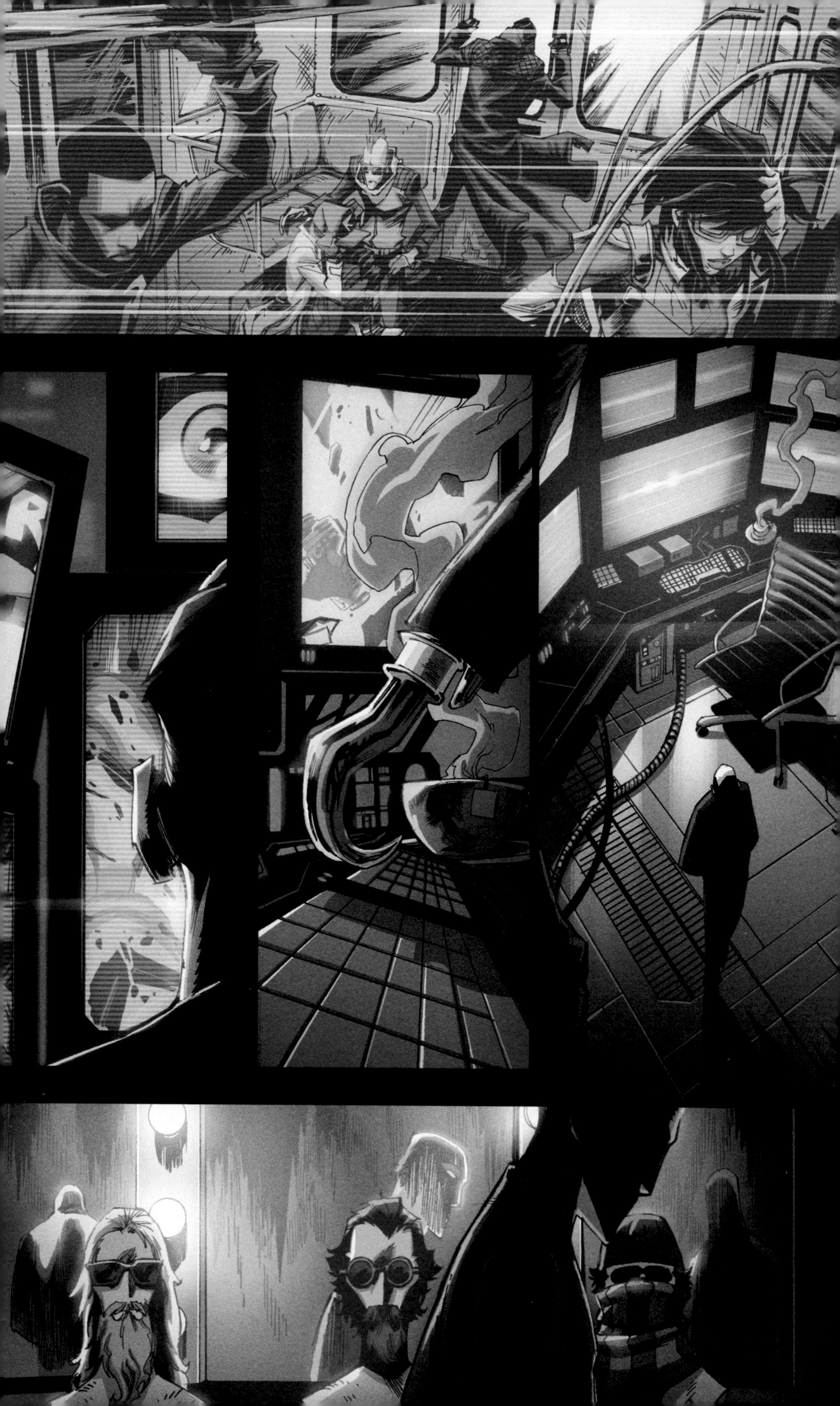

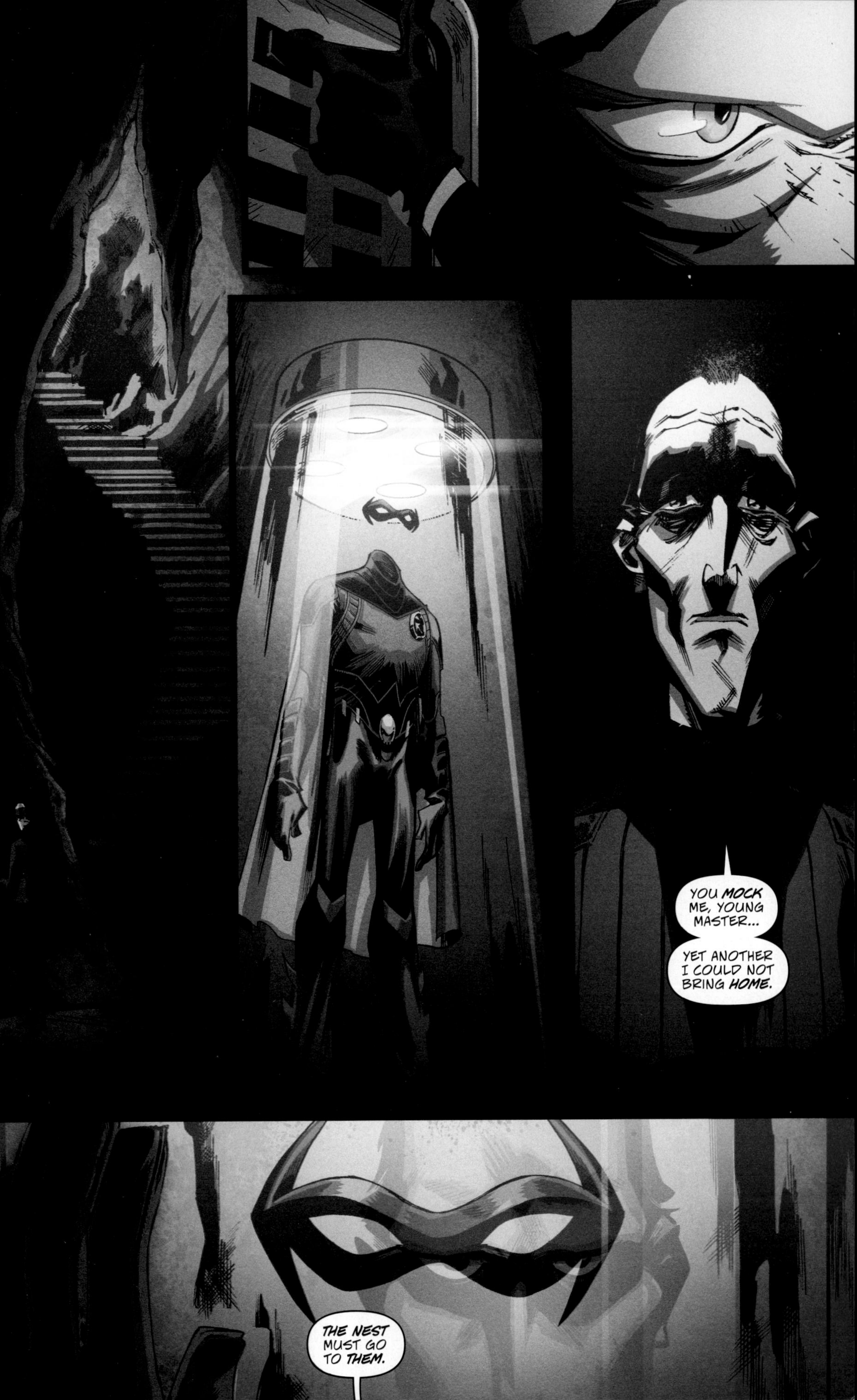
YOU MOCK ME, YOUNG MASTER...
YET ANOTHER I COULD NOT BRING HOME.
THE NEST MUST GO TO THEM.

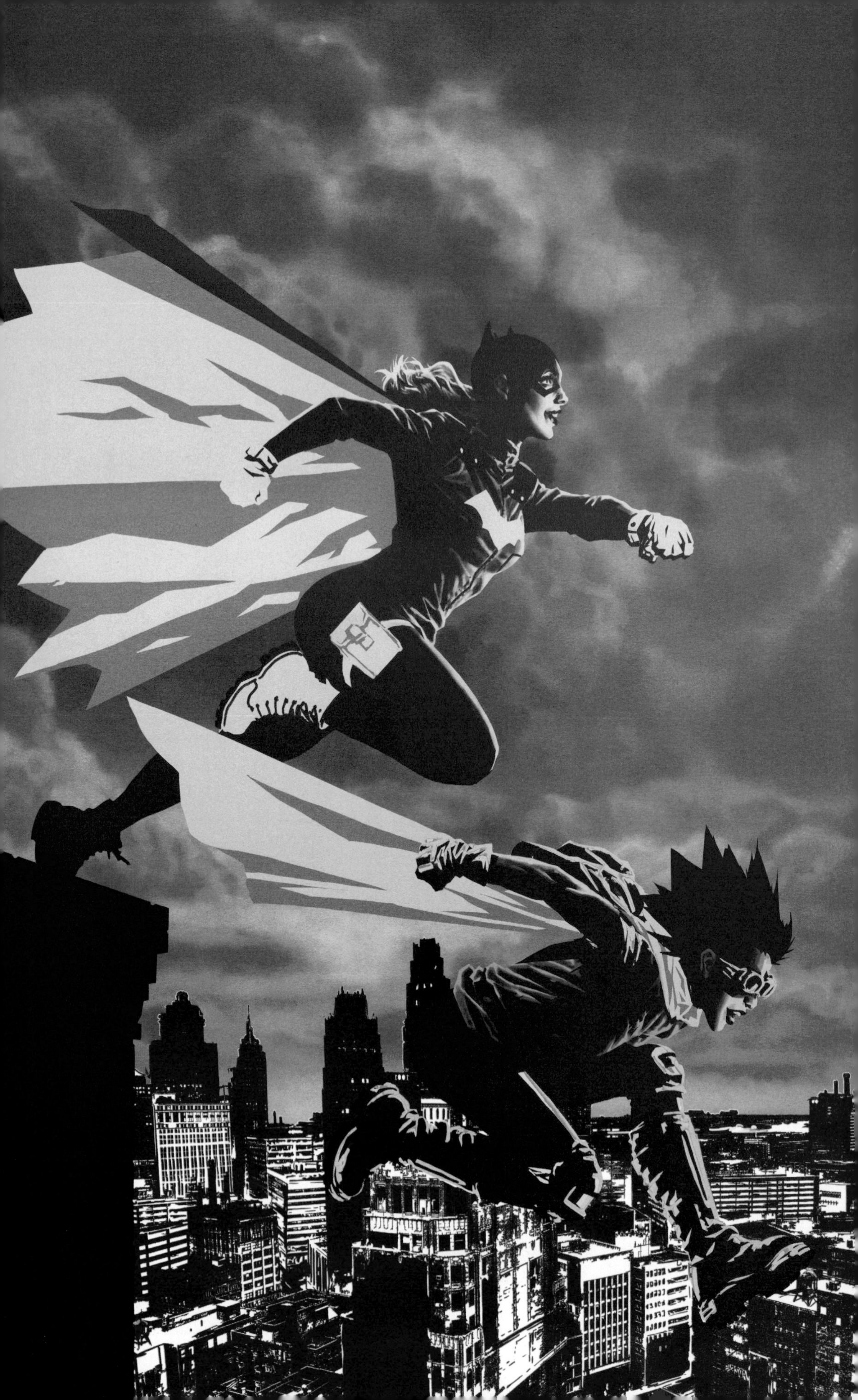

ROLE MODEL

writer **LEE BERMEJO**
penciller **JAMES HARVEY**
inks **JAMES HARVEY**

colors **JAMES HARVEY**
letters **JARED K. FLETCHER**
cover **LEE BERMEJO**

IT WAS A BEAUTIFUL DREAM.

IT *STILL* IS.

THE *FREEDOM* PART.

THE BLOOD OF PATRIOTS IS THE PART THAT MAKES YOU WAKE UP.

...PARENTS OF "ROBIN" TROY WALKER CHOKE BACK THE TEARS AS THEY BURY THEIR ONLY SON TODAY, THE SEVENTEEN-YEAR-OLD VICTIM KILLED IN LAST WEEK'S TERRIBLE BOMBING.

BREAKING NEWS
PARENTS OF TEEN KILLED IN BLAST
JOYCE AND STEVEN WALKER, PARE
GCN

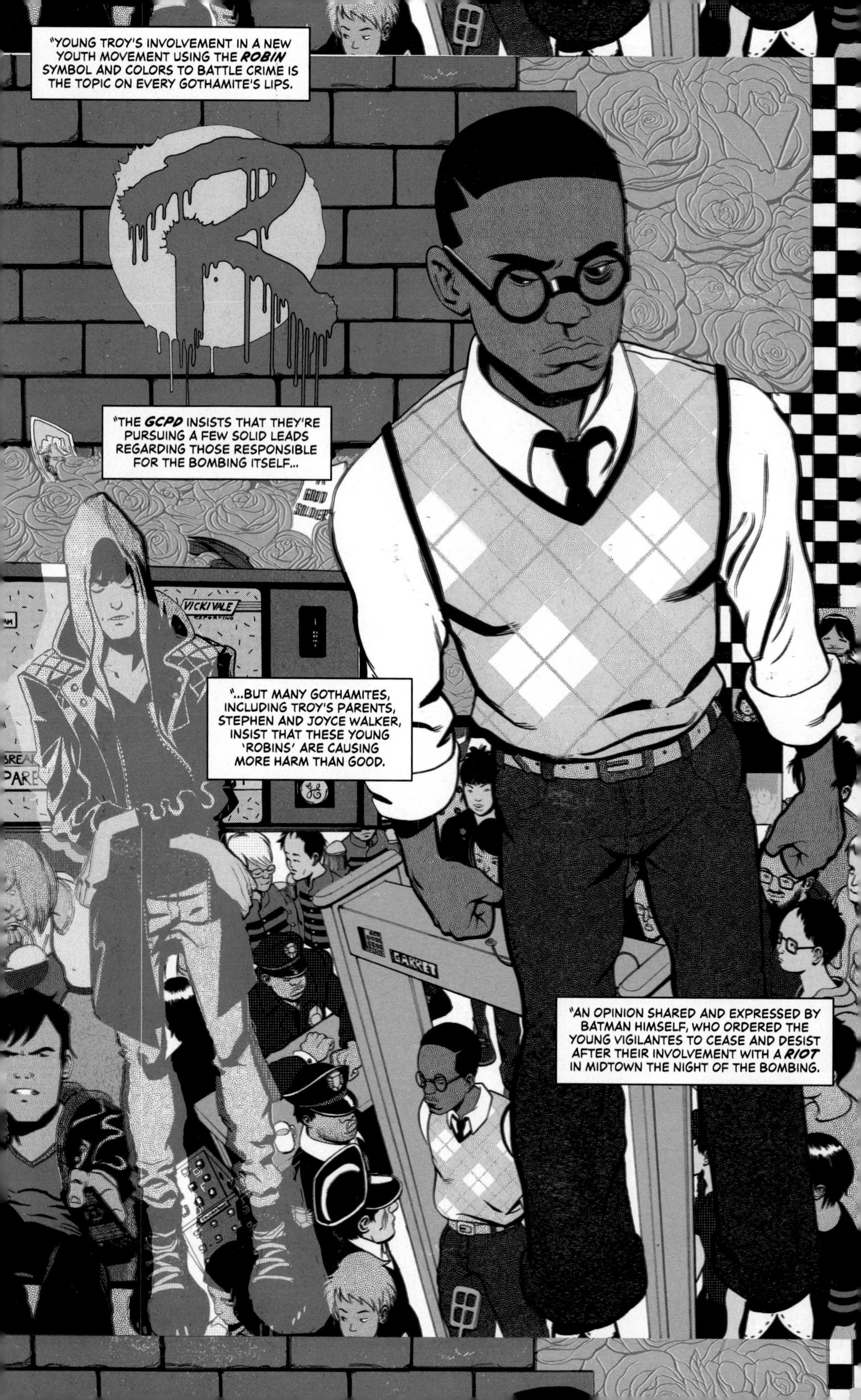
"YOUNG TROY'S INVOLVEMENT IN A NEW YOUTH MOVEMENT USING THE *ROBIN* SYMBOL AND COLORS TO BATTLE CRIME IS THE TOPIC ON EVERY GOTHAMITE'S LIPS.
"THE *GCPD* INSISTS THAT THEY'RE PURSUING A FEW SOLID LEADS REGARDING THOSE RESPONSIBLE FOR THE BOMBING ITSELF...
VICKI VALE
"...BUT MANY GOTHAMITES, INCLUDING TROY'S PARENTS, STEPHEN AND JOYCE WALKER, INSIST THAT THESE YOUNG 'ROBINS' ARE CAUSING MORE HARM THAN GOOD.
GARRET
"AN OPINION SHARED AND EXPRESSED BY BATMAN HIMSELF, WHO ORDERED THE YOUNG VIGILANTES TO CEASE AND DESIST AFTER THEIR INVOLVEMENT WITH A *RIOT* IN MIDTOWN THE NIGHT OF THE BOMBING.

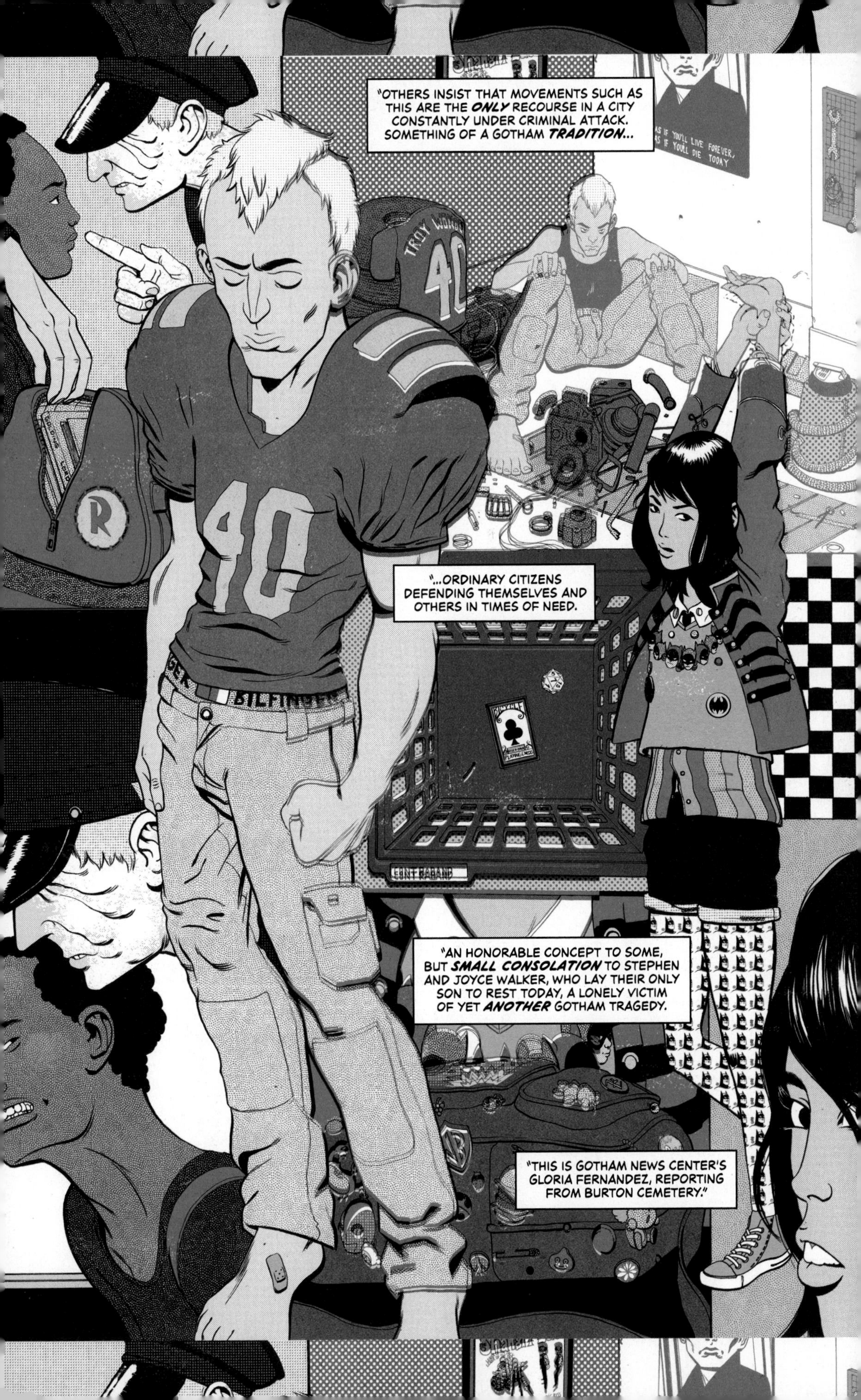
"OTHERS INSIST THAT MOVEMENTS SUCH AS THIS ARE THE ONLY RECOURSE IN A CITY CONSTANTLY UNDER CRIMINAL ATTACK. SOMETHING OF A GOTHAM TRADITION...
AS IF YOU'LL LIVE FOREVER,
AS IF YOU'LL DIE TODAY
"...ORDINARY CITIZENS DEFENDING THEMSELVES AND OTHERS IN TIMES OF NEED.
"AN HONORABLE CONCEPT TO SOME, BUT SMALL CONSOLATION TO STEPHEN AND JOYCE WALKER, WHO LAY THEIR ONLY SON TO REST TODAY, A LONELY VICTIM OF YET ANOTHER GOTHAM TRAGEDY.
"THIS IS GOTHAM NEWS CENTER'S GLORIA FERNANDEZ, REPORTING FROM BURTON CEMETERY."

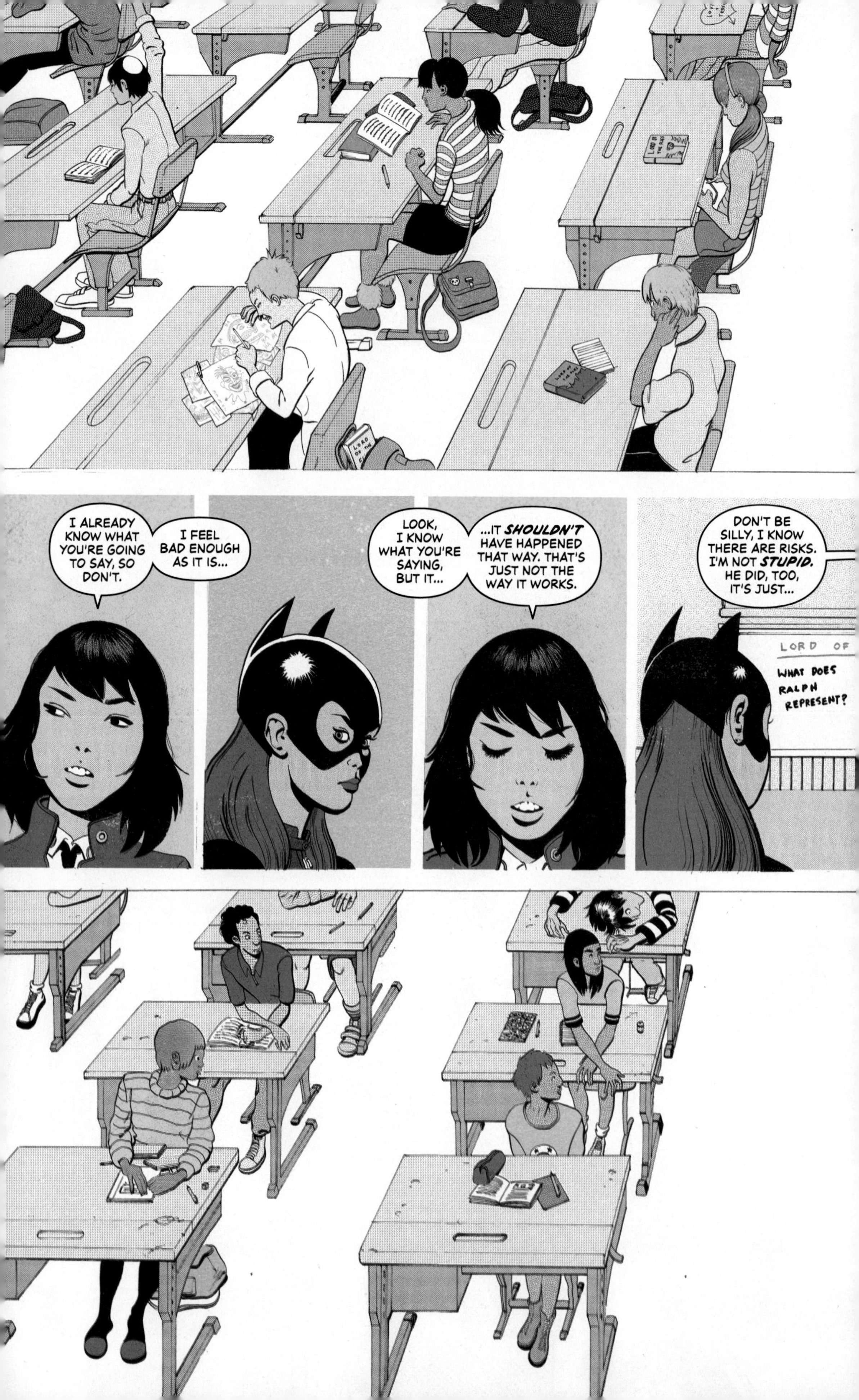
I ALREADY KNOW WHAT YOU'RE GOING TO SAY, SO DON'T.
I FEEL BAD ENOUGH AS IT IS...
LOOK, I KNOW WHAT YOU'RE SAYING, BUT IT...
...IT **SHOULDN'T** HAVE HAPPENED THAT WAY. THAT'S JUST NOT THE WAY IT WORKS.
DON'T BE SILLY, I KNOW THERE ARE RISKS. I'M NOT **STUPID.** HE DID, TOO, IT'S JUST...
LORD OF
WHAT DOES RALPH REPRESENT?

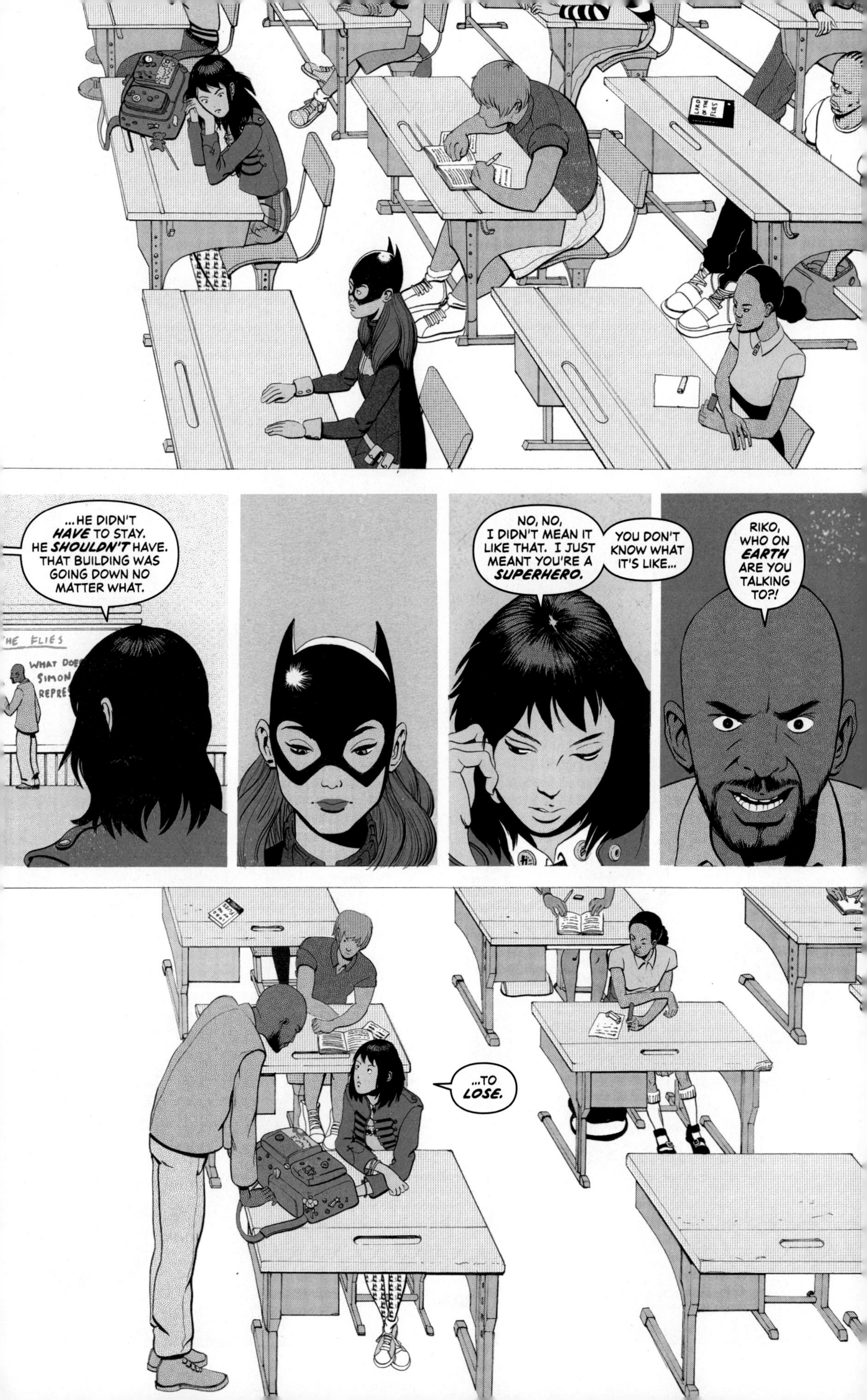
...HE DIDN'T HAVE TO STAY. HE SHOULDN'T HAVE. THAT BUILDING WAS GOING DOWN NO MATTER WHAT.
NO, NO, I DIDN'T MEAN IT LIKE THAT. I JUST MEANT YOU'RE A SUPERHERO.
YOU DON'T KNOW WHAT IT'S LIKE...
RIKO, WHO ON EARTH ARE YOU TALKING TO?!
...TO LOSE.

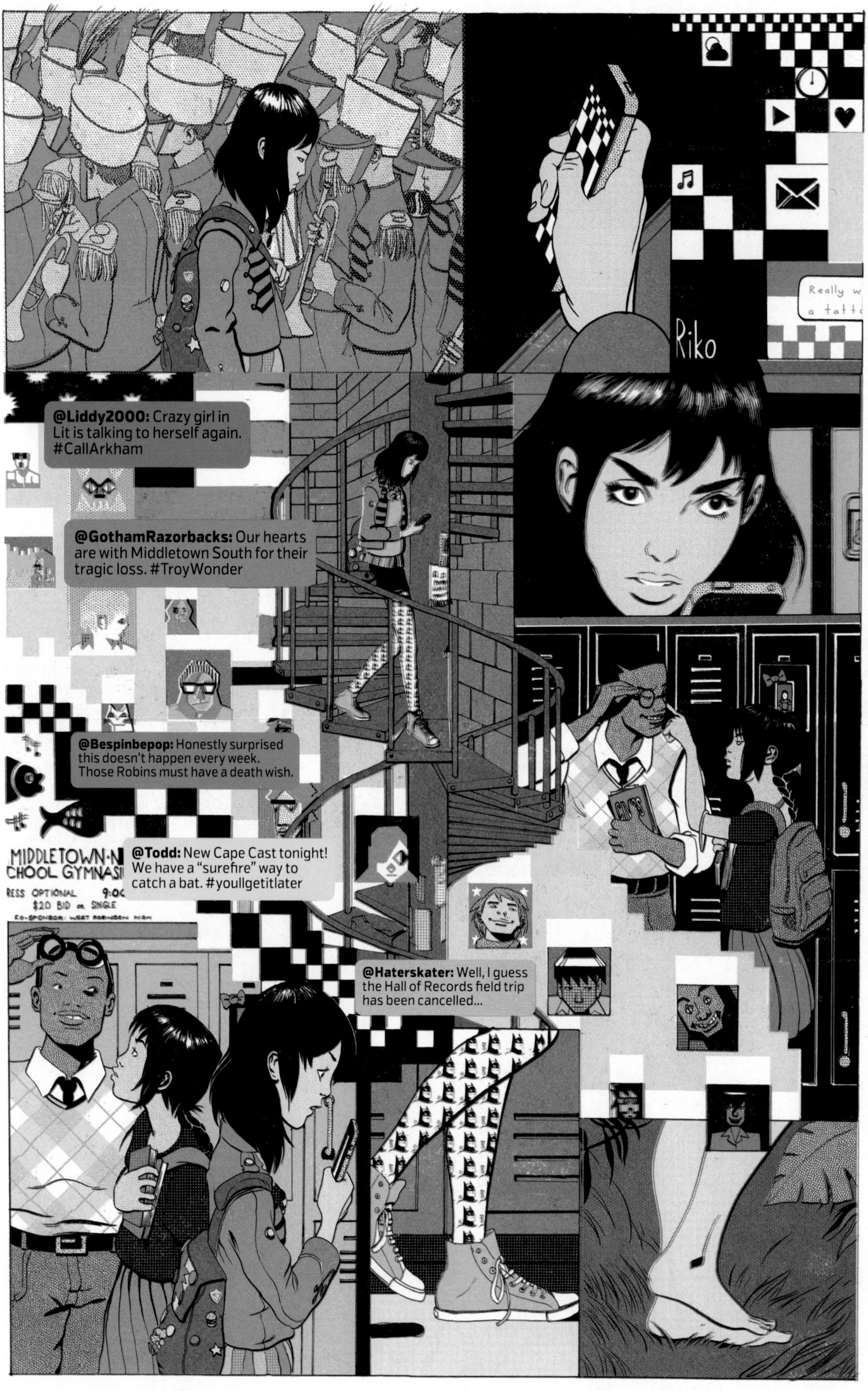

Really w
a tatto
Riko
@Liddy2000: Crazy girl in Lit is talking to herself again. #CallArkham
@GothamRazorbacks: Our hearts are with Middletown South for their tragic loss. #TroyWonder
@Bespinbepop: Honestly surprised this doesn't happen every week. Those Robins must have a death wish.
MIDDLETOWN·N
CHOOL GYMNASI
RESS OPTIONAL 9:0
$20 BID ea. SINGLE
@Todd: New Cape Cast tonight! We have a "surefire" way to catch a bat. #youllgetitlater
@Haterskater: Well, I guess the Hall of Records field trip has been cancelled...

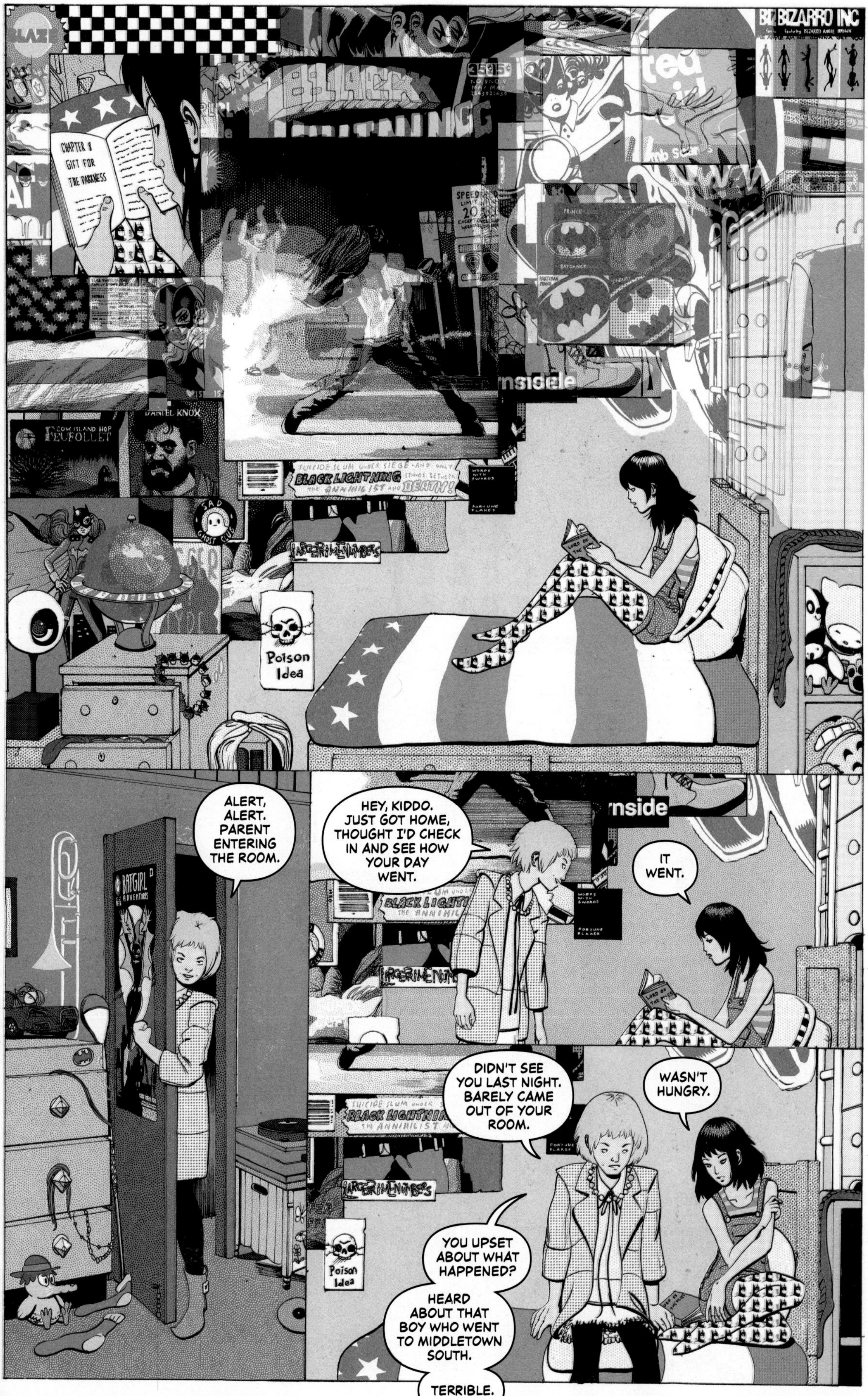
BIZARRO INC
CHAPTER 8
GIFT FOR THE DARKNESS
BLACK LIGHTNING
SPEED LIMIT
BATDANCE
DANIEL KNOX
COW ISLAND HOP
FEUFOLLET
SAD GHOST CLUB
SUICIDE SLUM UNDER SIEGE—AND ONLY BLACK LIGHTNING STANDS BETWEEN THE ANNIHILIST AND DEATH!
WORDS WITH SWORDS
FORTUNE FLAKES
LARGER THAN NUMBERS
Poison Idea
LORD OF THE FLIES
BATGIRL ADVENTURES
ALERT, ALERT. PARENT ENTERING THE ROOM.
HEY, KIDDO. JUST GOT HOME, THOUGHT I'D CHECK IN AND SEE HOW YOUR DAY WENT.
IT WENT.
DIDN'T SEE YOU LAST NIGHT. BARELY CAME OUT OF YOUR ROOM.
WASN'T HUNGRY.
YOU UPSET ABOUT WHAT HAPPENED?
HEARD ABOUT THAT BOY WHO WENT TO MIDDLETOWN SOUTH.
TERRIBLE.

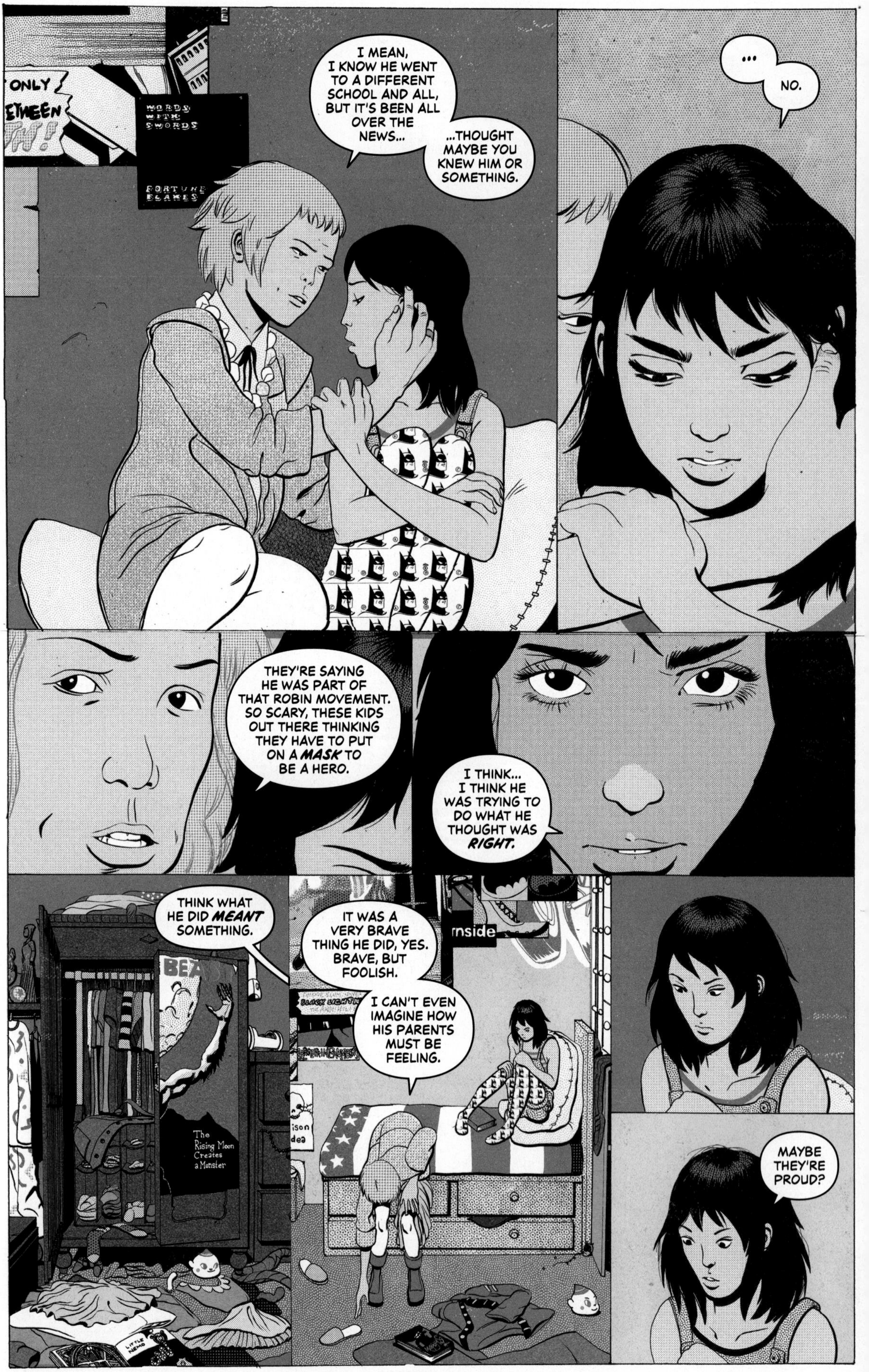
WORDS WITH SWORDS
FORTUNE FLAKES
I MEAN, I KNOW HE WENT TO A DIFFERENT SCHOOL AND ALL, BUT IT'S BEEN ALL OVER THE NEWS...
...THOUGHT MAYBE YOU KNEW HIM OR SOMETHING.
...
NO.
THEY'RE SAYING HE WAS PART OF THAT ROBIN MOVEMENT. SO SCARY, THESE KIDS OUT THERE THINKING THEY HAVE TO PUT ON A ***MASK*** TO BE A HERO.
I THINK... I THINK HE WAS TRYING TO DO WHAT HE THOUGHT WAS ***RIGHT.***
THINK WHAT HE DID ***MEANT*** SOMETHING.
The Rising Moon Creates a Monster
IT WAS A VERY BRAVE THING HE DID, YES. BRAVE, BUT FOOLISH.
I CAN'T EVEN IMAGINE HOW HIS PARENTS MUST BE FEELING.
MAYBE THEY'RE PROUD?

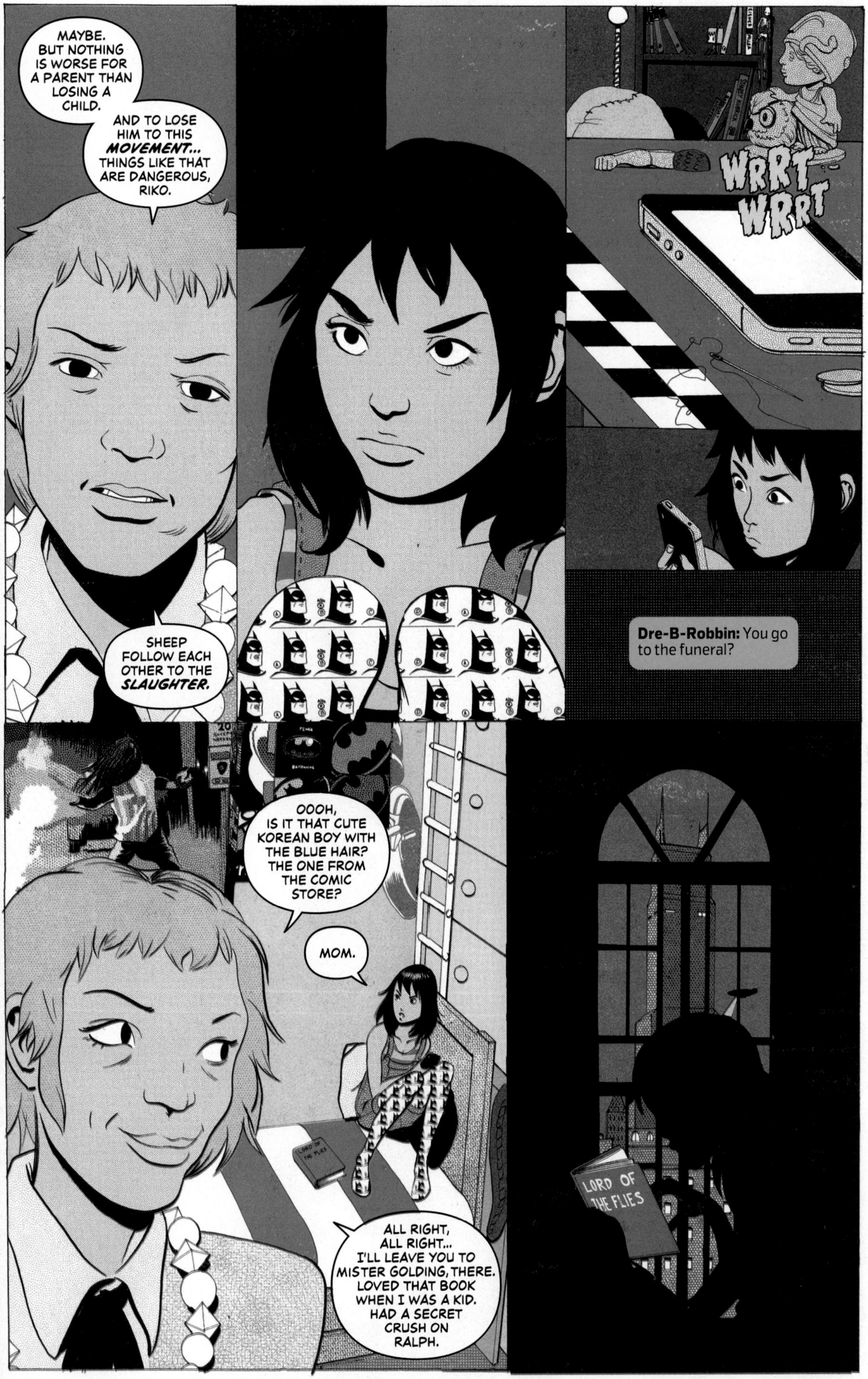

MAYBE. BUT NOTHING IS WORSE FOR A PARENT THAN LOSING A CHILD.
AND TO LOSE HIM TO THIS *MOVEMENT...* THINGS LIKE THAT ARE DANGEROUS, RIKO.
SHEEP FOLLOW EACH OTHER TO THE *SLAUGHTER.*
WRRT WRRT
Dre-B-Robbin: You go to the funeral?
OOOH, IS IT THAT CUTE KOREAN BOY WITH THE BLUE HAIR? THE ONE FROM THE COMIC STORE?
MOM.
ALL RIGHT, ALL RIGHT... I'LL LEAVE YOU TO MISTER GOLDING, THERE. LOVED THAT BOOK WHEN I WAS A KID. HAD A SECRET CRUSH ON RALPH.
LORD OF THE FLIES

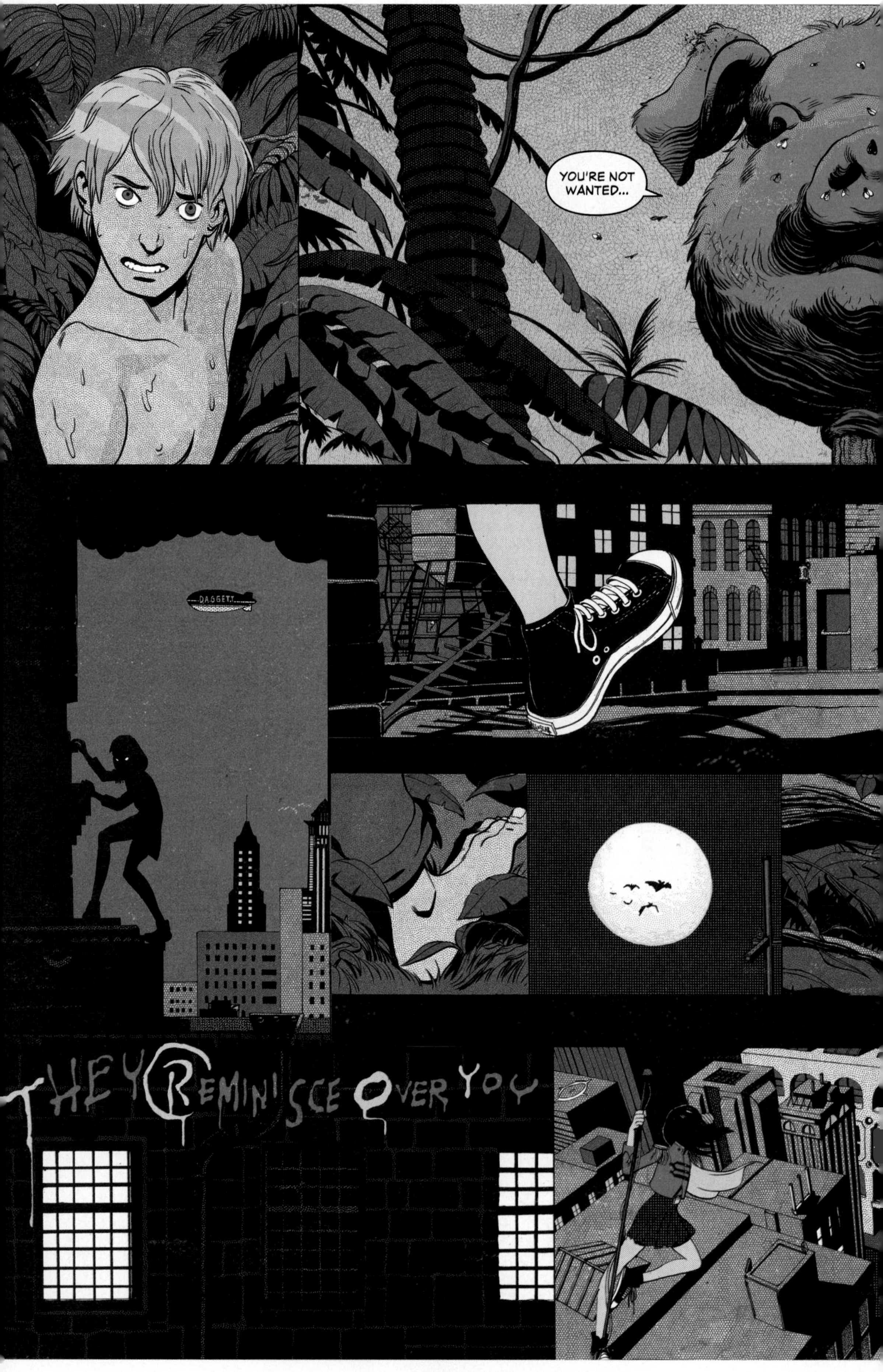
YOU'RE NOT WANTED...
DAGGETT
THEY REMINISCE OVER YOU

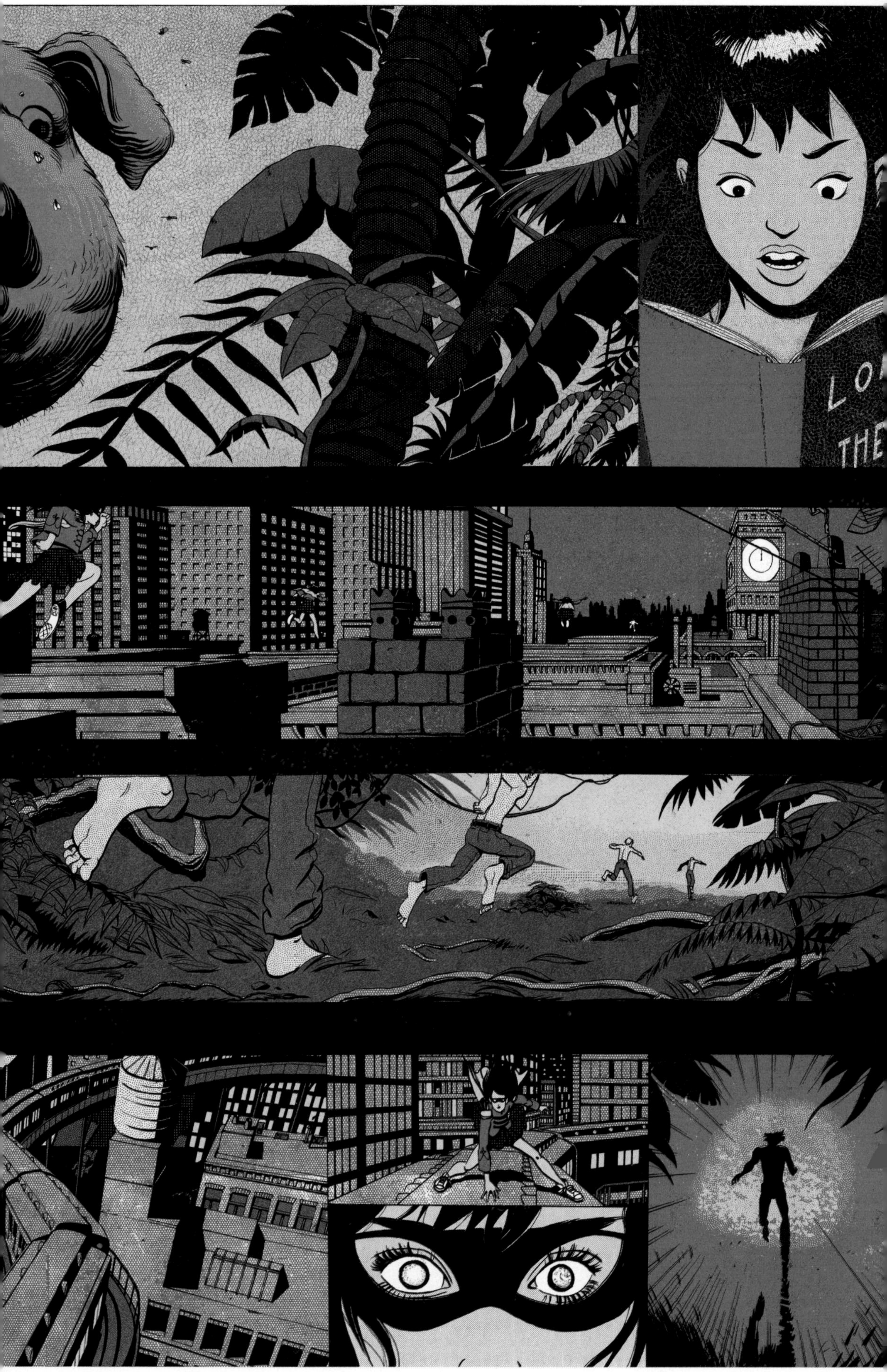

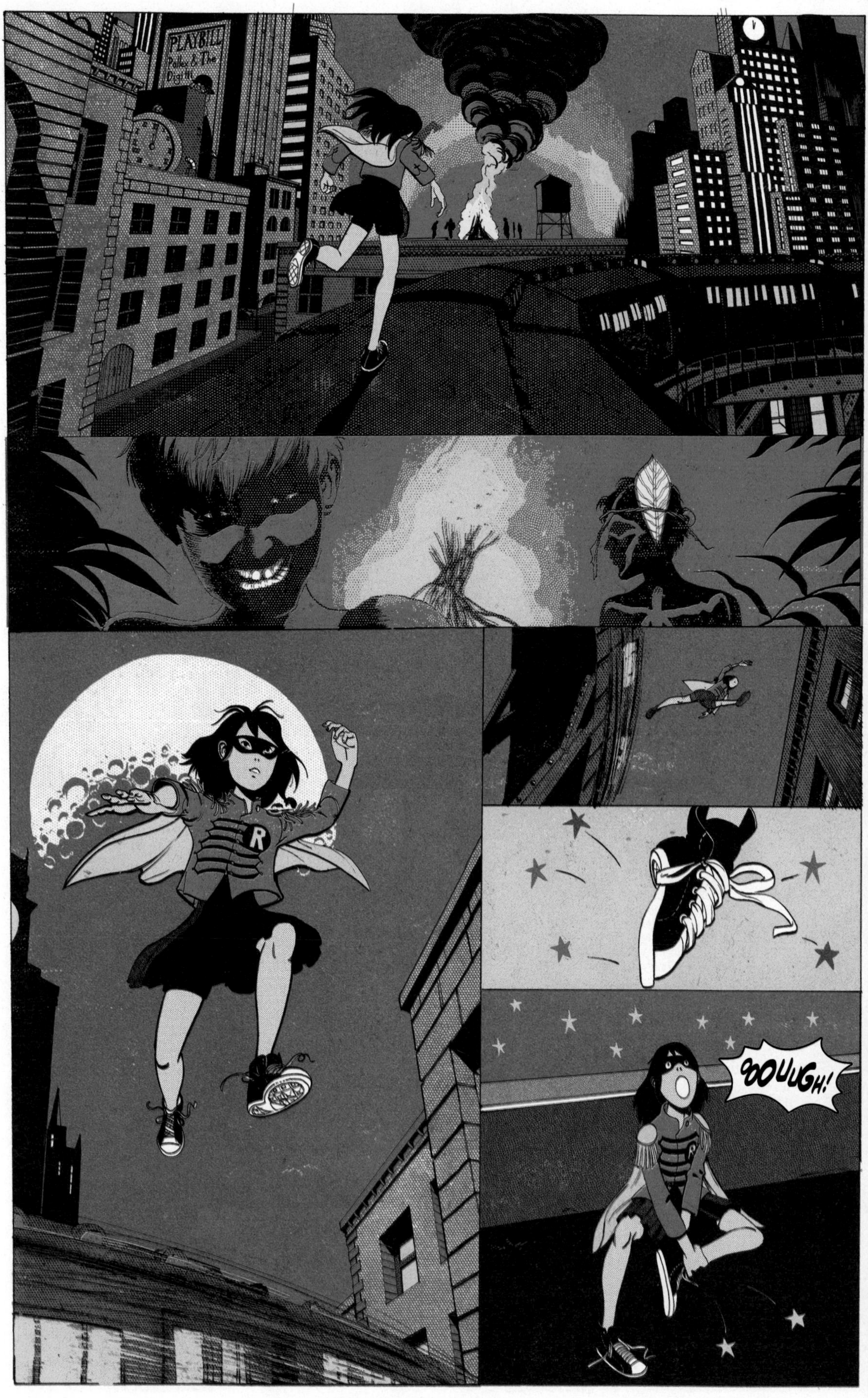
PLAYBILL
Pollex & The Digiti
OOOUUGH!

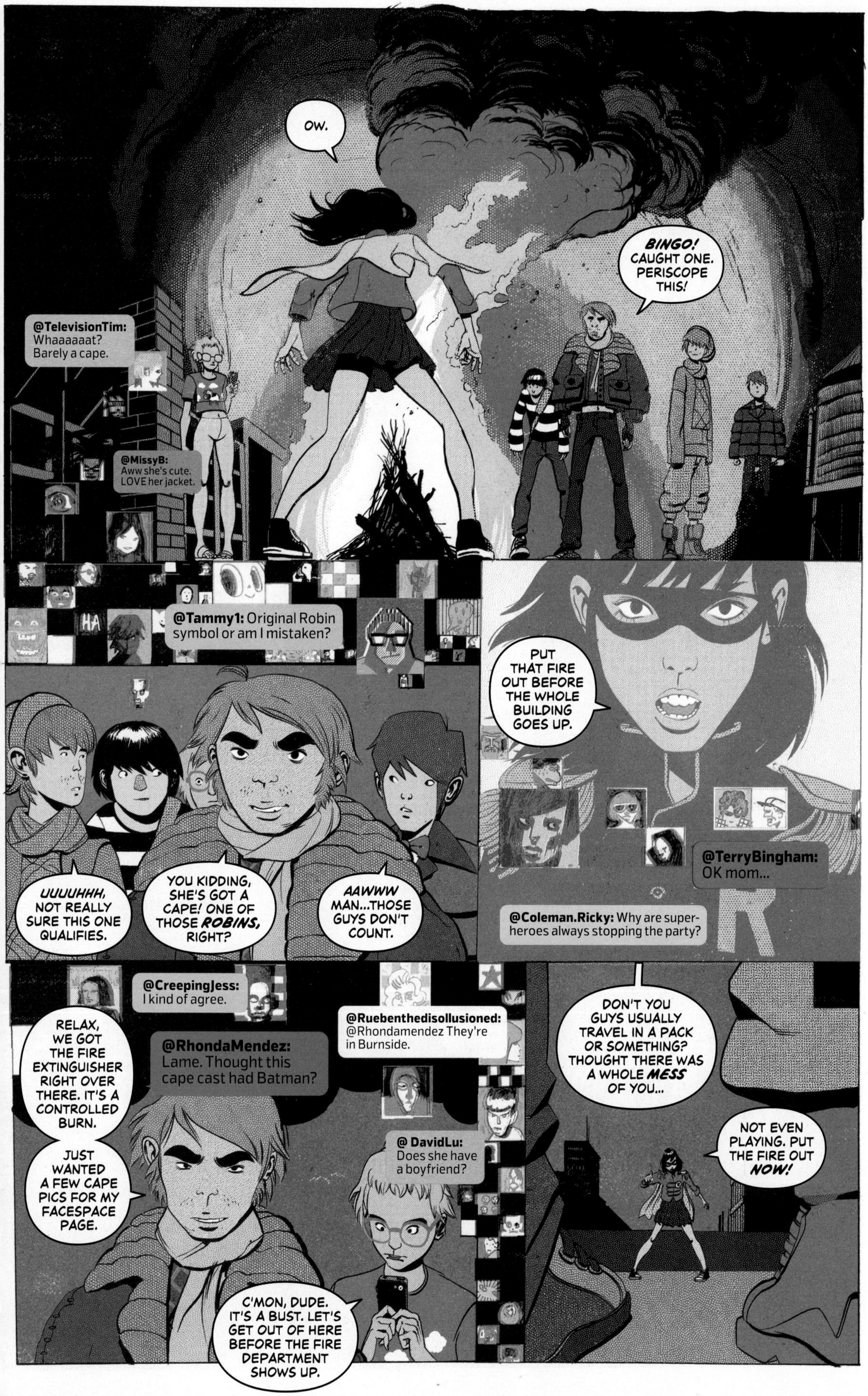
OW.
@TelevisionTim: Whaaaaaat? Barely a cape.
@MissyB: Aww she's cute. LOVE her jacket.
BINGO! CAUGHT ONE. PERISCOPE THIS!
@Tammy1: Original Robin symbol or am I mistaken?
UUUUHHH, NOT REALLY SURE THIS ONE QUALIFIES.
YOU KIDDING, SHE'S GOT A CAPE! ONE OF THOSE ROBINS, RIGHT?
AAWWW MAN...THOSE GUYS DON'T COUNT.
PUT THAT FIRE OUT BEFORE THE WHOLE BUILDING GOES UP.
@TerryBingham: OK mom...
@Coleman.Ricky: Why are superheroes always stopping the party?
@CreepingJess: I kind of agree.
RELAX, WE GOT THE FIRE EXTINGUISHER RIGHT OVER THERE. IT'S A CONTROLLED BURN.
JUST WANTED A FEW CAPE PICS FOR MY FACESPACE PAGE.
@RhondaMendez: Lame. Thought this cape cast had Batman?
@Ruebenthedisollusioned: @Rhondamendez They're in Burnside.
@ DavidLu: Does she have a boyfriend?
C'MON, DUDE. IT'S A BUST. LET'S GET OUT OF HERE BEFORE THE FIRE DEPARTMENT SHOWS UP.
DON'T YOU GUYS USUALLY TRAVEL IN A PACK OR SOMETHING? THOUGHT THERE WAS A WHOLE MESS OF YOU...
NOT EVEN PLAYING. PUT THE FIRE OUT NOW!

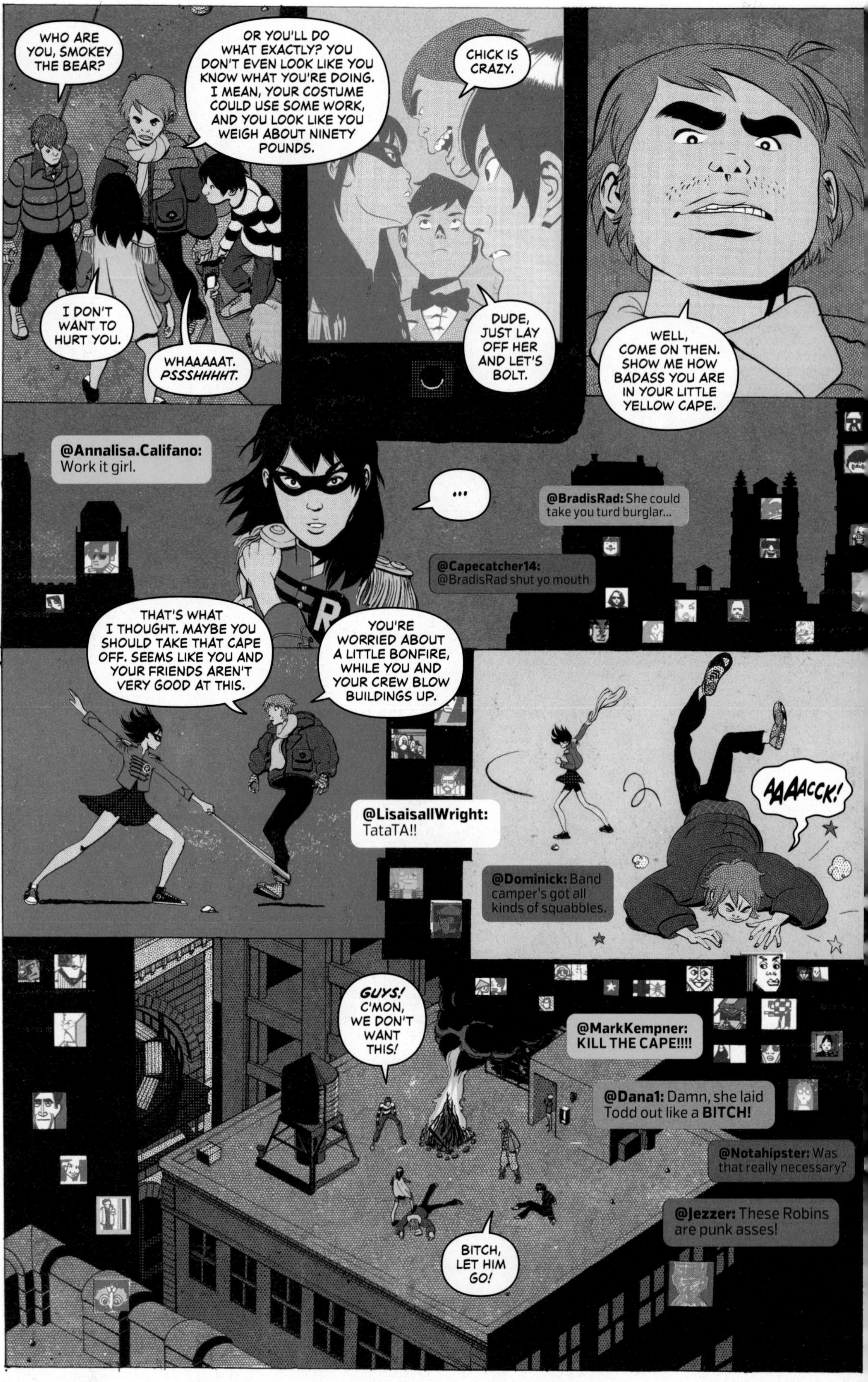
WHO ARE YOU, SMOKEY THE BEAR?
OR YOU'LL DO WHAT EXACTLY? YOU DON'T EVEN LOOK LIKE YOU KNOW WHAT YOU'RE DOING. I MEAN, YOUR COSTUME COULD USE SOME WORK, AND YOU LOOK LIKE YOU WEIGH ABOUT NINETY POUNDS.
I DON'T WANT TO HURT YOU.
WHAAAAAT. PSSSHHHHT.
CHICK IS CRAZY.
DUDE, JUST LAY OFF HER AND LET'S BOLT.
WELL, COME ON THEN. SHOW ME HOW BADASS YOU ARE IN YOUR LITTLE YELLOW CAPE.
@Annalisa.Califano: Work it girl.
...
@BradisRad: She could take you turd burglar...
@Capecatcher14: @BradisRad shut yo mouth
THAT'S WHAT I THOUGHT. MAYBE YOU SHOULD TAKE THAT CAPE OFF. SEEMS LIKE YOU AND YOUR FRIENDS AREN'T VERY GOOD AT THIS.
YOU'RE WORRIED ABOUT A LITTLE BONFIRE, WHILE YOU AND YOUR CREW BLOW BUILDINGS UP.
@LisaisallWright: TataTA!!
AAAACCK!
@Dominick: Band camper's got all kinds of squabbles.
GUYS! C'MON, WE DON'T WANT THIS!
@MarkKempner: KILL THE CAPE!!!!
@Dana1: Damn, she laid Todd out like a BITCH!
@Notahipster: Was that really necessary?
@Jezzer: These Robins are punk asses!
BITCH, LET HIM GO!

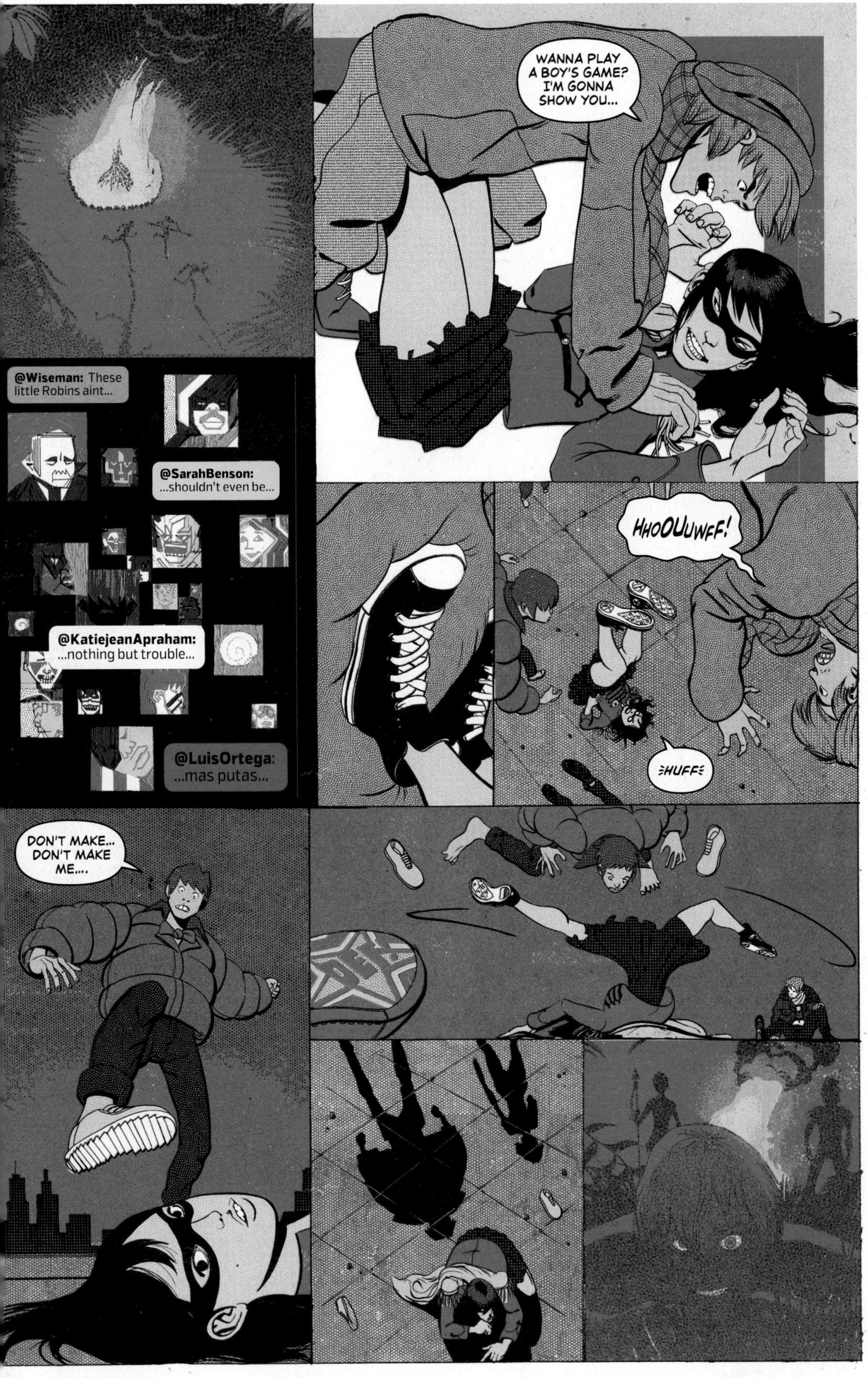
WANNA PLAY A BOY'S GAME? I'M GONNA SHOW YOU...
@Wiseman: These little Robins aint...
@SarahBenson: ...shouldn't even be...
@KatiejeanApraham: ...nothing but trouble...
@LuisOrtega: ...mas putas...
HHOOUuwFF!
HUFF
DON'T MAKE... DON'T MAKE ME....

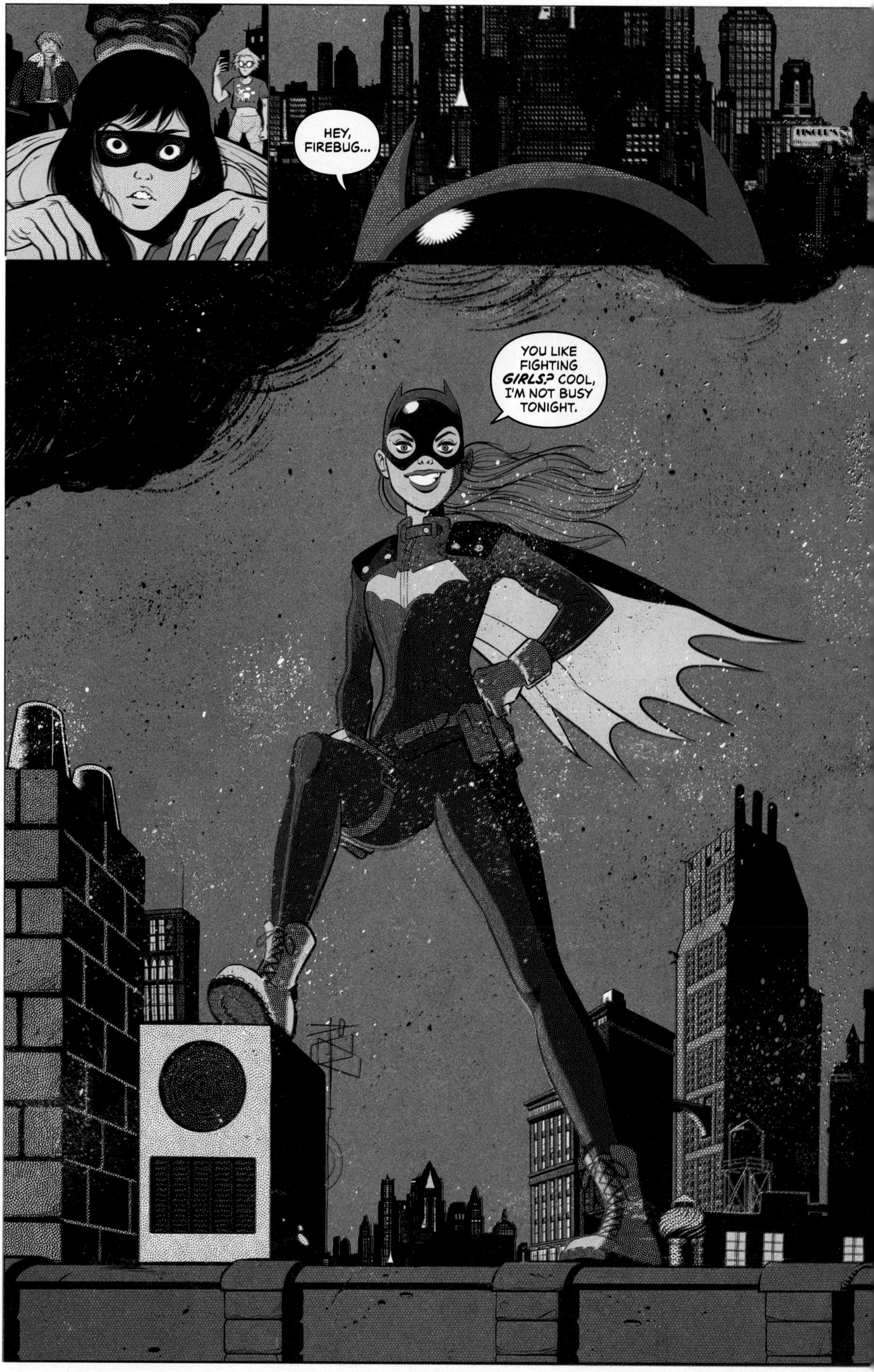
HEY, FIREBUG...
FINGER'S
YOU LIKE FIGHTING GIRLS? COOL, I'M NOT BUSY TONIGHT.

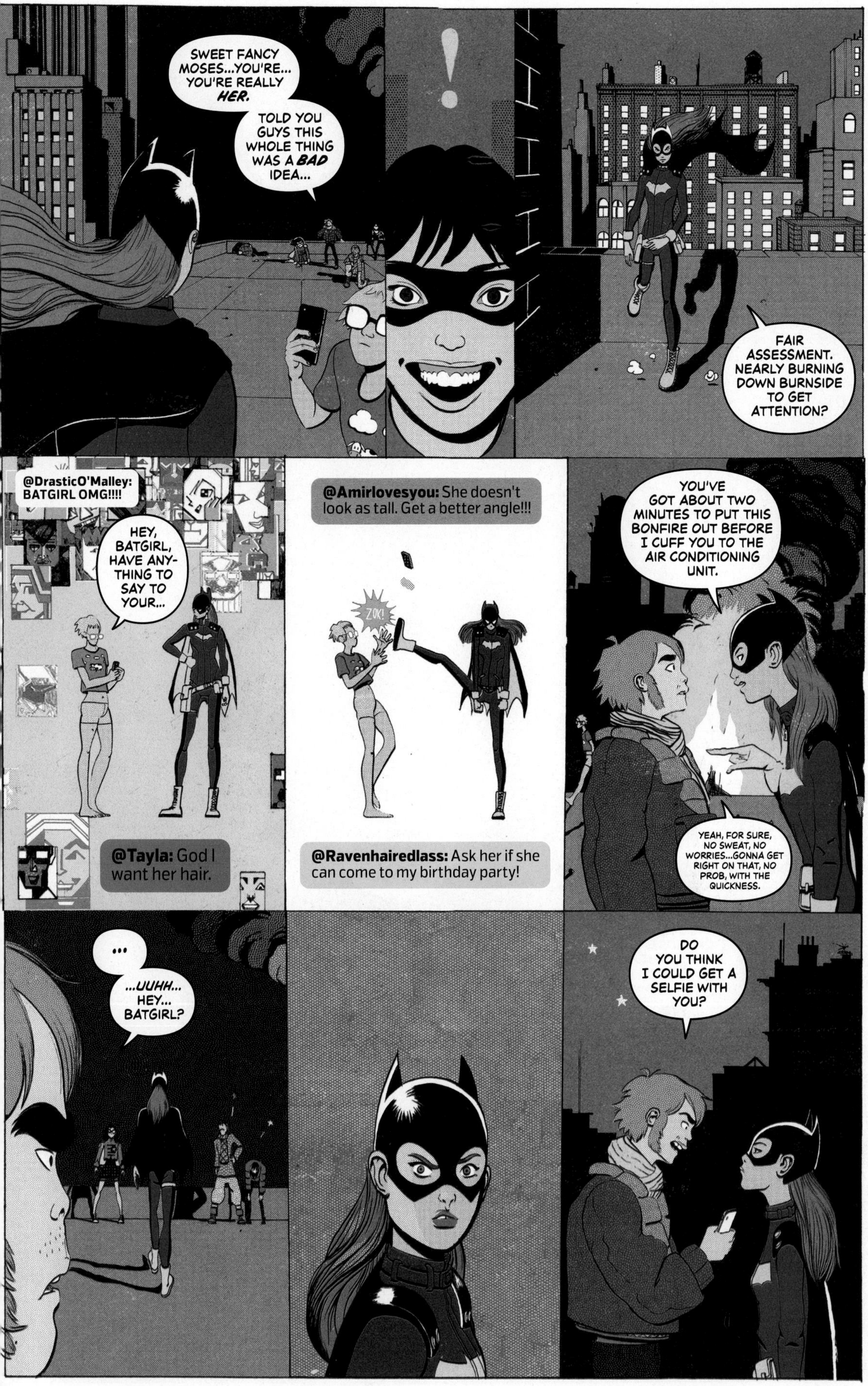

SWEET FANCY MOSES...YOU'RE... YOU'RE REALLY HER.
TOLD YOU GUYS THIS WHOLE THING WAS A BAD IDEA...
!
FAIR ASSESSMENT. NEARLY BURNING DOWN BURNSIDE TO GET ATTENTION?
@DrasticO'Malley: BATGIRL OMG!!!!
HEY, BATGIRL, HAVE ANY-THING TO SAY TO YOUR...
@Tayla: God I want her hair.
@Amirlovesyou: She doesn't look as tall. Get a better angle!!!
ZOK!
@Ravenhairedlass: Ask her if she can come to my birthday party!
YOU'VE GOT ABOUT TWO MINUTES TO PUT THIS BONFIRE OUT BEFORE I CUFF YOU TO THE AIR CONDITIONING UNIT.
YEAH, FOR SURE, NO SWEAT, NO WORRIES...GONNA GET RIGHT ON THAT, NO PROB, WITH THE QUICKNESS.
...
...UUHH... HEY... BATGIRL?
DO YOU THINK I COULD GET A SELFIE WITH YOU?

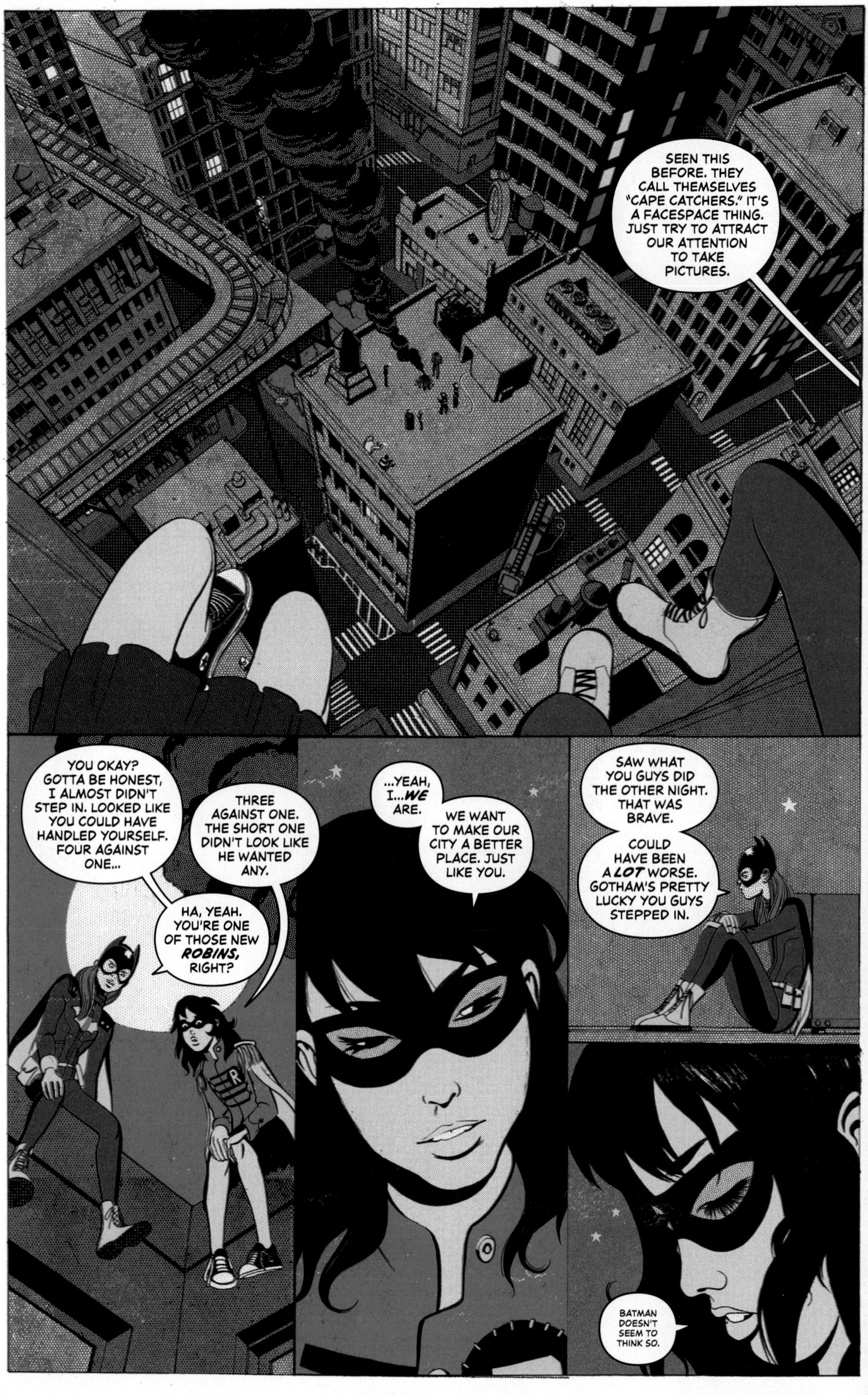
SEEN THIS BEFORE. THEY CALL THEMSELVES "CAPE CATCHERS." IT'S A FACESPACE THING. JUST TRY TO ATTRACT OUR ATTENTION TO TAKE PICTURES.
YOU OKAY? GOTTA BE HONEST, I ALMOST DIDN'T STEP IN. LOOKED LIKE YOU COULD HAVE HANDLED YOURSELF. FOUR AGAINST ONE...
THREE AGAINST ONE. THE SHORT ONE DIDN'T LOOK LIKE HE WANTED ANY.
HA, YEAH. YOU'RE ONE OF THOSE NEW ROBINS, RIGHT?
...YEAH, I...WE ARE.
WE WANT TO MAKE OUR CITY A BETTER PLACE. JUST LIKE YOU.
SAW WHAT YOU GUYS DID THE OTHER NIGHT. THAT WAS BRAVE.
COULD HAVE BEEN A LOT WORSE. GOTHAM'S PRETTY LUCKY YOU GUYS STEPPED IN.
BATMAN DOESN'T SEEM TO THINK SO.

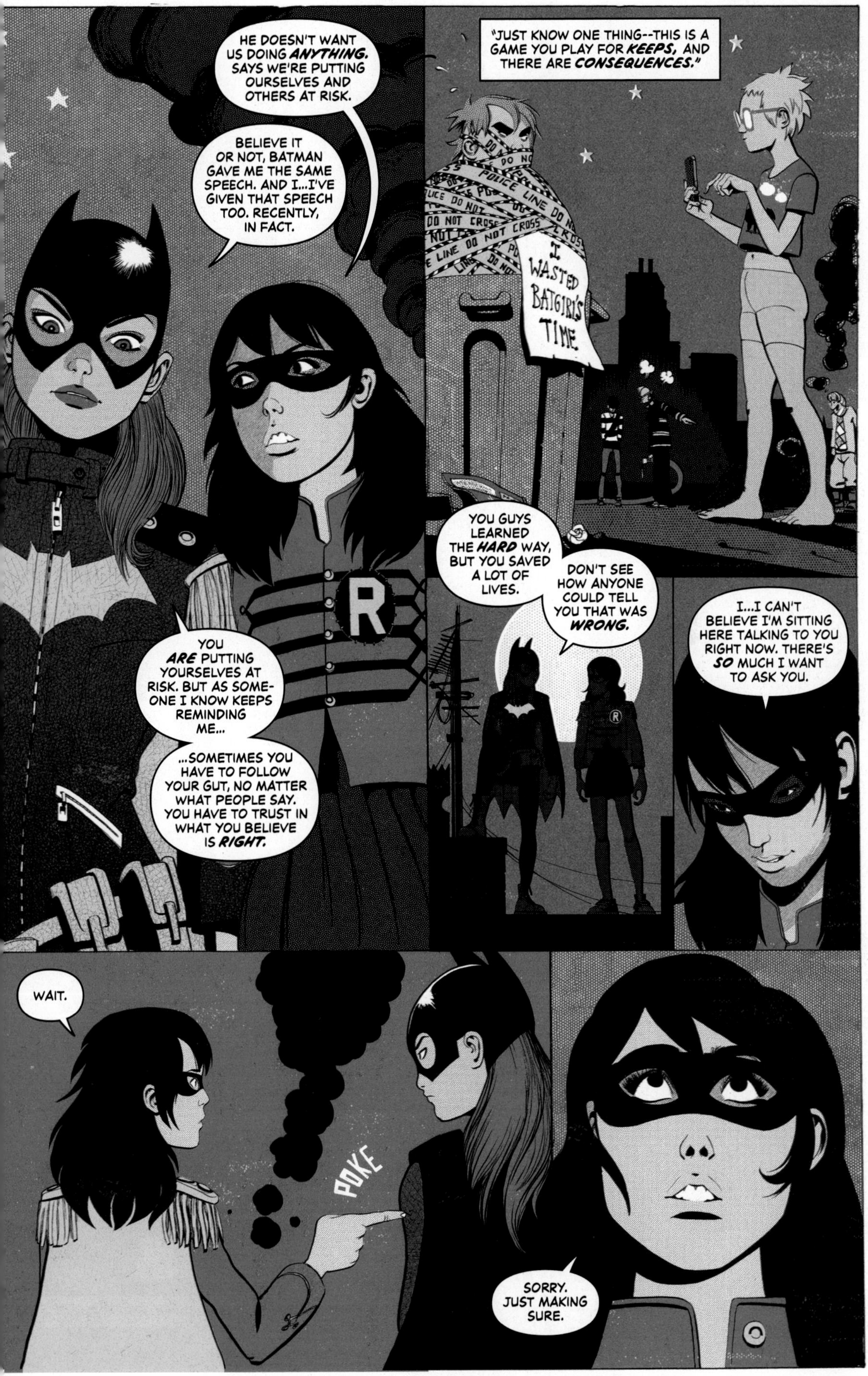
HE DOESN'T WANT US DOING ANYTHING. SAYS WE'RE PUTTING OURSELVES AND OTHERS AT RISK.
BELIEVE IT OR NOT, BATMAN GAVE ME THE SAME SPEECH. AND I...I'VE GIVEN THAT SPEECH TOO. RECENTLY, IN FACT.
YOU ARE PUTTING YOURSELVES AT RISK. BUT AS SOME-ONE I KNOW KEEPS REMINDING ME...
...SOMETIMES YOU HAVE TO FOLLOW YOUR GUT, NO MATTER WHAT PEOPLE SAY. YOU HAVE TO TRUST IN WHAT YOU BELIEVE IS RIGHT.
"JUST KNOW ONE THING--THIS IS A GAME YOU PLAY FOR KEEPS, AND THERE ARE CONSEQUENCES."
POLICE LINE DO NOT CROSS
I WASTED BATGIRL'S TIME
YOU GUYS LEARNED THE HARD WAY, BUT YOU SAVED A LOT OF LIVES.
DON'T SEE HOW ANYONE COULD TELL YOU THAT WAS WRONG.
I...I CAN'T BELIEVE I'M SITTING HERE TALKING TO YOU RIGHT NOW. THERE'S SO MUCH I WANT TO ASK YOU.
WAIT.
POKE
SORRY. JUST MAKING SURE.

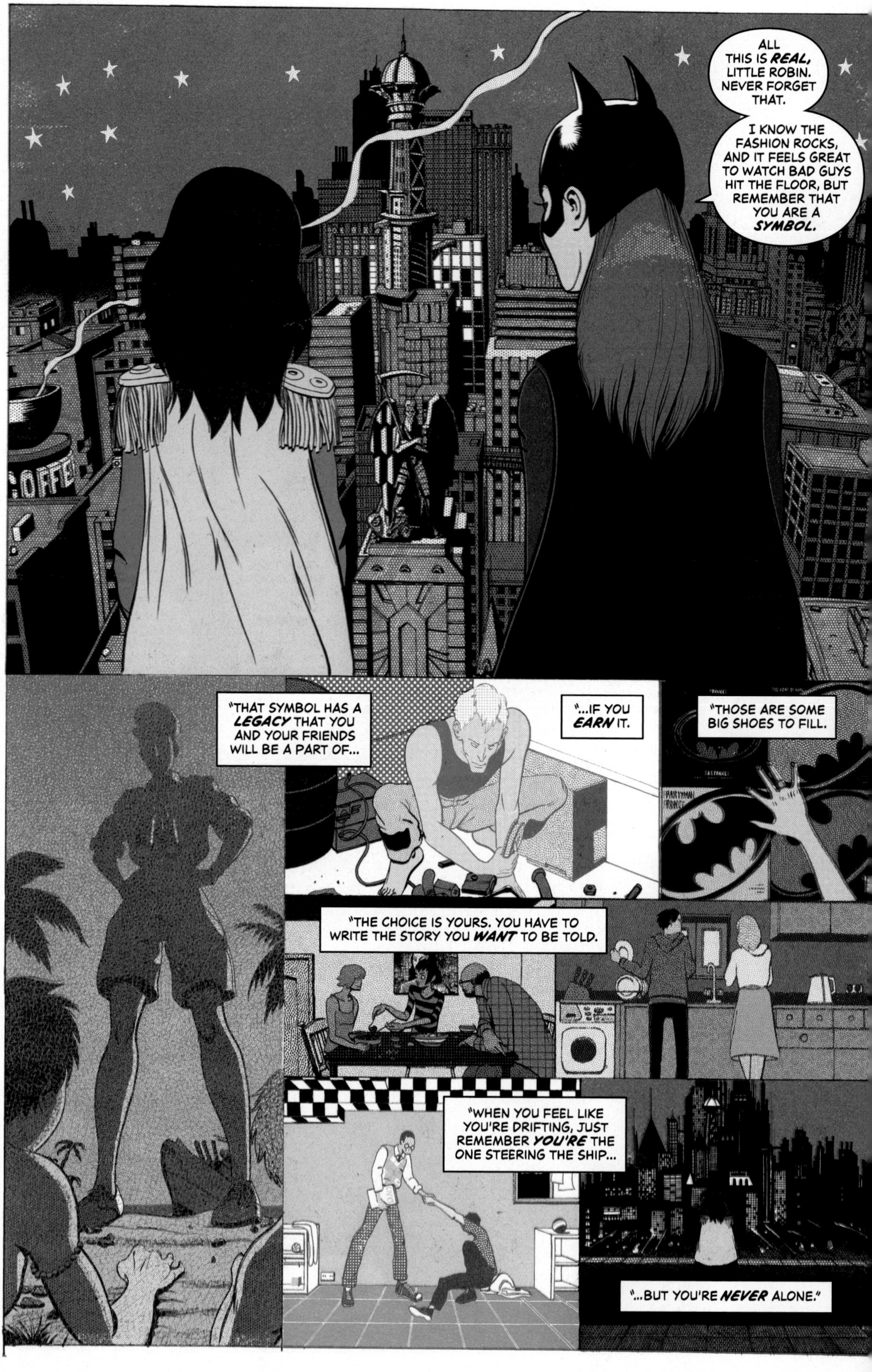
ALL THIS IS *REAL,* LITTLE ROBIN. NEVER FORGET THAT.
I KNOW THE FASHION ROCKS, AND IT FEELS GREAT TO WATCH BAD GUYS HIT THE FLOOR, BUT REMEMBER THAT YOU ARE A *SYMBOL.*
"THAT SYMBOL HAS A *LEGACY* THAT YOU AND YOUR FRIENDS WILL BE A PART OF...
"...IF YOU *EARN* IT.
"THOSE ARE SOME BIG SHOES TO FILL.
"THE CHOICE IS YOURS. YOU HAVE TO WRITE THE STORY YOU *WANT* TO BE TOLD.
"WHEN YOU FEEL LIKE YOU'RE DRIFTING, JUST REMEMBER *YOU'RE* THE ONE STEERING THE SHIP...
"...BUT YOU'RE *NEVER* ALONE."

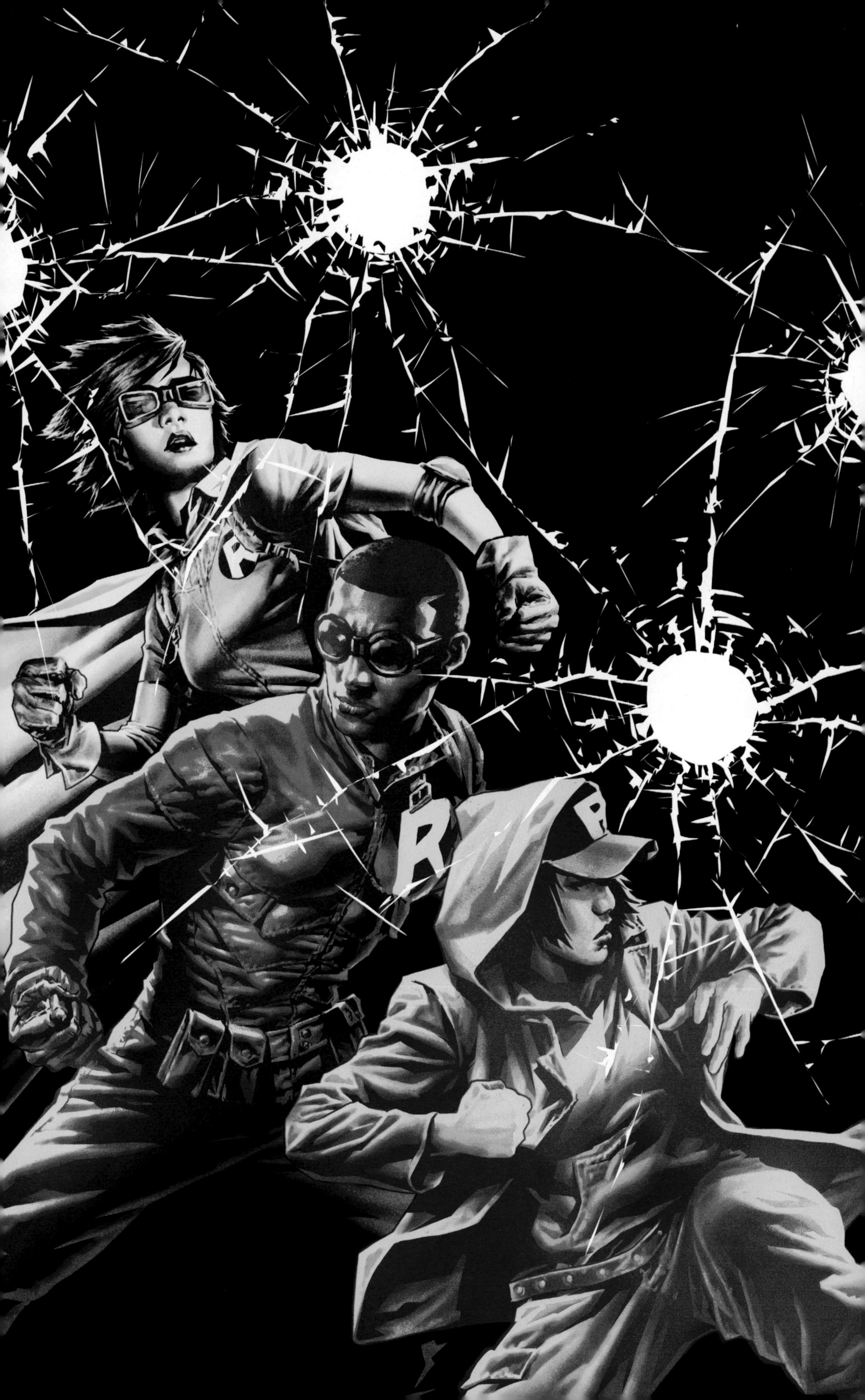

SIBLING RIVALRY

LEE BERMEJO story
JORGE CORONA art
ROB HAYNES breakdowns
TRISH MULVIHILL with
CHRISTINE DUART PETER colors
CARMINE DI GIANDOMENICO epilogue art
ALLEN PASSALAQUA epilogue colors
JARED K. FLETCHER letters
LEE BERMEJO cover

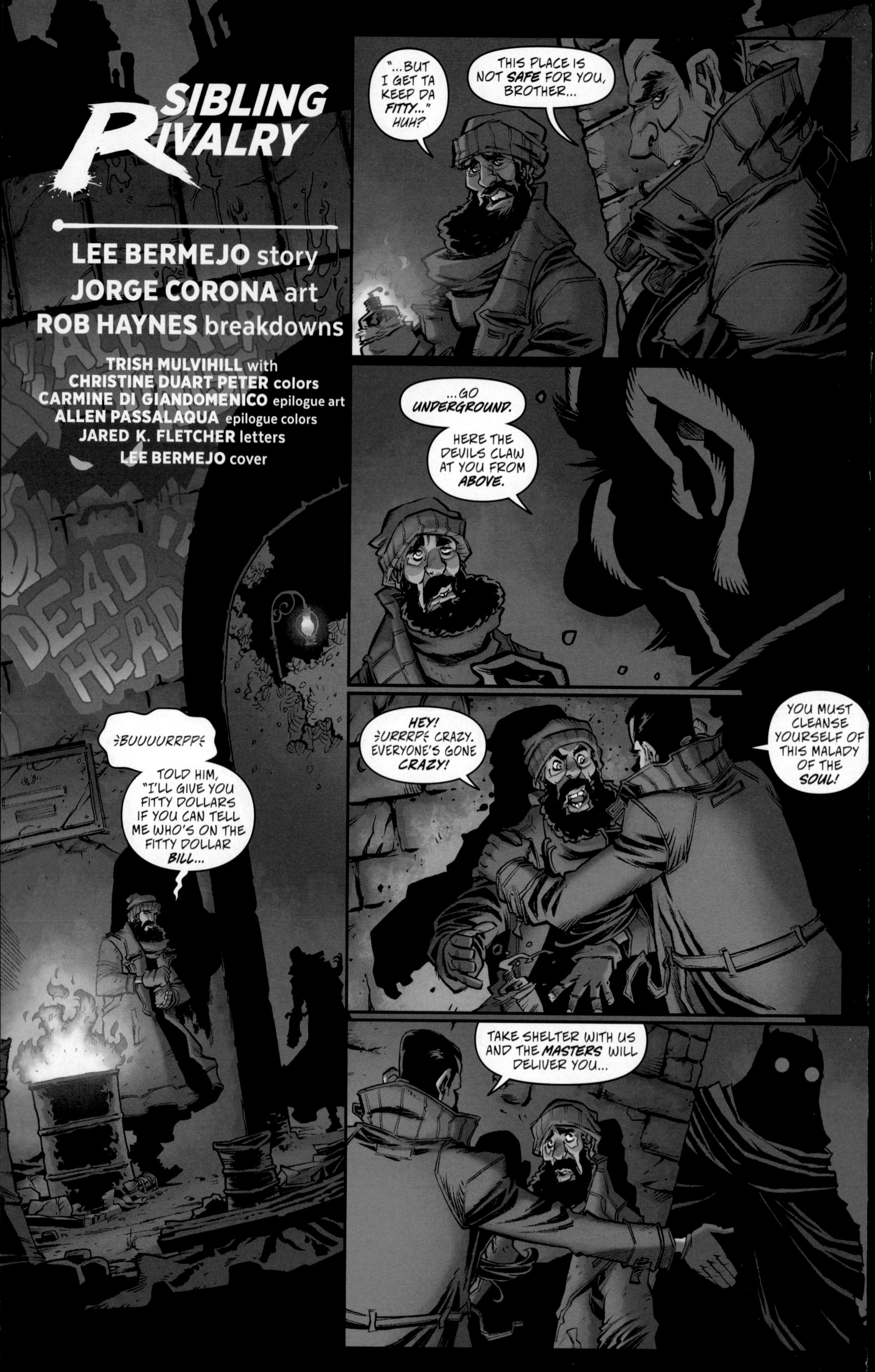

DEAD HEAD
BUUUURRPP
TOLD HIM, "I'LL GIVE YOU FITTY DOLLARS IF YOU CAN TELL ME WHO'S ON THE FITTY DOLLAR BILL...
"...BUT I GET TA KEEP DA FITTY..." HUH?
THIS PLACE IS NOT SAFE FOR YOU, BROTHER...
...GO UNDERGROUND.
HERE THE DEVILS CLAW AT YOU FROM ABOVE.
HEY! URRRP CRAZY. EVERYONE'S GONE CRAZY!
YOU MUST CLEANSE YOURSELF OF THIS MALADY OF THE SOUL!
TAKE SHELTER WITH US AND THE MASTERS WILL DELIVER YOU...

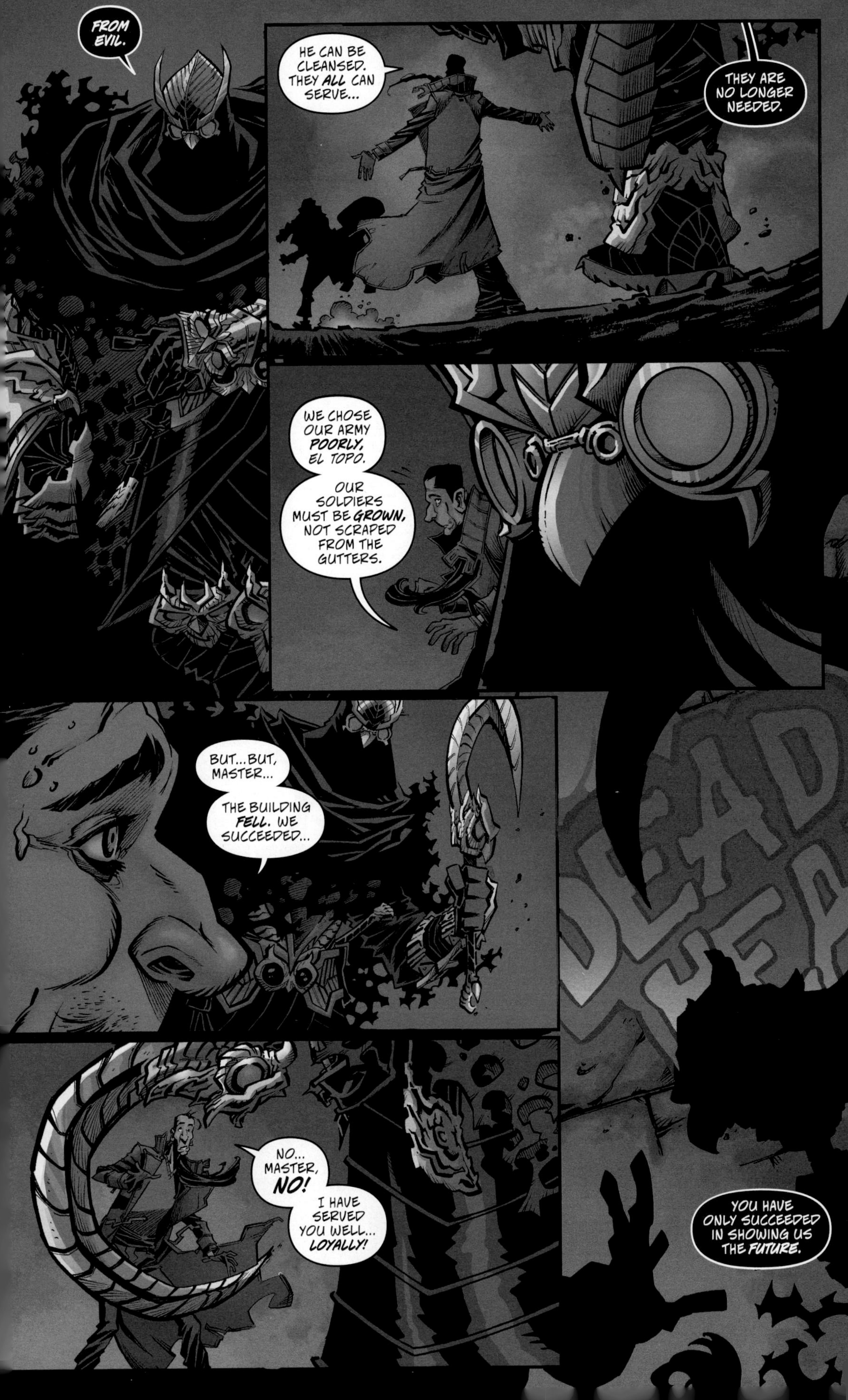
FROM EVIL.
HE CAN BE CLEANSED. THEY ALL CAN SERVE...
THEY ARE NO LONGER NEEDED.
WE CHOSE OUR ARMY POORLY, EL TOPO.
OUR SOLDIERS MUST BE GROWN, NOT SCRAPED FROM THE GUTTERS.
BUT...BUT, MASTER...
THE BUILDING FELL. WE SUCCEEDED...
NO... MASTER, NO!
I HAVE SERVED YOU WELL... LOYALLY!
YOU HAVE ONLY SUCCEEDED IN SHOWING US THE FUTURE.

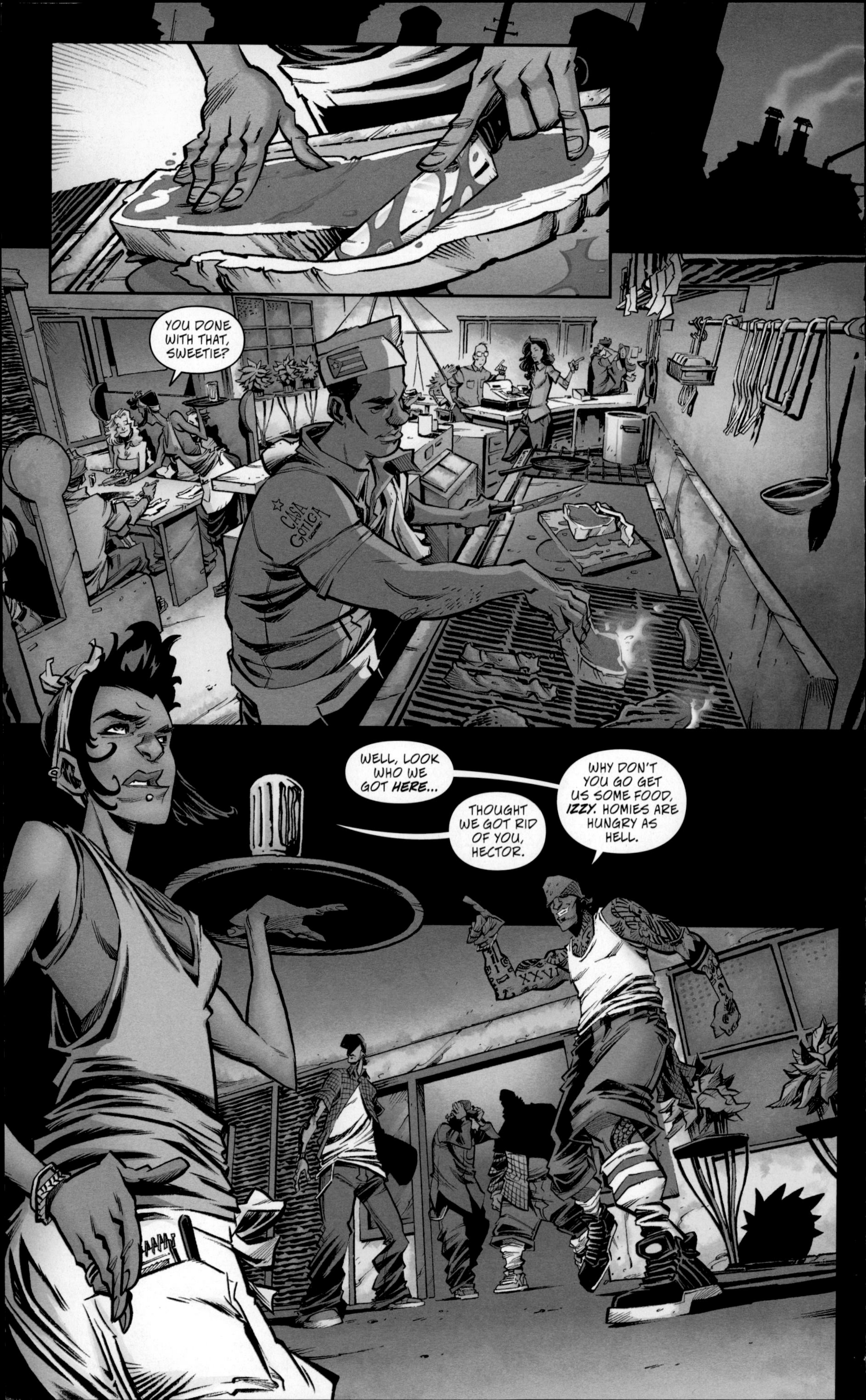
YOU DONE WITH THAT, SWEETIE?
CASA GOTICA
WELL, LOOK WHO WE GOT HERE...
THOUGHT WE GOT RID OF YOU, HECTOR.
WHY DON'T YOU GO GET US SOME FOOD, IZZY. HOMIES ARE HUNGRY AS HELL.

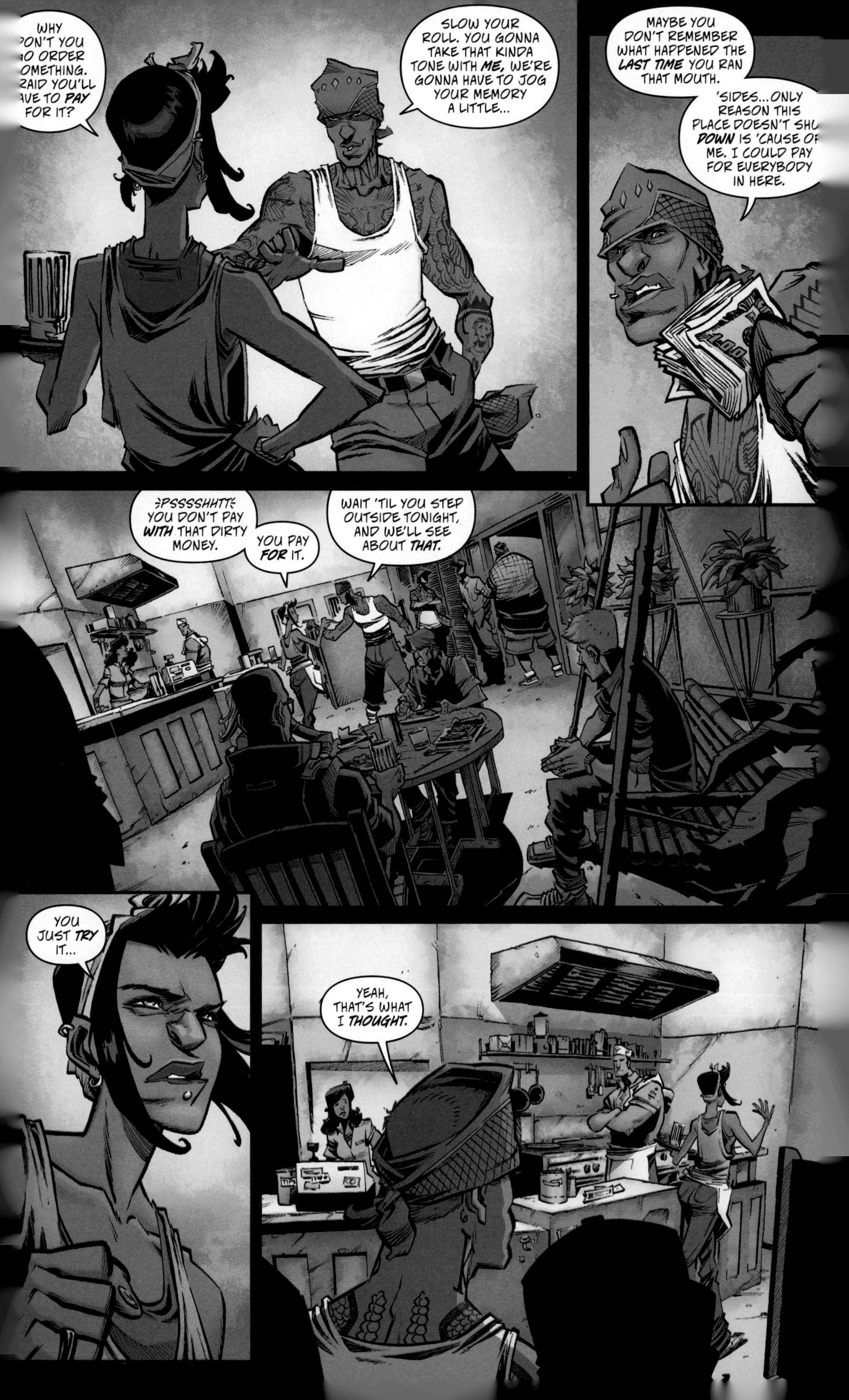
WHY
ON'T YOU
O ORDER
OMETHING.
RAID YOU'LL
AVE TO *PAY*
FOR IT?
SLOW YOUR ROLL. YOU GONNA TAKE THAT KINDA TONE WITH *ME,* WE'RE GONNA HAVE TO JOG YOUR MEMORY A LITTLE...
MAYBE YOU DON'T REMEMBER WHAT HAPPENED THE *LAST TIME* YOU RAN THAT MOUTH.
'SIDES...ONLY REASON THIS PLACE DOESN'T SHU
DOWN IS 'CAUSE OF
ME. I COULD PAY FOR EVERYBODY IN HERE.
PSSSSHHTT YOU DON'T PAY *WITH* THAT DIRTY MONEY.
YOU PAY *FOR* IT.
WAIT 'TIL YOU STEP OUTSIDE TONIGHT, AND WE'LL SEE ABOUT *THAT.*
YOU JUST *TRY* IT...
YEAH, THAT'S WHAT I *THOUGHT.*

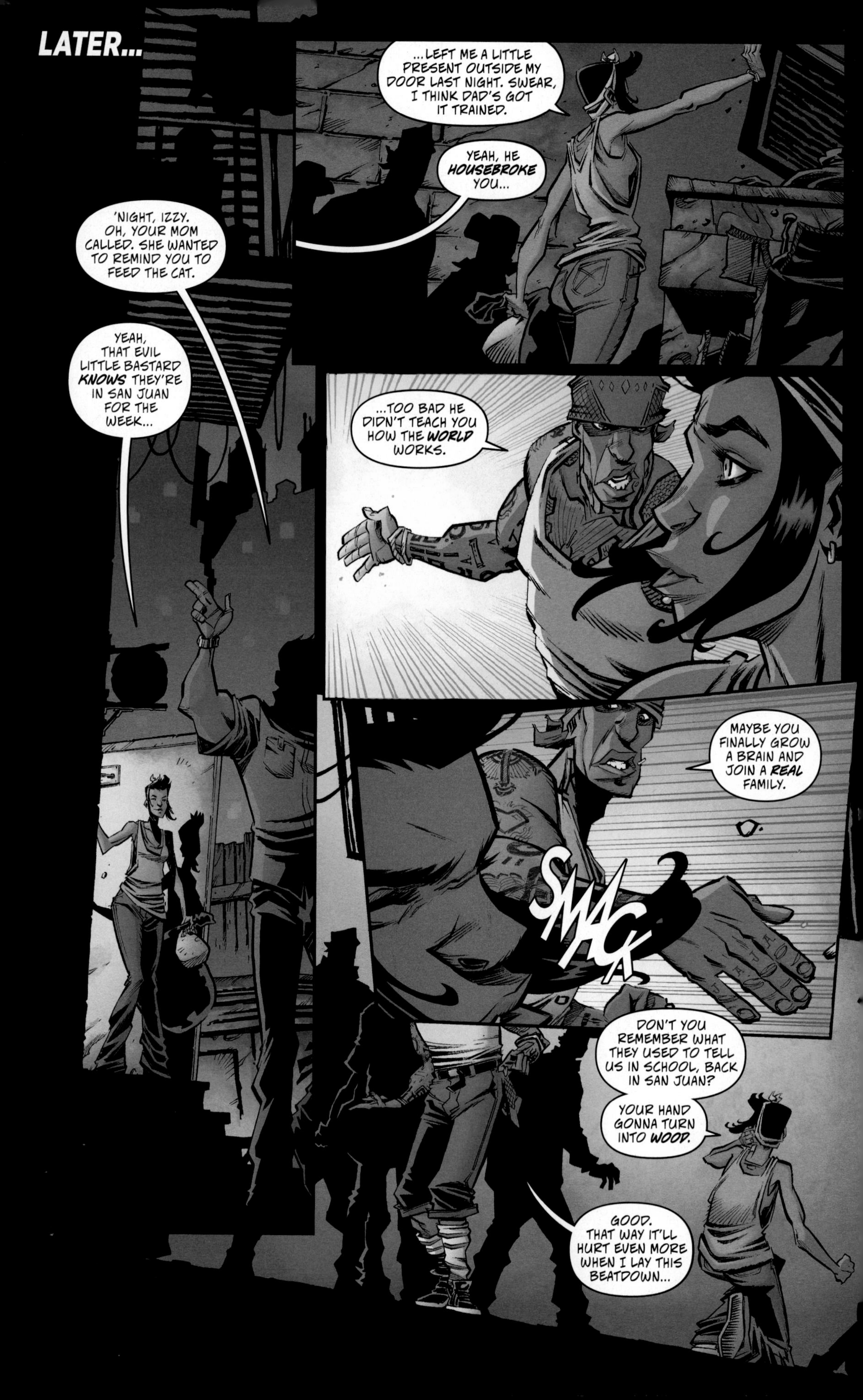
LATER...
...LEFT ME A LITTLE PRESENT OUTSIDE MY DOOR LAST NIGHT. SWEAR, I THINK DAD'S GOT IT TRAINED.
YEAH, HE HOUSEBROKE YOU...
'NIGHT, IZZY. OH, YOUR MOM CALLED. SHE WANTED TO REMIND YOU TO FEED THE CAT.
YEAH, THAT EVIL LITTLE BASTARD KNOWS THEY'RE IN SAN JUAN FOR THE WEEK...
...TOO BAD HE DIDN'T TEACH YOU HOW THE WORLD WORKS.
MAYBE YOU FINALLY GROW A BRAIN AND JOIN A REAL FAMILY.
SMACK
DON'T YOU REMEMBER WHAT THEY USED TO TELL US IN SCHOOL, BACK IN SAN JUAN?
YOUR HAND GONNA TURN INTO WOOD.
GOOD. THAT WAY IT'LL HURT EVEN MORE WHEN I LAY THIS BEATDOWN...

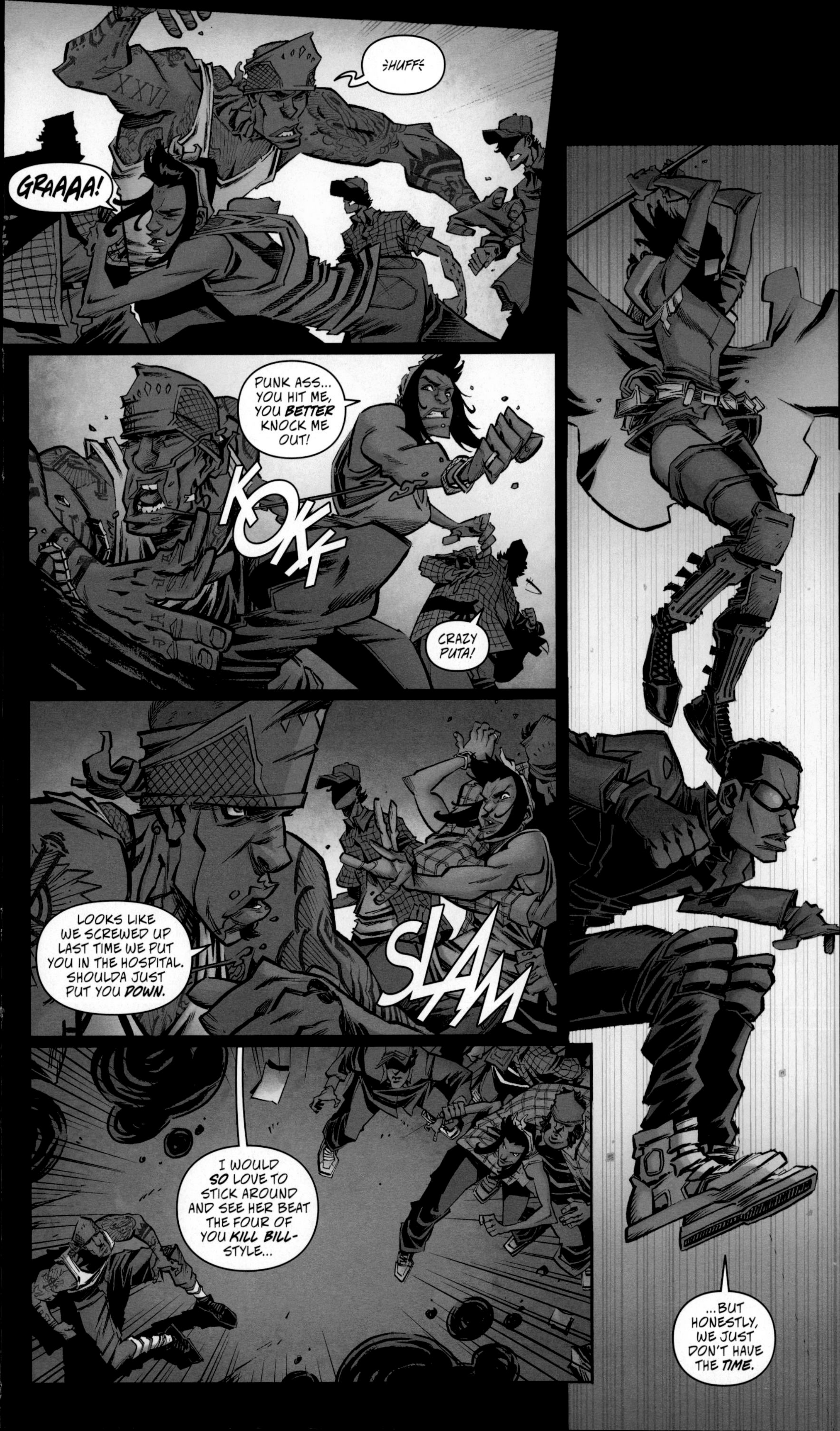

HUFF
GRAAAA!
PUNK ASS... YOU HIT ME, YOU **BETTER** KNOCK ME OUT!
KOKK
CRAZY *PUTA!*
LOOKS LIKE WE SCREWED UP LAST TIME WE PUT YOU IN THE HOSPITAL. SHOULDA JUST PUT YOU **DOWN.**
SLAM
I WOULD **SO** LOVE TO STICK AROUND AND SEE HER BEAT THE FOUR OF YOU ***KILL BILL-***STYLE...
...BUT HONESTLY, WE JUST DON'T HAVE THE ***TIME.***

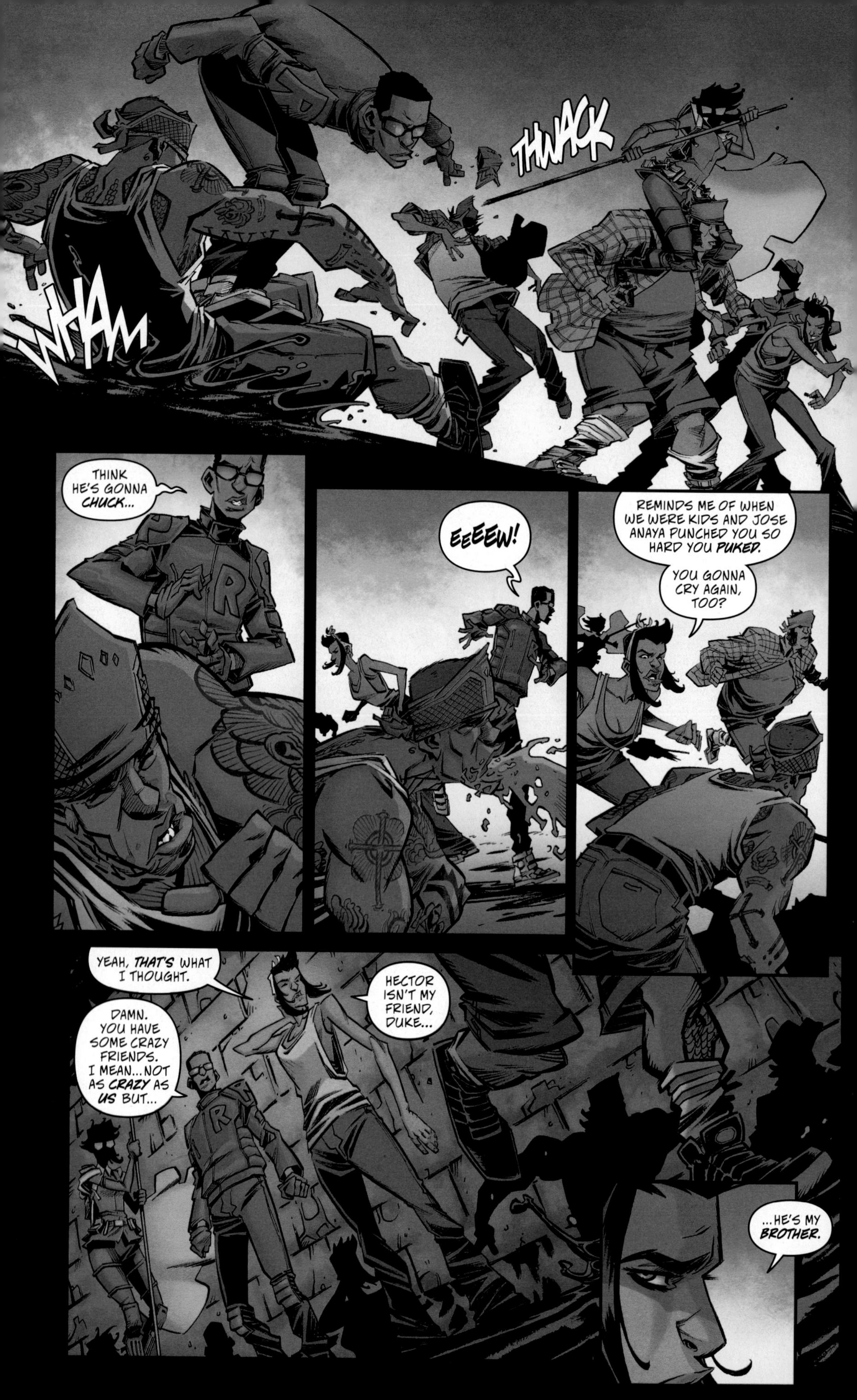
THWACK
WHAM
THINK HE'S GONNA CHUCK...
EEEEW!
REMINDS ME OF WHEN WE WERE KIDS AND JOSE ANAYA PUNCHED YOU SO HARD YOU PUKED.
YOU GONNA CRY AGAIN, TOO?
YEAH, THAT'S WHAT I THOUGHT.
DAMN. YOU HAVE SOME CRAZY FRIENDS. I MEAN...NOT AS CRAZY AS US BUT...
HECTOR ISN'T MY FRIEND, DUKE...
...HE'S MY BROTHER.

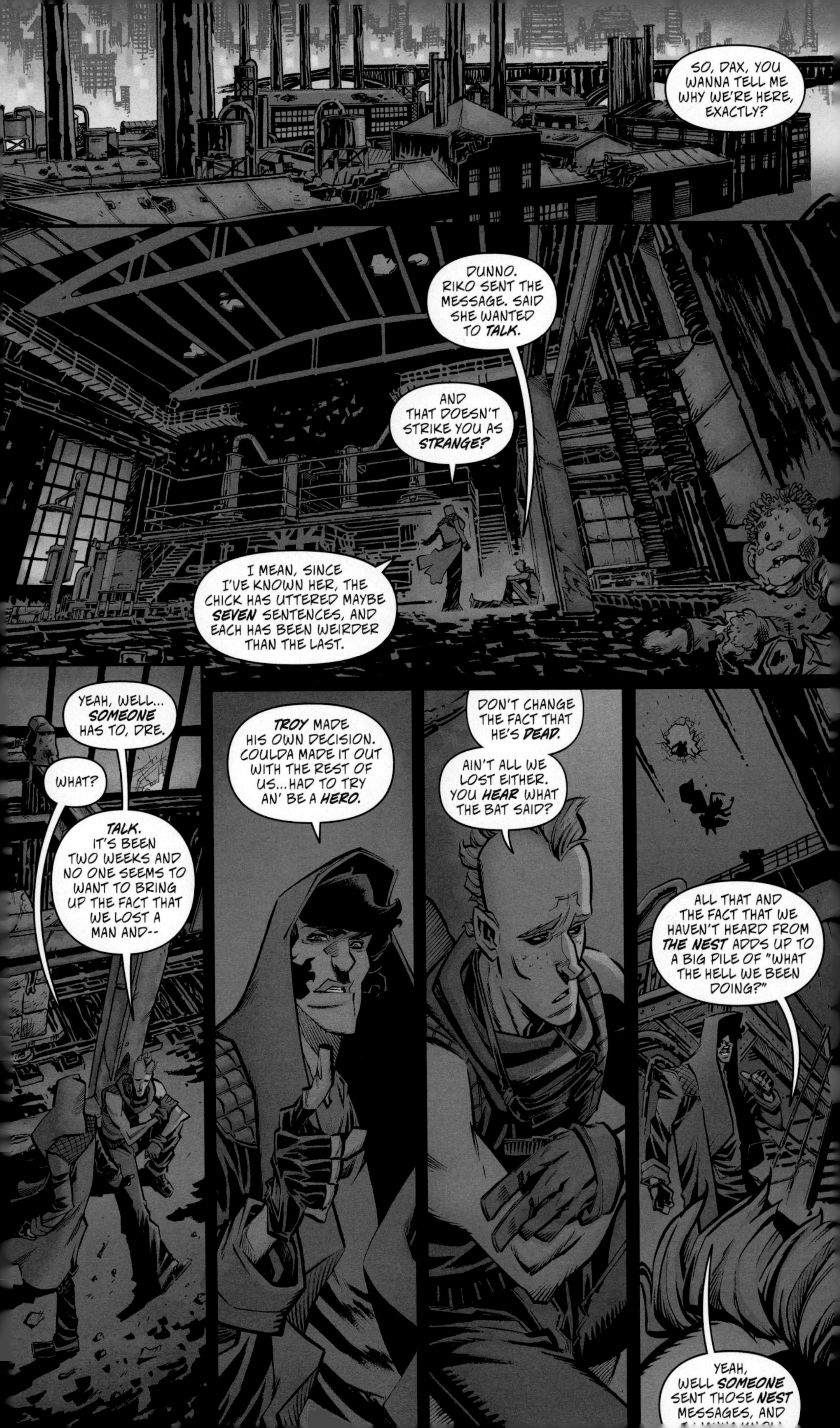
SO, DAX, YOU WANNA TELL ME WHY WE'RE HERE, EXACTLY?
DUNNO. RIKO SENT THE MESSAGE. SAID SHE WANTED TO *TALK.*
AND THAT DOESN'T STRIKE YOU AS *STRANGE?*
I MEAN, SINCE I'VE KNOWN HER, THE CHICK HAS UTTERED MAYBE *SEVEN* SENTENCES, AND EACH HAS BEEN WEIRDER THAN THE LAST.
YEAH, WELL... *SOMEONE* HAS TO, DRE.
WHAT?
TALK. IT'S BEEN TWO WEEKS AND NO ONE SEEMS TO WANT TO BRING UP THE FACT THAT WE LOST A MAN AND--
TROY MADE HIS OWN DECISION. COULDA MADE IT OUT WITH THE REST OF US...HAD TO TRY AN' BE A *HERO.*
DON'T CHANGE THE FACT THAT HE'S *DEAD.*
AIN'T ALL WE LOST EITHER. YOU *HEAR* WHAT THE BAT SAID?
ALL THAT AND THE FACT THAT WE HAVEN'T HEARD FROM *THE NEST* ADDS UP TO A BIG PILE OF "WHAT THE HELL WE BEEN DOING?"
YEAH, WELL *SOMEONE* SENT THOSE *NEST* MESSAGES, AND

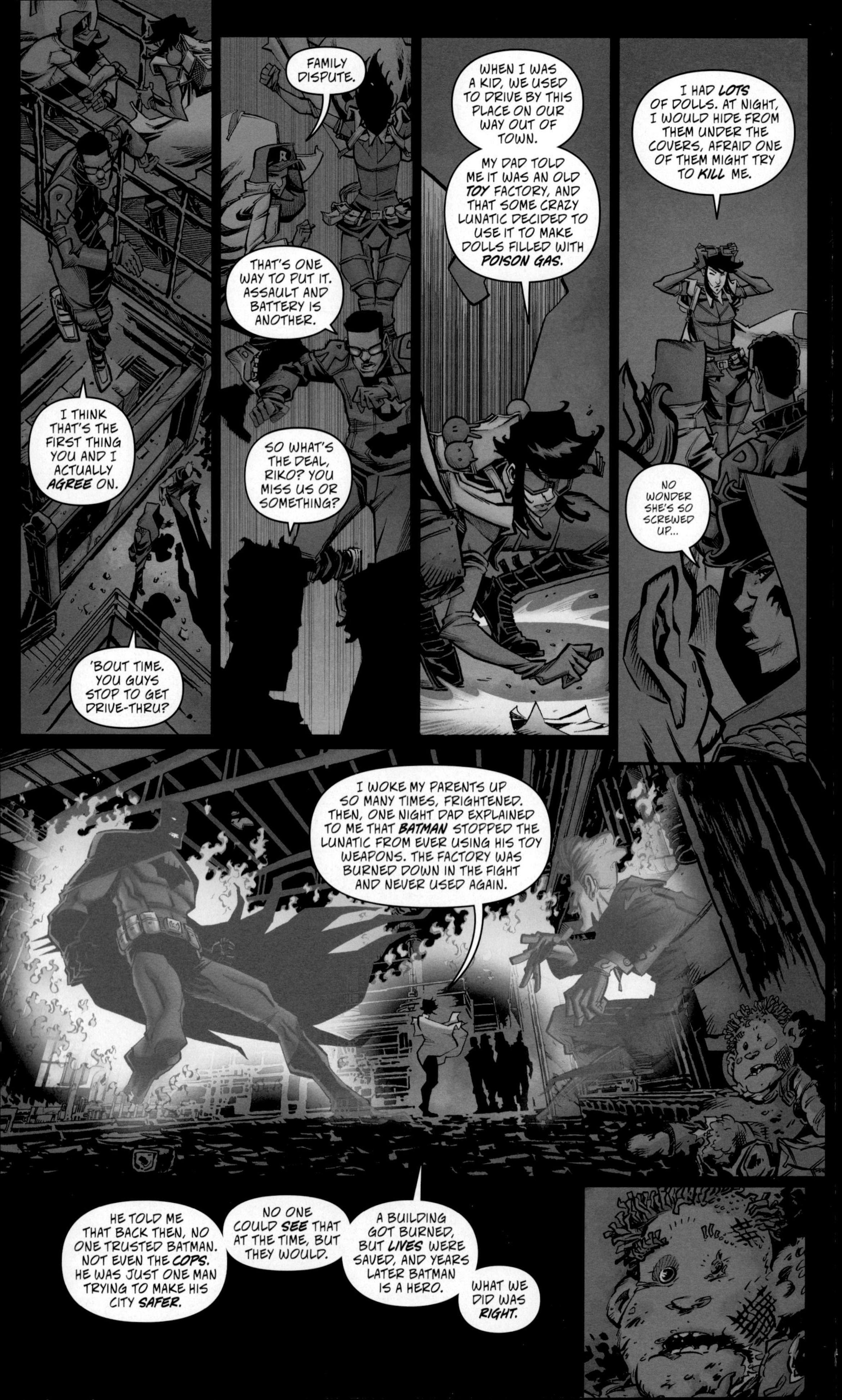

I THINK THAT'S THE FIRST THING YOU AND I ACTUALLY AGREE ON.
'BOUT TIME. YOU GUYS STOP TO GET DRIVE-THRU?
FAMILY DISPUTE.
THAT'S ONE WAY TO PUT IT. ASSAULT AND BATTERY IS ANOTHER.
SO WHAT'S THE DEAL, RIKO? YOU MISS US OR SOMETHING?
WHEN I WAS A KID, WE USED TO DRIVE BY THIS PLACE ON OUR WAY OUT OF TOWN.
MY DAD TOLD ME IT WAS AN OLD TOY FACTORY, AND THAT SOME CRAZY LUNATIC DECIDED TO USE IT TO MAKE DOLLS FILLED WITH POISON GAS.
I HAD LOTS OF DOLLS. AT NIGHT, I WOULD HIDE FROM THEM UNDER THE COVERS, AFRAID ONE OF THEM MIGHT TRY TO KILL ME.
NO WONDER SHE'S SO SCREWED UP...
I WOKE MY PARENTS UP SO MANY TIMES, FRIGHTENED. THEN, ONE NIGHT DAD EXPLAINED TO ME THAT BATMAN STOPPED THE LUNATIC FROM EVER USING HIS TOY WEAPONS. THE FACTORY WAS BURNED DOWN IN THE FIGHT AND NEVER USED AGAIN.
HE TOLD ME THAT BACK THEN, NO ONE TRUSTED BATMAN. NOT EVEN THE COPS. HE WAS JUST ONE MAN TRYING TO MAKE HIS CITY SAFER.
NO ONE COULD SEE THAT AT THE TIME, BUT THEY WOULD.
A BUILDING GOT BURNED, BUT LIVES WERE SAVED, AND YEARS LATER BATMAN IS A HERO.
WHAT WE DID WAS RIGHT.

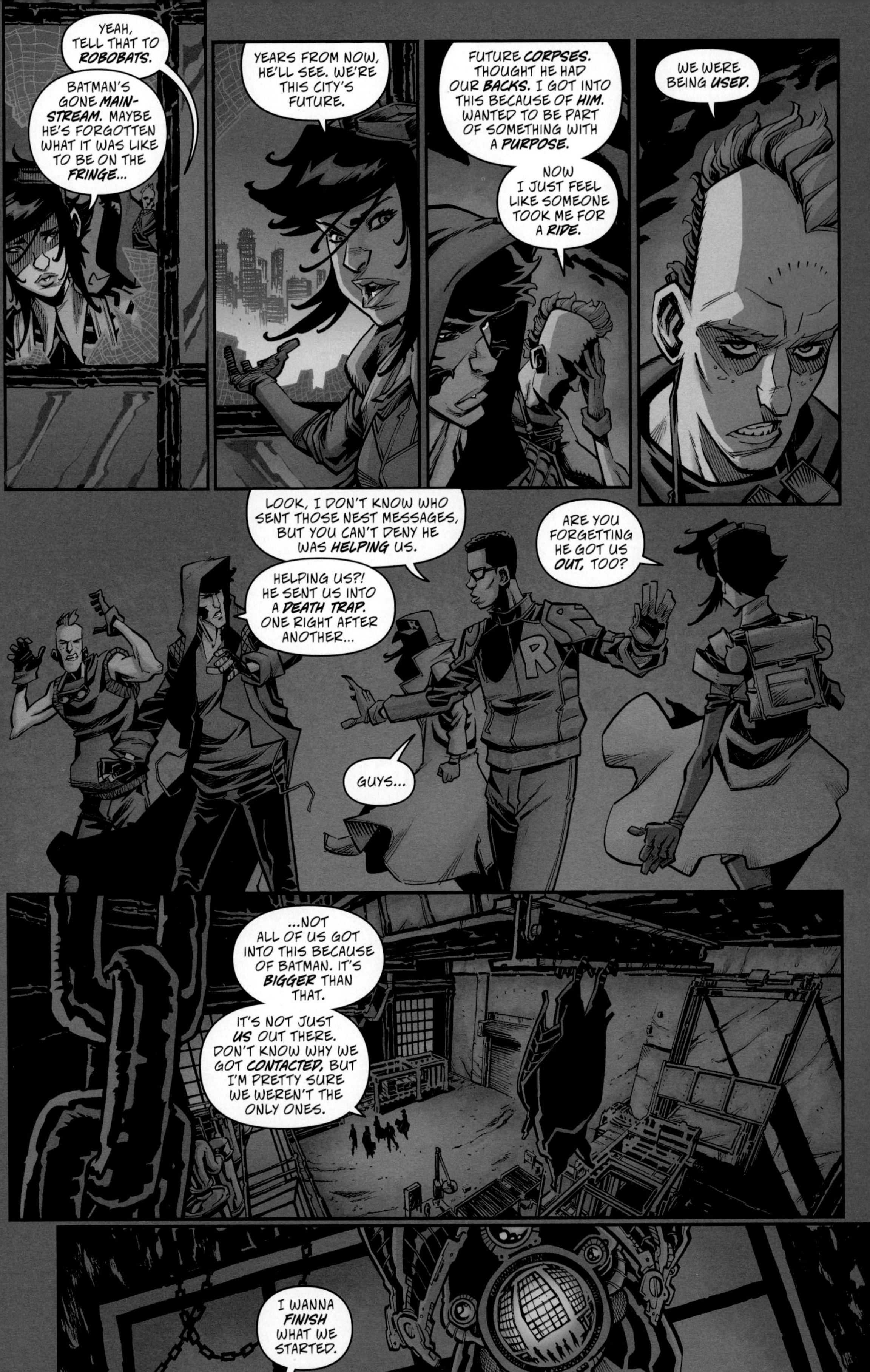
YEAH, TELL THAT TO ROBOBATS.
BATMAN'S GONE MAIN-STREAM. MAYBE HE'S FORGOTTEN WHAT IT WAS LIKE TO BE ON THE FRINGE...
YEARS FROM NOW, HE'LL SEE. WE'RE THIS CITY'S FUTURE.
FUTURE CORPSES. THOUGHT HE HAD OUR BACKS. I GOT INTO THIS BECAUSE OF HIM. WANTED TO BE PART OF SOMETHING WITH A PURPOSE.
NOW I JUST FEEL LIKE SOMEONE TOOK ME FOR A RIDE.
WE WERE BEING USED.
LOOK, I DON'T KNOW WHO SENT THOSE NEST MESSAGES, BUT YOU CAN'T DENY HE WAS HELPING US.
HELPING US?! HE SENT US INTO A DEATH TRAP. ONE RIGHT AFTER ANOTHER...
ARE YOU FORGETTING HE GOT US OUT, TOO?
GUYS...
...NOT ALL OF US GOT INTO THIS BECAUSE OF BATMAN. IT'S BIGGER THAN THAT.
IT'S NOT JUST US OUT THERE. DON'T KNOW WHY WE GOT CONTACTED, BUT I'M PRETTY SURE WE WEREN'T THE ONLY ONES.
I WANNA FINISH WHAT WE STARTED.

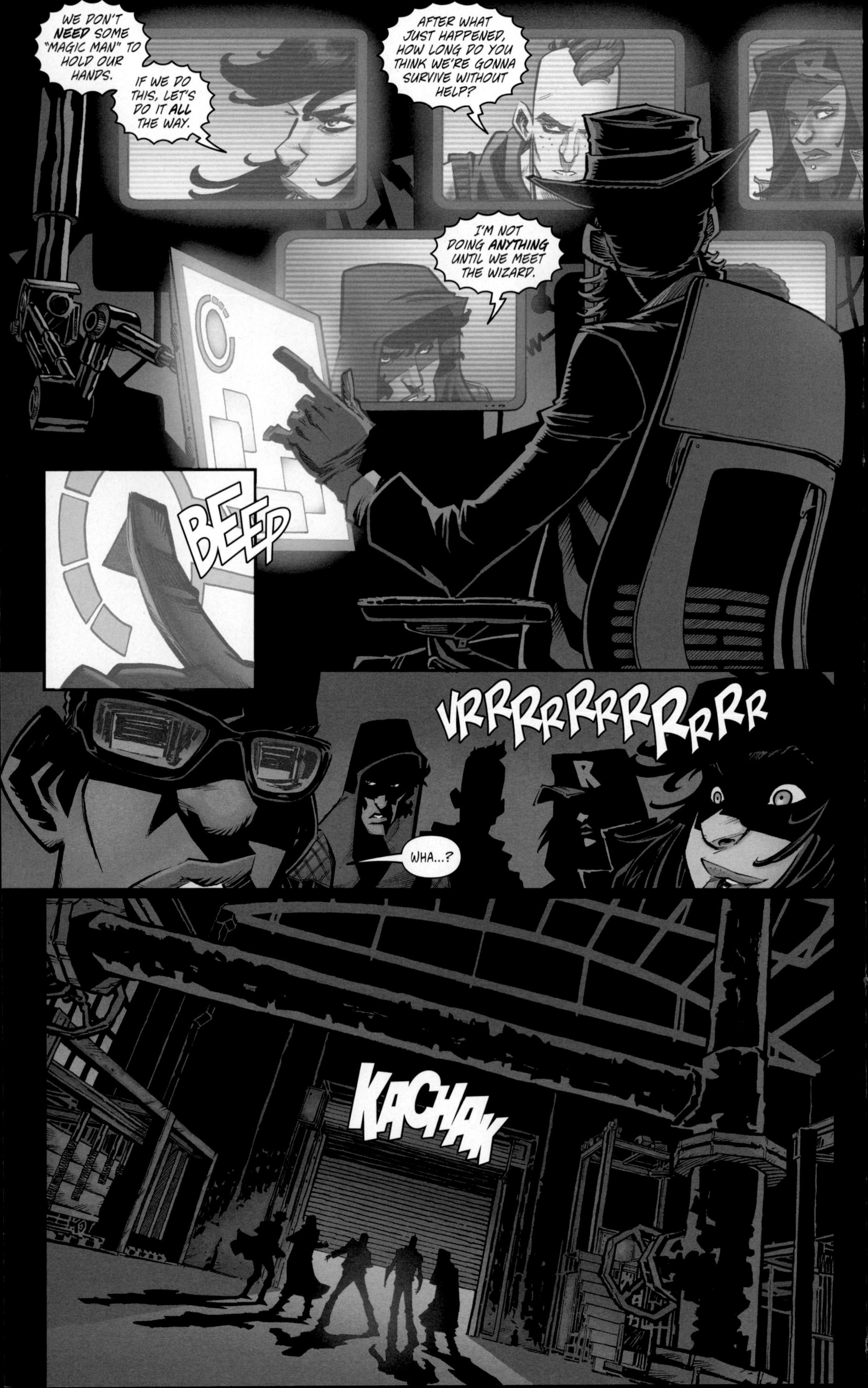

WE DON'T NEED SOME "MAGIC MAN" TO HOLD OUR HANDS.
IF WE DO THIS, LET'S DO IT ALL THE WAY.
AFTER WHAT JUST HAPPENED, HOW LONG DO YOU THINK WE'RE GONNA SURVIVE WITHOUT HELP?
I'M NOT DOING ANYTHING UNTIL WE MEET THE WIZARD.
BEEP
VRRRRRRRRRRRR
WHA...?
KACHAK

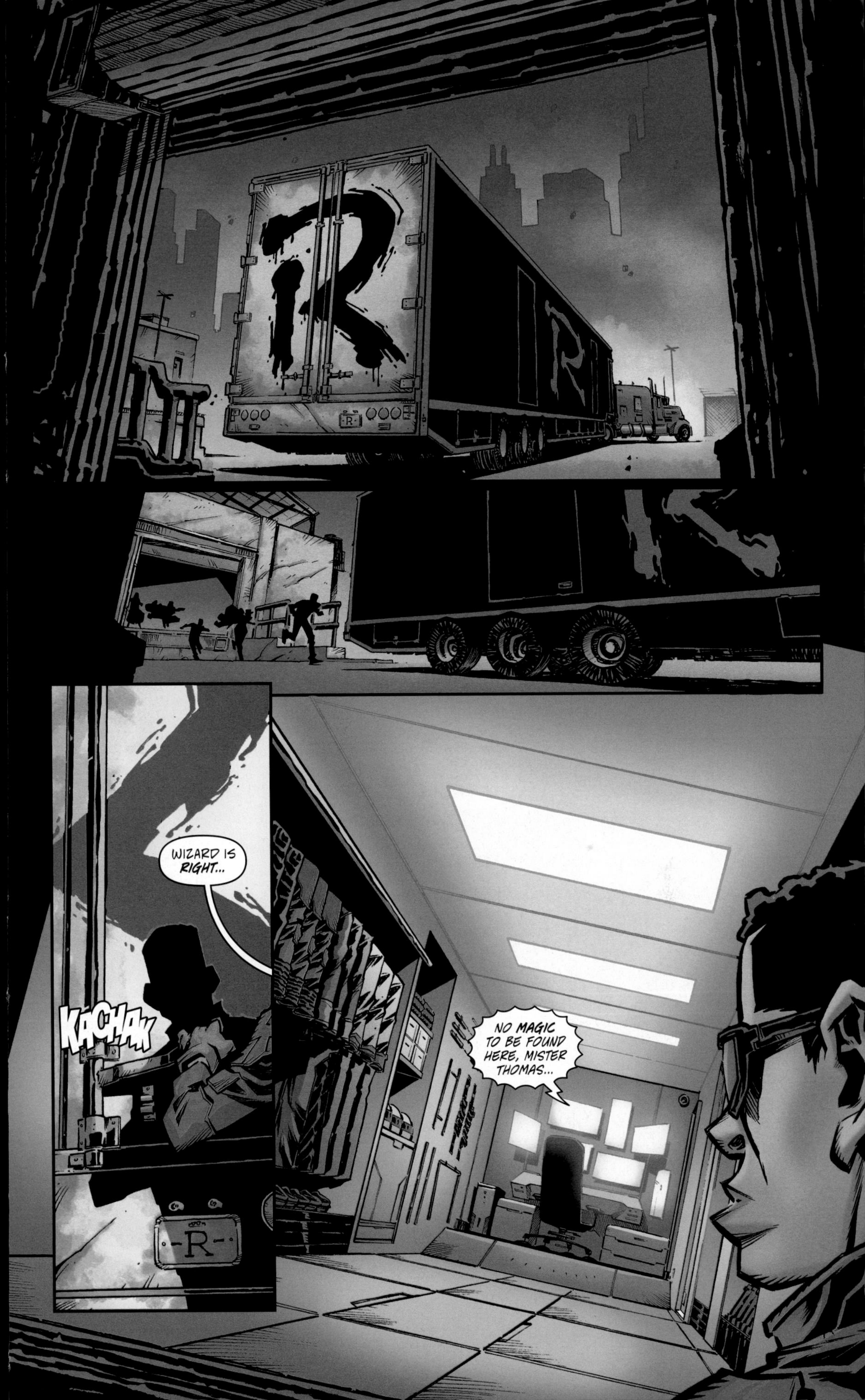
WIZARD IS RIGHT...
KACHAK
NO MAGIC TO BE FOUND HERE, MISTER THOMAS...

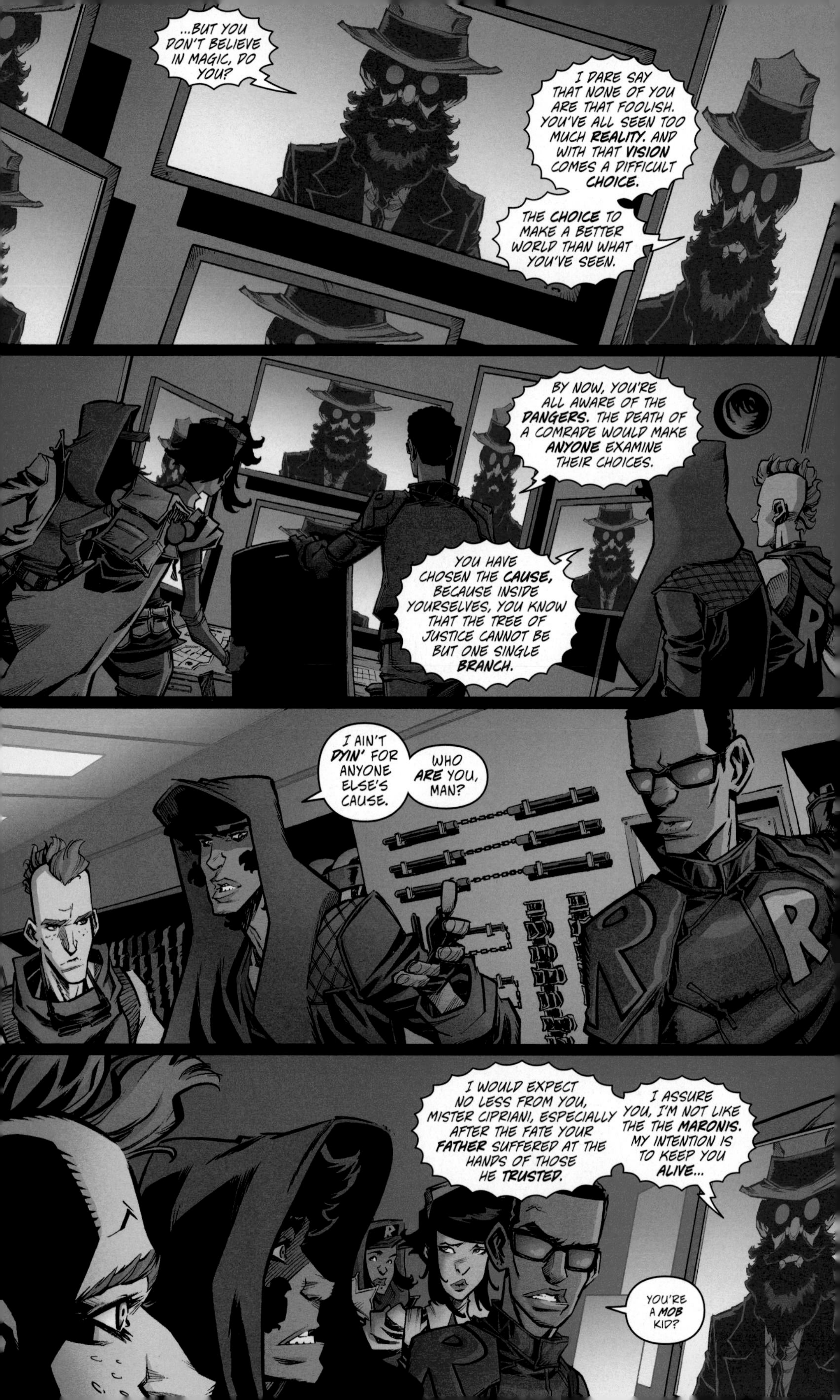

...BUT YOU DON'T BELIEVE IN MAGIC, DO YOU?
I DARE SAY THAT NONE OF YOU ARE THAT FOOLISH. YOU'VE ALL SEEN TOO MUCH REALITY. AND WITH THAT VISION COMES A DIFFICULT CHOICE.
THE CHOICE TO MAKE A BETTER WORLD THAN WHAT YOU'VE SEEN.
BY NOW, YOU'RE ALL AWARE OF THE DANGERS. THE DEATH OF A COMRADE WOULD MAKE ANYONE EXAMINE THEIR CHOICES.
YOU HAVE CHOSEN THE CAUSE, BECAUSE INSIDE YOURSELVES, YOU KNOW THAT THE TREE OF JUSTICE CANNOT BE BUT ONE SINGLE BRANCH.
I AIN'T DYIN' FOR ANYONE ELSE'S CAUSE.
WHO ARE YOU, MAN?
I WOULD EXPECT NO LESS FROM YOU, MISTER CIPRIANI, ESPECIALLY AFTER THE FATE YOUR FATHER SUFFERED AT THE HANDS OF THOSE HE TRUSTED.
I ASSURE YOU, I'M NOT LIKE THE THE MARONIS. MY INTENTION IS TO KEEP YOU ALIVE...
YOU'RE A MOB KID?

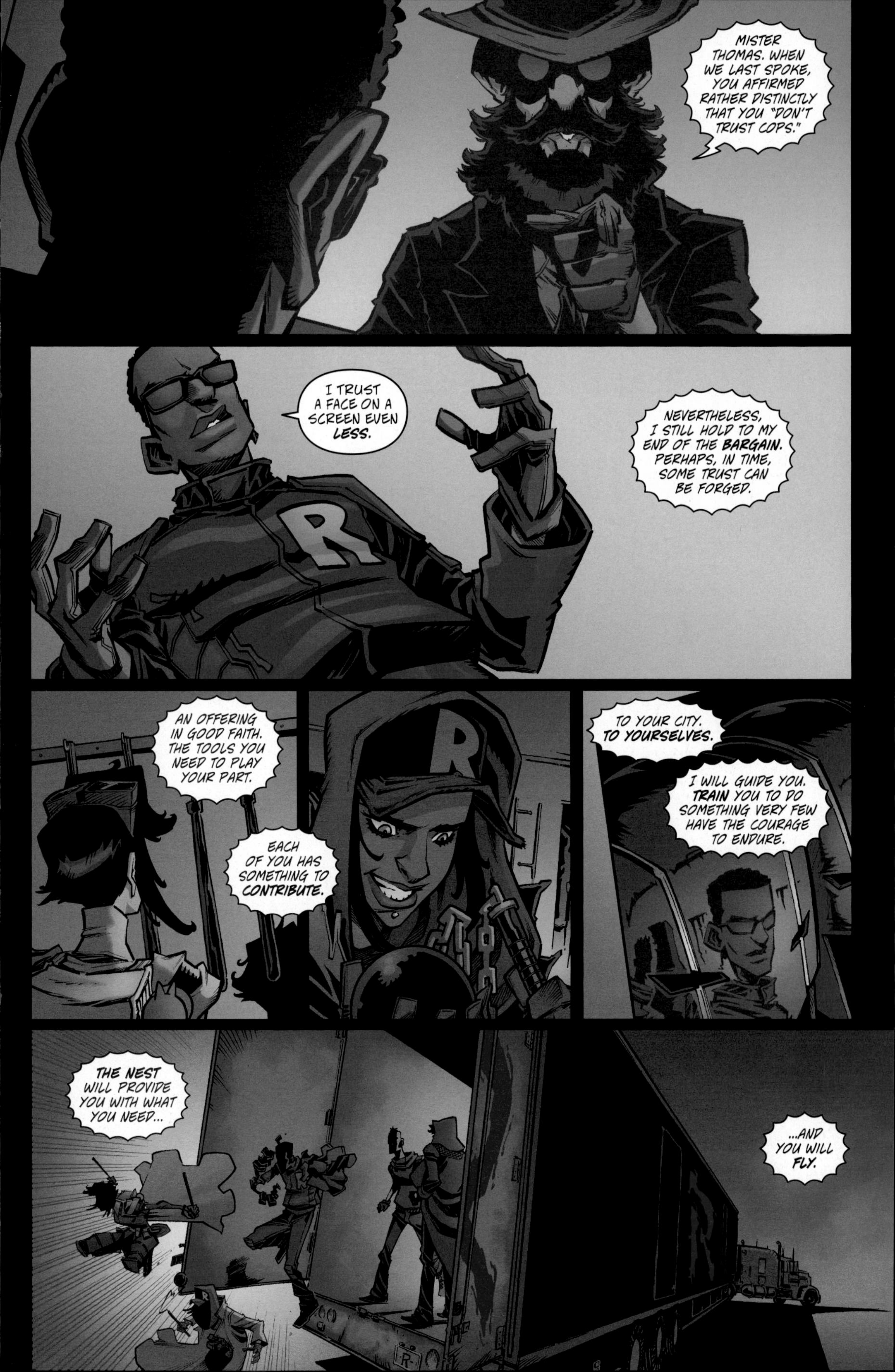
MISTER THOMAS. WHEN WE LAST SPOKE, YOU AFFIRMED RATHER DISTINCTLY THAT YOU "DON'T TRUST COPS."
I TRUST A FACE ON A SCREEN EVEN **LESS**.
NEVERTHELESS, I STILL HOLD TO MY END OF THE **BARGAIN**. PERHAPS, IN TIME, SOME TRUST CAN BE FORGED.
AN OFFERING IN GOOD FAITH. THE TOOLS YOU NEED TO PLAY YOUR PART.
EACH OF YOU HAS SOMETHING TO **CONTRIBUTE**.
TO YOUR CITY. **TO YOURSELVES.**
I WILL GUIDE YOU. **TRAIN** YOU TO DO SOMETHING VERY FEW HAVE THE COURAGE TO ENDURE.
THE NEST WILL PROVIDE YOU WITH WHAT YOU NEED...
...AND YOU WILL **FLY**.

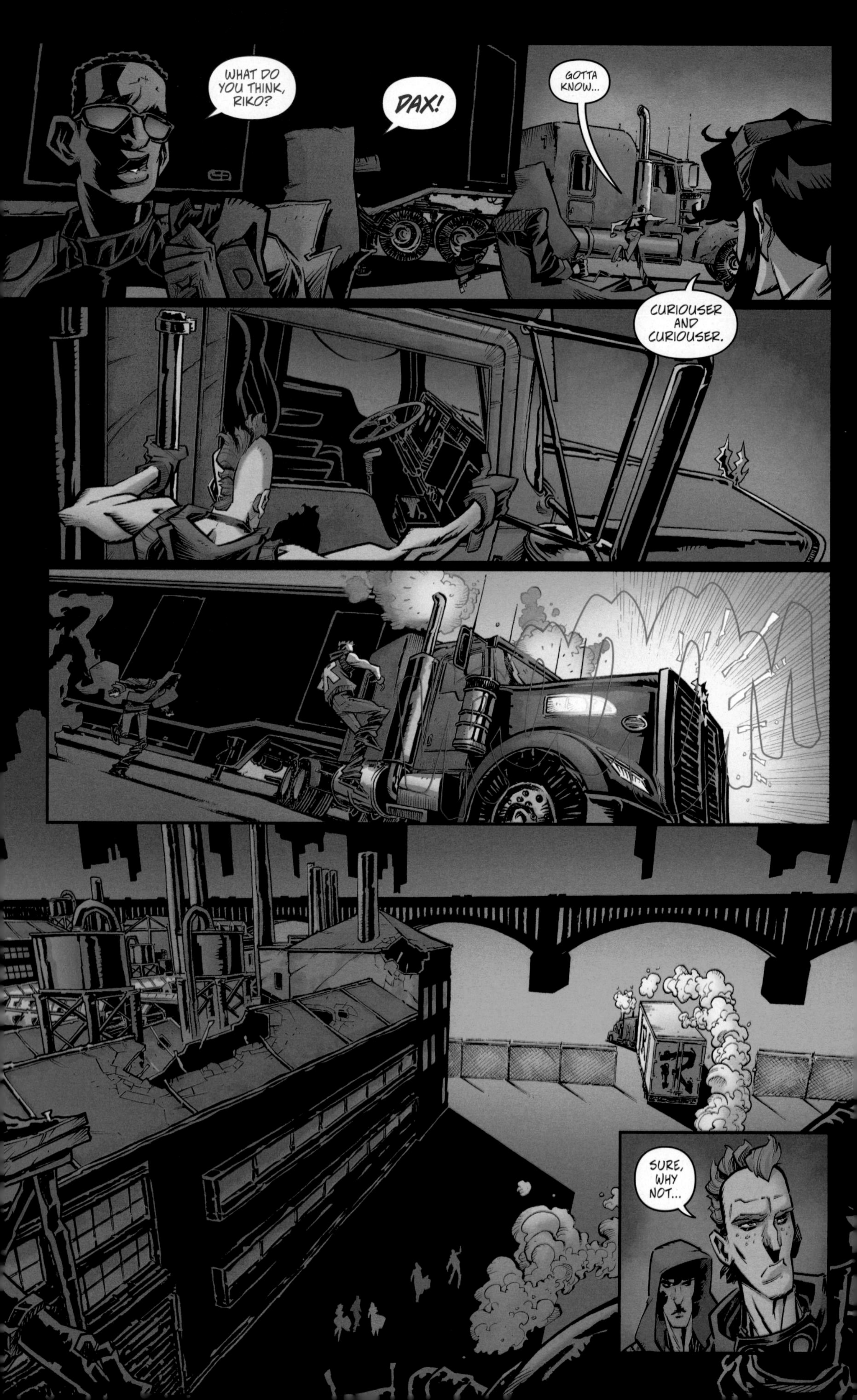
WHAT DO YOU THINK, RIKO?
DAX!
GOTTA KNOW...
CURIOUSER AND CURIOUSER.
SURE, WHY NOT...

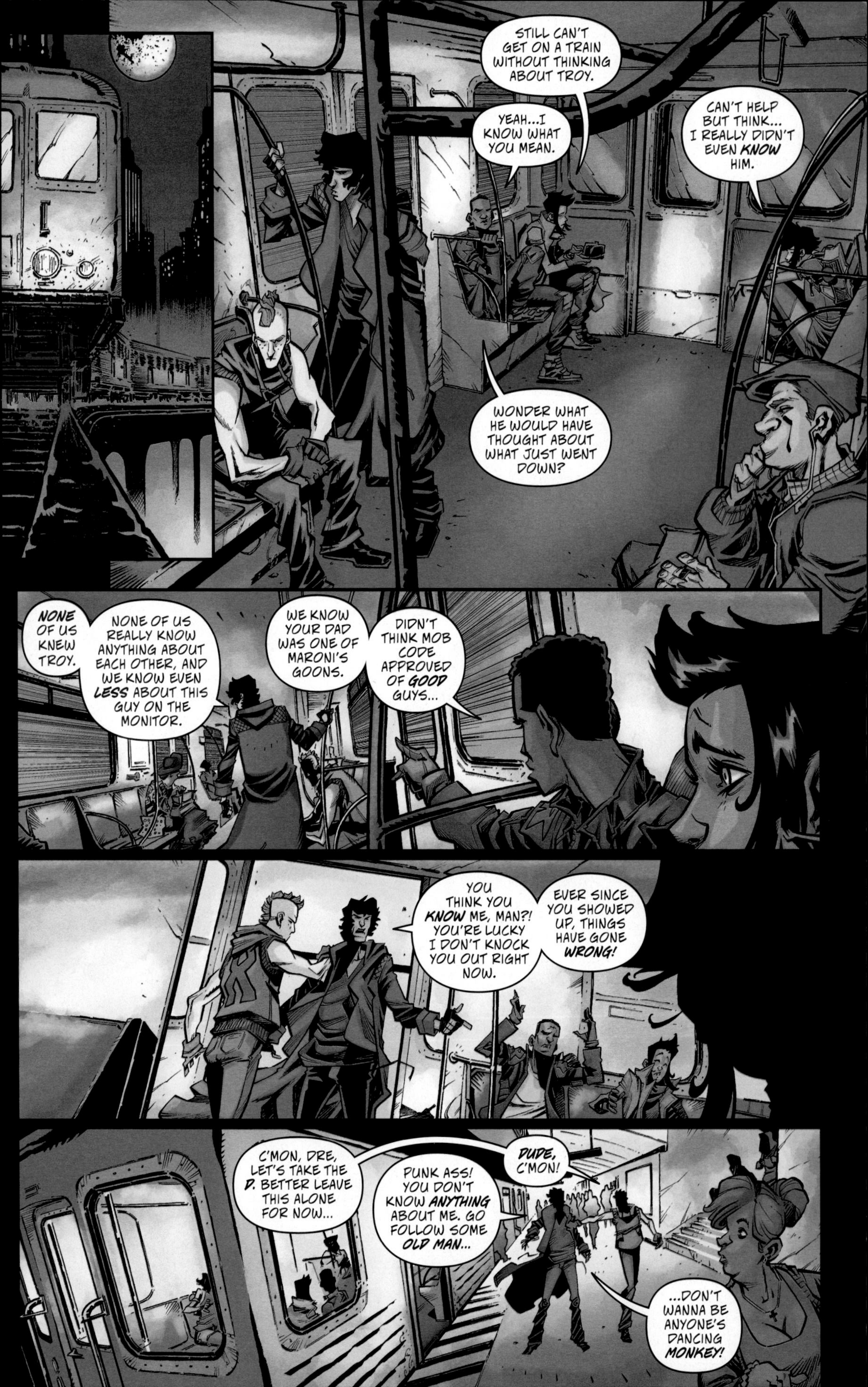
STILL CAN'T GET ON A TRAIN WITHOUT THINKING ABOUT TROY.
YEAH...I KNOW WHAT YOU MEAN.
CAN'T HELP BUT THINK... I REALLY DIDN'T EVEN KNOW HIM.
WONDER WHAT HE WOULD HAVE THOUGHT ABOUT WHAT JUST WENT DOWN?
NONE OF US KNEW TROY.
NONE OF US REALLY KNOW ANYTHING ABOUT EACH OTHER, AND WE KNOW EVEN LESS ABOUT THIS GUY ON THE MONITOR.
WE KNOW YOUR DAD WAS ONE OF MARONI'S GOONS.
DIDN'T THINK MOB CODE APPROVED OF GOOD GUYS...
YOU THINK YOU KNOW ME, MAN?! YOU'RE LUCKY I DON'T KNOCK YOU OUT RIGHT NOW.
EVER SINCE YOU SHOWED UP, THINGS HAVE GONE WRONG!
C'MON, DRE, LET'S TAKE THE D. BETTER LEAVE THIS ALONE FOR NOW...
PUNK ASS! YOU DON'T KNOW ANYTHING ABOUT ME. GO FOLLOW SOME OLD MAN...
DUDE, C'MON!
...DON'T WANNA BE ANYONE'S DANCING MONKEY!

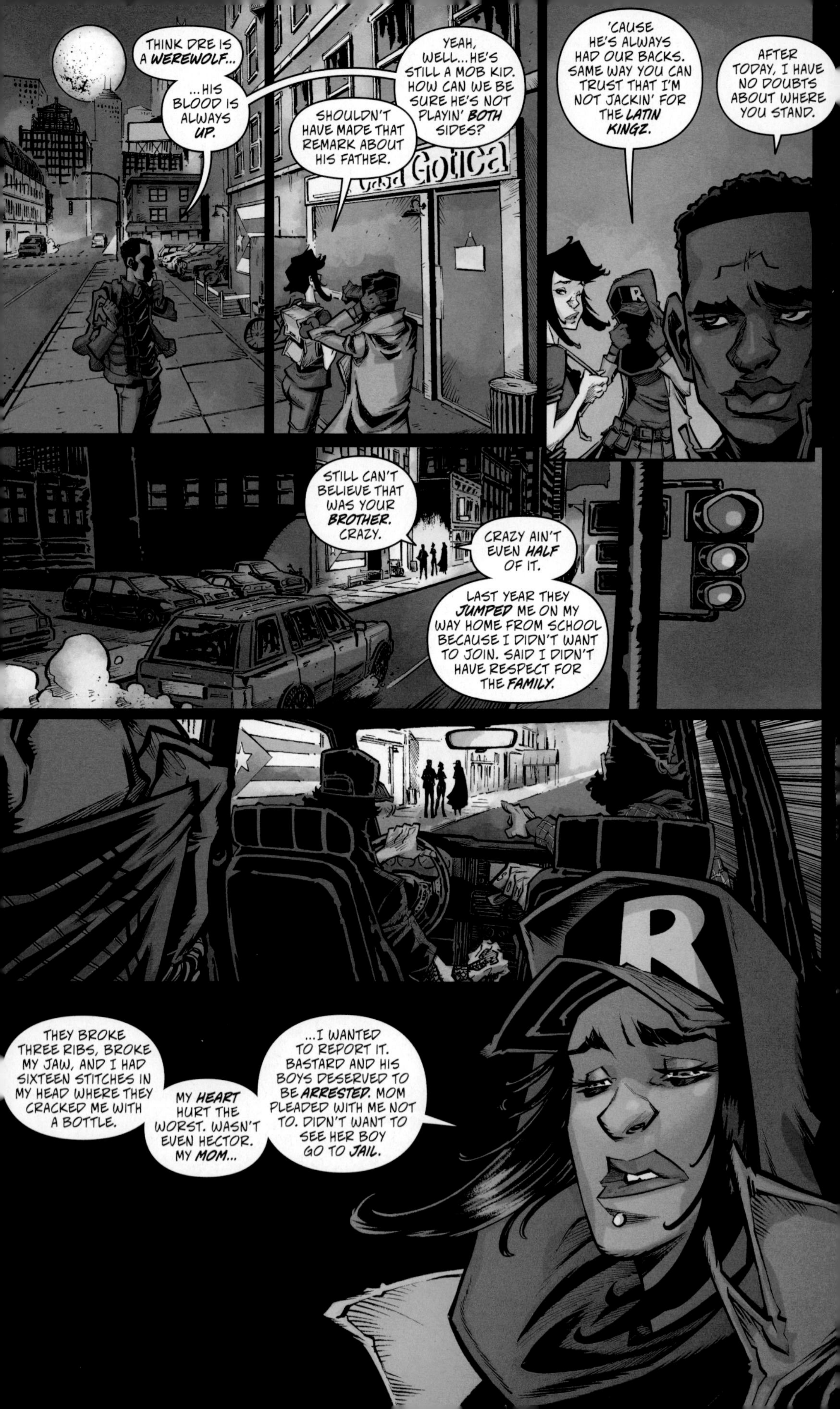
THINK DRE IS A WEREWOLF...
...HIS BLOOD IS ALWAYS UP.
YEAH, WELL...HE'S STILL A MOB KID. HOW CAN WE BE SURE HE'S NOT PLAYIN' BOTH SIDES?
SHOULDN'T HAVE MADE THAT REMARK ABOUT HIS FATHER.
'CAUSE HE'S ALWAYS HAD OUR BACKS. SAME WAY YOU CAN TRUST THAT I'M NOT JACKIN' FOR THE LATIN KINGZ.
AFTER TODAY, I HAVE NO DOUBTS ABOUT WHERE YOU STAND.
STILL CAN'T BELIEVE THAT WAS YOUR BROTHER. CRAZY.
CRAZY AIN'T EVEN HALF OF IT.
LAST YEAR THEY JUMPED ME ON MY WAY HOME FROM SCHOOL BECAUSE I DIDN'T WANT TO JOIN. SAID I DIDN'T HAVE RESPECT FOR THE FAMILY.
THEY BROKE THREE RIBS, BROKE MY JAW, AND I HAD SIXTEEN STITCHES IN MY HEAD WHERE THEY CRACKED ME WITH A BOTTLE.
MY HEART HURT THE WORST. WASN'T EVEN HECTOR. MY MOM...
...I WANTED TO REPORT IT. BASTARD AND HIS BOYS DESERVED TO BE ARRESTED. MOM PLEADED WITH ME NOT TO. DIDN'T WANT TO SEE HER BOY GO TO JAIL.

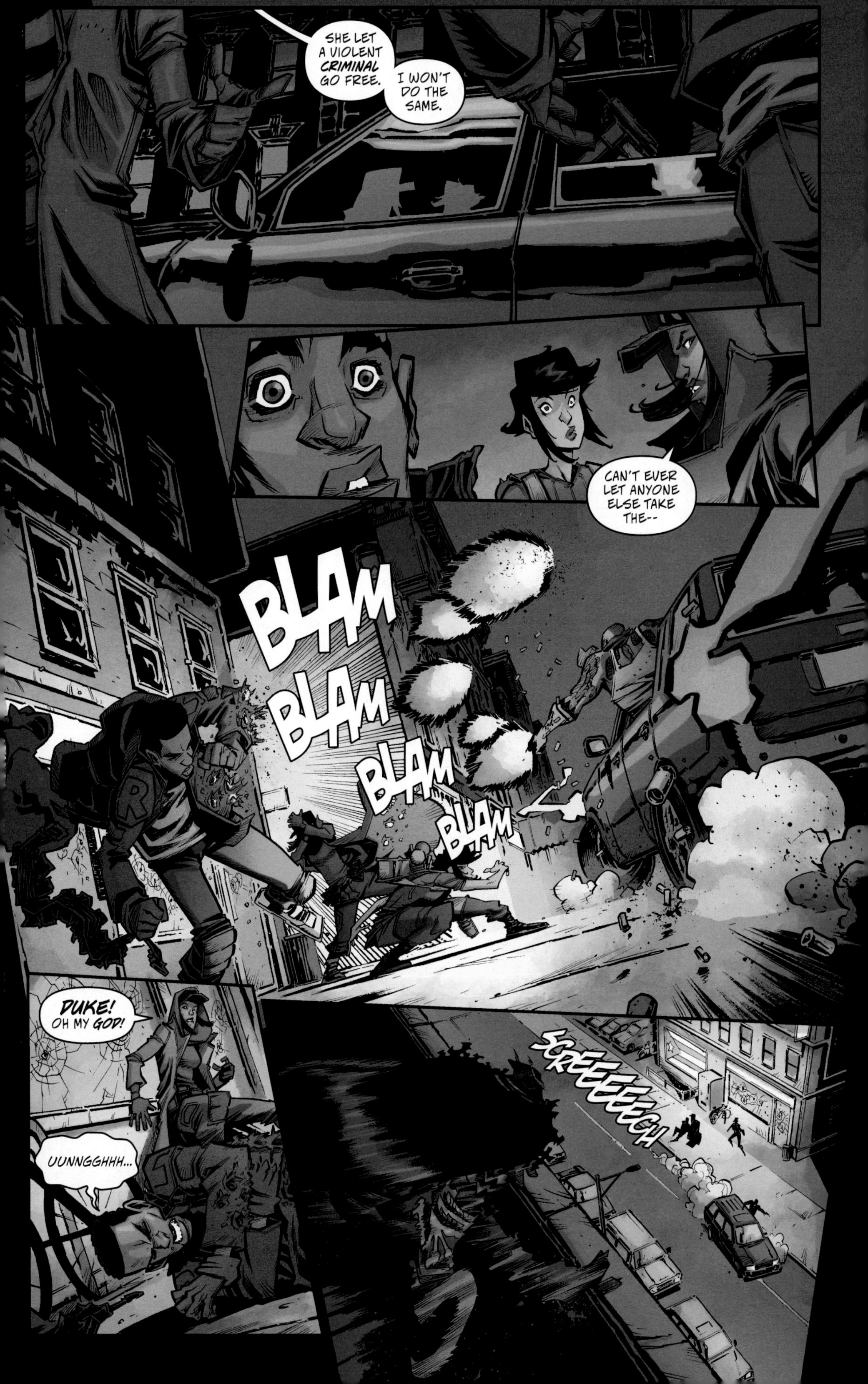

SHE LET A VIOLENT CRIMINAL GO FREE.
I WON'T DO THE SAME.
CAN'T EVER LET ANYONE ELSE TAKE THE--
BLAM
BLAM
BLAM
BLAM
DUKE! OH MY GOD!
UUNNGGHHH...
SCREEEEEECH

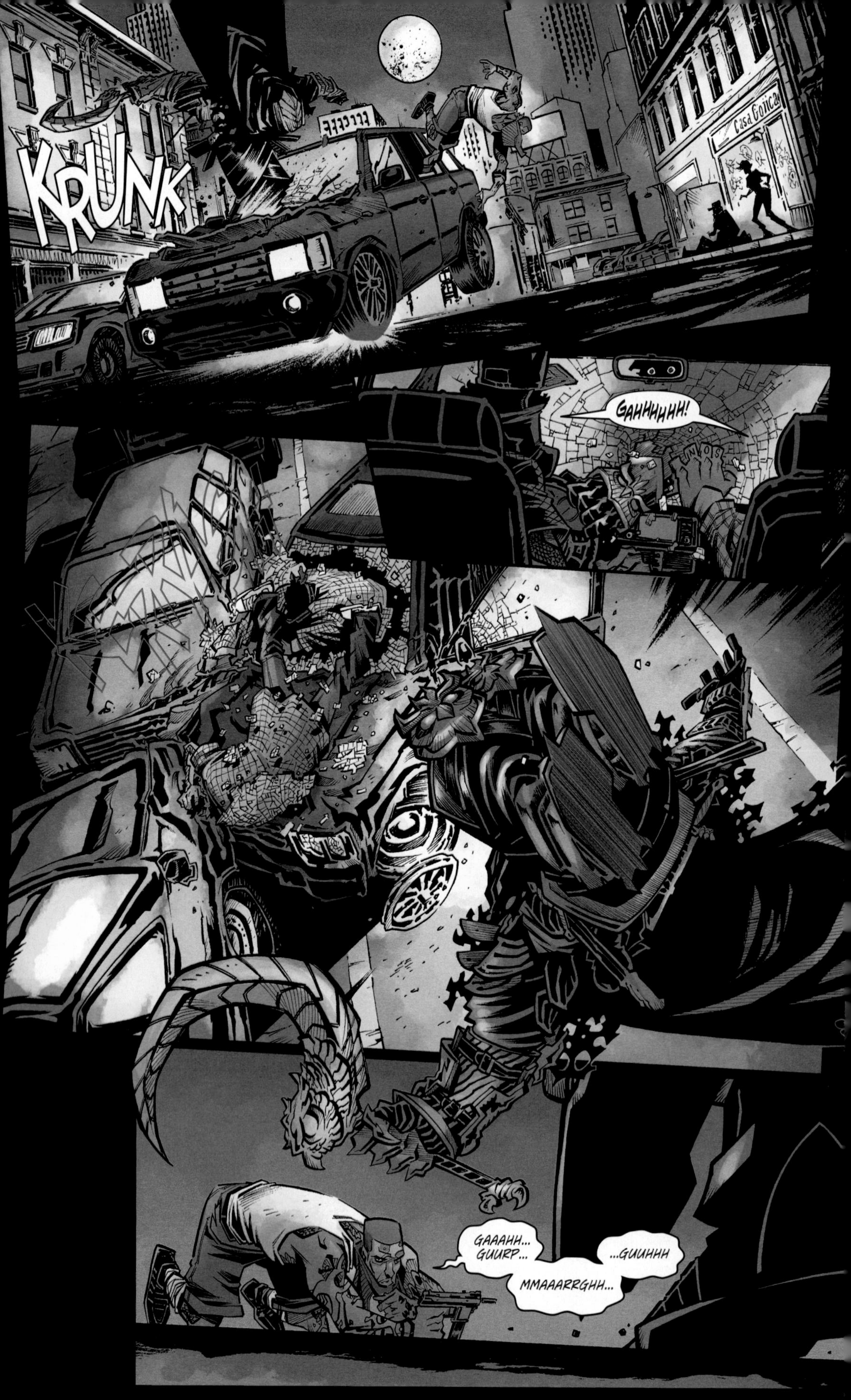

KRUNK
Casa Gotica
GAHHHHHH!
GAAAHH...
GUURP...
...GUUHHH
MMAAARRGHH...

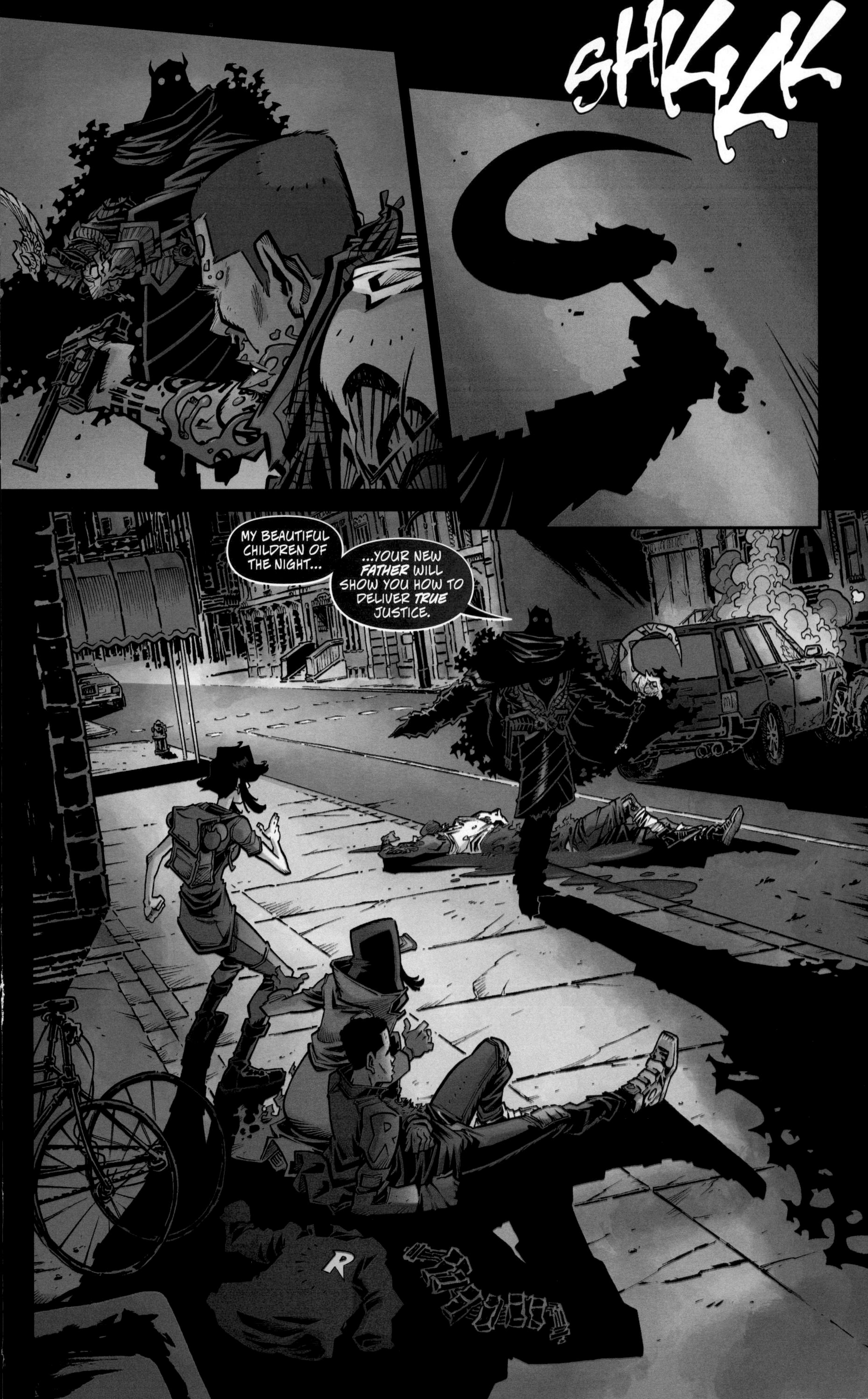
SHKKK
MY BEAUTIFUL CHILDREN OF THE NIGHT...
...YOUR NEW FATHER WILL SHOW YOU HOW TO DELIVER TRUE JUSTICE.

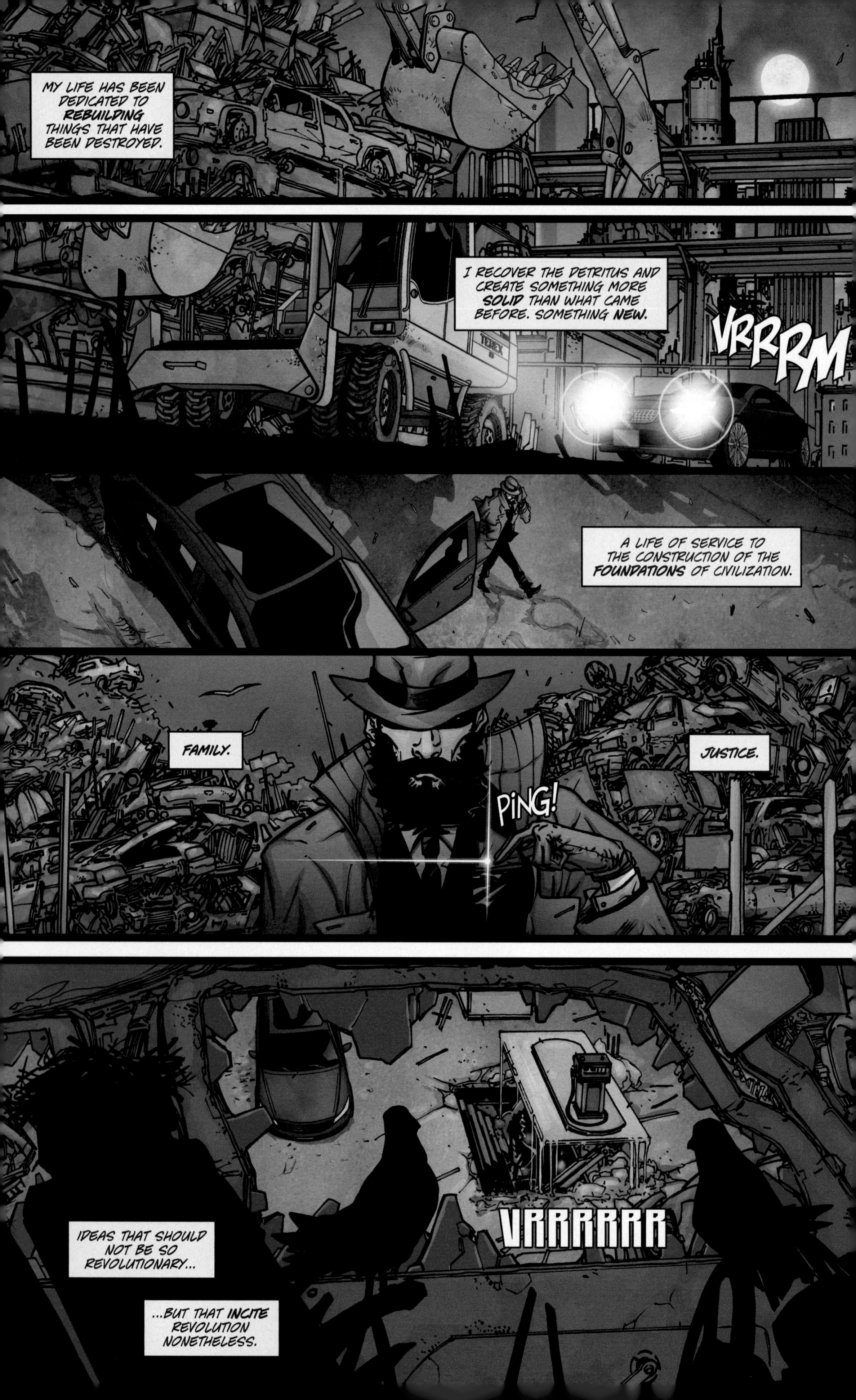
MY LIFE HAS BEEN DEDICATED TO REBUILDING THINGS THAT HAVE BEEN DESTROYED.
I RECOVER THE DETRITUS AND CREATE SOMETHING MORE SOLID THAN WHAT CAME BEFORE. SOMETHING NEW.
TEREX
VRRRM
A LIFE OF SERVICE TO THE CONSTRUCTION OF THE FOUNDATIONS OF CIVILIZATION.
FAMILY.
JUSTICE.
PING!
IDEAS THAT SHOULD NOT BE SO REVOLUTIONARY...
...BUT THAT INCITE REVOLUTION NONETHELESS.
VRRRRRR

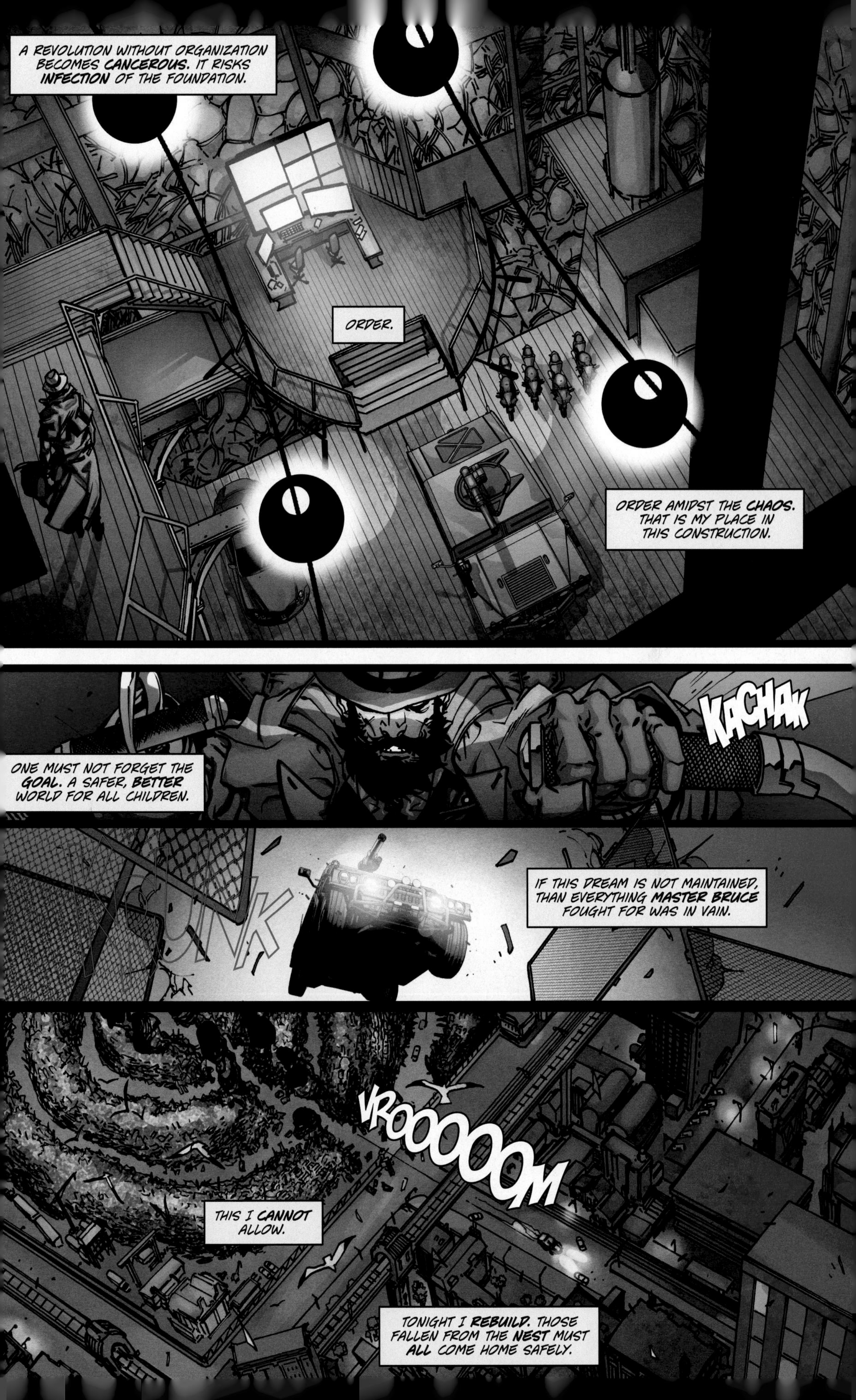
A REVOLUTION WITHOUT ORGANIZATION BECOMES CANCEROUS. IT RISKS INFECTION OF THE FOUNDATION.
ORDER.
ORDER AMIDST THE CHAOS. THAT IS MY PLACE IN THIS CONSTRUCTION.
ONE MUST NOT FORGET THE GOAL. A SAFER, BETTER WORLD FOR ALL CHILDREN.
KACHAK
IF THIS DREAM IS NOT MAINTAINED, THAN EVERYTHING MASTER BRUCE FOUGHT FOR WAS IN VAIN.
VROOOOOOM
THIS I CANNOT ALLOW.
TONIGHT I REBUILD. THOSE FALLEN FROM THE NEST MUST ALL COME HOME SAFELY.

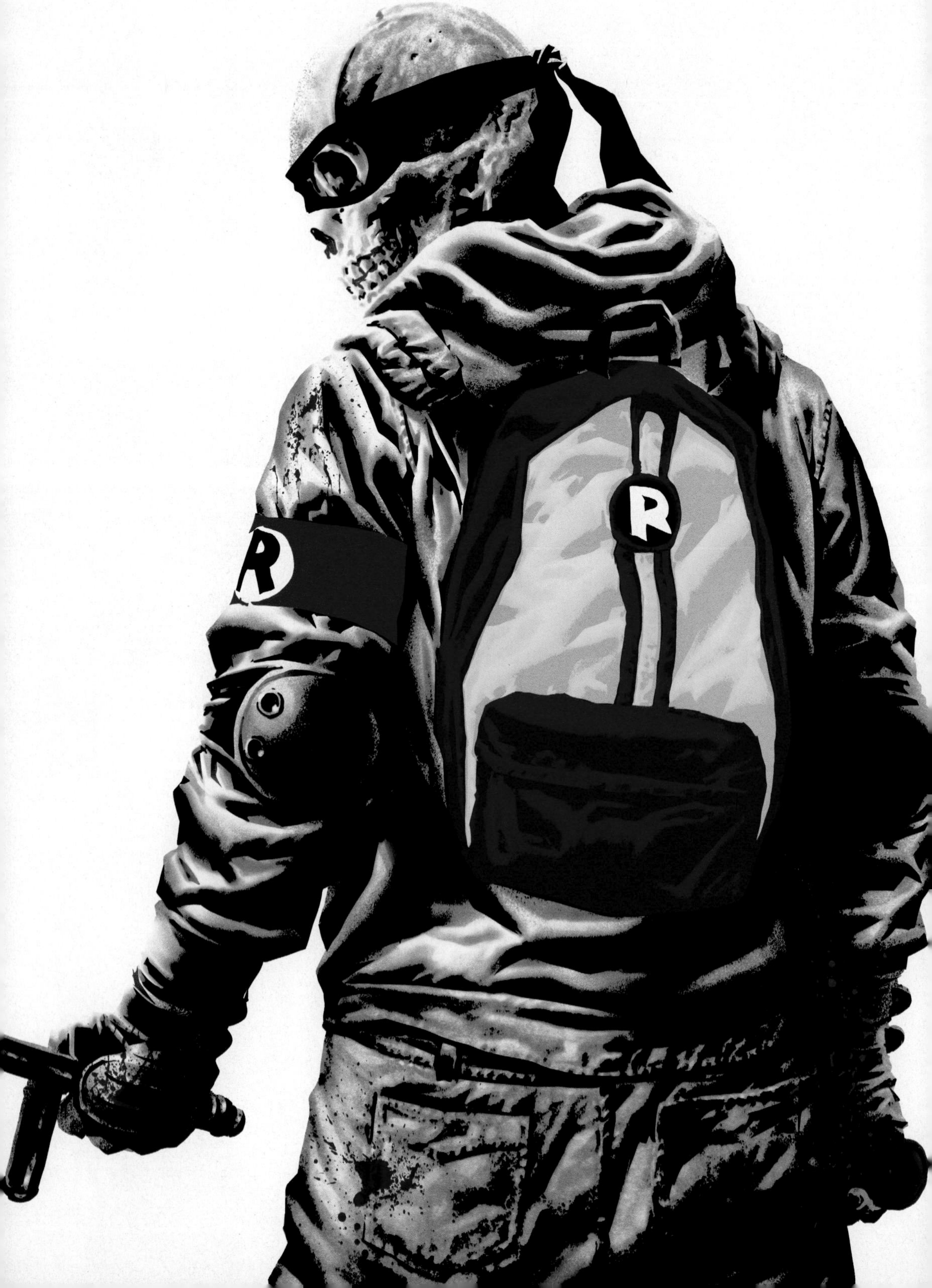

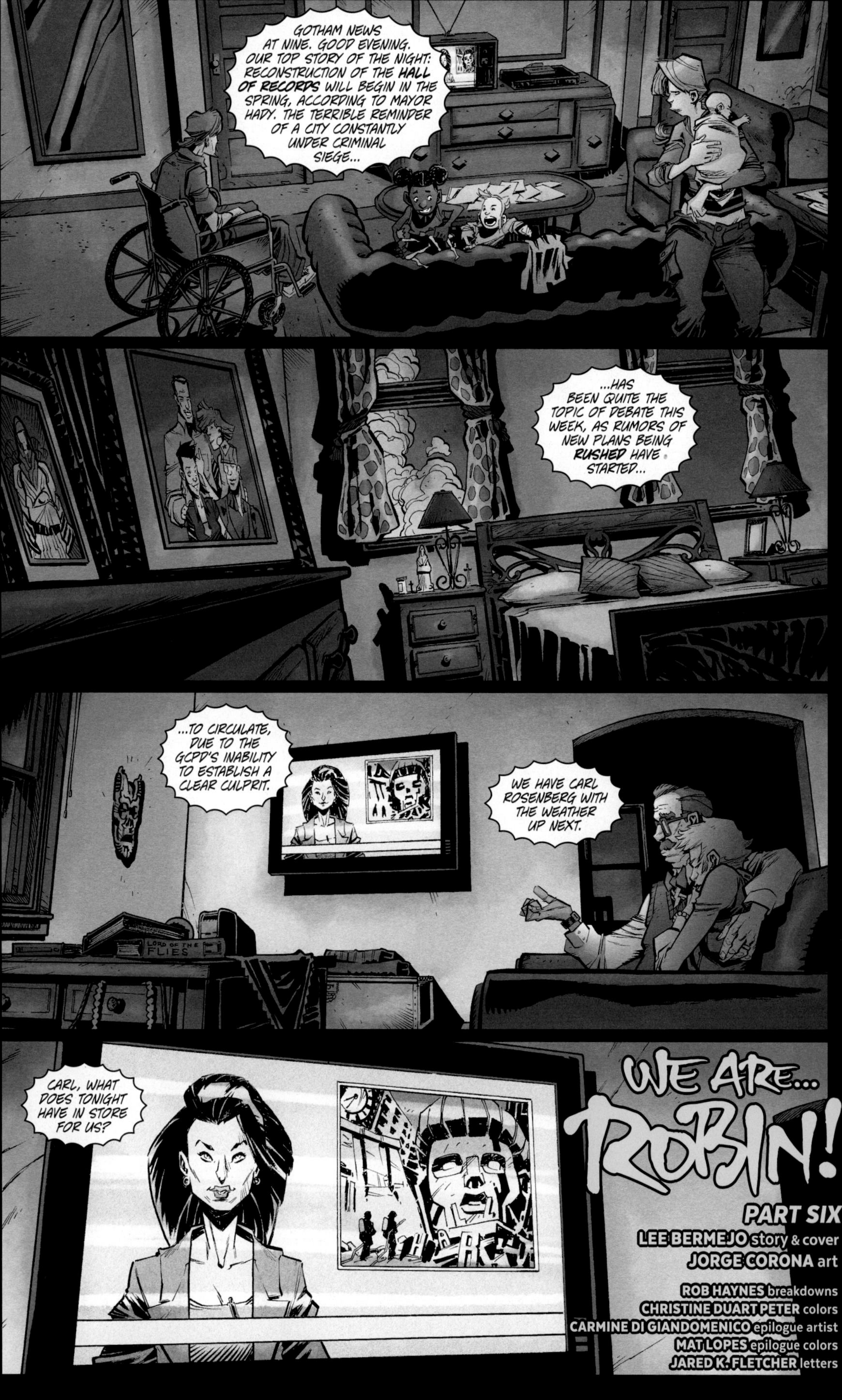
GOTHAM NEWS AT NINE. GOOD EVENING. OUR TOP STORY OF THE NIGHT: RECONSTRUCTION OF THE HALL OF RECORDS WILL BEGIN IN THE SPRING, ACCORDING TO MAYOR HADY. THE TERRIBLE REMINDER OF A CITY CONSTANTLY UNDER CRIMINAL SIEGE...
...HAS BEEN QUITE THE TOPIC OF DEBATE THIS WEEK, AS RUMORS OF NEW PLANS BEING RUSHED HAVE STARTED...
...TO CIRCULATE, DUE TO THE GCPD'S INABILITY TO ESTABLISH A CLEAR CULPRIT.
WE HAVE CARL ROSENBERG WITH THE WEATHER UP NEXT.
LORD OF THE FLIES
CARL, WHAT DOES TONIGHT HAVE IN STORE FOR US?
WE ARE... ROBIN!
PART SIX
LEE BERMEJO story & cover
JORGE CORONA art
ROB HAYNES breakdowns
CHRISTINE DUART PETER colors
CARMINE DI GIANDOMENICO epilogue artist
MAT LOPES epilogue colors
JARED K. FLETCHER letters

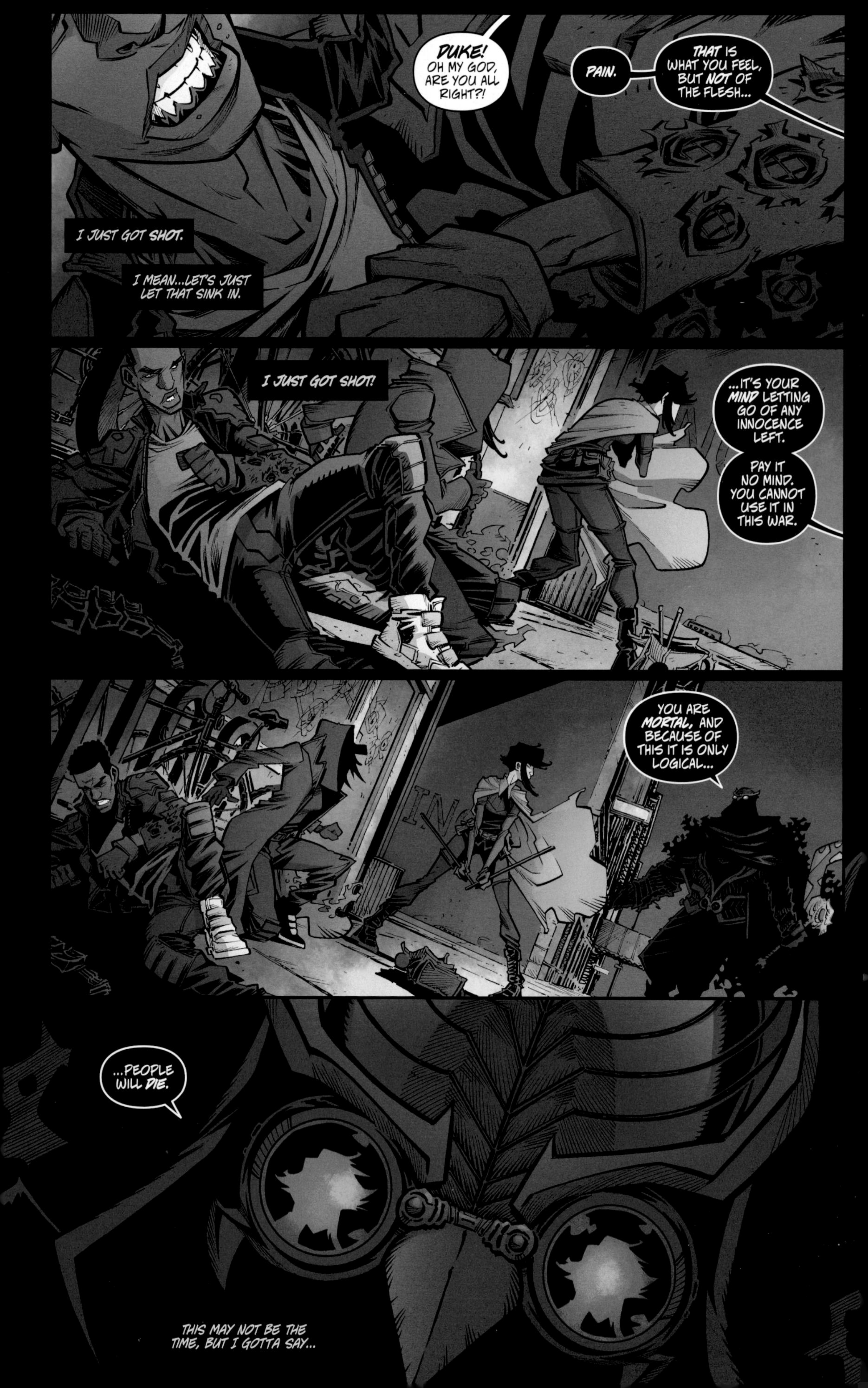
DUKE! OH MY GOD, ARE YOU ALL RIGHT?!
PAIN.
THAT IS WHAT YOU FEEL, BUT NOT OF THE FLESH...
I JUST GOT SHOT.
I MEAN...LET'S JUST LET THAT SINK IN.
I JUST GOT SHOT!
...IT'S YOUR MIND LETTING GO OF ANY INNOCENCE LEFT.
PAY IT NO MIND. YOU CANNOT USE IT IN THIS WAR.
YOU ARE MORTAL, AND BECAUSE OF THIS IT IS ONLY LOGICAL...
...PEOPLE WILL DIE.
THIS MAY NOT BE THE TIME, BUT I GOTTA SAY...

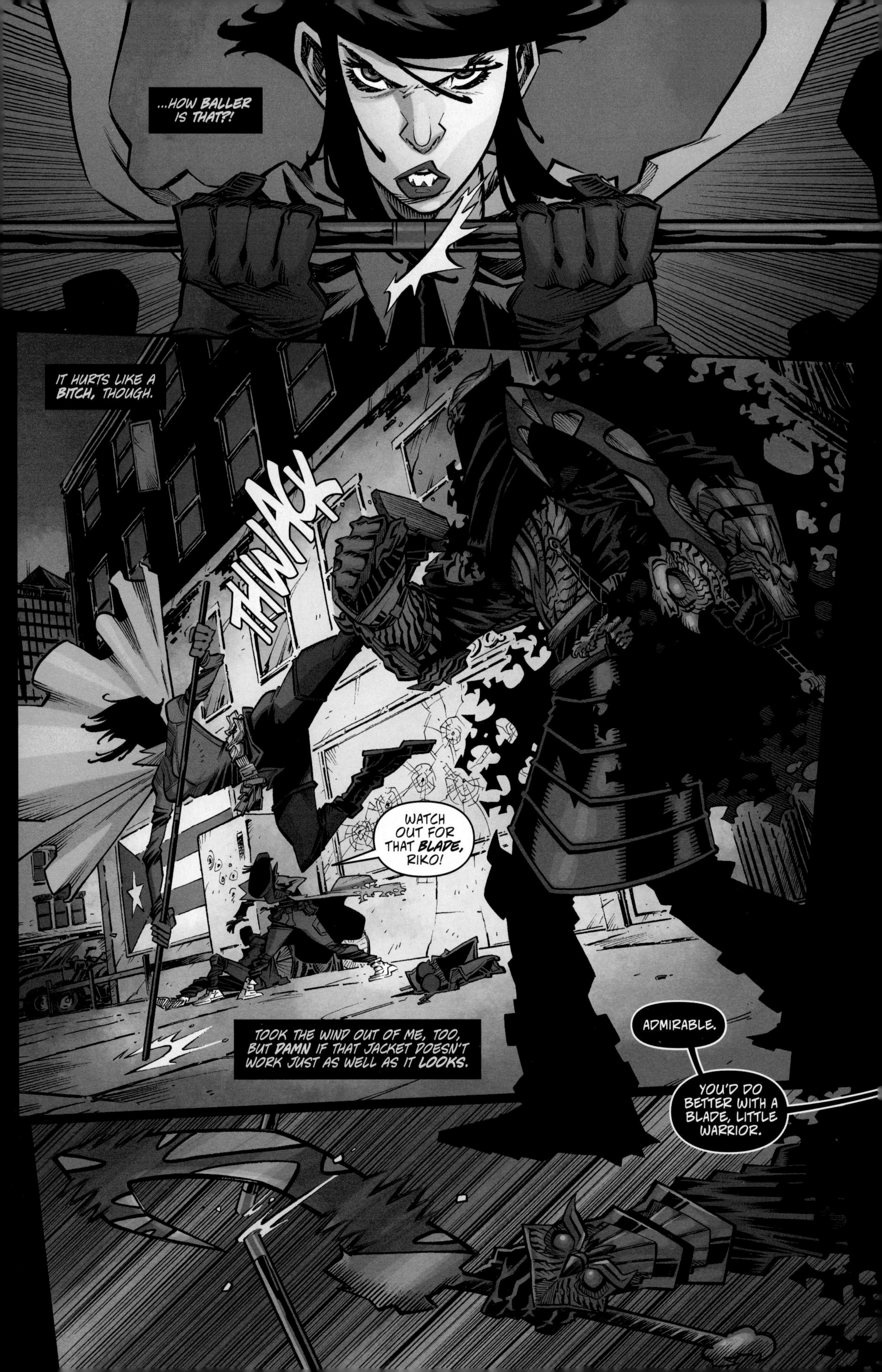
...HOW BALLER IS THAT?!
IT HURTS LIKE A BITCH, THOUGH.
THWACK
WATCH OUT FOR THAT BLADE, RIKO!
TOOK THE WIND OUT OF ME, TOO, BUT DAMN IF THAT JACKET DOESN'T WORK JUST AS WELL AS IT LOOKS.
ADMIRABLE.
YOU'D DO BETTER WITH A BLADE, LITTLE WARRIOR.

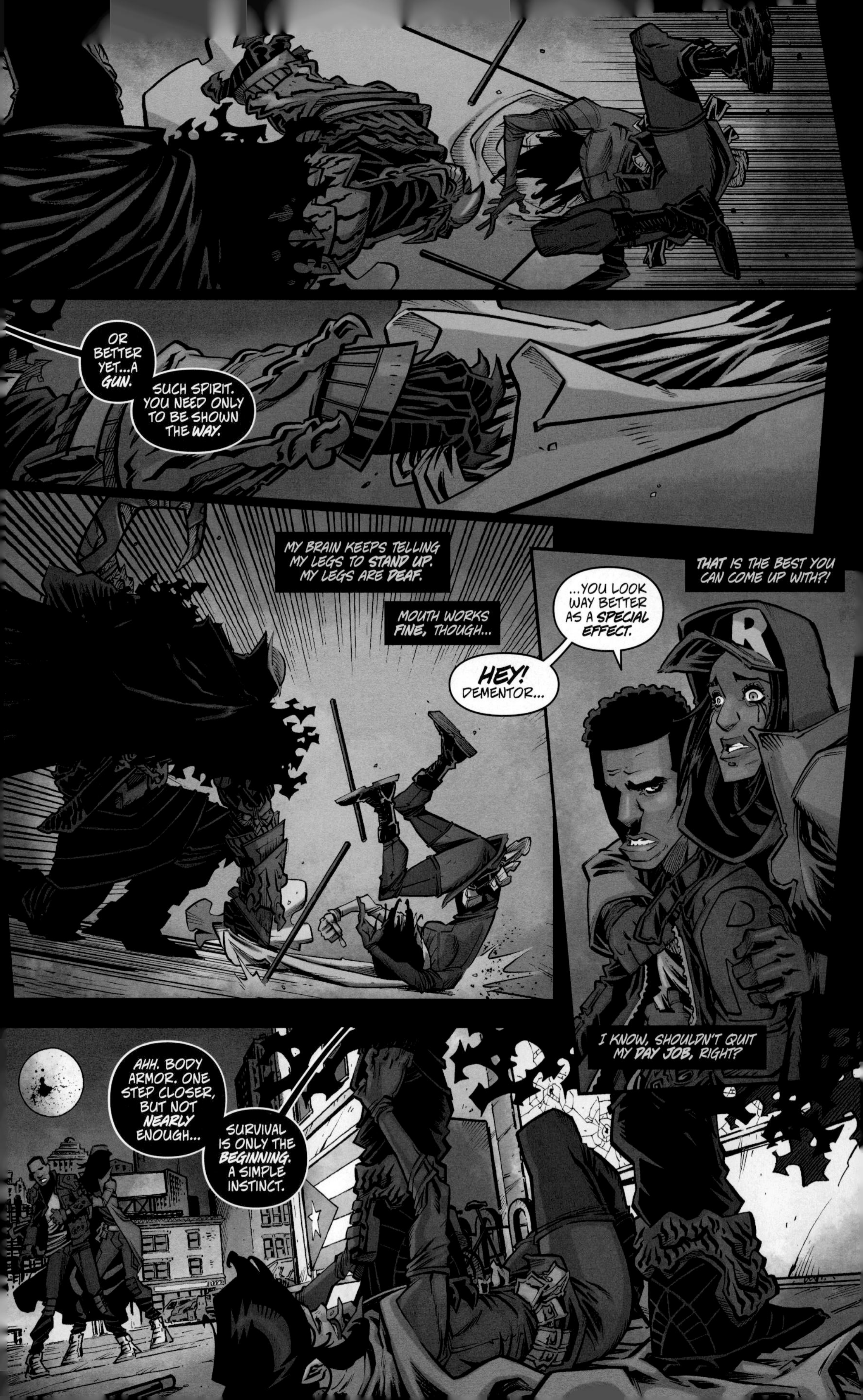
OR BETTER YET...A GUN.
SUCH SPIRIT. YOU NEED ONLY TO BE SHOWN THE WAY.
MY BRAIN KEEPS TELLING MY LEGS TO STAND UP. MY LEGS ARE DEAF.
MOUTH WORKS FINE, THOUGH...
HEY! DEMENTOR...
...YOU LOOK WAY BETTER AS A SPECIAL EFFECT.
THAT IS THE BEST YOU CAN COME UP WITH?!
I KNOW, SHOULDN'T QUIT MY DAY JOB, RIGHT?
AHH. BODY ARMOR. ONE STEP CLOSER, BUT NOT NEARLY ENOUGH...
SURVIVAL IS ONLY THE BEGINNING. A SIMPLE INSTINCT.

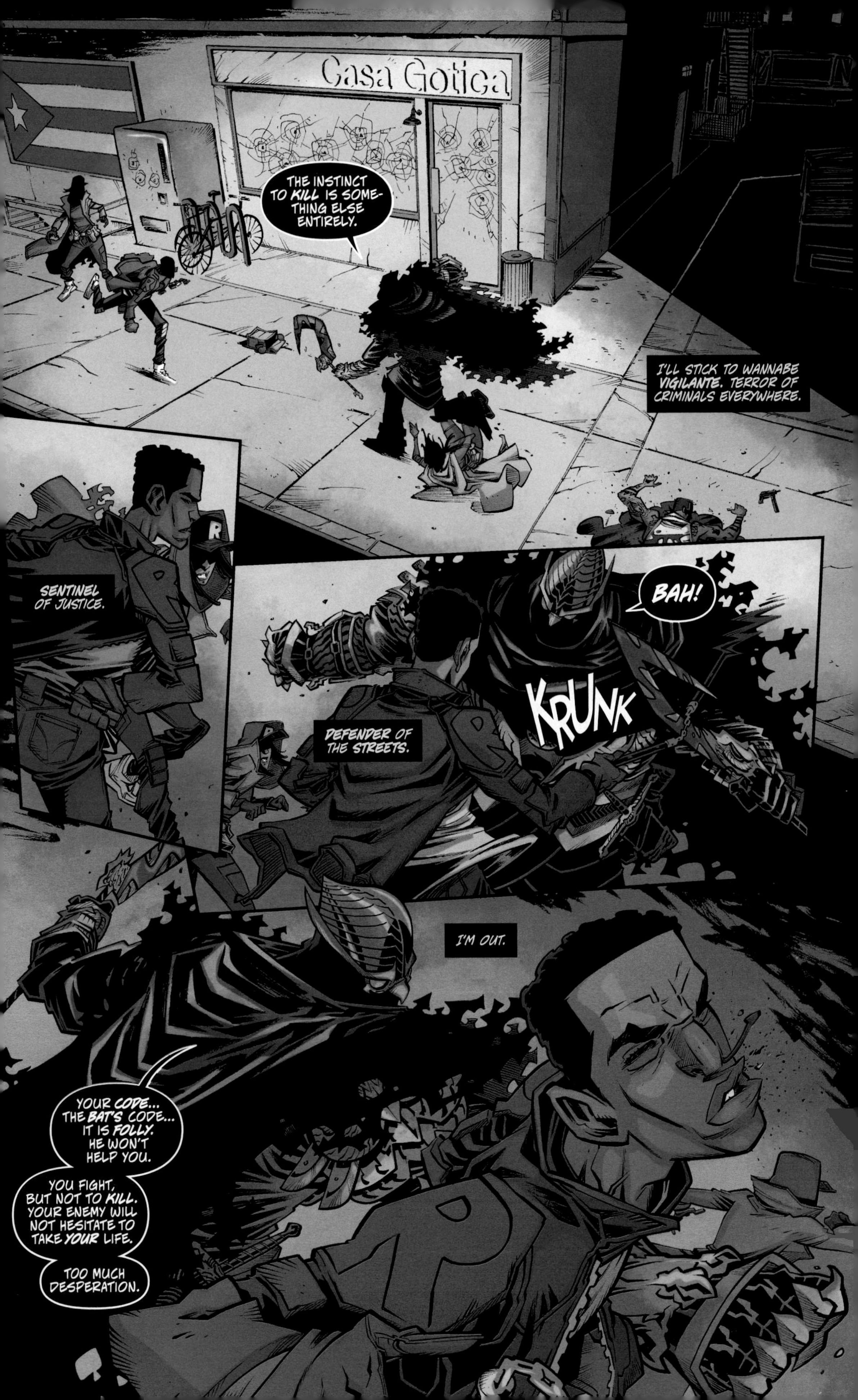

Casa Gotica
THE INSTINCT TO KILL IS SOMETHING ELSE ENTIRELY.
I'LL STICK TO WANNABE VIGILANTE. TERROR OF CRIMINALS EVERYWHERE.
SENTINEL OF JUSTICE.
BAH!
DEFENDER OF THE STREETS.
KRUNK
I'M OUT.
YOUR CODE... THE BAT'S CODE... IT IS FOLLY. HE WON'T HELP YOU.
YOU FIGHT, BUT NOT TO KILL. YOUR ENEMY WILL NOT HESITATE TO TAKE YOUR LIFE.
TOO MUCH DESPERATION.

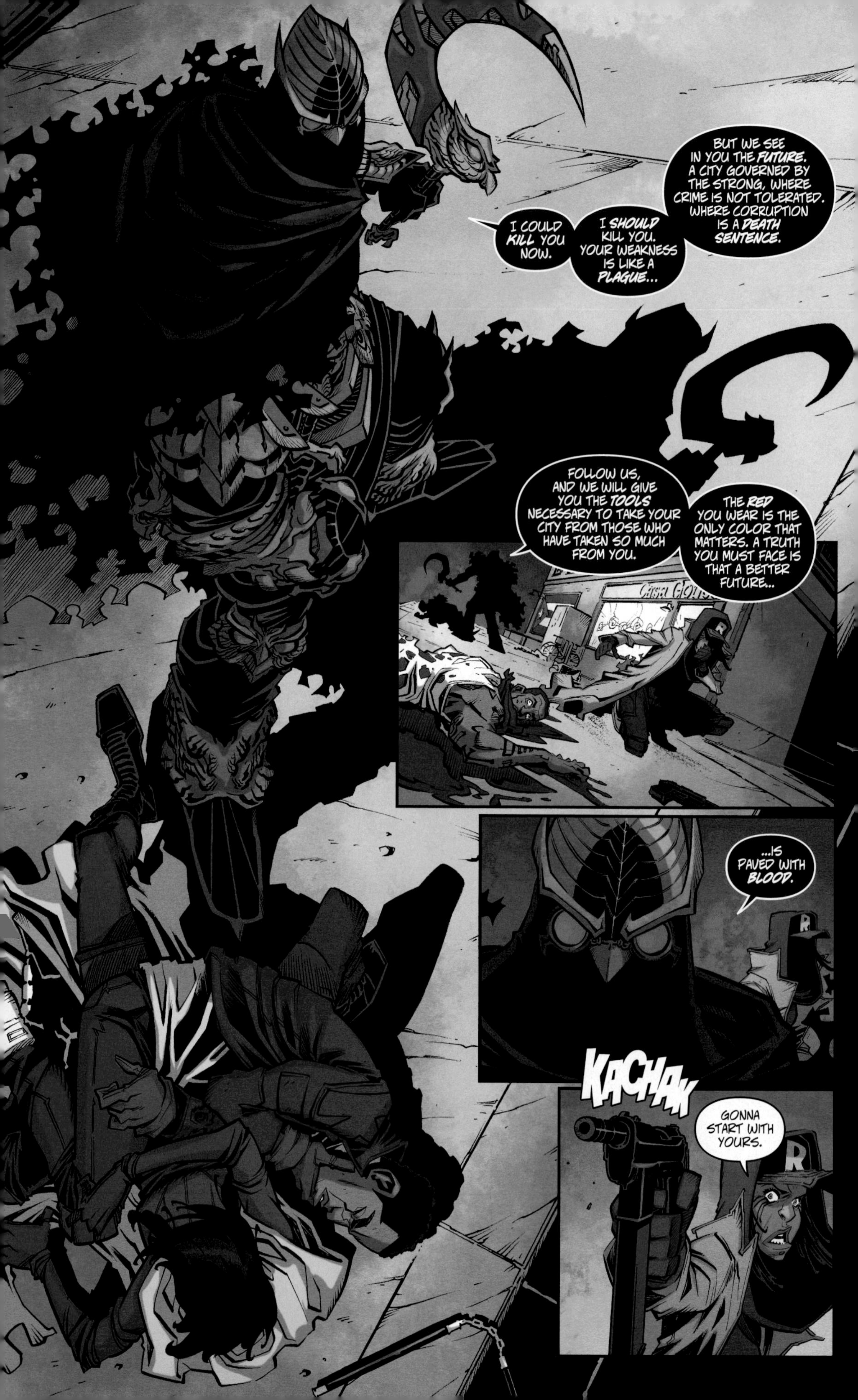
I COULD KILL YOU NOW.
I SHOULD KILL YOU. YOUR WEAKNESS IS LIKE A PLAGUE...
BUT WE SEE IN YOU THE FUTURE. A CITY GOVERNED BY THE STRONG, WHERE CRIME IS NOT TOLERATED. WHERE CORRUPTION IS A DEATH SENTENCE.
FOLLOW US, AND WE WILL GIVE YOU THE TOOLS NECESSARY TO TAKE YOUR CITY FROM THOSE WHO HAVE TAKEN SO MUCH FROM YOU.
THE RED YOU WEAR IS THE ONLY COLOR THAT MATTERS. A TRUTH YOU MUST FACE IS THAT A BETTER FUTURE...
...IS PAVED WITH BLOOD.
KACHAK
GONNA START WITH YOURS.

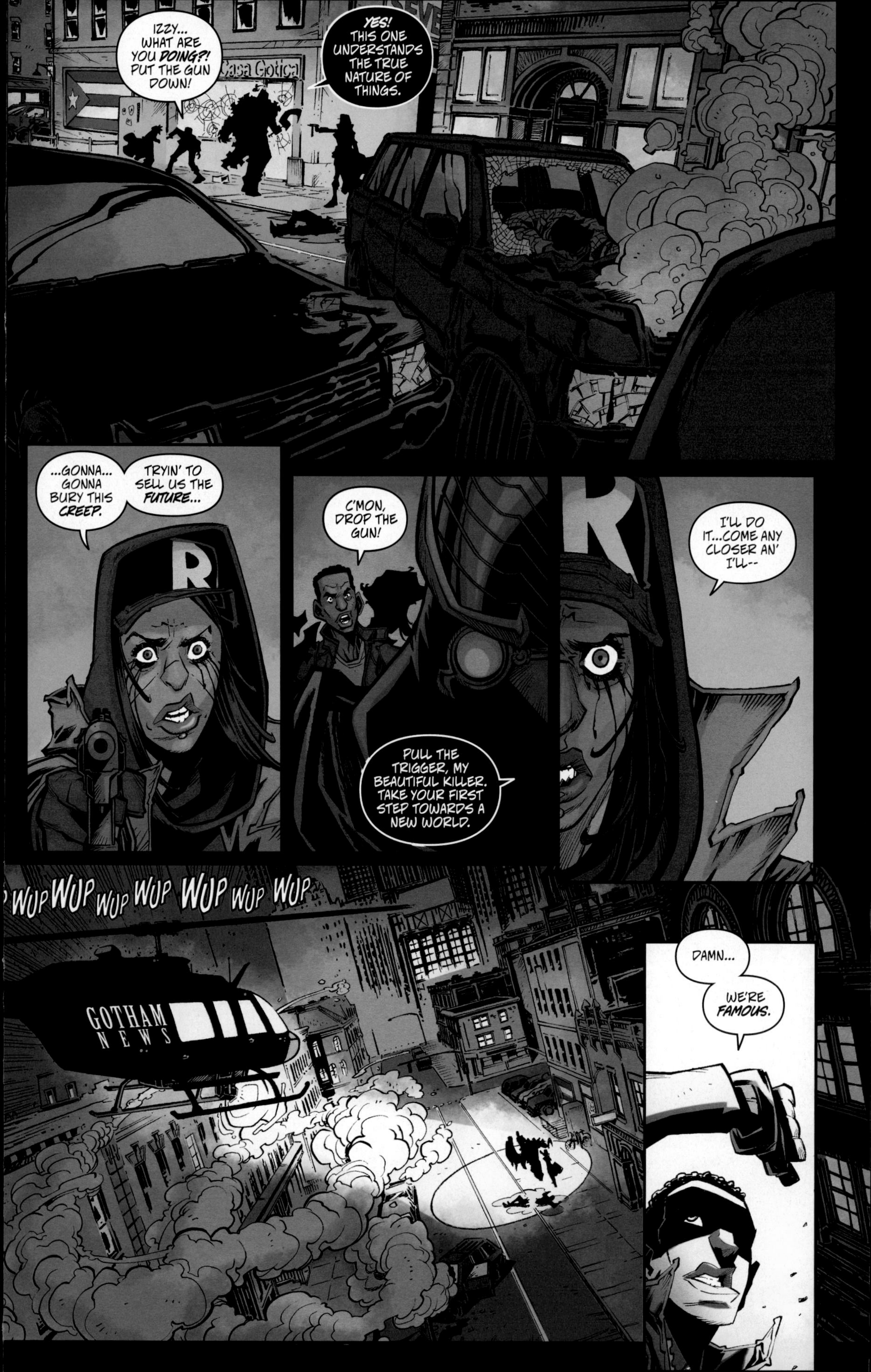
IZZY... WHAT ARE YOU DOING?! PUT THE GUN DOWN!
YES! THIS ONE UNDERSTANDS THE TRUE NATURE OF THINGS.
Casa Gotica
...GONNA... GONNA BURY THIS CREEP.
TRYIN' TO SELL US THE FUTURE...
C'MON, DROP THE GUN!
I'LL DO IT...COME ANY CLOSER AN' I'LL--
PULL THE TRIGGER, MY BEAUTIFUL KILLER. TAKE YOUR FIRST STEP TOWARDS A NEW WORLD.
WUP WUP WUP WUP WUP WUP WUP
GOTHAM NEWS
DAMN...
WE'RE FAMOUS.

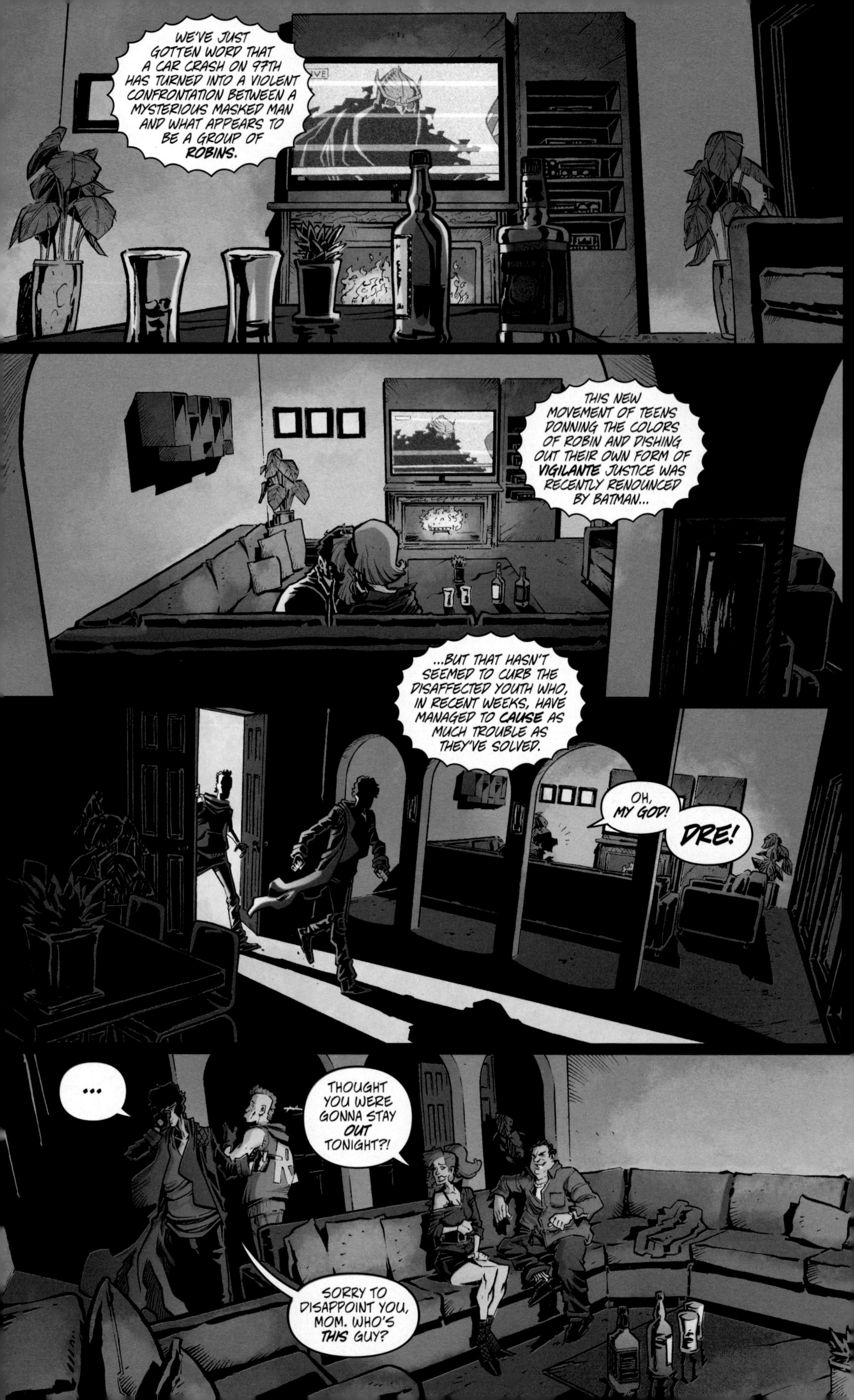
WE'VE JUST GOTTEN WORD THAT A CAR CRASH ON 97TH HAS TURNED INTO A VIOLENT CONFRONTATION BETWEEN A MYSTERIOUS MASKED MAN AND WHAT APPEARS TO BE A GROUP OF ROBINS.
LIVE
THIS NEW MOVEMENT OF TEENS DONNING THE COLORS OF ROBIN AND DISHING OUT THEIR OWN FORM OF VIGILANTE JUSTICE WAS RECENTLY RENOUNCED BY BATMAN...
...BUT THAT HASN'T SEEMED TO CURB THE DISAFFECTED YOUTH WHO, IN RECENT WEEKS, HAVE MANAGED TO CAUSE AS MUCH TROUBLE AS THEY'VE SOLVED.
OH, MY GOD!
DRE!
...
THOUGHT YOU WERE GONNA STAY OUT TONIGHT?!
SORRY TO DISAPPOINT YOU, MOM. WHO'S THIS GUY?
R

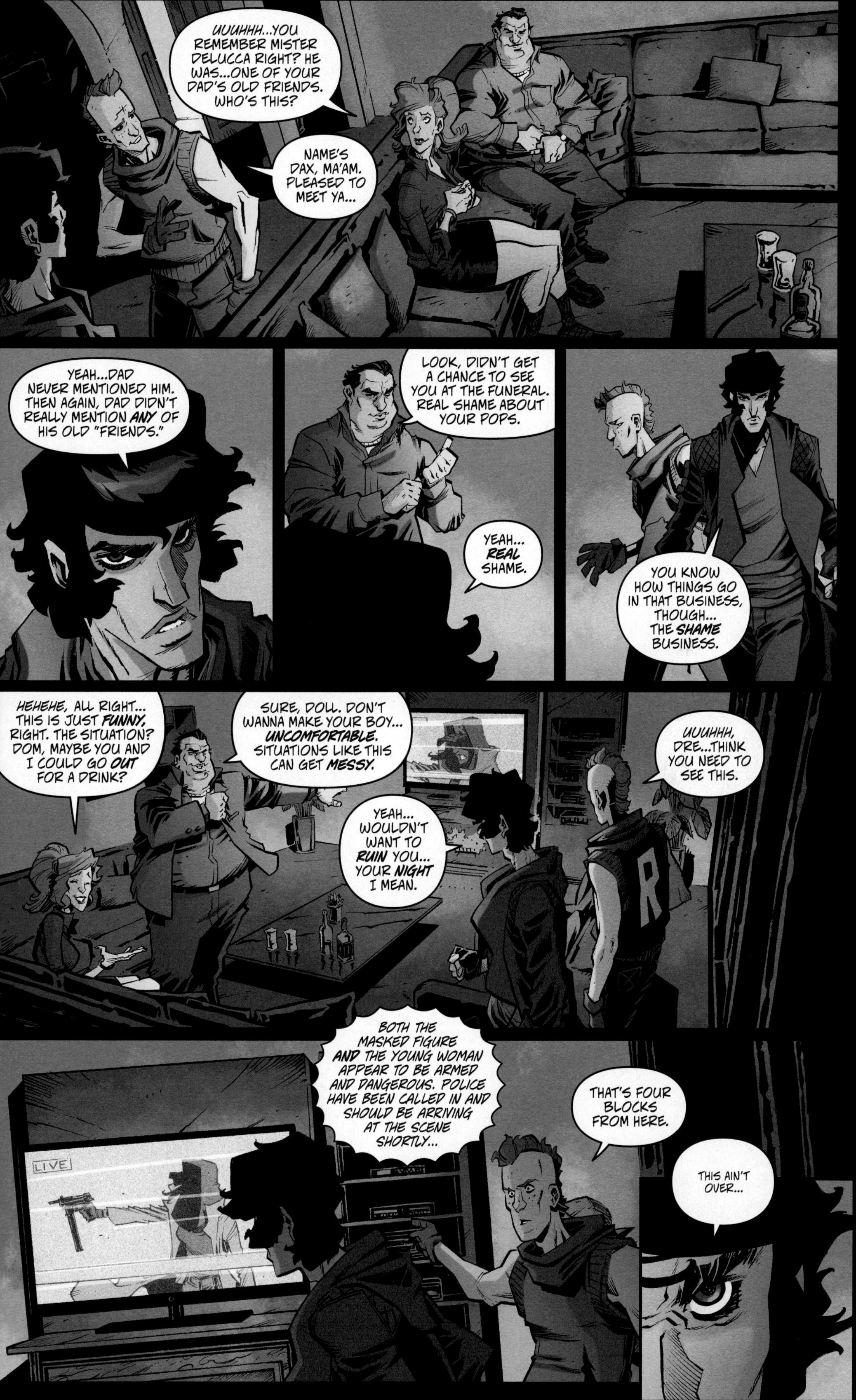
UUUHHH...YOU REMEMBER MISTER DELUCCA RIGHT? HE WAS...ONE OF YOUR DAD'S OLD FRIENDS. WHO'S THIS?
NAME'S DAX, MA'AM. PLEASED TO MEET YA...
YEAH...DAD NEVER MENTIONED HIM. THEN AGAIN, DAD DIDN'T REALLY MENTION ANY OF HIS OLD "FRIENDS."
LOOK, DIDN'T GET A CHANCE TO SEE YOU AT THE FUNERAL. REAL SHAME ABOUT YOUR POPS.
YEAH... REAL SHAME.
YOU KNOW HOW THINGS GO IN THAT BUSINESS, THOUGH... THE SHAME BUSINESS.
HEHEHE, ALL RIGHT... THIS IS JUST FUNNY, RIGHT. THE SITUATION? DOM, MAYBE YOU AND I COULD GO OUT FOR A DRINK?
SURE, DOLL. DON'T WANNA MAKE YOUR BOY... UNCOMFORTABLE. SITUATIONS LIKE THIS CAN GET MESSY.
YEAH... WOULDN'T WANT TO RUIN YOU... YOUR NIGHT I MEAN.
UUUHHH, DRE...THINK YOU NEED TO SEE THIS.
R
BOTH THE MASKED FIGURE AND THE YOUNG WOMAN APPEAR TO BE ARMED AND DANGEROUS. POLICE HAVE BEEN CALLED IN AND SHOULD BE ARRIVING AT THE SCENE SHORTLY...
LIVE
THAT'S FOUR BLOCKS FROM HERE.
THIS AIN'T OVER...

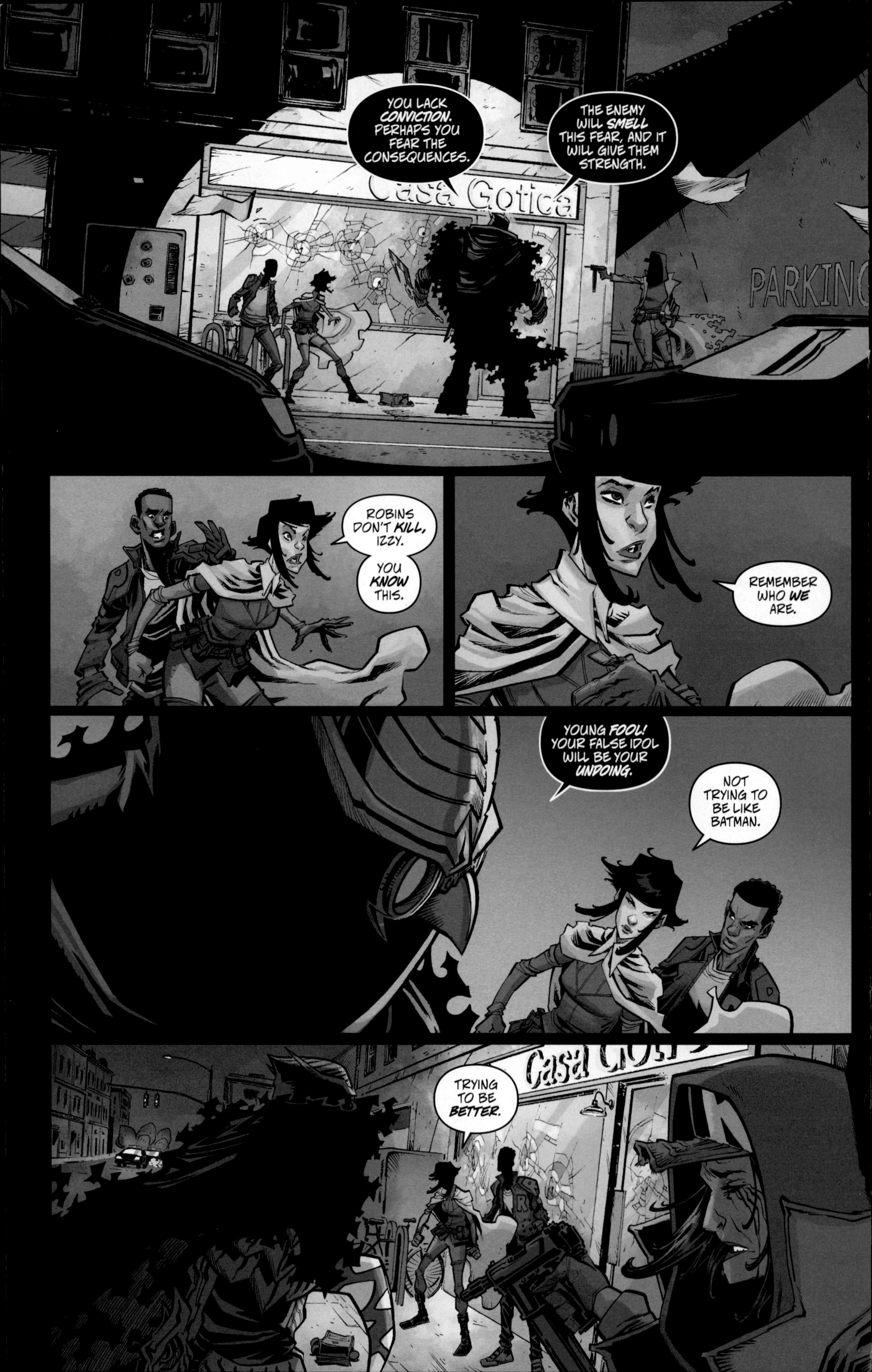

YOU LACK CONVICTION. PERHAPS YOU FEAR THE CONSEQUENCES.
THE ENEMY WILL SMELL THIS FEAR, AND IT WILL GIVE THEM STRENGTH.
Casa Gotica
PARKING
ROBINS DON'T KILL, IZZY.
YOU KNOW THIS.
REMEMBER WHO WE ARE.
YOUNG FOOL! YOUR FALSE IDOL WILL BE YOUR UNDOING.
NOT TRYING TO BE LIKE BATMAN.
TRYING TO BE BETTER.

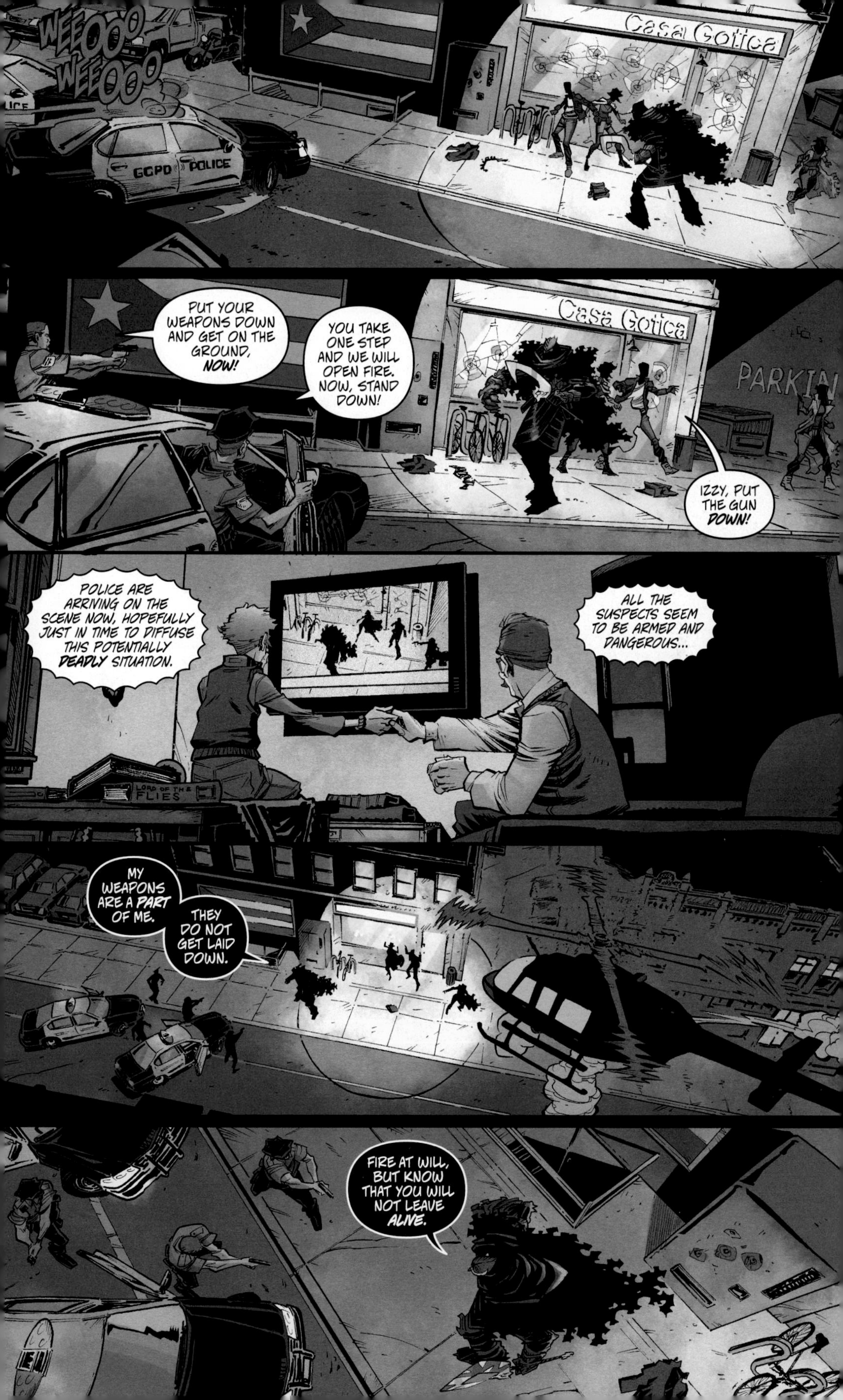
WEEOOO
WEEOOO
Casa Gotica
GCPD POLICE
PUT YOUR WEAPONS DOWN AND GET ON THE GROUND, **NOW!**
YOU TAKE ONE STEP AND WE WILL OPEN FIRE. NOW, STAND DOWN!
Casa Gotica
PARKIN
IZZY, PUT THE GUN **DOWN!**
POLICE ARE ARRIVING ON THE SCENE NOW, HOPEFULLY JUST IN TIME TO DIFFUSE THIS POTENTIALLY **DEADLY** SITUATION.
ALL THE SUSPECTS SEEM TO BE ARMED AND DANGEROUS...
LORD OF THE FLIES
MY WEAPONS ARE A **PART** OF ME.
THEY DO NOT GET LAID DOWN.
FIRE AT WILL, BUT KNOW THAT YOU WILL NOT LEAVE **ALIVE.**

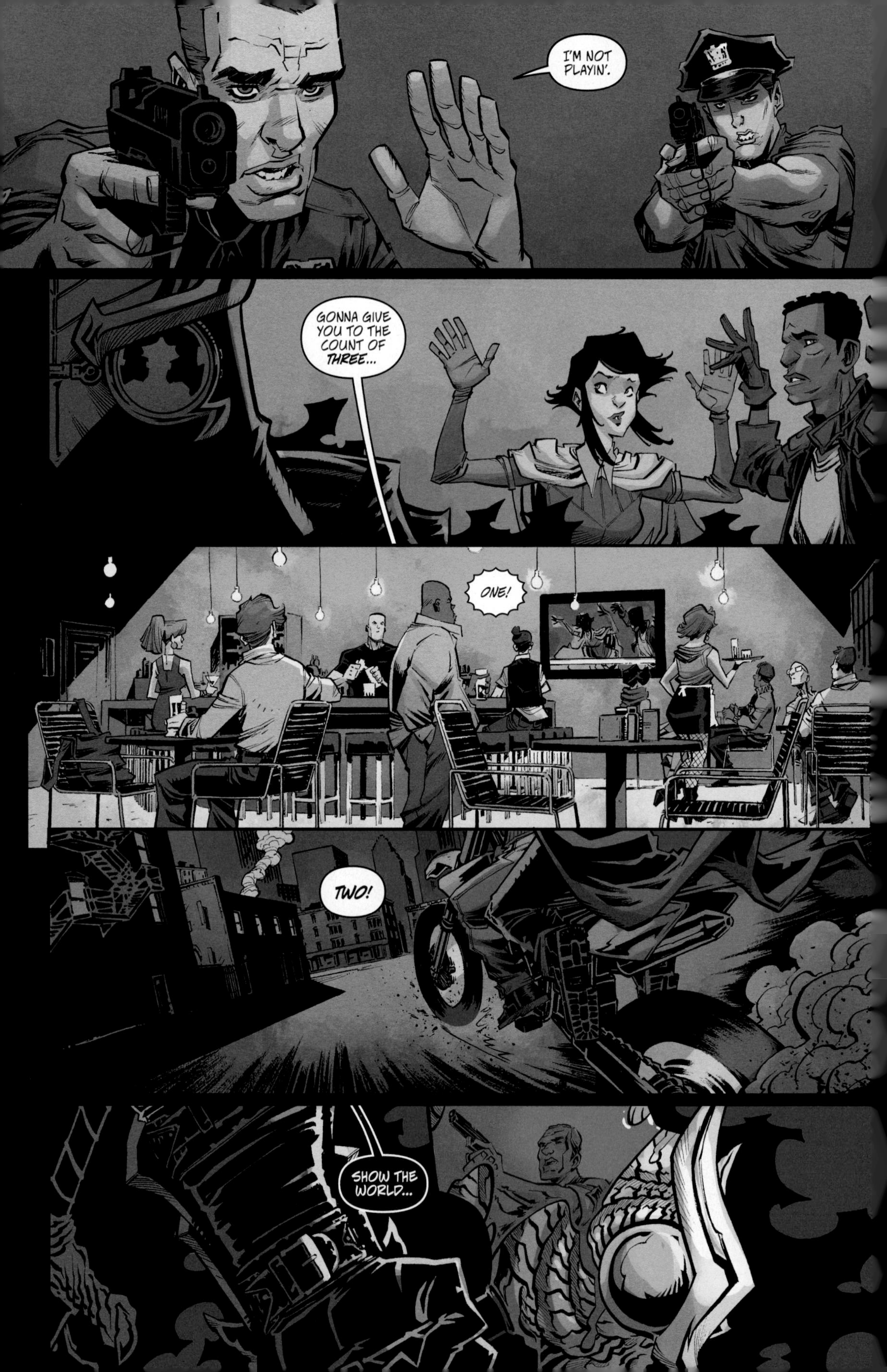
I'M NOT PLAYIN'.
GONNA GIVE YOU TO THE COUNT OF THREE...
ONE!
TWO!
SHOW THE WORLD...

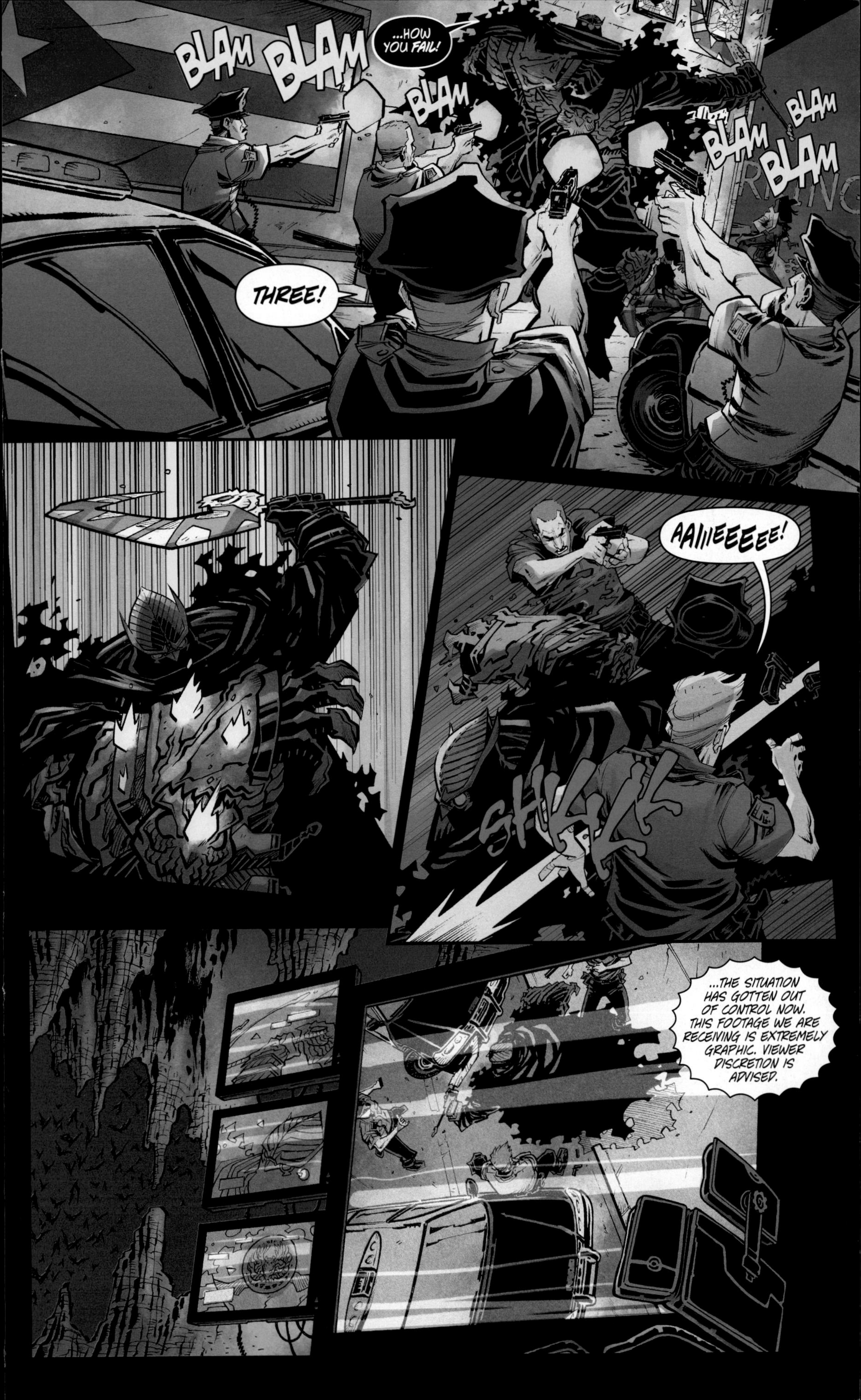
BLAM
BLAM
...HOW YOU FAIL!
BLAM
BLAM
BLAM
BLAM
THREE!
AAIIIEEEEee!
SHKKK
...THE SITUATION HAS GOTTEN OUT OF CONTROL NOW. THIS FOOTAGE WE ARE RECEIVING IS EXTREMELY GRAPHIC. VIEWER DISCRETION IS ADVISED.

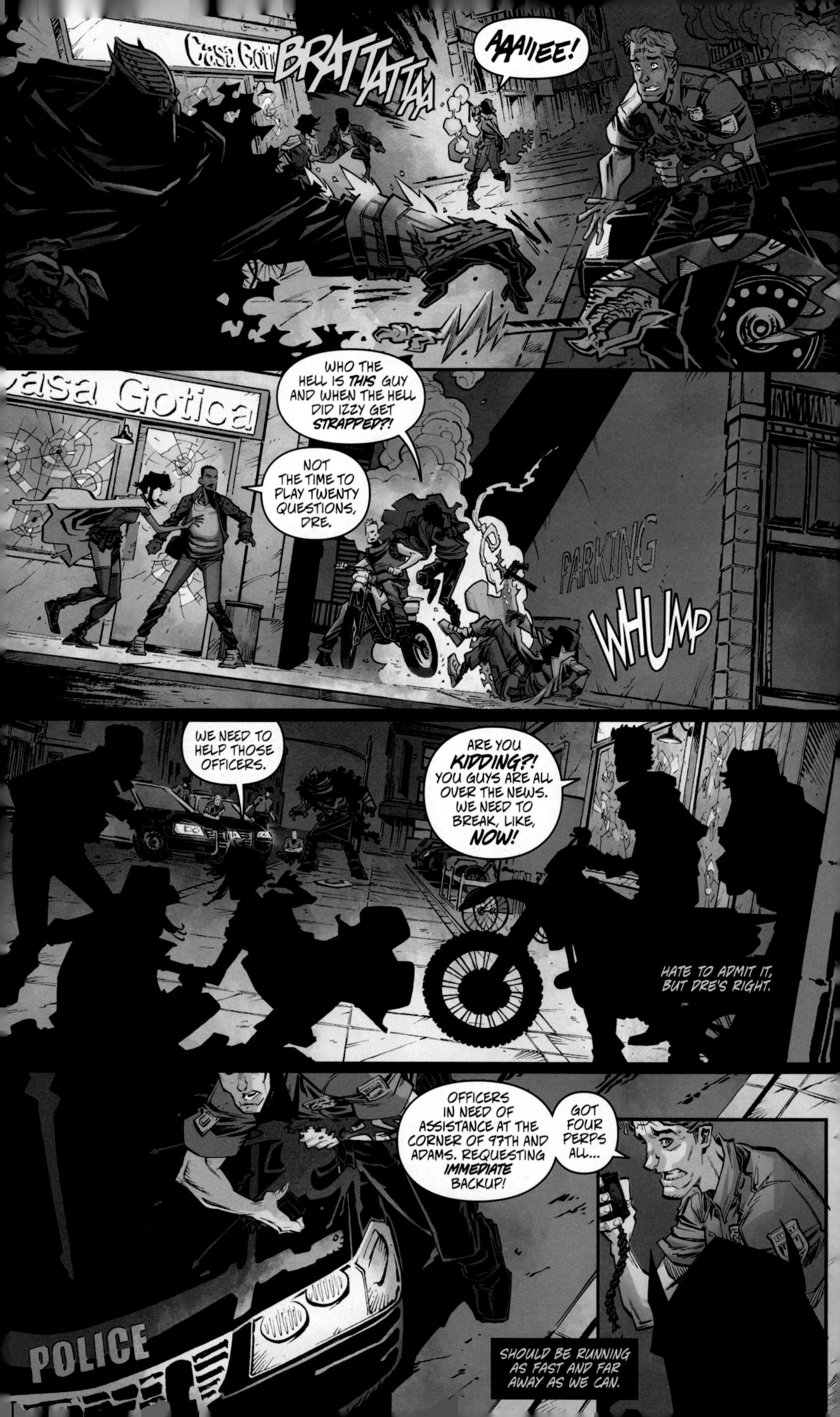
Casa Gotic
BRATTATTAA
AAAIIEE!
Casa Gotica
WHO THE HELL IS THIS GUY AND WHEN THE HELL DID IZZY GET STRAPPED?!
NOT THE TIME TO PLAY TWENTY QUESTIONS, DRE.
PARKING
WHUMP
WE NEED TO HELP THOSE OFFICERS.
ARE YOU KIDDING?! YOU GUYS ARE ALL OVER THE NEWS. WE NEED TO BREAK, LIKE, NOW!
HATE TO ADMIT IT, BUT DRE'S RIGHT.
OFFICERS IN NEED OF ASSISTANCE AT THE CORNER OF 97TH AND ADAMS. REQUESTING IMMEDIATE BACKUP!
GOT FOUR PERPS ALL...
POLICE
SHOULD BE RUNNING AS FAST AND FAR AWAY AS WE CAN.

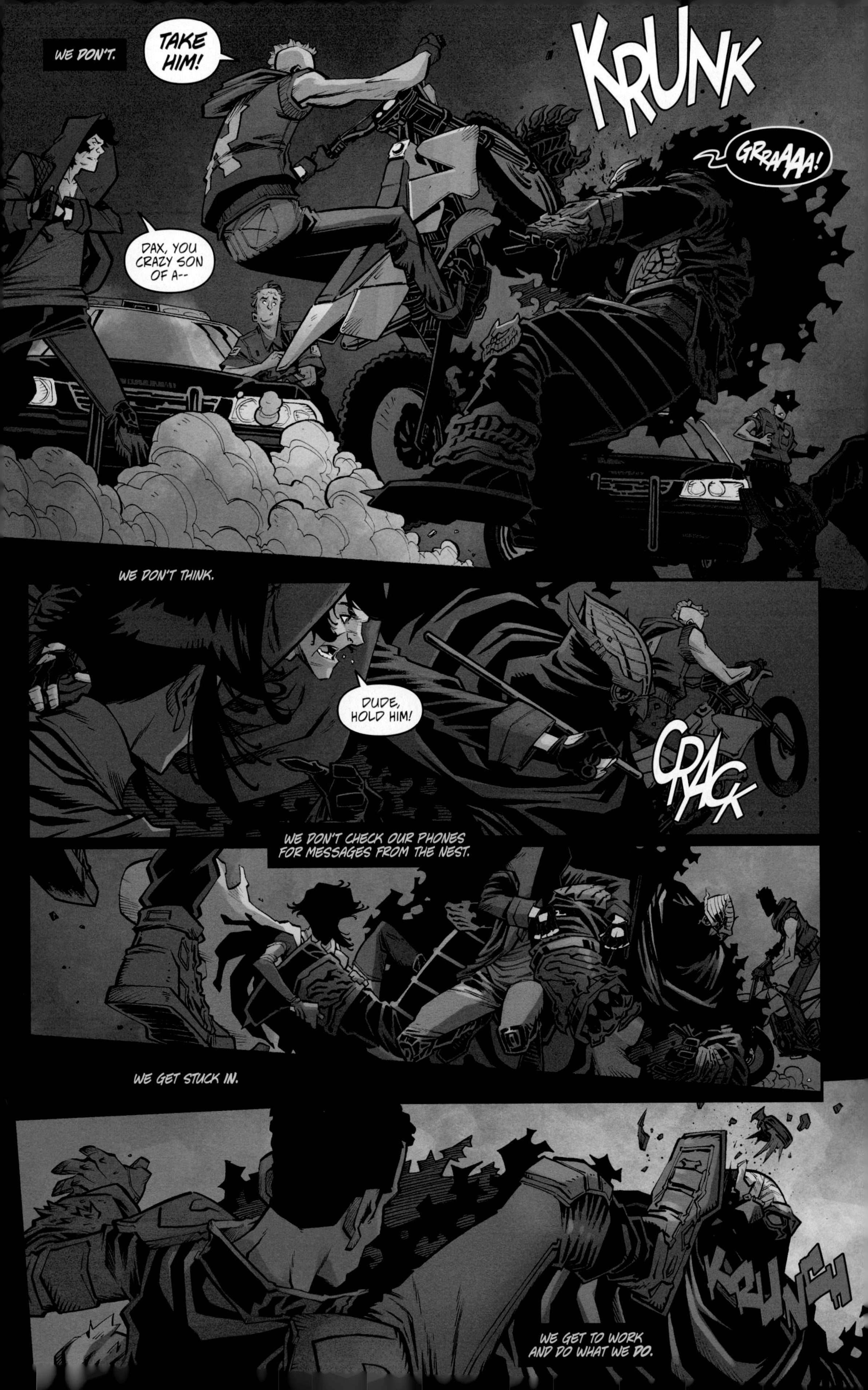
WE DON'T.
TAKE HIM!
KRUNK
GRRAAAA!
DAX, YOU CRAZY SON OF A--
WE DON'T THINK.
DUDE, HOLD HIM!
CRACK
WE DON'T CHECK OUR PHONES FOR MESSAGES FROM THE NEST.
WE GET STUCK IN.
KRUNCH
WE GET TO WORK AND DO WHAT WE DO.

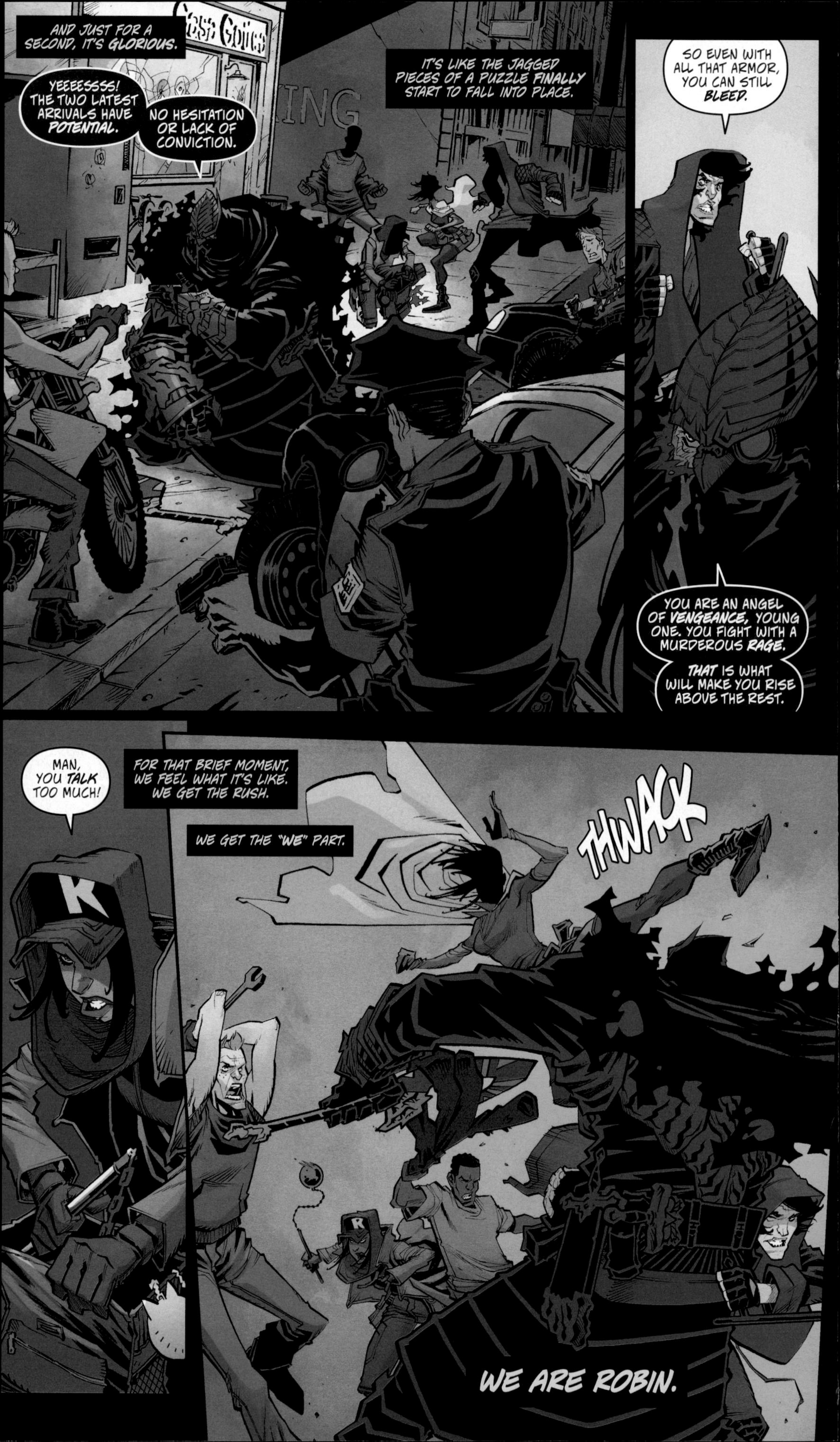
AND JUST FOR A SECOND, IT'S GLORIOUS.
YEEEESSSS! THE TWO LATEST ARRIVALS HAVE POTENTIAL.
NO HESITATION OR LACK OF CONVICTION.
IT'S LIKE THE JAGGED PIECES OF A PUZZLE FINALLY START TO FALL INTO PLACE.
SO EVEN WITH ALL THAT ARMOR, YOU CAN STILL BLEED.
YOU ARE AN ANGEL OF VENGEANCE, YOUNG ONE. YOU FIGHT WITH A MURDEROUS RAGE.
THAT IS WHAT WILL MAKE YOU RISE ABOVE THE REST.
MAN, YOU TALK TOO MUCH!
FOR THAT BRIEF MOMENT, WE FEEL WHAT IT'S LIKE. WE GET THE RUSH.
WE GET THE "WE" PART.
THWACK
WE ARE ROBIN.

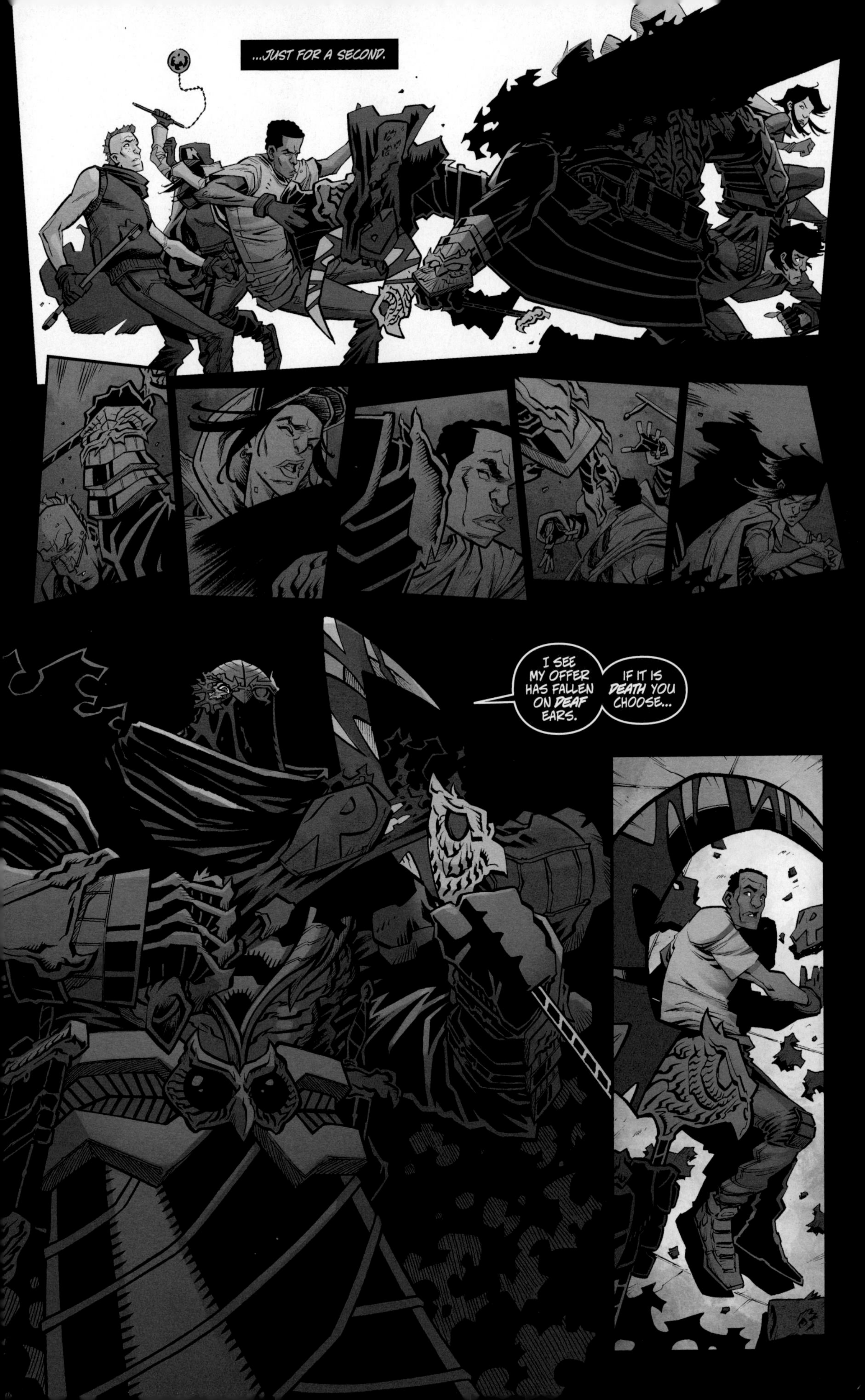
...JUST FOR A SECOND.
I SEE MY OFFER HAS FALLEN ON DEAF EARS.
IF IT IS DEATH YOU CHOOSE...

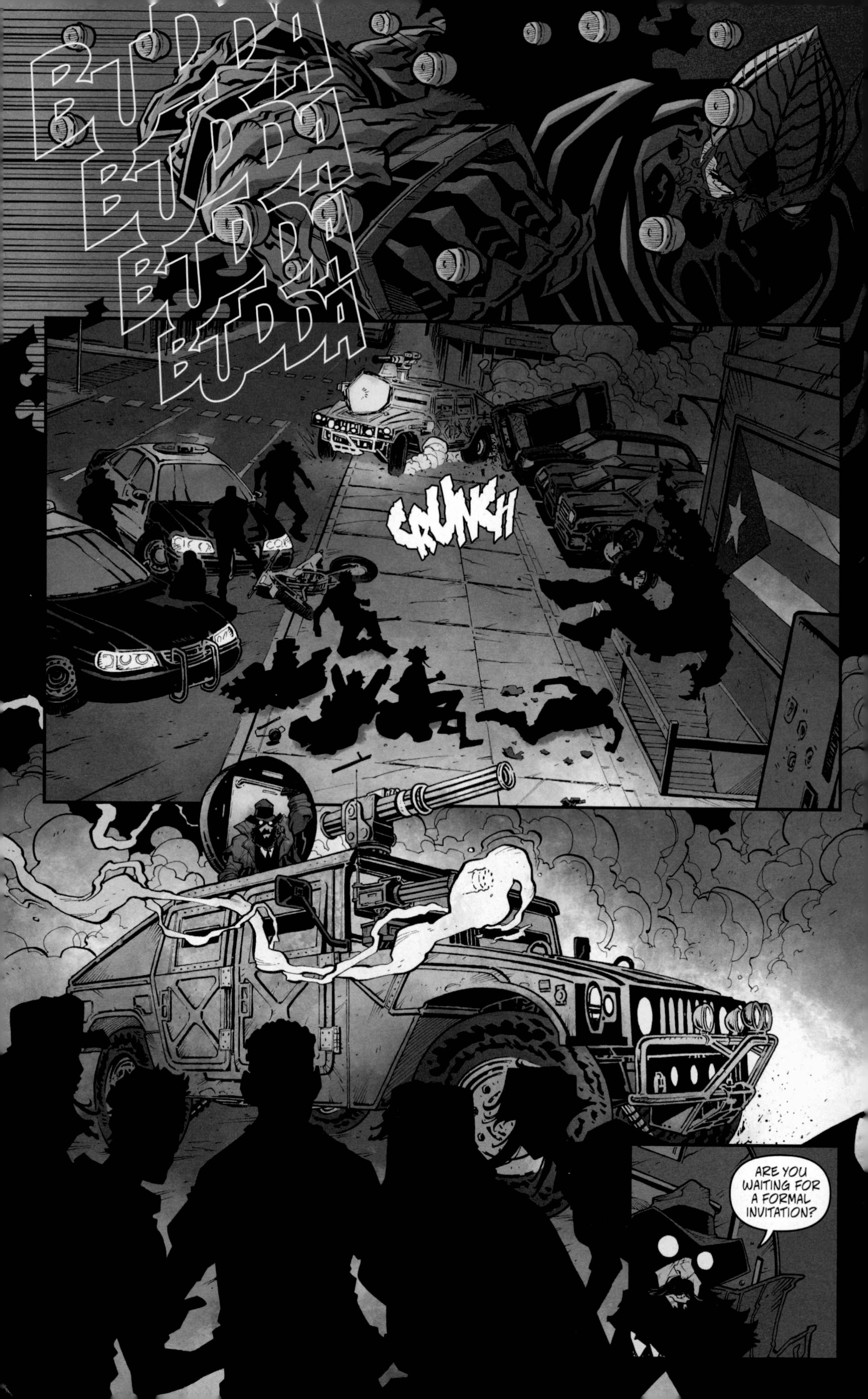
BUDDA BUDDA BUDDA BUDDA
CRUNCH
ARE YOU WAITING FOR A FORMAL INVITATION?

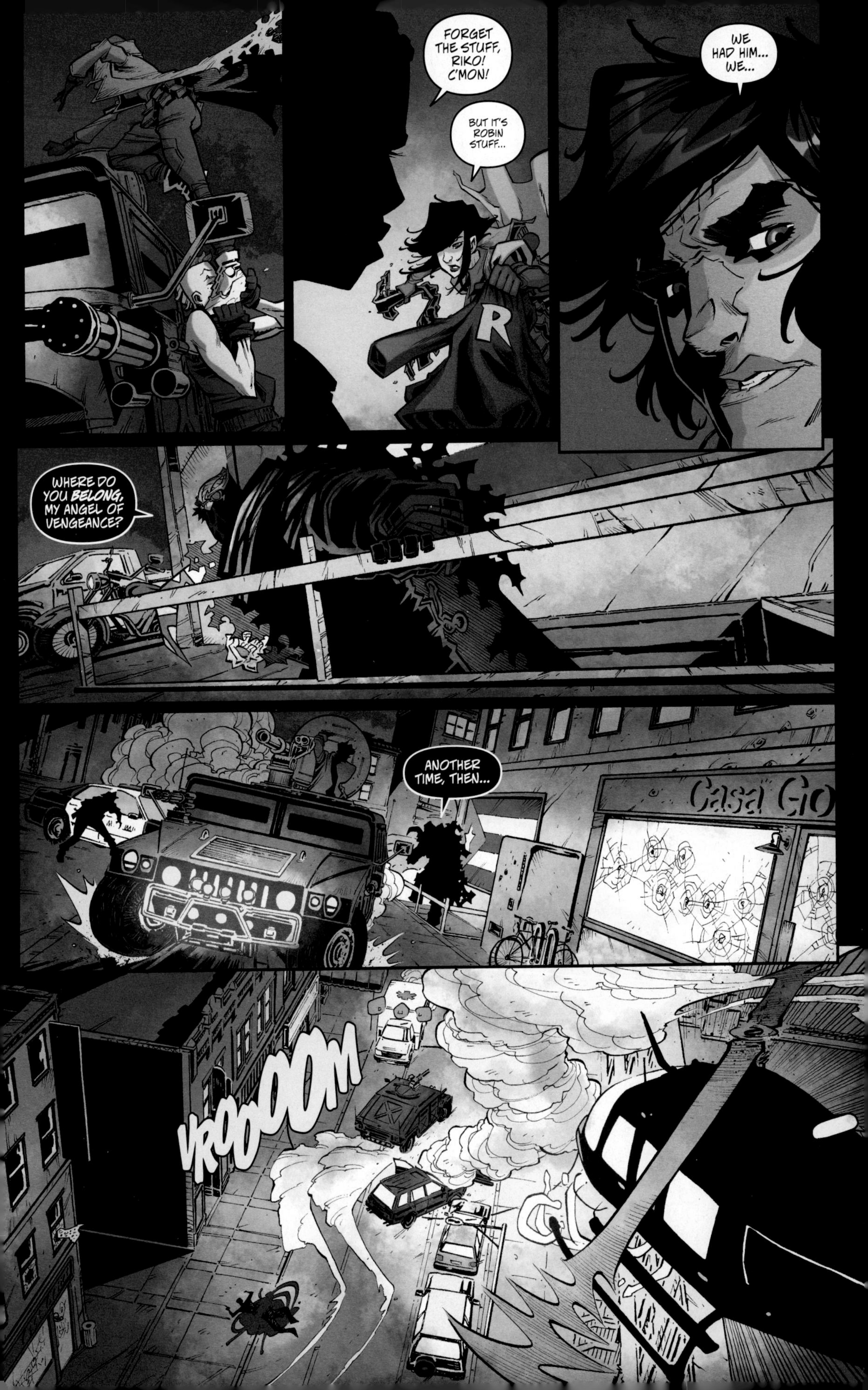
FORGET THE STUFF, RIKO! C'MON!
BUT IT'S ROBIN STUFF...
WE HAD HIM... WE...
WHERE DO YOU BELONG, MY ANGEL OF VENGEANCE?
ANOTHER TIME, THEN...
Casa Go
VROOOOM

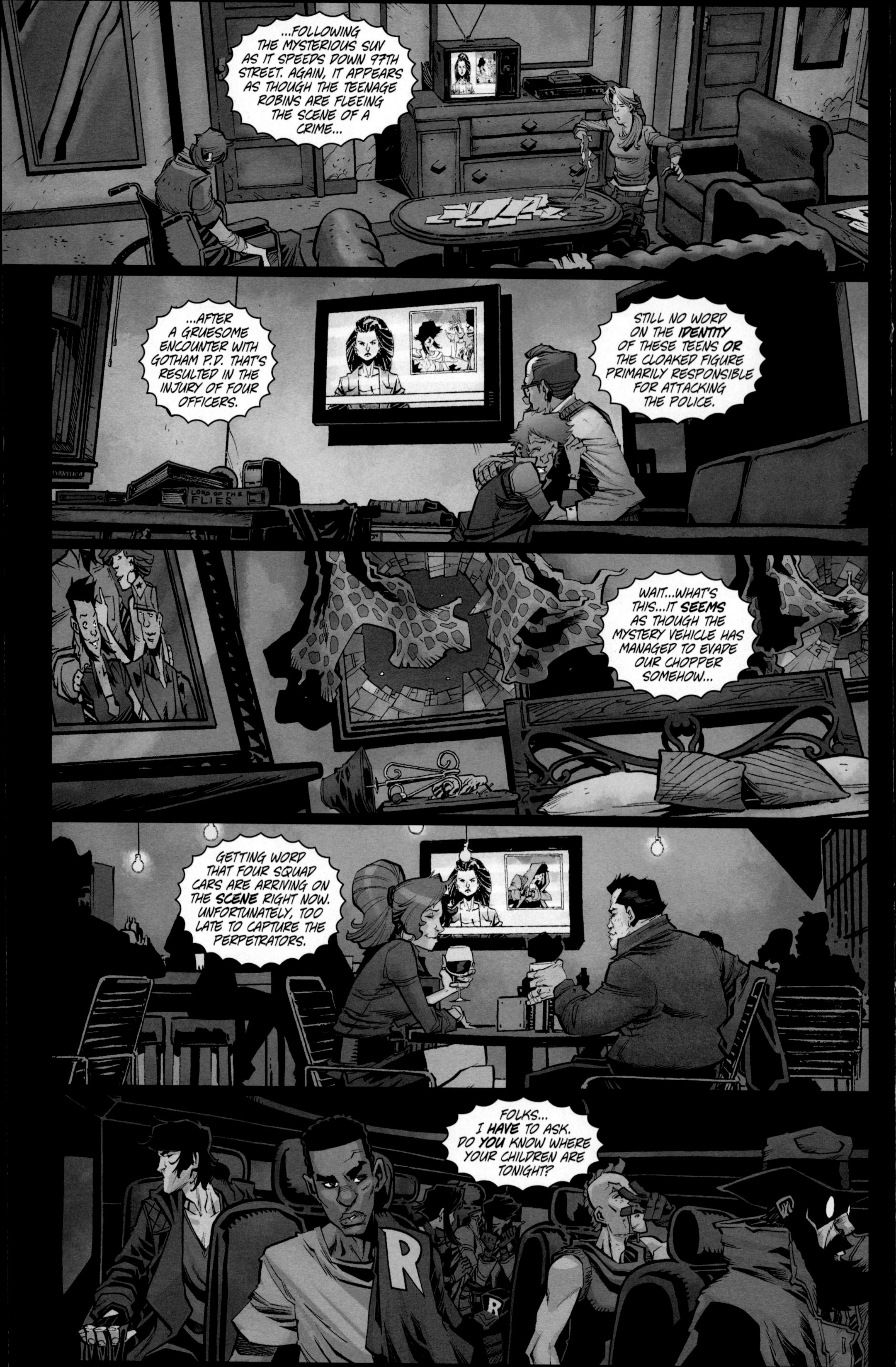
...FOLLOWING THE MYSTERIOUS SUV AS IT SPEEDS DOWN 97TH STREET. AGAIN, IT APPEARS AS THOUGH THE TEENAGE ROBINS ARE FLEEING THE SCENE OF A CRIME...
...AFTER A GRUESOME ENCOUNTER WITH GOTHAM P.D. THAT'S RESULTED IN THE INJURY OF FOUR OFFICERS.
STILL NO WORD ON THE **IDENTITY** OF THESE TEENS **OR** THE CLOAKED FIGURE PRIMARILY RESPONSIBLE FOR ATTACKING THE POLICE.
LORD OF THE FLIES
WAIT...WHAT'S THIS...IT **SEEMS** AS THOUGH THE MYSTERY VEHICLE HAS MANAGED TO EVADE OUR CHOPPER SOMEHOW...
GETTING WORD THAT FOUR SQUAD CARS ARE ARRIVING ON THE **SCENE** RIGHT NOW. UNFORTUNATELY, TOO LATE TO CAPTURE THE PERPETRATORS.
FOLKS... I **HAVE** TO ASK. DO **YOU** KNOW WHERE YOUR CHILDREN ARE TONIGHT?

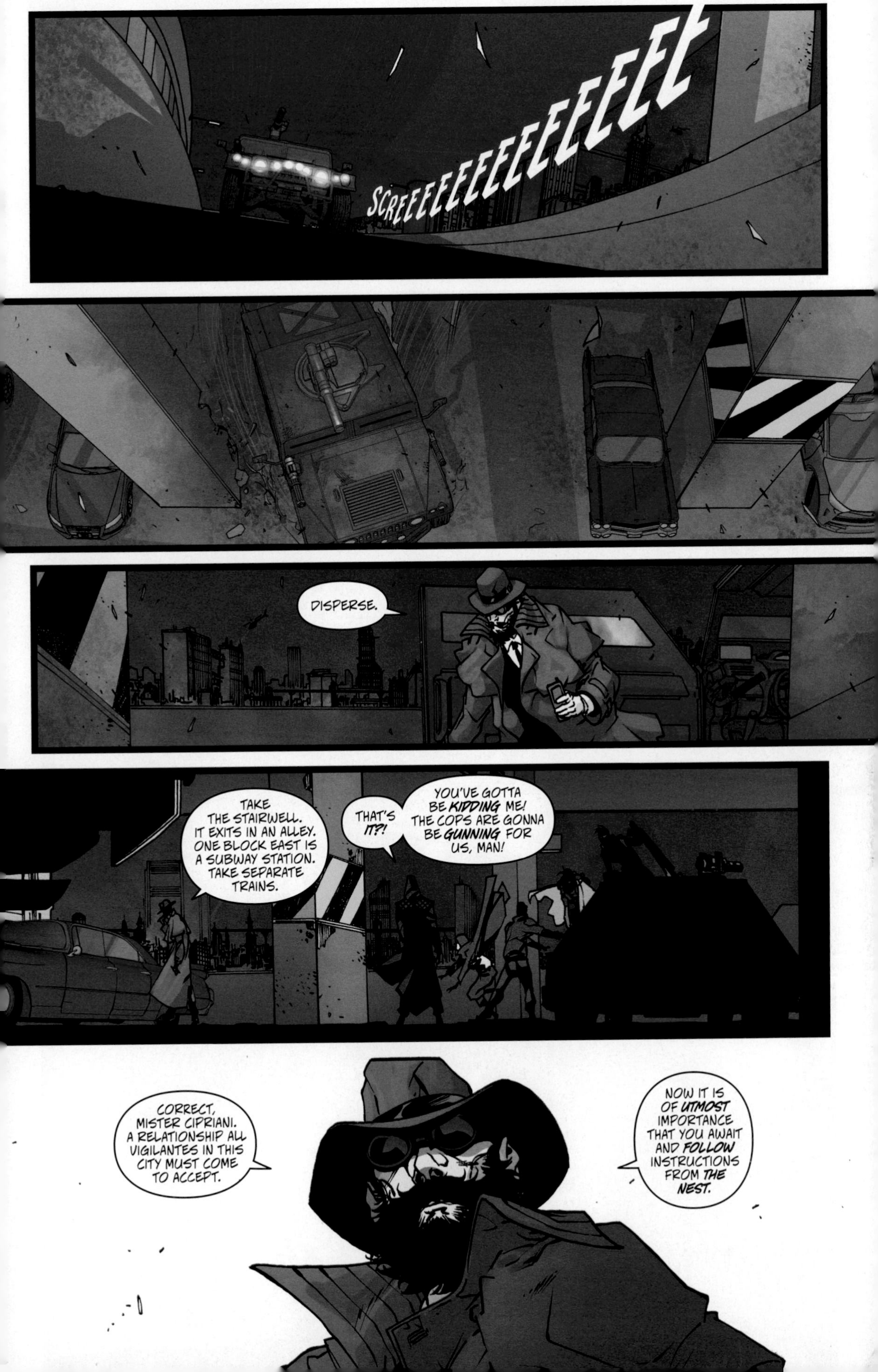
SCREEEEEEEEEEEEEEEEEEEET
DISPERSE.
TAKE THE STAIRWELL. IT EXITS IN AN ALLEY. ONE BLOCK EAST IS A SUBWAY STATION. TAKE SEPARATE TRAINS.
THAT'S IT?!
YOU'VE GOTTA BE KIDDING ME! THE COPS ARE GONNA BE GUNNING FOR US, MAN!
CORRECT, MISTER CIPRIANI. A RELATIONSHIP ALL VIGILANTES IN THIS CITY MUST COME TO ACCEPT.
NOW IT IS OF UTMOST IMPORTANCE THAT YOU AWAIT AND FOLLOW INSTRUCTIONS FROM THE NEST.

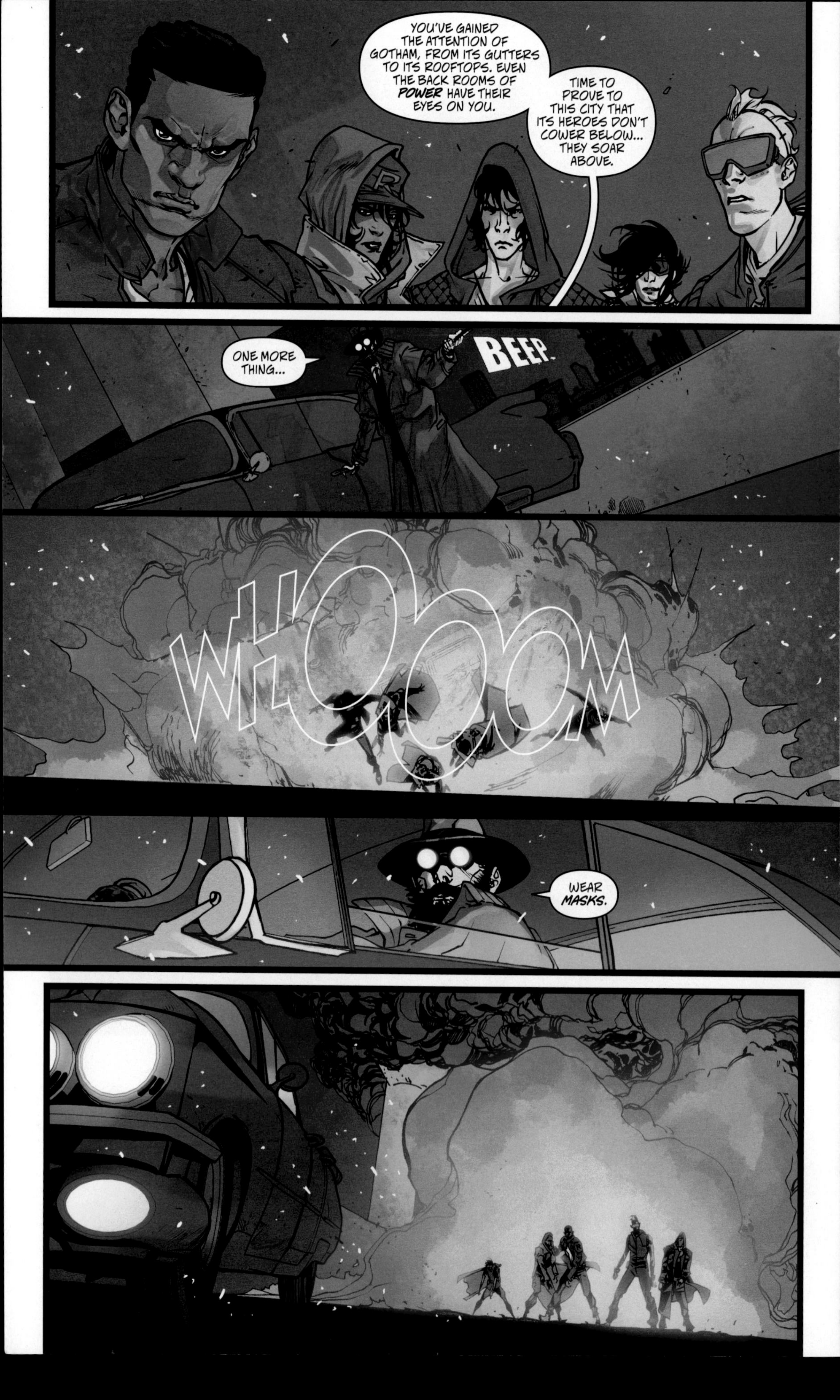
YOU'VE GAINED THE ATTENTION OF GOTHAM, FROM ITS GUTTERS TO ITS ROOFTOPS. EVEN THE BACK ROOMS OF POWER HAVE THEIR EYES ON YOU.
TIME TO PROVE TO THIS CITY THAT ITS HEROES DON'T COWER BELOW... THEY SOAR ABOVE.
ONE MORE THING...
BEEP
WHOOOOM
WEAR MASKS.

WHO ARE THE ROBINS?

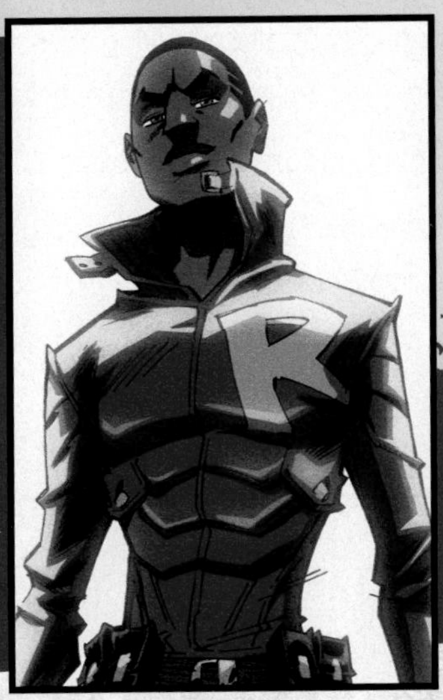

DUKE THOMAS

AGE 16

Currently a student at Middletown North. Subject to change. GPA does not reflect potential. Needs to be challenged frequently.

Hobbies include collectible card games, puzzles, and film. Shows potential as a writer. Ran track first year. Athletic, but not driven by competition. Motivations are internal.

Parents' current whereabouts unknown. Temporary foster parent: Raymond Mendez.

RIKO SHERIDAN

AGE 16

Username: R-iko

Current student at Middletown North. 4.2 GPA. Marching band freshman year. Drama student, but refuses to perform.

Hobbies include costume design, sewing, manga, anime, music, wing chu, kung fu san zoo. Batgirl fanatic.

Adoptive parents are David and Rita Harris-Sheridan. Birth parents killed in auto accident.

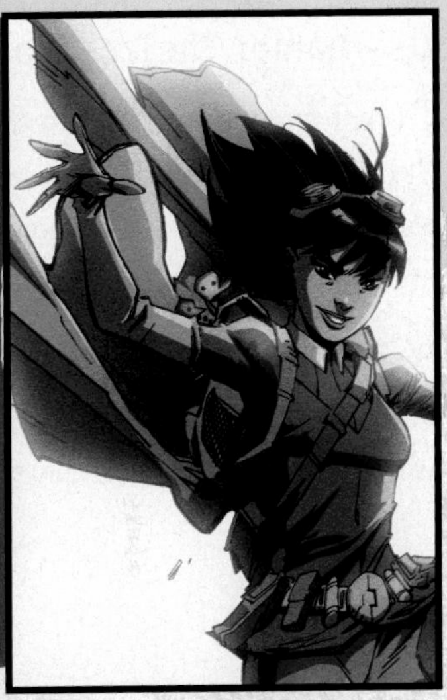

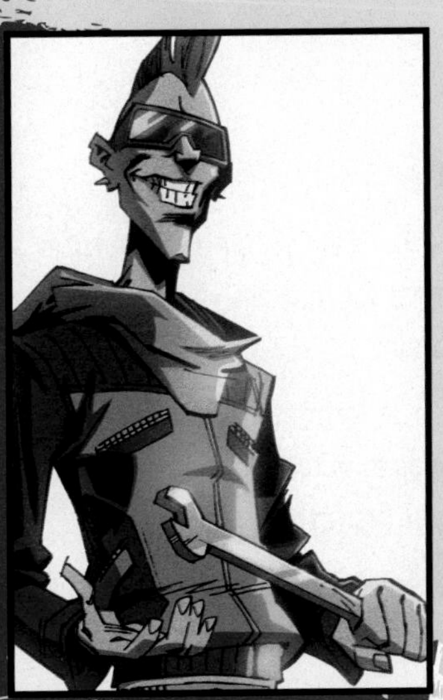

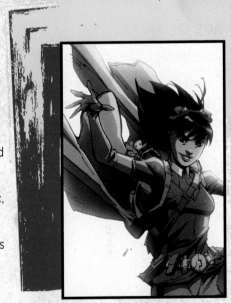

DAXTON 'DAX' [redacted]

AGE 17

Username: DaxAtax

Current student at Miller Valley Technical High School. 2.7 GPA. Discipline problem. Two suspensions. Attendance nightmare. Lacks drive/interest. Shows incredible loyalty and dedication to friends. A believer.

Hobbies include mechanics, motor cross, and NASCAR. Plays guitar (badly). Briefly performed in hardcore band, Scuzzy Muff. Left to join punk group, The Frown Clown.

Parents are [redacted]. Father's whereabouts unknown. Mother suffers from frequent migraines due to alcohol abuse.

ISABELLA ORTIZ

AGE 17
Username: Robina

Current student at West Robinson High. GPA 3.2. Transferred to Gotham sophomore year. Excels at language. Bilingual, but also studying French and Latin. Attendance problems sophomore year. Suspected gang activity.

Hobbies include dancing, gymnastics, singing, Judo, and kick-boxing.

Parents are Umberto Ortiz and Maria Fernanda Santiago. Two siblings. Older brother, Hector, and younger sister, Mia.

TROY WALKER

AGE 17

Username: TheTroyWonder, DECEASED

Current student at Middletown South. GPA 3.5. Star athlete. Varsity Strong Safety for the Middletown Cougars. All-State two years in a row. Hoping to play for Notre Dame and eventually go pro. Above average student with interests in political activism, history, and philosophy.

Hobbies include football, baseball, video games, and cross-fit.

Parents are Stephen and Joyce Walker. Stephen Walker, construction worker, injured on the job during Joker Toxin incident. Receiving disability.

ANRE 'DRE' CIPRIANI

AGE 17

Username: Dre-b-Robbin

Current student at Middletown South. GPA 2.5. One suspension for fighting. Written up multiple times for aggressive displays of disobedience. Argumentative. Arrogant.

Hobbies include MMA, boxing, true crime novels, forensic science, and cooking. As a child was a musical prodigy. Piano. Completely abandoned music after his father's murder.

Parents are Gianfranco Cipriani (deceased) and Angela Mancuso. Father, a "made" member of the Maroni crime family, murdered by the Falcones when Dre was eight.

WE ARE ROBIN #1
VARIANT BY JAMES HARVEY

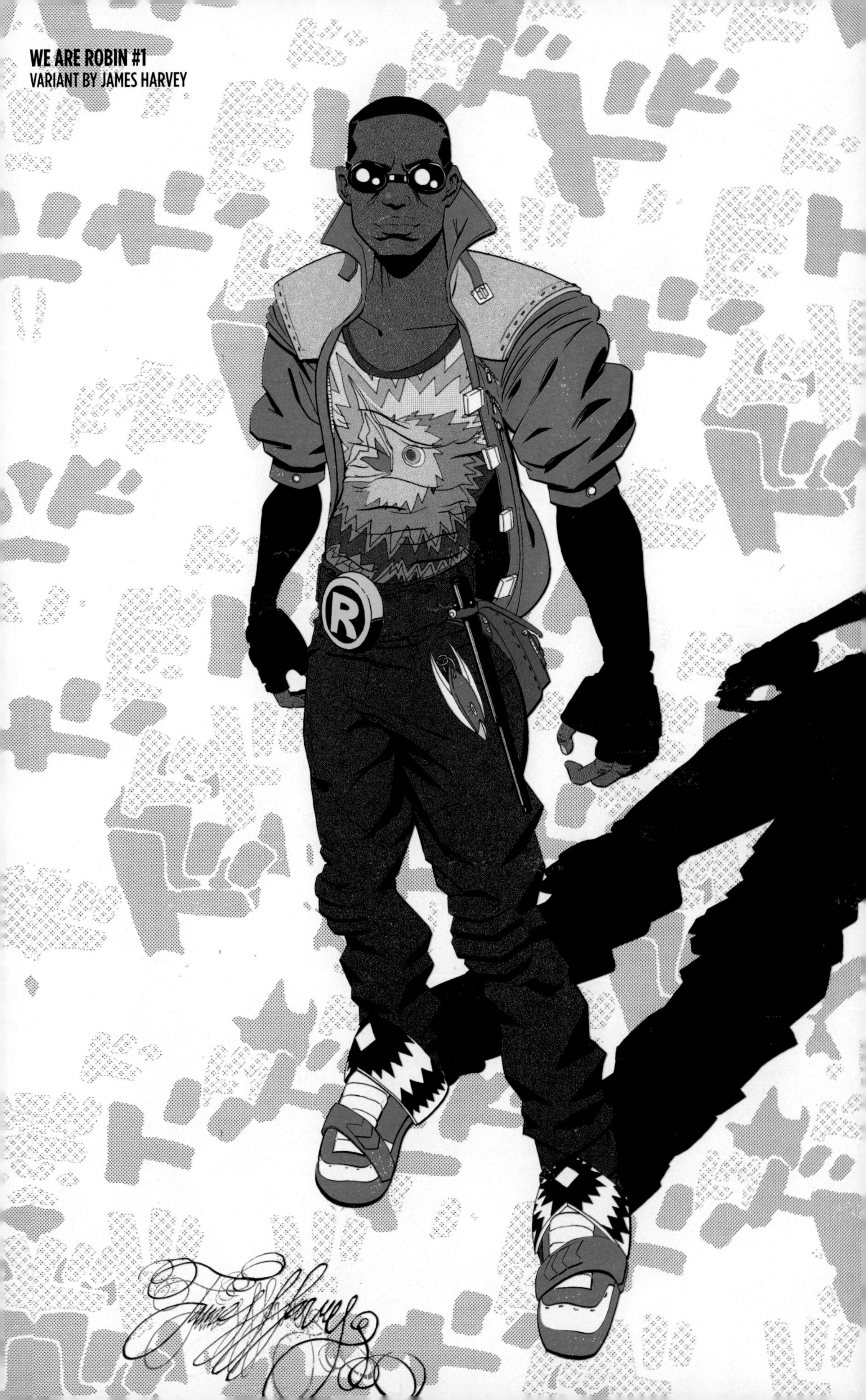

WE ARE ROBIN #2
VARIANT BY JAMES HARVEY

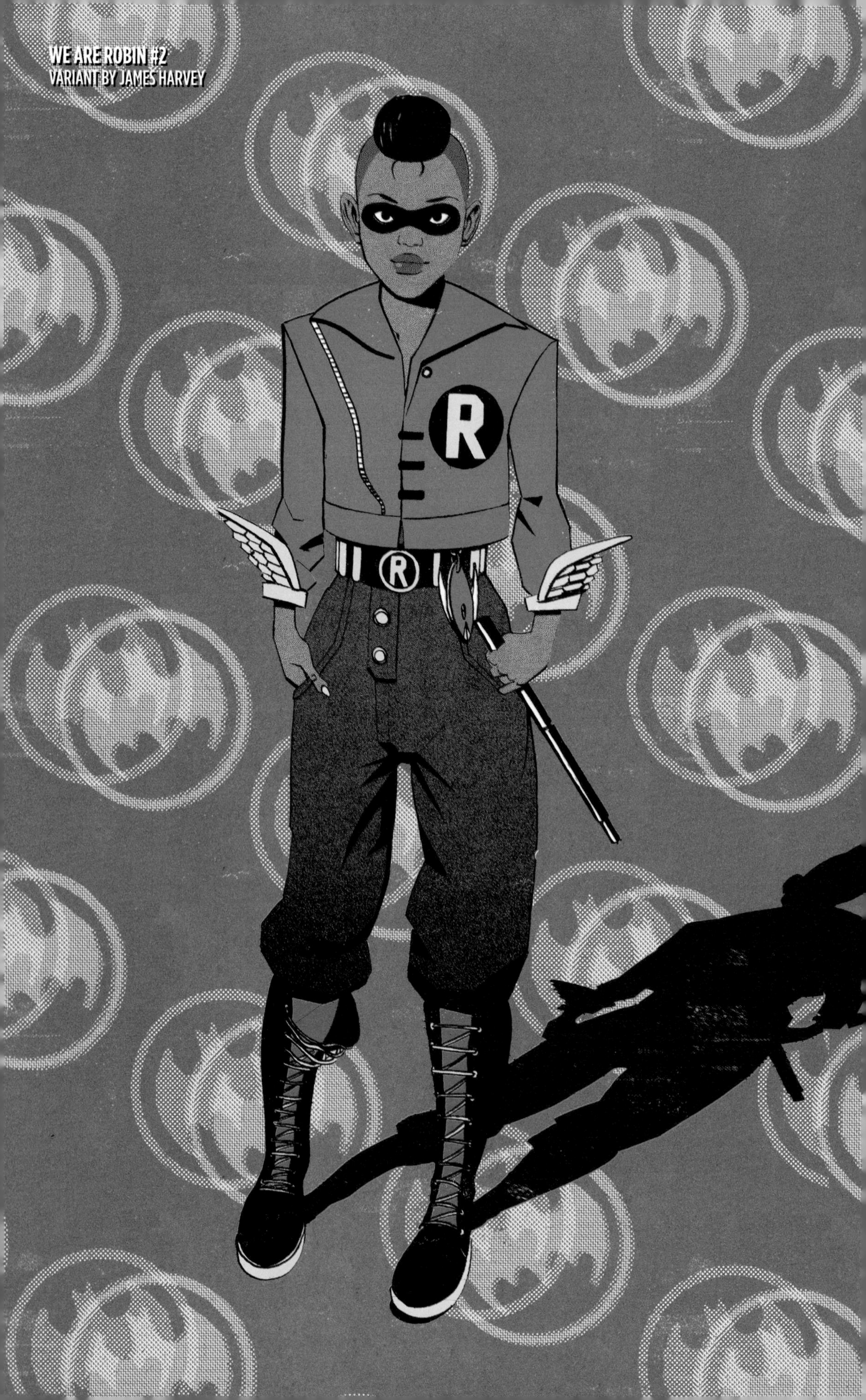

WE ARE ROBIN #3
VARIANT BY JAMES HARVEY

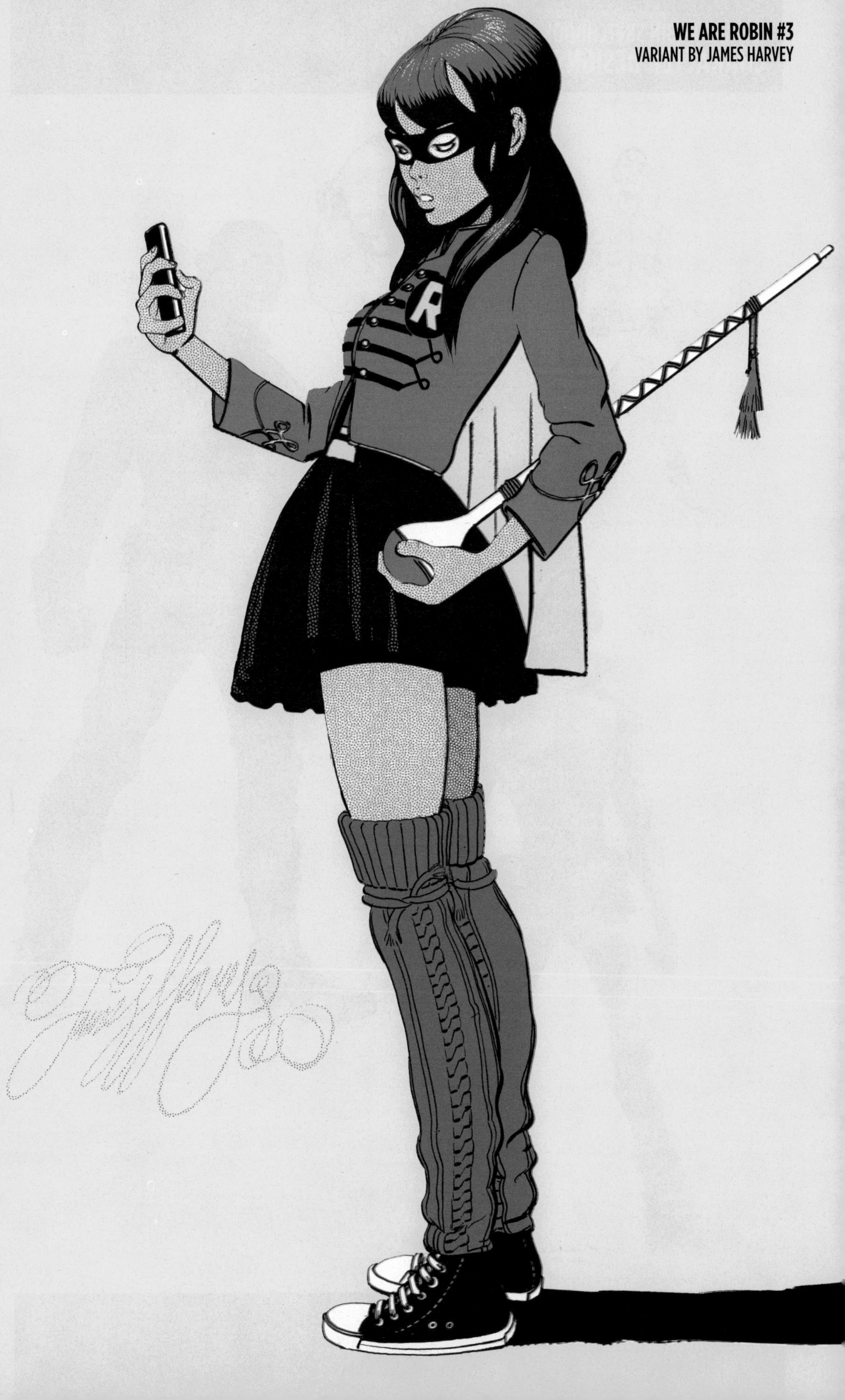

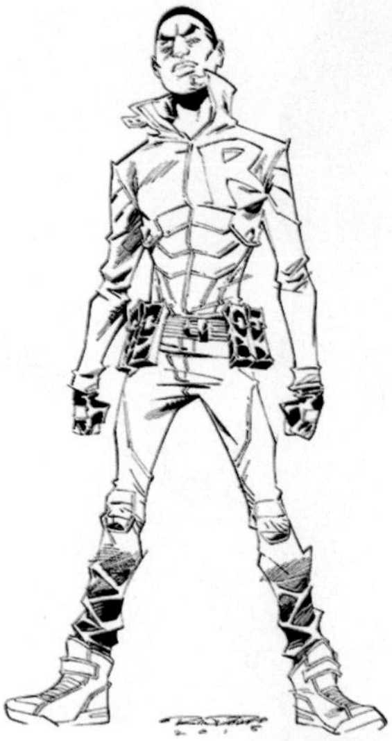

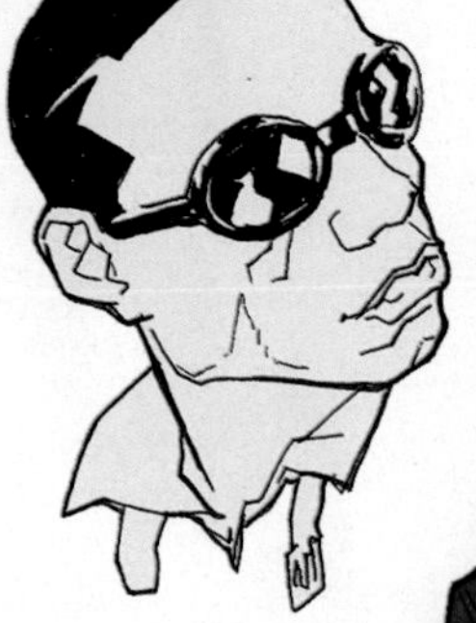

LEE BERMEJO

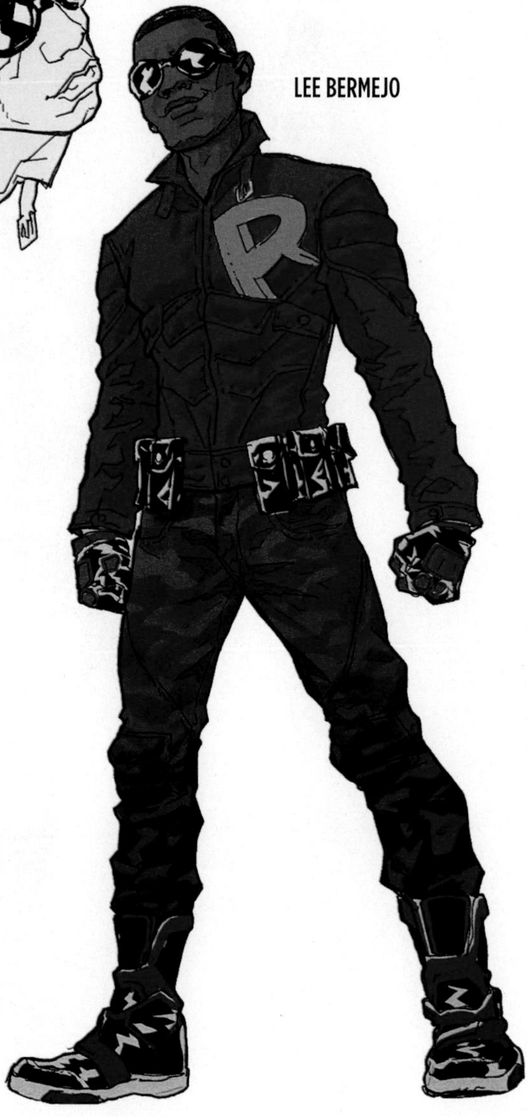

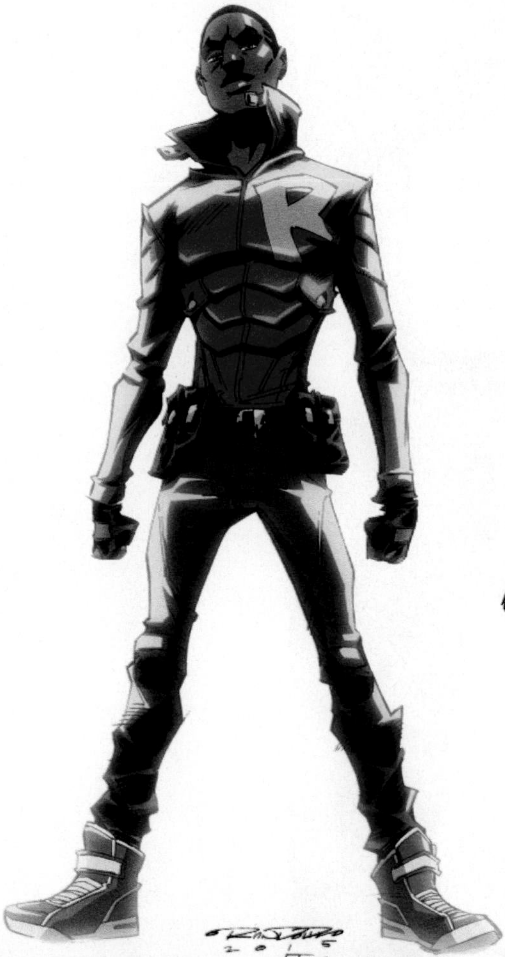

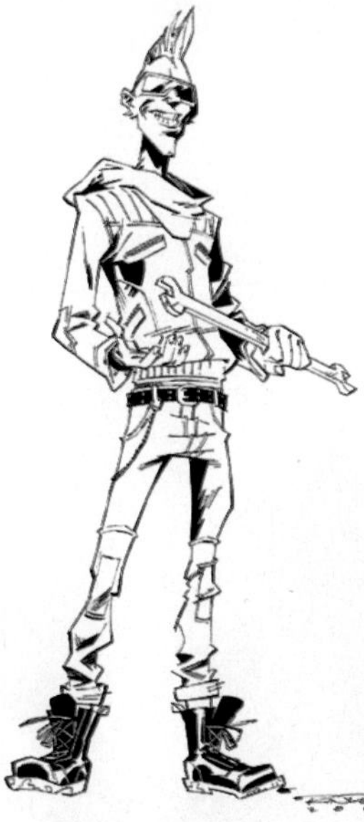

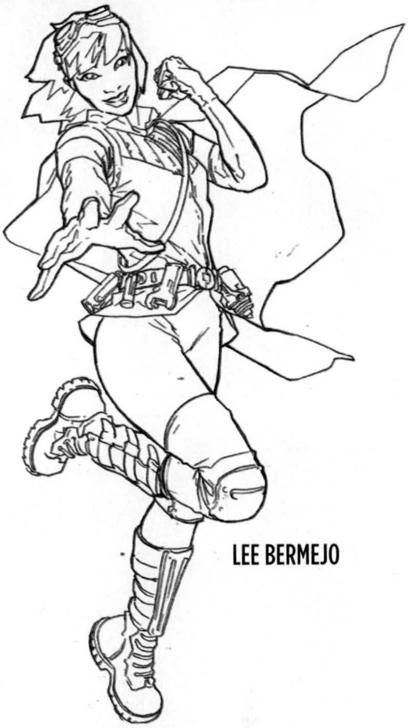

LEE BERMEJO

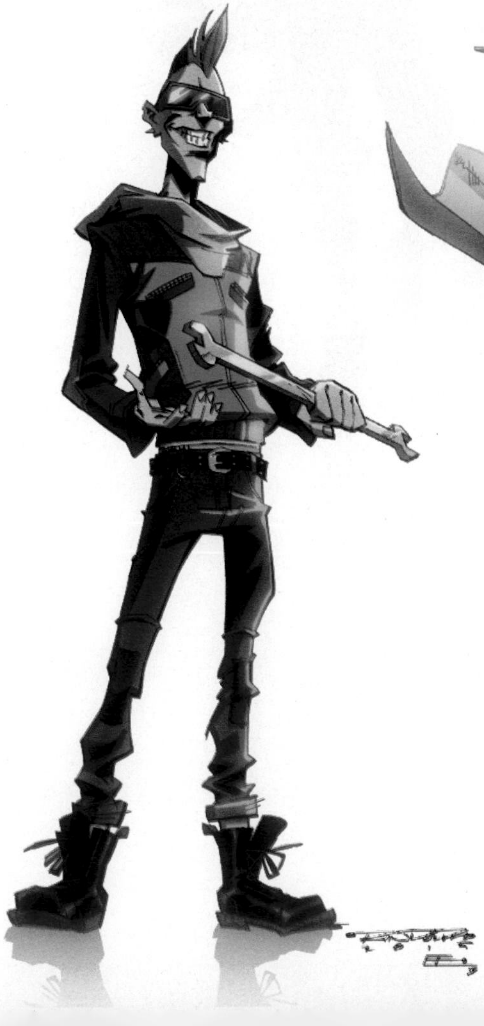

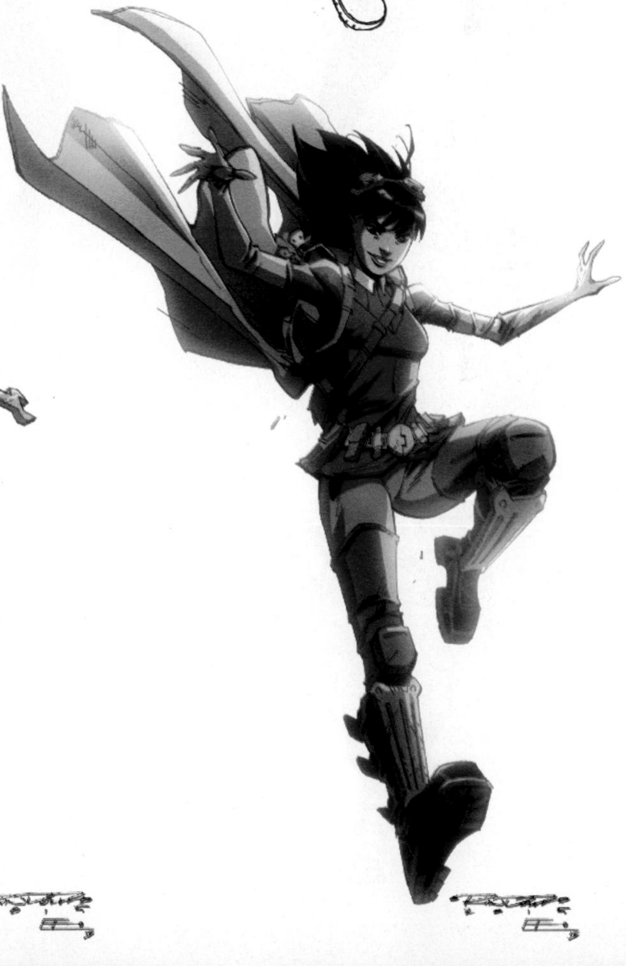

LEE BERMEJO

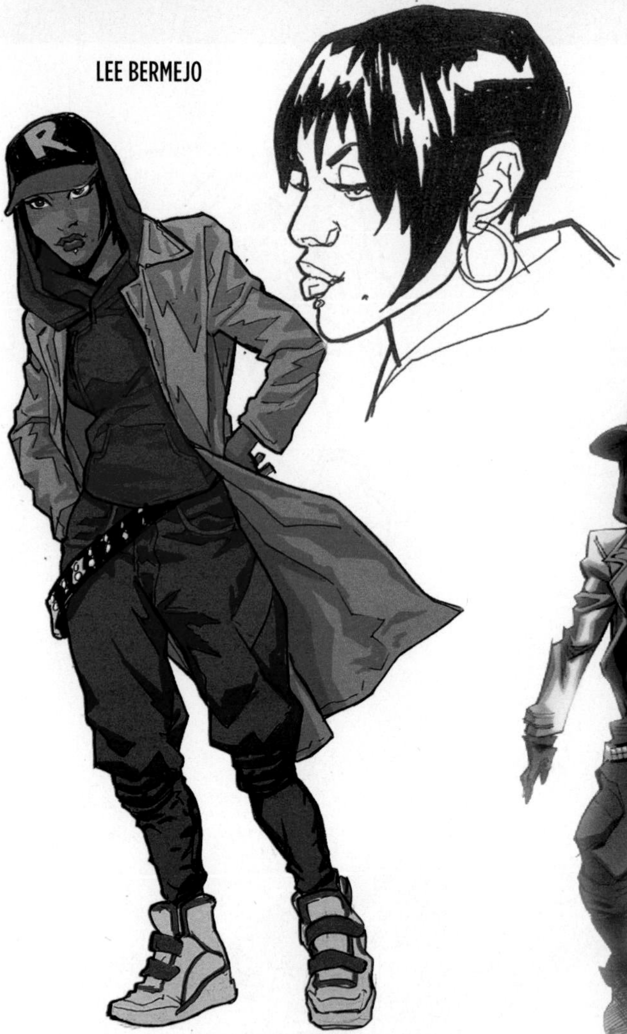

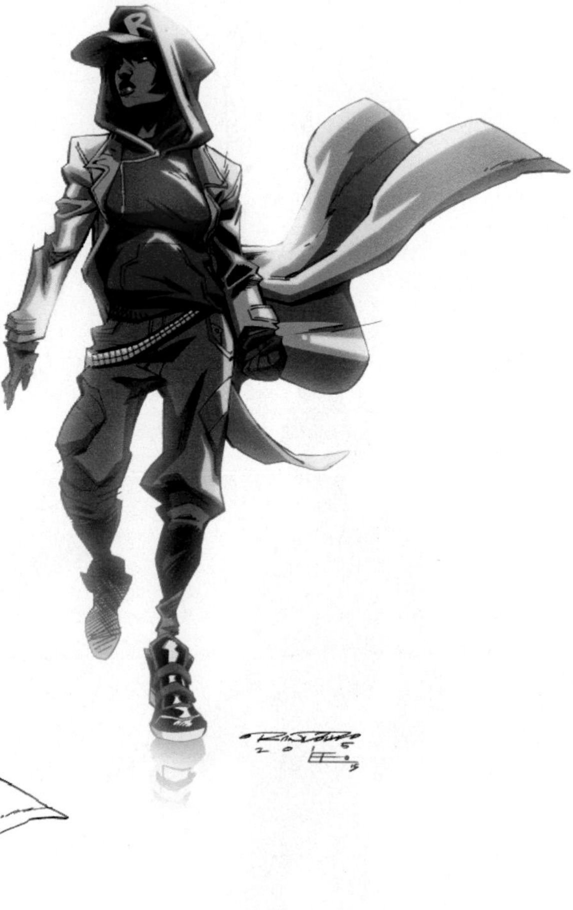

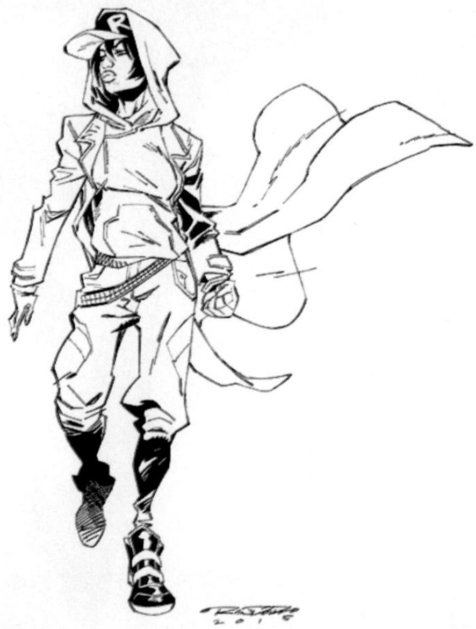

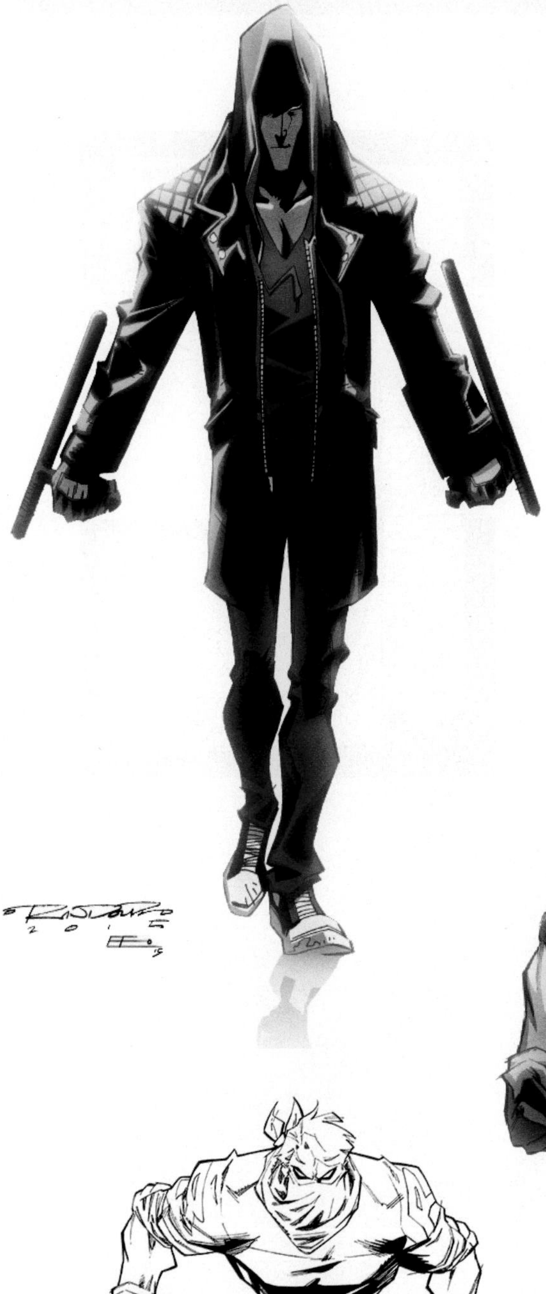

LEE BERMEJO

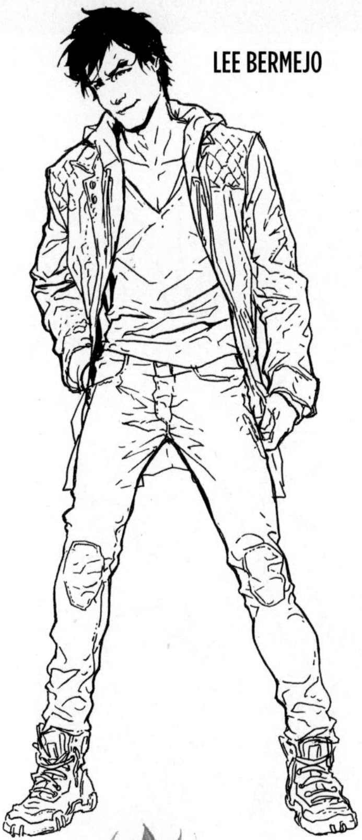

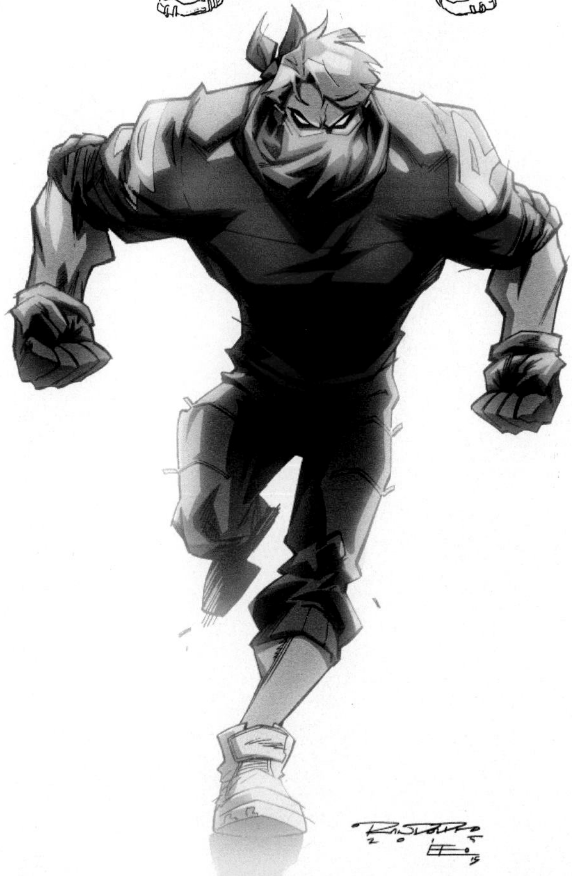

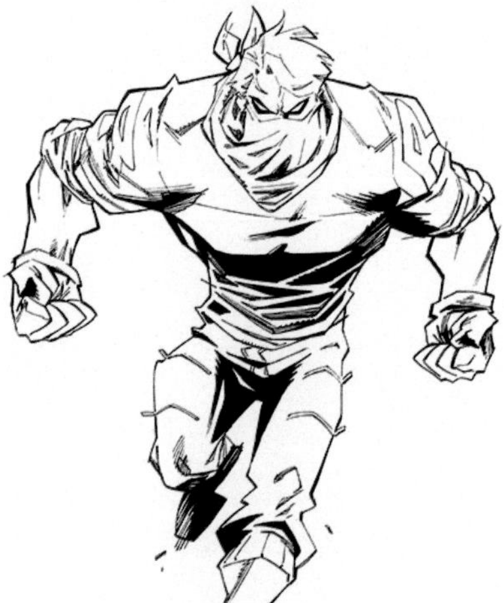

PAGE PROCESS
COMPARISON OF ROB HAYNES' LAYOUTS (ABOVE) & JORGE CORONA'S PENCILS (BELOW) FOR WE ARE ROBIN #1, PAGES #1-4

SOMEONE TOLD ME THAT THE PROBLEM WITH YOUTH IS THE INABILITY TO ACCEPT YOUR OWN MORTALITY.

I WOULDN'T CONSIDER THIS ONE OF MY PROBLEMS.
NEXT TIME I CATCH YOU WITH MY SISTER, I'M GONNA PUT YOU IN THE GROUND!!
KICK HIS SKINNY ASS, SMILEY!!!
DAMN, RELAX KID ... SHE TOLD ME I SMELLED GOOD. BLAME THE COLOGNE.
PLUS, SHE'S HOT AS HELL...
HELPS WHEN YOU DON'T SMELL LIKE WEED AND CHICKEN FLAUTAS...
PINCHE CAVRÓN!!!
AFTER YOU'VE SEEN A MURDERING PSYCHOPATH USE YOUR PARENTS FOR BAIT, AND YOUR CITY OVERTAKEN BY ZOMBIES, THE FRAGILITY OF LIFE BECOMES SO CLEAR IT MIGHT AS WELL BE IN IMAX.

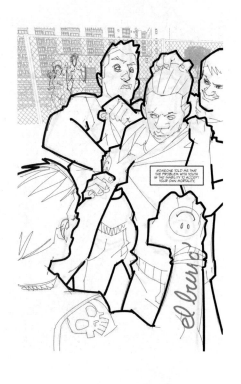

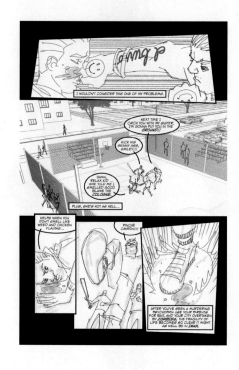

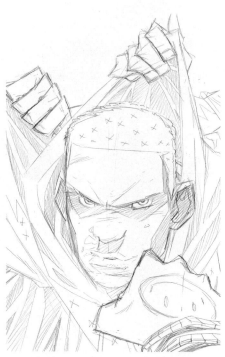

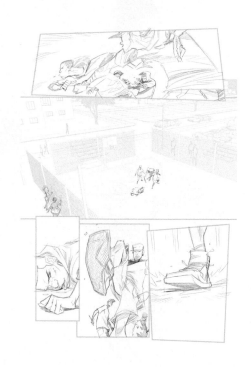